DIGITAL COMPUTER ARITHMETIC
Design and Implementation

McGraw-Hill Computer Science Series

Ahuja: *Design and Analysis of Computer Communication Networks*
Barbacci and Siewiorek: *The Design and Analysis of Instruction Set Processors*
Cavanagh: *Digital Computer Arithmetic: Design and Implementation*
Donovan: *Systems Programming*
Filman and Friedman: *Coordinated Computing: Tools and Techniques for Distributed Software*
Givone: *Introduction to Switching Circuit Theory*
Goodman and Hedetniemi: *Introduction to the Design and Analysis of Algorithms*
Katzan: *Microprogramming Primer*
Keller: *A First Course in Computer Programming Using Pascal*
Kohavi: *Switching and Finite Automata Theory*
Liu: *Elements of Discrete Mathematics*
Liu: *Introduction to Combinatorial Mathematics*
MacEwen: *Introduction to Computer Systems: Using the PDP-11 and Pascal*
Madnick and Donovan: *Operating Systems*
Manna: *Mathematical Theory of Computation*
Newman and Sproull: *Principles of Interactive Computer Graphics*
Payne: *Introduction to Simulation: Programming Techniques and Methods of Analysis*
Révész: *Introduction to Formal Languages*
Rice: *Matrix Computations and Mathematical Software*
Salton and McGill: *Introduction to Modern Information Retrieval*
Shooman: *Software Engineering: Design, Reliability, and Management*
Tremblay and Bunt: *An Introduction to Computer Science: An Algorithmic Approach*
Tremblay and Bunt: *An Introduction to Computer Science: An Algorithmic Approach, Short Edition*
Tremblay and Manohar: *Discrete Mathematical Structures with Applications to Computer Science*
Tremblay and Sorenson: *An Introduction to Data Structures with Applications*
Tucker: *Programming Languages*
Wiederhold: *Database Design*

McGraw-Hill Series in Computer Organization and Architecture

Bell and Newell: *Computer Structures: Readings and Examples*
Gear: *Computer Organization and Programming*
Hamacher, Vranesic, and Zaky: *Computer Organization*
Hayes: *Computer Architecture and Organization*
Hayes: *Digital System Design and Microprocessors*
Hwang and Briggs: *Computer Architecture and Parallel Processing*
Kogge: *The Architecture of Pipelined Computers*
Siewiorek, Bell, and Newell: *Computer Structures: Principles and Examples*
Stone: *Introduction to Computer Organization and Data Structures*
Stone and Siewiorek: *Introduction to Computer Organization and Data Structures: PDP-11 Edition*

DIGITAL
COMPUTER
ARITHMETIC
Design and Implementation

Joseph J. F. Cavanagh

University of Santa Clara

McGraw-Hill Book Company

New York   St. Louis   San Francisco   Auckland   Bogotá   Hamburg
Johannesburg   London   Madrid   Mexico   Montreal   New Delhi
Panama   Paris   São Paulo   Singapore   Sydney   Tokyo   Toronto

To MY WIFE,
Madeline,
whose help and encouragement
made this book possible.

This book was set in Times Roman by Gloria's Graphics.
The editors were Eric M. Munson and Joseph F. Murphy;
the production supervisor was Joe Campanella.
The drawings were done by Joseph J. F. Cavanagh.
Halliday Lithograph Corporation was printer and binder.

DIGITAL COMPUTER ARITHMETIC
Design and Implementation

234567890HALHAL8987654

ISBN 0-07-010282-1

Library of Congress Cataloging in Publication Data
Cavanagh, Joseph J. F.
    Digital computer arithmetic

    (McGraw-Hill computer science series)   (McGraw-Hill series
in computer organization and architecture)
    Bibliography: p.
    Includes index.
    1. Computer arithmetic.   I. Title.   II. Series.
III. Series: McGraw-Hill series in computer organization and architecture.
QA76.9.C62C38 1983   519.4   83-9401
ISBN 0-07-010282-1

CONTENTS

PREFACE

Computation speeds have increased dramatically during the past three decades—resulting primarily from faster, denser technologies and new concepts in computer architecture. The speed of large-scale processors has doubled approximately every 3 years. An essential ingredient of a high-speed processor is a high-speed execution unit. The execution unit performs all arithmetic and logical operations on operands as well as shifting and data manipulation.

The purpose of this book is to present digital computer arithmetic covering fixed-point, binary-coded decimal, and floating point number representations for the operations of addition, subtraction, multiplication, and division as employed in a high-speed execution unit. The arithmetic algorithms, processor architectures, and design methodologies are presented in sufficient detail to permit both ease of understanding and hardware design implementation. Logic diagrams accompany each of the methods presented and use technolgoy-independent VLSI. New methods of computer arithmetic are also described—methods that are currently being designed into future high-speed processors.

Emphasis is placed on the design of high-speed addition, subtraction, multiplication, and division. Several different methods are described for each of the four operations in each of the three different number representations. Each method provides a detailed presentation of:

The theory for the method
Examples using the theory
The architecture (organization)
Examples using the architecture
The gate-level design of the architecture

The book is intended to be tutorial, and as such, is comprehensive and self-contained. Because the book covers computer arithmetic exclusively, many different methods can be presented—and in much greater detail than books on architecture. No statement in this book purports, "It is obvious that . . . ." In my experience, I have found that it is usually not obvious. All equations are carried though to completion, and all architectural organizations are designed in detail at the gate level. Nothing is left unfinished or partially designed. Therefore, this book can be used as a practical design guide for digital computer arithmetic units. The arithmetic algorithms are illustrated by flowcharts, processor organizations, and logic diagrams. Further understanding of the algorithms is aided by numerous arithmetic and logical equations.

Chapter 1 introduces the fixed-point, binary-coded decimal, and floating-point number representations that are used in digital computers. It includes the encoding schemes for sign magnitude, diminished-radix complement, and radix complement. It also includes a review of logic design. This review includes boolean algebra, minimization techniques, combinational logic, and sequential logic, covering synthesizing techniques for both synchronous and asynchronous logic circuits. An introduction to VLSI technology and design automation systems is also included in Chap. 1.

Chapter 2 presents fixed-point arithmetic for addition and subtraction. The main emphasis for addition and subtraction is on the carry lookahead principle, which performs high-speed add/subtract operations. The chapter also includes carry-select and conditional-sum addition.

Chapter 3 presents several different methods for performing fixed-point multiplication, including the standard sequential add-shift technique for lower-speed applications. The Booth algorithm and multiplier bit-pair recoding methods are included where higher-speed multiplication is required with a minimum of additional hardware over that of the sequential method. Two types of iterative cellular array multipliers are introduced for high-speed multiplication applications. A table lookup approach for multiplication is presented; this approach provides a noticeable increase in speed over the multiplier recoding method, but it is slower than array multiplication.

Chapter 4 covers fixed-point division, which includes sections on the sequential restoring/nonrestoring methods. Also included is SRT division, which skips 0s and 1s in the dividend or partial remainder, and two techniques of convergence division. Convergence division is not as fast as array division, but it requires less hardware because it can utilize the high-speed array multiplier that may already be incorporated in the multiply unit. Finally, different types of array dividers are presented.

Chapter 5 covers different methods of decimal arithmetic for the four operations of addition, subtraction, multiplication, and division. Several addition/subtraction techniques are illustrated. Architectural organizations are presented for multiplication using ROMs and table lookup. Decimal division, which uses a table lookup method that is analogous to the binary search technique utilized in programming, is discussed.

Chapter 6 presents floating-point arithmetic, starting with fundamental concepts and features that are unique to floating-point processors for the four basic operations. The additional hardware required for floating-point operations is relatively complex and adds to the cost of the computer, but the operation of the machine is more efficient.

Chapter 7 presents additional floating-point topics, such as unnormalized floating-point arithmetic. Rounding methods are also discussed and a section on guard digits illustrates the importance of these additional bits during the intermediate steps, thus permitting maximum accuracy to be retained in the result. Overflow and underflow, multiple precision, and a hexadecimal radix description are also covered. A summary of IEEE proposed standard for floating-point arithmetic completes this chapter on additional floating-point topics.

The information in this text represents more than two decades of computer equipment design by the author and an extensive literature survey. The book is used as the text for a graduate course in digital computer arithmetic in the electrical engineering and computer science department of the University of Santa Clara.

The book is not intended as a text on logic design, although this subject is reviewed in Chap. 1. It is assumed that a reader who is interested in digital computer arithmetic will have an adequate background in combinational and sequential logic design. The book presents basic and advanced concepts of high-speed computer arithmetic and is designed for practicing engineers and computer scientists; graduate students in electrical engineering, computer science, and mathematical sciences; and senior-level undergraduate students.

Finally, I would like to express my appreciation and thanks to all those who helped in the preparation of this book: in particular, to my wife, Madeline, for her encouragement and support and for typing the original manuscript and revisions; to Professor V. Carl Hamacher of the University of Toronto and Professor John P. Hayes of the University of Michigan for their many helpful suggestions and comments; and to Professor Daniel W. Lewis of the University of Santa Clara for his moral support.

Joseph J. F. Cavanagh

Strive always for a simple and uncluttered design as one of the most important design objectives, because the simplest original design will eventually become many times more complicated than anyone expected.

NUMBER SYSTEMS, LOGIC DESIGN, AND VERY LARGE SCALE INTEGRATION

1.1 NUMBER SYSTEMS

Arithmetic processors are used to perform arithmetic operations on numerical data and thus to generate solutions to computational problems. Large-scale integration (LSI) and very large scale integration (VLSI) technologies have made it possible to design sophisticated, high-performance arithmetic processors for modern digital computers. These processors are usually designed to operate with two or more different number representations. The architectural design of an arithmetic processor is guided primarily by the number representation to be utilized and also by the technology to be employed in the system.

Machine arithmetic differs from real arithmetic (using the set of real numbers) primarily in number precision. Because of fixed word length, arithmetic processors can produce only finite-precision results, whereas real arithmetic can produce results to any degree of precision. Also, because of fixed-word-length registers, rounding of a result may be required, which transforms a more precise number into a less precise number, so that the result can be accommodated by a fixed-length register.

Digital computer arithmetic is a subset of computer architecture, which also includes logic design. This text will present computer arithmetic as it applies to three number representations: fixed point, decimal, and floating point. Positional number systems and their relationship to the three number representations will also be described. Each number representation will be presented in relationship to the four operations of addition, subtraction, multiplication, and division. Several methods will be described for each operation in each number representation, and the architecture and algorithms will be described in detail.

1.1.1 Positional Number System

The binary number system is the most conventional and easily implemented system for internal use in a digital computer. It is also a positional number system. In this mode of representation, a number is encoded as a vector of n bits (or digits) in which each bit is weighted according to its position in the vector. Associated with each number system is a radix (or base) r. Each bit has an integer value in the range 0 to $r - 1$. In the binary system, where $r = 2$, each bit has the value of 0 or 1.

Consider an n-bit vector of the form

$$A = a_{n-1} a_{n-2} \cdots a_1 a_0$$

where $a_i = 0$ or 1 for $0 \leqslant i \leqslant n - 1$. This vector can represent positive integer values V in the range 0 to $2^n - 1$, where

$$V = a_{n-1} \times 2^{n-1} + \cdots + a_1 \times 2^1 + a_0 \times 2^0 \tag{1.1}$$

Thus, the value for A, which is usually denoted by $|A|$, can be described as

$$A = \sum_{i=0}^{n-1} a_i r^i \tag{1.2}$$

The above representation is for positive integers. This can be extended to include fractions, for example,

$$|A| = a_{n-1} \times 2^{n-1} + \cdots + a_1 \times 2^1 + a_0 \times 2^0$$

$$+ a_{-1} \times 2^{-1} + a_{-2} \times 2^{-2} + \cdots + a_{-m} \times 2^{-m} \tag{1.3}$$

The string of binary digits 1 0 1 1 0 1 . 1 1 0 1 (with radix point) can be interpreted to represent the quantity

$$1 \times 2^5 + 0 \times 2^4 + 1 \times 2^3 + 1 \times 2^2 + 0 \times 2^1 + 1 \times 2^0$$

$$+ 1 \times 2^{-1} + 1 \times 2^{-2} + 0 \times 2^{-3} + 1 \times 2^{-4} = 45 \frac{13}{16}$$

It was previously stated that each bit in a number system has an integer value in the range 0 to $r - 1$. This produces a digit set S

$$S = \{0, 1, 2, \cdots, r-1\} \tag{1.4}$$

in which all the digits of the set are positively weighted. It is also possible to have a digit set in which both positive- and negative-weighted digits are allowed, such as,

$$T = \{-l, \cdots, -1, 0, 1, \cdots, l\} \tag{1.5}$$

where l is a positive integer representing the upper and lower limit of the set. This is considered to be a redundant number system, because there may be more than one way to represent a given number.

Each digit of a redundant number system can assume the $2(l+1)$ values of Eq. 1.5. The range of l is

$$\left\lceil \frac{r-1}{2} \right\rceil \leqslant l \leqslant r-1 \tag{1.6}$$

where $\left\lceil \frac{r-1}{2} \right\rceil$ is called the ceiling of $\frac{r-1}{2}$. For any real number x, the ceiling of x, denoted by $\lceil x \rceil$, is the smallest integer not less than x. The floor of x, denoted by $\lfloor x \rfloor$, is the largest integer not greater than x. Since the integer $l \geqslant 1$ and $r \geqslant 2$, then the maximum magnitude of l will be

$$l = \left\lfloor \frac{r}{2} \right\rfloor \tag{1.7}$$

Thus, for $r = 2$, the digit set is

$$T_{r=2} = \{-1, 0, 1\} \tag{1.8}$$

For $r = 4$, the digit set is

$$T_{r=4} = \{-2, -1, 0, 1, 2\} \tag{1.9}$$

For example, for $n = 4$ and $r = 2$, the number $A = -5$ has four representations as shown below. It is this multirepresentation that makes redundant number

		2^3	2^2	2^1	2^0
A	$=$	0	-1	0	-1
	$=$	0	-1	-1	1
	$=$	-1	0	1	1
	$=$	-1	1	0	-1

systems difficult to use for certain arithmetic operations. Also, since each signed digit may require more than one bit to represent the digit, this may increase both the storage requirements and the width of the storage bus.

1.1.2 Binary, Octal, and Hexadecimal Representation

Other radices used in digital computers are octal (radix 8), decimal (radix 10), and hexadecimal (radix 16). The 8 symbols for octal are 0, 1, 2, 3, 4, 5, 6, and 7. The 10 symbols for decimal are 0, 1, 2, 3, 4, 5, 6, 7, 8, and 9. The 16 symbols for hexadecimal are 0, 1, 2, 3, 4, 5, 6, 7, 8, 9, A, B, C, D, E, and F. The last six symbols in the hexadecimal radix system represent the adopted convention and correspond to the decimal numbers 10, 11, 12, 13, 14, and 15, respectively.

Most current digital computers use the binary ($r = 2$) number system. There is a disadvantage in converting to and from the externally used decimal system, but this is compensated for by the ease of implementing the four basic operations: addition, subtraction, multiplication, and division. The fractional point is inserted when using paper and pencil to perform computations, but is implied within the internal structure of the computer; that is, there is no specific storage element assigned to contain the fractional point.

Since $2^3 = 8$ and $2^4 = 16$, each octal digit corresponds to three binary bits and each hexadecimal digit corresponds to four binary bits. Conversion from binary to octal is easily accomplished by partitioning the binary number into groups of three bits per group. A corresponding octal digit is then assigned to each group, and the string of octal digits thus obtained is equivalent to the binary representation of the number. This is illustrated in Fig. 1.1. There are two implied 0s to the left of the high-order (leftmost) binary digit. This facilitates the assignment of the octal digit.

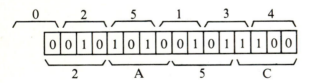

Figure 1.1 Binary, octal, and hexadecimal representation.

Similarly, conversion from binary to hexadecimal is accomplished by partitioning the binary number into groups of four bits. A corresponding hexadecimal digit is then assigned to each group, and the string of hexadecimal digits thus obtained is equivalent to the binary representation of the number. This is also shown in Fig. 1.1, which represents a particular example of a 16-bit register. Since a binary number consists of a string of 0s and 1s, the 16-bit register of Fig. 1.1 can contain a binary number in the range 0 to $2^{16} - 1$. For the particular example shown, the binary number $0\,0\,1\,0\,1\,0\,1\,0\,0\,1\,0\,1\,1\,1\,0\,0_2$ is equivalent to $10,844_{10}$, 025134_8, and $2A5C_{16}$.

Tables 1.1 and 1.2 list some octal and hexadecimal numbers, respectively, and their corresponding representation in decimal and binary-coded form. The binary-coded form is obtained from the procedure explained previously. The same binary bit configuration can be represented in both octal and hexadecimal. For example, the binary equivalent of decimal 117_{10} is 1 1 1 0 1 0 1. The binary-coded octal equivalent is 165_8 with two implied leading 0s. The binary-coded hexadecimal equivalent is 75_{16} with one implied leading 0. In all cases, the bit configuration is the same. Long strings of 1s and 0s are inconvenient to represent in true binary form. It is for this reason that computer manuals and printouts invariably choose either octal or hexadecimal designation when specifying the contents of registers in a computer.

The binary number system is the most natural system for a computer, but human beings are accustomed to using the decimal numbers 0–9. One way to bridge this difference is to convert the decimal inputs to a computer into binary, to perform the required computation, and then to convert the binary results into decimal. However, it is also possible to perform arithmetic operations on decimal numbers directly, provided they are placed in the registers in the proper form.

A binary number is a group of n bits that can assume 2^n different combinations of the values of the n bits. The binary-coded decimal (BCD) representation consists of four bits per digit, giving a total of $2^4 = 16$ combinations. However, only ten of these combinations are valid, because the decimal digits consist of the numbers 0–9 only. The bit assignment most commonly used for the 10 decimal digits in BCD notation is shown in Table 1.3. The decimal number 134 is 1 0 0 0 0 1 1 0 in binary, but when encoded in BCD it is represented as 0 0 0 1   0 0 1 1   0 1 0 0. The only difference between a decimal number

Table 1.1 Binary-coded octal numbers

Octal number	Binary-coded octal			Decimal equivalent
0			0 0 0	0
1			0 0 1	1
2			0 1 0	2
3			0 1 1	3
4			1 0 0	4
5			1 0 1	5
6			1 1 0	6
7			1 1 1	7
10		0 0 1	0 0 0	8
11		0 0 1	0 0 1	9
12		0 0 1	0 1 0	10
23		0 1 0	0 1 1	19
56		1 0 1	1 1 0	46
124	0 0 1	0 1 0	1 0 0	84
362	0 1 1	1 1 0	0 1 0	242
571	1 0 1	1 1 1	0 0 1	377

Table 1.2 Binary-coded hexadecimal numbers

Hexadecimal number	Binary-coded hexadecimal		Decimal equivalent
0		0 0 0 0	0
1		0 0 0 0	1
2		0 0 1 0	2
3		0 0 1 1	3
4		0 1 0 0	4
5		0 1 0 1	5
6		0 1 1 0	6
7		0 1 1 1	7
8		1 0 0 0	8
9		1 0 0 1	9
A		1 0 1 0	10
B		1 0 1 1	11
C		1 1 0 0	12
D		1 1 0 1	13
E		1 1 1 0	14
F		1 1 1 1	15
12	0 0 0 1	0 0 1 0	18
16	0 0 0 1	0 1 1 0	22
19	0 0 0 1	1 0 0 1	25
2A	0 0 1 0	1 0 1 0	42
B6	1 0 1 1	0 1 1 0	182
CD	1 1 0 0	1 1 0 1	205
F4	1 1 1 1	0 1 0 0	244

Table 1.3 Binary-coded decimal (BCD) numbers

Decimal number	Binary-coded decimal number		
0			0 0 0 0
1			0 0 0 1
2			0 0 1 0
3			0 0 1 1
4			0 1 0 0
5			0 1 0 1
6			0 1 1 0
7			0 1 1 1
8			1 0 0 0
9			1 0 0 1
17		0 0 0 1	0 1 1 1
26		0 0 1 0	0 1 1 0
72		0 1 1 1	0 0 1 0
134	0 0 0 1	0 0 1 1	0 1 0 0
573	0 1 0 1	0 1 1 1	0 0 1 1
999	1 0 0 1	1 0 0 1	1 0 0 1

represented by the decimal digits 0–9 and a BCD number of the same value is in the symbols used to represent the digits—the number itself is exactly the same.

1.1.3 Number Representations

All mathematical functions can be expressed in terms of the four basic arithmetic operations: addition, subtraction, multiplication, and division. These operations can be executed in three operation modes corresonding to the three major types of number representations: fixed point, decimal, and floating point.

Fixed-point arithmetic is used primarily on problems where the data is represented with a fixed radix point; that is, the radix point (binary point when radix = 2) remains in a fixed position within the number. Fixed-point operations can be subdivided into two categories. In integer arithmetic, the radix point is to the right of the number, so that an integer number represented in fixed-point notation has an implied radix point to the right of the register containing the number. In fractional arithmetic, the radix point is to the left of the number. The two formats are shown below. Most computer designers adopt the integer method.

Integer format | X   X   X   · ·   X | •

Fraction format   • | X   X   X   · ·   X |

where x = 0 or 1.

Decimal arithmetic is used for arithmetic, shifting, and editing operations on decimal data. Decimal digits may be represented in either packed or unpacked format. In the packed format, each byte (eight bits) contains two decimal digits. Provision is also made for a sign digit, which is also four bits. In the unpacked format, the rightmost four bits of a byte constitute the decimal digit; the leftmost four bits are not used to represent decimal data. (They serve as "packing" to make each digit one byte long, or to expand the range to include alphabetic and special characters.) The two formats are shown below.

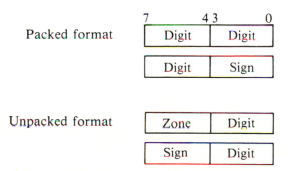

Floating-point arithmetic is used mainly for scientific and engineering computations, in which frequent magnitude scaling is required. Floating-point operations can also be subdivided into two categories. Normalized operations require that all data entering into a computation be normalized; that is, the numbers are represented in fractional form and the bit to the immediate right of the radix point is 1. Unnormalized operations also represent the numbers in fractional form, but the bit to the immediate right of the radix point can be 1 or 0. Both formats are shown below. Most computers are designed to operate with normalized numbers.

Normalized format • | 1   x   x · · · x |

Unnormalized format • | x   x   x · · · x |

where x = 0 or 1.

1.1.4 Integer Representations

If only positive integers were to be represented in fixed-point notation, then an n-bit word would permit a range from 0 to $2^n - 1$. However, both positive and negative integers are used in computations and an encoding scheme must be devised in which both positive and negative numbers are distributed as evenly as possible. There must also be an easy way to distinguish between positive and negative numbers, that is, an easy sign test. Detection of 0s must be simple, and the execution of the four basic operations must be easily implemented.

A signed radix number must be either positive or negative. The left-most (high-order) digit is usually reserved for the sign. Consider the following number A with radix r,

$$A = (a_{n-1} \, a_{n-2} \, \cdots \, a_1 \, a_0)_r$$

where the sign digit a_{n-1} has the following value:

$$a_{n-1} = \begin{cases} 0 & \text{if } |A| \geqslant 0 \\ r-1 & \text{if } |A| < 0 \end{cases} \tag{1.10}$$

For binary numbers, where $r = 2$, Eq. 1.10 becomes

$$a_{n-1} = \begin{cases} 0 & \text{if } |A| \geqslant 0 \\ 1 & \text{if } |A| < 0 \end{cases} \tag{1.11}$$

The remaining digits in A indicate either the true magnitude of A or the magnitude of A in a complemented form. There are three conventional ways to represent positive and negative numbers in a positional number system: sign magnitude, diminished-radix complement, and radix complement.

Sign magnitude In this representation, the high-order bit indicates the sign of the integer (0 for +, 1 for −). A positive number has a range of 0 to $2^{n-1} - 1$, and a negative number has a range of 0 to $-(2^{n-1} - 1)$. Thus, a positive number can be represented as

$$A = (0 \, a_{n-2} \, a_{n-3} \cdots a_1 \, a_0)_r \qquad (1.12)$$

and a negative number as

$$-A = [(r-1) \, a_{n-2} \, a_{n-3} \cdots a_1 \, a_0]_r \qquad (1.13)$$

For $r = 2$, Eqs. 1.12 and 1.13 become

$$A = 0 \, a_{n-2} \, a_{n-3} \cdots a_1 \, a_0 \qquad (1.14)$$

and

$$-A = 1 \, a_{n-2} \, a_{n-3} \cdots a_1 \, a_0 \qquad (1.15)$$

respectively. In sign-magnitude notation, the positive version A differs from the negative version $-A$ only in the sign digit position. The magnitude portion $a_{n-2} \, a_{n-3} \cdots a_1 \, a_0$ is identical for both positive and negative numbers (Table 1.4).

One problem with sign-magnitude notation is the dual representation of the number 0, namely +0 and −0. A second problem occurs when adding two numbers of opposite sign; the magnitudes must be compared to determine the sign of the result. This is not required in the other two methods. Sign-magnitude notation is still frequently used in the representation of fractions in floating-point formats.

Diminished-radix complement In binary notation, the diminished-radix $(r-1)$ complement is the 1s complement. Positive integers in the range 0 to $2^{n-1} - 1$ are still represented as in the binary positional system, that is,

$$A = 0 \, a_{n-2} \, a_{n-3} \cdots a_1 \, a_0$$

Negative numbers in the range 0 to $-(2^{n-1} - 1)$ are represented by first obtaining their absolute value (the numerical value of the number regardless of sign) as above, and then complementing each bit of the corresponding positive value; that is, change 0s to 1s and change 1s to 0s. Thus, a positive number is

Table 1.4 Signed-integer representation

$a_3\ a_2\ a_1\ a_0$	Sign magnitude	1s complement	2s complement
0 1 1 1	+ 7	+ 7	+ 7
0 1 1 0	+ 6	+ 6	+ 6
0 1 0 1	+ 5	+ 5	+ 5
0 1 0 0	+ 4	+ 4	+ 4
0 0 1 1	+ 3	+ 3	+ 3
0 0 1 0	+ 2	+ 2	+ 2
0 0 0 1	+ 1	+ 1	+ 1
0 0 0 0	+ 0	+ 0	+ 0
1 0 0 0	− 0	− 7	− 8
1 0 0 1	− 1	− 6	− 7
1 0 1 0	− 2	− 5	− 6
1 0 1 1	− 3	− 4	− 5
1 1 0 0	− 4	− 3	− 4
1 1 0 1	− 5	− 2	− 3
1 1 1 0	− 6	− 1	− 2
1 1 1 1	− 7	− 0	− 1

Note: The most negative number in 2s complement representation, for $n = 4$, is $1\,0\,0\,0_2$ (-8_{10}). When adding $0\,1\,1\,1_2$ ($+7_{10}$) to $0\,0\,0\,1_2$ ($+1_{10}$), the result is $1\,0\,0\,0_2$ ($+8_{10}$). This should not be confused with $1\,0\,0\,0_2$ (-8_{10}), because the result of the addition produces an overflow condition (Sec. 2.2.1) resulting in invalid data for $n = 4$. The result is valid, however, for $n = 5$.

represented by

$$A = 0\, a_{n-2}\, a_{n-3}\ \cdots\ a_1\, a_0 \tag{1.16}$$

and the same absolute value is represented as a negative number by

$$\overline{A} = 1\, \overline{a}_{n-2}\, \overline{a}_{n-3}\ \cdots\ \overline{a}_1\, \overline{a}_0 \tag{1.17}$$

or, more generally,

$$\overline{A} = [\,(r-1)\,\overline{a}_{n-2}\, \overline{a}_{n-3}\ \cdots\ \overline{a}_1\, \overline{a}_0\,]_r \tag{1.18}$$

where $\overline{a}_i = (r-1) - a_i$.

Comparing the signs of two numbers is straightforward, because the leftmost bit is a 0 for positive numbers and a 1 for negative numbers. Unfortunately, there is still a dual representation for 0, because a word of all 0s (+ 0) becomes a word of all 1s (− 0) when complemented.

Radix complement In binary notation, the radix complement is the 2s complement. Positive numbers in the range 0 to $2^{n-1} - 1$ are still represented in the usual binary positional system; that is,

$$A = 0\, a_{n-2}\, a_{n-3} \, \cdots \, a_1\, a_0$$

Negative numbers are obtained by adding 1 to the 1s complement representation of the desired negative value. Thus, a negative number is represented by

$$(\overline{A})_{+1} = (1\, \overline{a}_{n-2}\, \overline{a}_{n-3} \, \cdots \, \overline{a}_1\, \overline{a}_0) + 1 \tag{1.19}$$

Therefore, to form a negative number in 2s complement notation, take the corresponding positive number, complement each bit, and add 1 to the low-order bit position. This addition may change all n bits of the number; for example, for $r = 2$, the 2s complement of 0 0 0 0 0 0 0 0 becomes

$$
\begin{array}{r}
1\;1\;1\;1\;1\;1\;1\;1 \\
+\qquad\qquad\quad 1 \\
\hline
1 \leftarrow 0\;0\;0\;0\;0\;0\;0\;0
\end{array}
$$

Generally, the radix complement of a negative number is represented by

$$(\overline{A})_{+1} = \{\,[\,(r-1)\, \overline{a}_{n-2}\, \overline{a}_{n-3} \, \cdots \, \overline{a}_1\, \overline{a}_0\,] + 1\,\}_r \tag{1.20}$$

or $(\overline{A})_{+1} = r^n - A$. The sign test is again a simple comparison of two bits. There is a unique representation of 0, because a string of 0s, when negated, becomes a string of 0s (the carry-out of the high-order bit position is discarded).

The range is represented by -2^{n-1} to $2^{n-1} - 1$, where -2^{n-1} is represented by a 1 followed by $(n-1)$ 0s. Addition and subtraction are easier here than in diminished-radix complement and the result is always in correct 2s complement notation. The above three representations are summarized in Table 1.5.

Table 1.5 Fixed-point (integer) representations of positive and negative binary numbers of the same absolute value

Number representation	Radix = 2	
	Positive numbers	Negative numbers
Sign magnitude	$0\, a_{n-2}\, a_{n-3} \, \cdots \, a_1\, a_0$	$1\, a_{n-2}\, a_{n-3} \, \cdots \, a_1\, a_0$
Diminished-radix complement (1s complement)	$0\, a_{n-2}\, a_{n-3} \, \cdots \, a_1\, a_0$	$1\, \overline{a}_{n-2}\, \overline{a}_{n-3} \, \cdots \, \overline{a}_1\, \overline{a}_0$
Radix complement (2s complement)	$0\, a_{n-2}\, a_{n-3} \, \cdots \, a_1\, a_0$	$1\, \overline{a}_{n-2}\, \overline{a}_{n-3} \, \cdots \, \overline{a}_1\, \overline{a}_0 +1$

Decimal integer representation Numbers represented in decimal use more storage space than an equivalent binary representation. Also, the circuits for decimal arithmetic are more complex than those for binary arithmetic. The advantages are that people are familiar with the decimal number system and most input/output data is in the decimal notation. There are three commonly used ways to represent fixed-point decimal numbers. These are the same as for binary numbers except for a radix change: sign magnitude, diminished-radix (9s) complement, and radix (10s) complement.

For all three representations, a positive decimal number can be represented by a 0 bit or 0 digit followed by the magnitude of the number. Some formats require the sign digit to be to the right of the low-order digit. It is for negative numbers where the representations differ. For sign-magnitude representation, the sign digit is 9 $(r - 1)$ and the magnitude is positive. For the 9s complement representation, the sign digit is 9 $(r - 1)$ and the magnitude is also in 9s complement. The 10s complement representation is the same as the 9s complement, but with a 1 added to the low-order digit. Table 1.6 shows the three representations for positive and negative decimal numbers.

Table 1.6 Fixed-point representations of positive and negative decimal numbers

Number representation	Radix = 10	
	Positive numbers	Negative numbers
Sign magnitude	$0\ a_{n-2}\ a_{n-3}\ \cdots\ a_1\ a_0$	$9\ a_{n-2}\ a_{n-3}\ \cdots\ a_1\ a_0$
Diminished-radix complement (9s complement)	$0\ a_{n-2}\ a_{n-3}\ \cdots\ a_1\ a_0$	$9\ \bar{a}_{n-2}\ \bar{a}_{n-3}\ \cdots\ \bar{a}_1\ \bar{a}_0$
Radix complement (10s complement)	$0\ a_{n-2}\ a_{n-3}\ \cdots\ a_1\ a_0$	$9\ \bar{a}_{n-2}\ \bar{a}_{n-3}\ \cdots\ \bar{a}_1\ \bar{a}_0 + 1$

1.2 LOGIC DESIGN

Digital computers operate on binary digits, which can have only one of two possible values: 0 or 1. Computation, therefore, must be done in a number system that has only two states. In mathematical logic, propositions are considered that are either true or false, permitting logical variables to be defined that have either true or false values. Thus, digital computers and mathematical logic are both two-variable systems, and much of the mathematics that has been developed for deductive mathematical systems can be applied to the analysis and synthesis of digital computers.

The purpose of this section on logic design is to review the axioms and theorems of boolean algebra, to present minimization techniques for boolean expressions, to introduce combinational and sequential logic circuits, and to present the theory and design of finite-state machines.

1.2.1 Boolean Algebra

In 1854 George Boole introduced a systematic treatment of logical operations, which is now called *boolean algebra*. The symbols most often used for boolean addition are $\vee$ or $+$. The symbols most often used for boolean multiplication are $\wedge$ or $\cdot$; in cases where the operation is obvious, no symbol is used. The addition symbols $\vee$ and $+$ are read as OR and are called the *OR operator*. Thus, $A \vee B$ is read as A OR B. The multiplication symbols $\wedge$ and $\cdot$ are read as AND and are called the *AND operator*. Thus, $A \wedge B$ is read A AND B. The symbols most often used for the complement operation (or negation) are the bar ($^{-}$) over the variable or the prime ($'$) symbol. Thus, $\overline{A}$ is read as NOT A. The symbols most often used for the EXCLUSIVE-OR (A OR B, but not both A AND B) function are $\veebar$ or $\oplus$.

In a book that deals with both arithmetic and logical operations, it is sometimes confusing to use the symbol $+$ to indicate both the operation of addition and also the logical connective OR. Therefore, this book will use the symbols listed below for the corresponding operations.

Operator	Function
$\vee$	OR
$\wedge$	AND
$\veebar$	EXCLUSIVE-OR
$\overline{A}, \neg A$	Negation
$+$	Addition
$-$	Subtraction
$\times$	Multiplication
$/, \div$	Division
$\cdot$	Concatenation (elements that are linked together in a series or chain, thus treating all of the elements as one unit)

Axioms and theorems Like any other deductive mathematical system, boolean algebra can be defined with a set of variables, a set of fundamental operators, and a set of axioms (or postulates). A *set* is a collection of objects having a common property. The objects are called the *elements* of the set to which they belong. If A is an element of set S, then this is written as $A \in S$. If B is not an element of set S, then this is written as $B \notin S$. Also, if set S consists of elements which are the numbers 1, 2, 3, and 4, then $S = \{ 1, 2, 3, 4 \}$. An *axiom* is a statement that is universally accepted as true; that is, the statement needs no proof, because its truth is obvious. The axioms of a mathematical system form the basis from which it is possible to derive theorems and other properties of the system. The four most common axioms used in boolean algebra are described below.

Axiom 1: Commutative laws There are two commutative laws in boolean algebra: one for the OR function and one for the AND function. Both commutative laws state that the order in which the variables appear in an expression is not important; the result is the same.

(*a*) Commutativity with respect to $\vee$:

$$A \vee B = B \vee A \qquad (1.21)$$

(*b*) Commutativity with respect to $\wedge$:

$$A \wedge B = B \wedge A \qquad (1.22)$$

Axiom 2: Distributive laws The distributive laws for boolean algebra are essentially the same as those for ordinary algebra. The interpretation, however, is different.

(*a*) $\vee$ is distributed over $\wedge$:

$$A \vee (B \wedge C) = (A \vee B) \wedge (A \vee C) \qquad (1.23)$$

(*b*) $\wedge$ is distributed over $\vee$:

$$A \wedge (B \vee C) = (A \wedge B) \vee (A \wedge C) \qquad (1.24)$$

Axiom 3: Identity laws There exists distinct identity elements 0 and 1, where

(*a*) 0 is an identity element with respect to $\vee$, such that

$$A \vee 0 = 0 \vee A = A \qquad (1.25)$$

(*b*) 1 is an identity element with respect to $\wedge$, such that

$$A \wedge 1 = 1 \wedge A = A \qquad (1.26)$$

Axiom 4: Complementation laws For every element $A \in S$, there exists an element $\overline{A}$ (called the *complement of A*), where $\overline{A} \in S$, such that

(*a*) $\qquad\qquad\qquad A \vee \overline{A} = 1 \qquad (1.27)$

(*b*) $\qquad\qquad\qquad A \wedge \overline{A} = 0 \qquad (1.28)$

Principle of duality The preceding axioms were listed in pairs and designated (*a*) and (*b*). One part may be obtained from the other by interchanging the binary operators and the identity elements. Thus, every algebraic expression or theorem that can be deduced from the axioms of boolean algebra can be transformed into a second valid expression or theorem if the operators $\vee$ and $\wedge$ and the identity elements 0 and 1 are interchanged. All axioms conform to the principle of duality. For example, if the dual of an algebraic expression is desired, simply interchange the OR and AND operators, and replace 0s with 1s and 1s with 0s.

Basic theorems The following theorems are derived by means of the axioms, and are listed in pairs; each relation in the pair is the dual of the other. To the right of each step in the proof is the number of the axiom or theorem that justifies the step.

Theorem 1: 0 and 1 associated with a variable For each element A in a boolean algebra,

(a) $$A \vee 1 = 1 \qquad (1.29)$$

PROOF

$$
\begin{aligned}
A \vee 1 &= 1 \wedge (A \vee 1) & \text{Axiom 3}(b) \\
&= (A \vee \bar{A}) \wedge (A \vee 1) & \text{Axiom 4}(a) \\
&= A \vee (\bar{A} \wedge 1) & \text{Axiom 2}(a) \\
&= A \vee \bar{A} & \text{Axiom 3}(b) \\
&= 1 & \text{Axiom 4}(a)
\end{aligned}
$$

(b) $$A \wedge 0 = 0 \qquad \text{by duality} \qquad (1.30)$$

Theorem 2: 0 and 1 complement The two-valued boolean algebra has two distinct elements, 0 and 1, such that $0 \neq 1$. Therefore, each of the identity elements is the complement of the other. Thus,

(a) $$\bar{0} = 1 \qquad (1.31)$$

(b) $$\bar{1} = 0 \qquad (1.32)$$

Theorem 3: Idempotent laws The first idempotent law states that if A is equal to 1, then A OR A will be equal to 1. Likewise, if A is equal to 0, then A OR A will be equal to 0. Thus, one of the A's is unnecessary and may be discarded. This is also referred to as the *law of tautology* and is implied for boolean addition and multiplication; that is, there is a needless repetition of the variable.

(a) $$A \vee A = A \qquad (1.33)$$

PROOF

$$A \lor A = (A \lor A) \land 1 \qquad \text{Axiom } 3(b)$$
$$= (A \lor A) \land (A \lor \overline{A}) \qquad \text{Axiom } 4(a)$$
$$= A \lor (A \land \overline{A}) \qquad \text{Axiom } 2(a)$$
$$= A \lor 0 \qquad \text{Axiom } 4(b)$$
$$= A \qquad \text{Axiom } 3(a)$$

(b) $\qquad\qquad A \land A = A \qquad$ by duality $\qquad\qquad$ (1.34)

The idempotent laws are true for any number of variables A. Thus,

$$A \lor A \lor A \lor \cdots \lor A = A$$

and

$$A \land A \land A \land \cdots \land A = A$$

Theorem 4: Involution law The involution law states that the complement of a complemented variable is the variable itself. This law is also referred to as the *law of double complementation*. Thus,

$$\overline{\overline{A}} = A \qquad\qquad (1.35)$$

PROOF Let $\overline{A}$ be the complement of A and $\overline{\overline{A}}$ be the complement of $\overline{A}$. Then,

$$\overline{\overline{A}} = \overline{\overline{A}} \lor 0 \qquad\qquad \text{Axiom } 3(a)$$
$$= \overline{\overline{A}} \lor (A \land \overline{A}) \qquad\qquad \text{Axiom } 4(b)$$
$$= (\overline{\overline{A}} \lor A) \land (\overline{\overline{A}} \lor \overline{A}) \qquad\qquad \text{Axiom } 2(a)$$
$$= (\overline{\overline{A}} \lor A) \land 1 \qquad\qquad \text{Axiom } 4(a)$$
$$= (\overline{\overline{A}} \lor A) \land (\overline{A} \lor A) \qquad\qquad \text{Axiom } 4(a)$$
$$= [(\overline{\overline{A}} \lor A) \land \overline{A}] \lor [(\overline{\overline{A}} \lor A) \land A] \qquad\qquad \text{Axiom } 2(b)$$
$$= (\overline{\overline{A}} \land \overline{A}) \lor (A \land \overline{A}) \lor (\overline{\overline{A}} \land A) \lor (A \land A) \qquad\qquad \text{Axiom } 2(b)$$
$$= 0 \lor 0 \lor (\overline{\overline{A}} \land A) \lor (A \land A) \qquad\qquad \text{Axiom } 4(b)$$
$$= (\overline{\overline{A}} \land A) \lor (A \land A) \qquad\qquad \text{Axiom } 3(a)$$
$$= (\overline{\overline{A}} \land A) \lor A \qquad\qquad \text{Theorem } 3(b)$$
$$= A \land (1 \lor \overline{\overline{A}}) \qquad\qquad \text{Axiom } 2(b)$$
$$= A \land 1 \qquad\qquad \text{Theorem } 1(a)$$
$$= A \qquad\qquad \text{Axiom } 3(b)$$

Theorem 5: Absorption laws The absorption laws state that some two-variable boolean expressions can be reduced to a single variable. The second variable can be removed from the expression without altering the result.

(*a*) $A \vee (A \wedge B) = A$ (does not imply $A \wedge B = 0$)   (1.36)

PROOF

$$
\begin{aligned}
A \vee (A \wedge B) &= (A \wedge 1) \vee (A \wedge B) & \text{Axiom 3(}b\text{)}\\
&= A \wedge (1 \vee B) & \text{Axiom 2(}b\text{)}\\
&= A \wedge (B \vee 1) & \text{Axiom 1(}a\text{)}\\
&= A \wedge 1 & \text{Theorem 1(}a\text{)}\\
&= A & \text{Axiom 3(}b\text{)}
\end{aligned}
$$

(*b*) $A \wedge (A \vee B) = A$ by duality   (1.37)

Theorem 6: Absorption laws (simplification) This is a different form of the absorption laws and is used for simplification of certain boolean expressions.

(*a*) $A \vee (\overline{A} \wedge B) = A \vee B$ (1.38)

PROOF

$$
\begin{aligned}
A \vee (\overline{A} \wedge B) &= (A \vee \overline{A}) \wedge (A \vee B) & \text{Axiom 2(}a\text{)}\\
&= 1 \wedge (A \vee B) & \text{Axiom 4(}a\text{)}\\
&= A \vee B & \text{Axiom 3(}b\text{)}
\end{aligned}
$$

(*b*) $A \wedge (\overline{A} \vee B) = A \wedge B$ by duality   (1.39)

Theorem 7: Associative laws The associative laws state that three or more variables can be combined by means of logical addition or multiplication. The variables can be combined in any order without changing the result. The associative law states that

(*a*) $(A \vee B) \vee C = A \vee (B \vee C)$ (by duality from Eq. 1.41)   (1.40)

(*b*) $(A \wedge B) \wedge C = A \wedge (B \wedge C)$ (1.41)

PROOF Let $X = (A \wedge B) \wedge C$ and $Y = A \wedge (B \wedge C)$. Prove that $X = Y$.

$$
\begin{aligned}
A \vee X = A \vee [(A \wedge B) \wedge C] \\
= [A \vee (A \wedge B)] \wedge (A \vee C) & \quad \text{Axiom 2(}a\text{)}\\
= A \wedge (A \vee C) & \quad \text{Theorem 5(}a\text{)}\\
= A & \quad \text{Theorem 5(}b\text{)}
\end{aligned}
$$

Also,

$$A \vee Y = A \vee [A \wedge (B \wedge C)]$$
$$= (A \vee A) \wedge [A \vee (B \wedge C)] \qquad \text{Axiom 2}(a)$$
$$= A \wedge [A \vee (B \wedge C)] \qquad \text{Theorem 3}(a)$$
$$= A \qquad \text{Theorem 5}(b)$$

Therefore, $A \vee X = A \vee Y$.

Now prove that $\overline{A} \vee X = \overline{A} \vee Y$.

$$\overline{A} \vee X = \overline{A} \vee [(A \wedge B) \wedge C]$$
$$= [\overline{A} \vee (A \wedge B)] \wedge (\overline{A} \vee C) \qquad \text{Axiom 2}(a)$$
$$= [(\overline{A} \vee A) \wedge (\overline{A} \vee B)] \wedge (\overline{A} \vee C) \qquad \text{Axiom 2}(a)$$
$$= [1 \wedge (\overline{A} \vee B)] \wedge (\overline{A} \vee C) \qquad \text{Axiom 4}(a)$$
$$= (\overline{A} \vee B) \wedge (\overline{A} \vee C) \qquad \text{Axiom 3}(b)$$
$$= \overline{A} \vee (B \wedge C) \qquad \text{Axiom 2}(a)$$

Also,

$$\overline{A} \vee Y = \overline{A} \vee [A \wedge (B \wedge C)]$$
$$= (\overline{A} \vee A) \wedge [\overline{A} \vee (B \wedge C)] \qquad \text{Axiom 2}(a)$$
$$= 1 \wedge [\overline{A} \vee (B \wedge C)] \qquad \text{Axiom 4}(a)$$
$$= \overline{A} \vee (B \wedge C) \qquad \text{Axiom 3}(b)$$
$$= \overline{A} \vee X \qquad \text{From above}$$

Therefore, $\overline{A} \vee X = \overline{A} \vee Y$. Thus,

$$(A \vee X) \wedge (\overline{A} \vee X) = (A \vee Y) \wedge (\overline{A} \vee Y)$$
$$[(A \vee X) \wedge \overline{A}] \vee [(A \vee X) \wedge X]$$
$$= [(A \vee Y) \wedge \overline{A}] \vee [(A \vee Y) \wedge Y] \qquad \text{Axiom 2}(b)$$

$$(\overline{A} \wedge A) \vee (\overline{A} \wedge X) \vee [(A \vee X) \wedge X]$$
$$= (\overline{A} \wedge A) \vee (\overline{A} \wedge Y) \vee [(A \vee Y) \wedge Y] \qquad \text{Axiom 2}(b)$$

$$(\overline{A} \wedge A) \vee (\overline{A} \wedge X) \vee X$$
$$= (\overline{A} \wedge A) \vee (\overline{A} \wedge Y) \vee Y \qquad \text{Theorem 5}(b)$$

$$(\overline{A} \wedge X) \vee X$$
$$= (\overline{A} \wedge Y) \vee Y \qquad \text{Axiom 4}(b)$$

$$X = Y \qquad \text{Theorem 5}(a)$$

Therefore, $(A \wedge B) \wedge C = A \wedge (B \wedge C)$.

Theorem 8: DeMorgan's laws Any equation in boolean algebra can be written in either of two fundamental forms: the minterm form or the maxterm form. A *minterm* is a term consisting of variables that are ANDed together; that is, it is a logical product of two or more variables. An example of a minterm is

$$A \wedge B \wedge C$$

A minterm form of equation is

$$f = (A \wedge B \wedge C) \vee (\overline{A} \wedge B \wedge \overline{C}) \qquad (1.42)$$

This is also referred to as a *sum of minterms,* in which each term contains all of the variables in either their true or complemented form. When the equation is composed of terms that do not contain all variables, then this is called a *sum of products.* An example of a sum of products is

$$f = (A \wedge B) \vee (A \wedge B \wedge \overline{C}) \vee \overline{B} \qquad (1.43)$$

A *maxterm* is a term consisting of variables that are ORed together; that is, it is a logical addition of two or more variables. An example of a maxterm is

$$A \vee B \vee C$$

A maxterm form of equation is

$$f = (A \vee B \vee C) \wedge (\overline{A} \vee B \vee \overline{C}) \qquad (1.44)$$

This is also referred to as a *product of maxterms,* in which each term contains all of the variables in either their true or complemented form. When the equation is composed of terms that do not contain all variables, then this is called a *product of sums.* An example of a product of sums is

$$f = (A \vee B) \wedge (A \vee B \vee \overline{C}) \wedge \overline{B}$$

DeMorgan's laws permit a boolean expression to be converted from a minterm form to an equivalent maxterm form, or vice versa. Thus,

(*a*) $$\overline{(A \vee B)} = \overline{A} \wedge \overline{B} \qquad (1.45)$$

PROOF Assume that $\overline{A} \wedge \overline{B}$ is the complement of $A \vee B$. Therefore, if it can be shown that

$$(A \vee B) \vee (\overline{A} \wedge \overline{B}) = 1 \qquad \text{Axiom 4}(a)$$

and

$$(A \vee B) \wedge (\overline{A} \wedge \overline{B}) = 0 \qquad \text{Axiom 4}(b)$$

then this implies that $(\overline{A \vee B}) = \overline{A} \wedge \overline{B}$.

$$
\begin{aligned}
(A \vee B) \vee (\overline{A} \wedge \overline{B}) &= [(A \vee B) \vee \overline{A}] \\
&\quad \wedge [(A \vee B) \vee \overline{B}] && \text{Axiom 2}(a) \\
&= [(B \vee A) \vee \overline{A}] \\
&\quad \wedge [(A \vee B) \vee \overline{B}] && \text{Axiom 1}(a) \\
&= [B \vee (A \vee \overline{A})] \\
&\quad \wedge [A \vee (B \vee \overline{B})] && \text{Theorem 7}(a) \\
&= (B \vee 1) \wedge (A \vee 1) && \text{Axiom 4}(a) \\
&= 1 \wedge 1 && \text{Theorem 1}(a) \\
&= 1 && \text{Axiom 3}(b)
\end{aligned}
$$

$$
\begin{aligned}
(A \vee B) \wedge (\overline{A} \wedge \overline{B}) &= (\overline{A} \wedge \overline{B}) \wedge (A \vee B) && \text{Axiom 1}(b) \\
&= [(\overline{A} \wedge \overline{B}) \wedge A] \\
&\quad \vee [(\overline{A} \wedge \overline{B}) \wedge B] && \text{Axiom 2}(b) \\
&= [(\overline{B} \wedge \overline{A}) \wedge A] \\
&\quad \vee [(\overline{A} \wedge \overline{B}) \wedge B] && \text{Axiom 1}(b) \\
&= [\overline{B} \wedge (\overline{A} \wedge A)] \\
&\quad \vee [\overline{A} \wedge (\overline{B} \wedge B)] && \text{Theorem 7}(b) \\
&= (\overline{B} \wedge 0) \vee (\overline{A} \wedge 0) && \text{Axiom 4}(b) \\
&= 0 \vee 0 && \text{Theorem 1}(b) \\
&= 0 && \text{Theorem 3}(a)
\end{aligned}
$$

Therefore, $(\overline{A \vee B}) = \overline{A} \wedge \overline{B}$.

(b) $\qquad\qquad (\overline{A \wedge B}) = \overline{A} \vee \overline{B} \qquad$ by duality $\qquad\qquad (1.46)$

Theorem 9: Generalized DeMorgan's laws DeMorgan's laws can be generalized for any number of variables such that

(a)

$$\overline{(A_0 \vee A_1 \vee A_2 \vee \cdots \vee A_n)}$$
$$= \overline{A_0} \wedge \overline{A_1} \wedge \overline{A_2} \wedge \cdots \wedge \overline{A_n} \qquad (1.47)$$

(b)

$$\overline{(A_0 \wedge A_1 \wedge A_2 \wedge \cdots \wedge A_n)}$$
$$= \overline{A_0} \vee \overline{A_1} \vee \overline{A_2} \vee \cdots \vee \overline{A_n} \qquad (1.48)$$

Truth tables A *truth table* is one of several notations commonly employed to express the relationship between binary variables. A truth table lists all possible combinations of the independent variables and shows the connection between the values of these variables and the result of the operation in terms of the dependent variable. This section examines the relationships between truth tables and equations. For each combination of values of the independent variables A and B, there is a value of the dependent variable f that is specified by the definition of the logical operation. For example, the truth tables for the operations AND, OR, and EXCLUSIVE-OR are listed in Table 1.7. These tables are constructed by listing all possible values of the variables when combined in pairs. The result of the operation for each pair of variables is listed in a separate column. The tables illustrate the definitions of the operations.

Table 1.7 Truth tables for operations AND, OR, and EXCLUSIVE-OR

AND			OR			EXCLUSIVE-OR		
A	B	$f = A \wedge B$	A	B	$f = A \vee B$	A	B	$f = A \not\vee B$
0	0	0	0	0	0	0	0	0
0	1	0	0	1	1	0	1	1
1	0	0	1	0	1	1	0	1
1	1	1	1	1	1	1	1	0

The output function f can be read directly from the truth table. For example, the OR function produces the following sum of minterms that corresponds to the rows, where $f = 1$:

$$f = (\overline{A} \wedge B) \vee (A \wedge \overline{B}) \vee (A \wedge B) \qquad (1.49)$$

This may not be the simplest expression for the function f, because there may be unnecessary variables in the equation. In fact, Eq. 1.49 reduces to $A \vee B$. This is accomplished by applying the preceding axioms and theorems as shown below.

$$(\overline{A} \wedge B) \vee (A \wedge \overline{B}) \vee (A \wedge B)$$

$$= (\overline{A} \wedge B) \vee [(A \wedge \overline{B}) \vee (A \wedge B)] \qquad \text{Theorem } 7(a)$$

$$= (\overline{A} \wedge B) \vee [A \wedge (\overline{B} \vee B)] \qquad \text{Axiom } 2(b)$$

$$= (\overline{A} \wedge B) \vee (A \wedge 1) \qquad \text{Axiom } 4(a)$$

$$= (\overline{A} \wedge B) \vee A \qquad \text{Axiom } 3(b)$$

$$= A \vee B \qquad \text{Theorem } 6(a)$$

The theorems of boolean algebra can be verified by the use of truth tables. The truth table in Table 1.8 confirms the absorption law of Theorem 5(a).

Table 1.8 Truth table for absorption law of Theorem 5(a)

A	B	$A \wedge B$	$f = A \vee (A \wedge B)$
0	0	0	0
0	1	0	0
1	0	0	1
1	1	1	1

$$\llcorner \_ A = A \vee (A \wedge B) \_\lrcorner$$

The algebraic proof for DeMorgan's law of Theorem 8(a) was long, but its validity is easily shown by means of the truth table in Table 1.9.

Table 1.9 Truth table for DeMorgan's law of Theorem 8(a)

A	B	$A \vee B$	$\overline{(A \vee B)}$	$\overline{A}$	$\overline{B}$	$(\overline{A} \wedge \overline{B})$
0	0	0	1	1	1	1
0	1	1	0	1	0	0
1	0	1	0	0	1	0
1	1	1	0	0	0	0

$$\llcorner \_ \overline{(A \vee B)} = \overline{A} \wedge \overline{B} \_\lrcorner$$

Each row of a truth table presents a unique n-tuple (n independent variables) and an associated 1-tuple (one dependent variable). The first independent variable can assume two values (0 or 1). The second can also assume two values. Thus, the first two variables can assume $2 \times 2 = 4 = 2^2$ possible combinations. Thus, n variables can assume 2^n combinations.

1.2.2 Minimization Techniques

This section will discuss various techniques for minimizing a boolean algebraic equation. A *literal* is an uncomplemented or complemented variable. Each term in a boolean equation consists of one or more literals. When a boolean function is implemented with logic gates, each literal specifies an input to a gate and each term represents a logic gate. It is important, therefore, to have the fewest number of literals in a term and the fewest number of terms in an equation. The minimum number of literals and terms reduces not only the amount of logic gates in a function but also the delay required to generate the function.

Algebraic manipulation. The number of literals and terms required to generate a boolean function can be minimized by algebraic manipulation. There are no specific rules or algorithms to follow that will guarantee a result with the fewest number of literals or terms. The only method available is an empirical procedure utilizing the axioms and theorems in much the same way that the theorems were proven from the axioms. The following examples illustrate this procedure.

Example 1.1 Simplify the following boolean function.

$$
\begin{aligned}
f(A,B,C) &= AB \vee \overline{A}C \vee BC \\
&= AB \vee \overline{A}C \vee BC\,(A \vee \overline{A}) && \text{Axiom } 4(a) \\
&= AB \vee \overline{A}C \vee ABC \vee \overline{A}BC && \text{Axiom } 2(b) \\
&= AB \vee ABC \vee \overline{A}C \vee \overline{A}BC && \text{Axiom } 1(a) \\
&= AB\,(1 \vee C) \vee \overline{A}C\,(1 \vee B) && \text{Axiom } 2(b) \\
&= (AB \wedge 1) \vee (\overline{A}C \wedge 1) && \text{Theorem } 1(a) \\
&= AB \vee \overline{A}C && \text{Axiom } 3(b)
\end{aligned}
$$

Example 1.1 illustrates the fact that an increase in the number of literals may produce a final simpler equation.

Example 1.2 Simplify the following boolean function.

$$
\begin{aligned}
f(A,B,C) &= AB \vee AC \vee A\overline{B}C \vee \overline{A}BC \vee \overline{A}B \\
&= AB \vee AC \vee A\overline{B}C \vee \overline{A}B\,(C \vee 1) && \text{Axiom } 2(b) \\
&= AB \vee AC \vee A\overline{B}C \vee \overline{A}B\,(1) && \text{Theorem } 1(a) \\
&= AB \vee AC \vee A\overline{B}C \vee \overline{A}B && \text{Axiom } 3(b) \\
&= AB \vee \overline{A}B \vee AC \vee A\overline{B}C && \text{Axiom } 1(a) \\
&= B\,(A \vee \overline{A}) \vee AC\,(1 \vee \overline{B}) && \text{Axiom } 2(b) \\
&= B\,(1) \vee AC\,(1) && \text{Axiom } 4(a), \text{ Theorem } 1(a) \\
&= B \vee AC && \text{Axiom } 3(b)
\end{aligned}
$$

Example 1.3 Simplify the following sum-of-minterms boolean function.

$$
\begin{aligned}
f(A,B,C,D) &= ABCD \lor AB\overline{C}D \lor A\overline{B}CD \lor A\overline{B}C\overline{D} \\
&= ABDC \lor ABD\overline{C} \lor A\overline{B}CD \lor A\overline{B}C\overline{D} & \text{Axiom 1}(b) \\
&= ABD\,(C \lor \overline{C}) \lor A\overline{B}C\,(D \lor \overline{D}) & \text{Axiom 2}(b) \\
&= ABD\,(1) \lor A\overline{B}C\,(1) & \text{Axiom 4}(a) \\
&= ABD \lor A\overline{B}C & \text{Axiom 3}(b)
\end{aligned}
$$

Literals may be combined and represented by a different literal for simplification, as shown in Example 1.4, which derives the three-variable form of DeMorgan's law.

Example 1.4

$$
\begin{aligned}
(\overline{A \lor B \lor C}) &= (\overline{A \lor X}) & \text{let } X = B \lor C \\
&= \overline{A} \land \overline{X} & \text{Theorem 8}(a) \\
&= \overline{A} \land (\overline{B \lor C}) & \text{substitute } B \lor C = X \\
&= \overline{A} \land (\overline{B} \land \overline{C}) & \text{Theorem 8}(a) \\
&= \overline{A} \land \overline{B} \land \overline{C} & \text{Theorem 7}(b)
\end{aligned}
$$

Karnaugh map The unsystematic procedures used in the previous section for minimizing boolean functions become tedious when large logical expressions are encountered. The *Karnaugh map* provides a simplified method for minimizing boolean functions. The map technique may become cumbersome for five or more variables, but is ideally suited for four or less variables. The map is a symbolic representation of the truth table and provides a systematic means of reducing the function.

The Karnaugh map is a diagram consisting of squares, in which each square represents a minterm. It can also be regarded as a two-dimensional representation of a truth table. Any boolean function can be expressed as a sum of minterms. Therefore, a boolean function can be represented on a Karnaugh map by an area consisting of those squares that contain the minterms. The map presents a diagram from which different patterns can be used to derive alternate boolean expressions for the same function. The simplest expression is then selected.

Figure 1.2 illustrates a two-variable Karnaugh map and the corresponding truth table. There are four minterms for two variables; thus, the map consists of four squares (or cells), one for each minterm. Figure 1.2(a) shows the four minterms that represent the two variables, and Fig. 1.2(b) shows the position of the minterms in the map. The relationship between the squares and the two variables is shown in Fig. 1.2(c). The 0s and 1s that label each row and column designate the value of the variables A and B.

The first step in using a Karnaugh map is to plot the equation to be simplified on the map. The lower right square in Fig. 1.2(c) corresponds to $A = B = 1$. A 1 is placed in the lower right square if AB is a minterm of the equation. Similarly, the lower left square contains a 1 if $A\overline{B}$ is a minterm. Thus, to obtain the complete Karnaugh map for two variables, the function is expanded into a sum of minterms; that is, the expanded form consists of terms, where each term contains the two literals, either uncomplemented or complemented.

$\overline{A}$	$\overline{B}$	
0	0	m_0 (minterm$_0$)
0	1	m_1
1	0	m_2
1	1	m_3

(a)

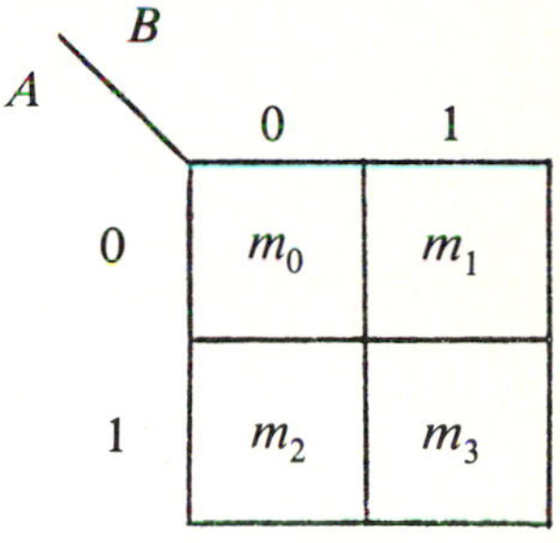

(b)

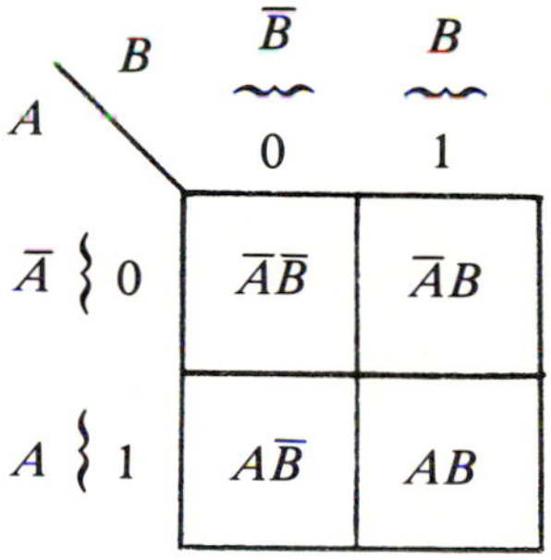

(c)

Figure 1.2 Two-variable Karnaugh map: (*a*) truth table, (*b*) minterm placement, and (*c*) Karnaugh map.

For example, to plot the function $A \vee \overline{A}B$ on a Karnaugh map, expand the expression into the sum-of-minterms form. Thus,

$$A \vee \overline{A}B = A(B \vee \overline{B}) \vee \overline{A}B \quad \text{Axiom 4}(a)$$
$$= AB \vee A\overline{B} \vee \overline{A}B \quad \text{Axiom 2}(b) \quad (1.50)$$

Next, place a 1 inside the squares that represent the three minterms. Since AB is equal to m_3, a 1 is placed inside the square representing m_3, that is, the square where $A = B = 1$. A 1 is then placed in the remaining squares represented by a minterm in the expression. Thus, the completed Karnaugh map for the function of Eq. 1.50 is shown in Fig. 1.3.

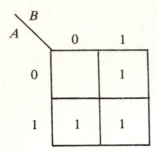

Figure 1.3 Karnaugh map for Eq. 1.50

The squares in the Karnaugh map are arranged so that any pair of minterms that can be reduced occupy adjacent squares. When an equation is plotted on a map, any pair of adjacent squares that contain 1s can be reduced to a single literal. For example, the minterms $A\overline{B}$ and AB in Eq. 1.50 that represent m_2 and m_3 in the Karnaugh map, respectively, can be reduced to the variable A. This can be verified by applying Axioms 2(b), 4(a), and 3(b)—in that order—to the expression $A\overline{B} \vee AB$. The same minterm can be combined more than once. Thus, in Fig. 1.3, m_3 is combined with m_2 to yield A and m_3 is also combined with m_1 to yield B. Therefore, the minimized form of Eq. 1.50 is $A \vee B$, which is verified by Theorem 6(a).

An alternative and simpler way to construct the map of Fig. 1.3 for Eq. 1.50 is to place 1s in squares m_2 and m_3 that represent the term A; that is, the condition where $A = 1$, regardless of the value of B. Then a 1 is placed in square m_1 that represents the minterm $\overline{A}B$. This produces the same map as was generated by expanding the expression into a sum-of-minterms form. In this way, the map can be constructed directly from the expression that is to be minimized. Squares located next to each other on a diagonal are not considered to be adjacent. Vertical edges and horizontal edges are adjacent as shown in the following discussion of three-variable Karnaugh maps.

A three-variable Karnaugh map and the corresponding truth table are shown in Fig. 1.4. There are eight minterms for three variables, thus the map consists of eight squares, one for each minterm. Note that the minterms (and thus the labels for the columns) are not arranged in an ascending binary sequence. This sequence is characterized by having only one bit change between adjacent columns. Thus, any two adjacent squares in the map differ by only one variable, which is uncomplemented in one square and complemented in the other. The reason for having only one variable change its value (or state) between adjacent squares is to prevent a race condition. A race condition results when two or more variables change their state at the same time, and the next state may not be the desired state. Races are discussed in more detail in Sec. 1.2.4.

The same procedure is used to represent a three-variable expression on a Karnaugh map as was used for two variables. Equation 1.51 specifies an expression that is to be minimized by means of a three-variable Karnaugh map.

$$f(A,B,C) = A\overline{B}C \lor AB\overline{C} \lor ABC \qquad (1.51)$$

The equation is plotted on the map of Fig. 1.5. The minterms that can be combined to form a term with fewer literals are enclosed by a loop. The loops may not enclose an odd number of 1s, but must enclose an even number of 1s, provided the number of 1s is a power of 2; that is, 2, 4, 8, but not 6, 10, 12, etc. Each loop represents a new combined term. An isolated 1 indicates a minterm that cannot be combined. Any variable that has both its uncomplemented and complemented form enclosed by the same loop can be dropped from the term.

Thus, the minimized form of Eq. 1.51 is

$$f(A,B,C) = A\overline{B}C \lor AB\overline{C} \lor ABC$$
$$= AC \lor AB \qquad (1.52)$$

A	B	C	
0	0	0	m_0
0	0	1	m_1
0	1	0	m_2
0	1	1	m_3
1	0	0	m_4
1	0	1	m_5
1	1	0	m_6
1	1	1	m_7

(a)

A\BC	00	01	11	10
0	m_0	m_1	m_3	m_2
1	m_4	m_5	m_7	m_6

(b)

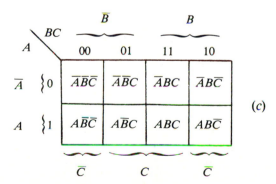

(c)

Figure 1.4 Three-variable Karnaugh map: (a) truth table, (b) minterm placement, and (c) Karnaugh map.

A Karnaugh map produces a minimized sum-of-products expression. Equation 1.52 represents 2 two-input AND gates with outputs that are ORed with a two-input OR gate. The number of gates can be reduced further by applying Axiom 2(*b*) to Eq. 1.52, yielding Eq. 1.53 as follows:

$$f(A,B,C) = AC \vee AB$$
$$= A (C \vee B) \qquad \text{Axiom 2(}b\text{)} \qquad (1.53)$$

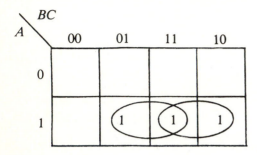

Fig. 1.5 Karnaugh map for Eq. 1.51.

Thus, the number of logic gates has been reduced to one AND gate and one OR gate, but the equation is no longer in sum-of-products form. This is of no consequence, because the number of logic levels remains the same.

Consider some additional examples. The function of Eq. 1.54 is plotted on the Karnaugh map of Fig. 1.6.

$$f(A,B,C) = \overline{A}\overline{B}C \vee \overline{A}BC \vee A\overline{B}C \vee ABC \qquad (1.54)$$

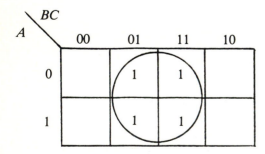

Figure 1.6 Karnaugh map for Eq. 1.54.

The loop encircles four squares containing 1s. Each square differs from its adjacent square only in the complementation of one variable. Therefore, the four minterms (m_1, m_3, m_5, and m_7) can be grouped together to form one term. The four minterms represent the minimized function. Thus, Eq. 1.54 reduces to

$$f(A,B,C) = \overline{A}\overline{B}C \vee \overline{A}BC \vee A\overline{B}C \vee ABC$$
$$= C \tag{1.55}$$

that is, all the squares where variable C has the value 1, regardless of the value of the other variables.

The minimization of Eq. 1.56 is shown in Fig. 1.7. The right and left edges of the map are considered to be in contact, as are the top and bottom edges; that is, opposite edges touch each other to form adjacent squares. Consider the map to be a vertical cylinder when the right and left edges make contact and a horizontal

$$f(A,B,C) = \overline{A}\overline{B}\overline{C} \vee \overline{A}B\overline{C} \vee A\overline{B}\overline{C} \vee AB\overline{C} \tag{1.56}$$

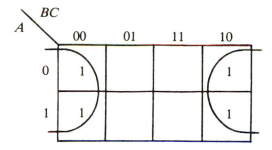

Figure 1.7 Karnaugh map for Eq. 1.56

cylinder when the top and bottom edges make contact. Thus, the minimized function of Eq. 1.56 is obtained from the map as

$$f(A,B,C) = \overline{A}\overline{B}\overline{C} \vee \overline{A}B\overline{C} \vee A\overline{B}\overline{C} \vee AB\overline{C}$$
$$= \overline{C} \tag{1.57}$$

The Karnaugh map for a four-variable boolean function is shown in Fig. 1.8. Figure 1.8(a) illustrates the truth table and the corresponding minterms; Fig. 1.8 (b) lists the 16 minterms and the square assigned to each; and Fig. 1.8(c) shows the relationship between the four variables and their placement on the map. The labels (or numbers) for the rows and columns permit only one variable to change between two adjacent rows or columns. The minterm corresponding to each square can be obtained by concatenating the row number with the column number. For example, the fourth row (10) and third column (11) give the binary number 1011 when concatenated, which is the equivalent of 11_{10}. Thus, the square in that position represents minterm m_{11}.

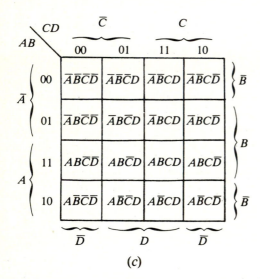

A	B	C	D	
0	0	0	0	m_0
0	0	0	1	m_1
0	0	1	0	m_2
0	0	1	1	m_3
0	1	0	0	m_4
0	1	0	1	m_5
0	1	1	0	m_6
0	1	1	1	m_7
1	0	0	0	m_8
1	0	0	1	m_9
1	0	1	0	m_{10}
1	0	1	1	m_{11}
1	1	0	0	m_{12}
1	1	0	1	m_{13}
1	1	1	0	m_{14}
1	1	1	1	m_{15}

(a)

AB \ CD	00	01	11	10
00	m_0	m_1	m_3	m_2
01	m_4	m_5	m_7	m_6
11	m_{12}	m_{13}	m_{15}	m_{14}
10	m_8	m_9	m_{11}	m_{10}

(b)

Figure 1.8 Four-variable Karnaugh map: (a) truth table, (b) minterm placement, and (c) Karnaugh map.

The minimization of a four-variable Karnaugh map is similar to the method used for three variables. The combination of adjacent squares that can be used during the minimization process is described below:

1. One square specifies one minterm, which represents a term of four literals.
2. Two adjacent squares specify two minterms, which represent a term of three literals.

3. Four adjacent squares represent a term with two literals.
4. Eight adjacent squares represent a term with one literal.
5. Sixteen adjacent squares represent a function that is equal to 1.

The minimization of Eq. 1.58 is demonstrated by use of the Karnaugh map of Fig. 1.9.

$$f(A,B,C,D) = A\overline{B}\overline{C} \lor \overline{A}\overline{B}\overline{C} \lor \overline{A}BCD \lor \overline{A}C\overline{D} \lor AB\overline{C}D \lor A\overline{B}C \quad (1.58)$$

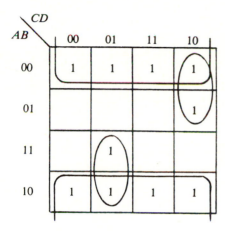

Figure 1.9 Karnaugh map for Eq. 1.58.

The minimized function is

$$f(A,B,C,D) = A\overline{B}\overline{C} \lor \overline{A}\overline{B}\overline{C} \lor \overline{A}BCD \lor \overline{A}C\overline{D} \lor AB\overline{C}D \lor A\overline{B}C$$
$$= \overline{B} \lor \overline{A}C\overline{D} \lor A\overline{C}D \quad (1.59)$$

Maps with more than four variables are not as easy to use as maps with four or less variables. The size of a Karnaugh map increases as 2^n, where n is the number of literals. Thus, as n becomes large, the map becomes awkward to use when combining adjacent squares. Figure 1.10 shows a five-variable map. As before, minterms can be combined in adjacent squares where there is a change in value of only one variable. Thus, m_{27} and m_{31} can be combined, as can m_3 and m_7. The heavy vertical line that divides the 2 four-variable maps can be considered a hinge, which permits the 2 four-variable maps to be superimposed on each other. Each square, therefore, is adjacent not only to the four neighboring squares, but also to its mirror image in the adjacent four-variable map.

If the number of literals is greater than or equal to 7, then the number of squares in the Karnaugh map becomes excessive, which complicates the selection

AB \ CDE	000	001	011	010	110	111	101	100
00	m_0	m_1	m_3	m_2	m_6	m_7	m_5	m_4
01	m_8	m_9	m_{11}	m_{10}	m_{14}	m_{15}	m_{13}	m_{12}
11	m_{24}	m_{25}	m_{27}	m_{26}	m_{30}	m_{31}	m_{29}	m_{28}
10	m_{16}	m_{17}	m_{19}	m_{18}	m_{22}	m_{23}	m_{21}	m_{20}

Figure 1.10 Five-variable Karnaugh map.

of adjacent squares. A simpler method of minimization should then be used. The Quine-McCluskey method resolves the problem of many literals by providing a step-by-step procedure that guarantees a minimized expression in the sum-of-products form. However, since the purpose of this book is computer arithmetic, the technique will not be presented here. Almost any book on logic design will have a section devoted to the Quine-McCluskey method of minimization.

1.2.3 Combinational Logic

Logic circuits in digital systems may be either combinational or sequential. A combinational circuit is one with outputs that at any given time are determined entirely from the present input signals to the circuit. The operation of combinational logic circuits can be expressed in terms of fundamental logical operations, such as AND, OR, and NOT (INVERT). The AND and OR functions are called *gates,* and their truth tables are shown in Table 1.7. The NOT function simply inverts (or changes) a high-level input signal to a low-level output signal, or vice versa. A sequential circuit also consists of AND, OR, and NOT functions, but contains one or more storage elements called *latches* or *flip-flops.* The outputs of a sequential circuit are a function of both the present input signals and the state of the storage elements. As a result, the outputs are dependent not only on present inputs but also on past inputs, and the circuit behavior of a sequential logical function must be specified by a time sequence of inputs and internal storage states.

The logic symbols in this text are drawn from Military Standard 806C and ANSI Standard Y32.14. The AND function can be represented three ways, as shown in Fig. 1.11. Although only two inputs are shown, both AND and OR cir-

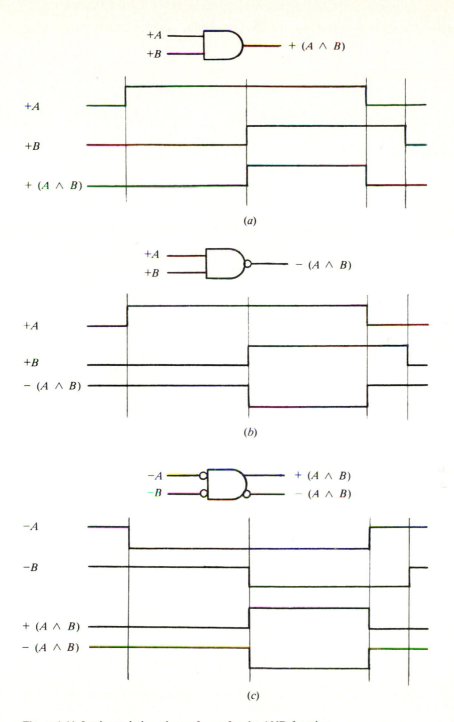

Figure 1.11 Logic symbols and waveforms for the AND function.

cuits can have three or more inputs. The maximum number of inputs per gate depends on the logic family technology that is used. The plus (+) and minus (−) symbols that are placed to the left of the variables indicate a high or low voltage level, respectively. This indicates the asserted (or active) voltage level for the variables, that is, the "logical 1" (or true) state, in contrast to the "logical 0" (or false) state. Thus, a signal can be asserted either plus or minus, depending upon the active condition of the signal at that point. For example, Figure 1.11(a) specifies that the AND function will be realized when both input A and input B are at their more positive potential, thus generating an output at its more positive potential. The word *positive*, as used here, does not necessarily mean a positive voltage level, but merely the more positive of two voltage levels. Therefore, the AND function for Fig. 1.11(a) can be written as $+ (A \wedge B)$. If, however, signal A was active minus and B was active plus, then the AND function would be $+ (\overline{A} \wedge B)$.

The logic symbol of Fig. 1.11(b) is a positive AND-inverter (NAND) in which inputs A and B must both be at their more positive potential for the output to be at its more negative potential. A circle at the input or output of a logic symbol (or logic block) indicates a more negative potential. Thus, when both A and B are plus, the output expression will be $- (A \wedge B)$. If, however, the signal (or line) A was active minus and B was active plus, then the output expression would be $- (\overline{A} \wedge B)$.

Figure 1.11(c) illustrates a negative AND with both inverted and noninverted outputs. The symbols for Fig. 1.11(a) and (b) are usually found in transistor-transistor logic (TTL), whereas the symbol in Fig. 1.11(c) is the dual of the NOR circuit used in emitter-coupled logic (ECL).

The logic symbol of Fig. 1.12(a) is a positive OR circuit. The output of an OR circuit is at its indicated polarity when one or more input is at its indicated polarity. Thus, the output of the OR circuit of Fig. 1.12(a) will be plus if either A or B is plus or if both A and B are plus. Figure 1.12(b) is a negative OR circuit that is the dual of the AND circuit of Fig. 1.11(b). When either A or B is minus or both A and B are minus, the output of the negative OR gate will be plus. Fig. 1.12(c) represents a positive OR/NOR circuit with both inverted and noninverted outputs and is found primarily in the ECL logic family.

The EXCLUSIVE-OR circuit is represented three ways, as shown in Fig. 1.13. Either Fig. 1.13(a) or (b) is acceptable as representing the sum-of-products function of Fig. 1.13(c). The EXCLUSIVE-NOR symbol is shown in Fig. 1.13(d). The truth table for the EXCLUSIVE-OR function is shown in Table 1.7. The NOT symbol is shown in Fig. 1.14. The output of a NOT circuit is of opposite potential to the input. As before, the circle at the output of a logic block means that the output must be at its least positive potential when the function of the block is satisfied.

The symbols for the AND, OR, EXCLUSIVE-OR, and NOT functions may also be drawn as rectangles, as shown in Fig. 1.15. This is useful for those computer companies in which a design automation system produces logic diagrams by

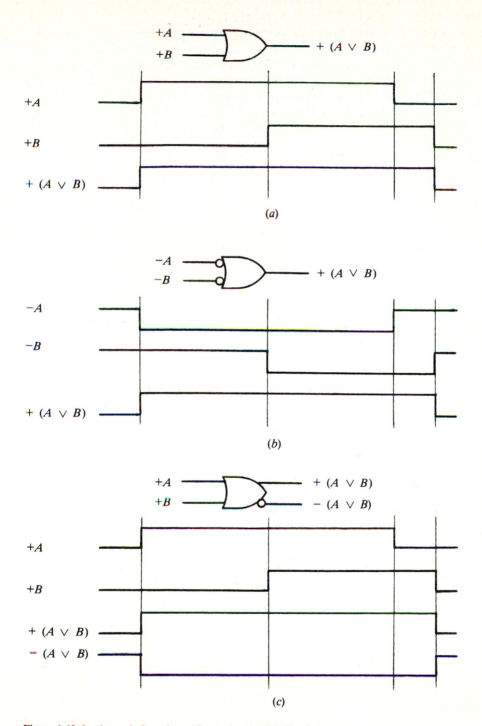

Figure 1.12 Logic symbols and waveforms for the OR function.

means of a high-speed printer. It is difficult for a printer to produce the symbol shapes shown in Figs. 1.11–1.14. Also, most computer-aided design (CAD) systems use the rectangular method for drawing logic diagrams.

If a set of operations can express any boolean function (AND, OR, NOT), then the set is said to be functionally complete. Both the NOR and NAND operators are functionally complete; that is, any boolean function can be expressed using only NOR gates or only NAND gates.

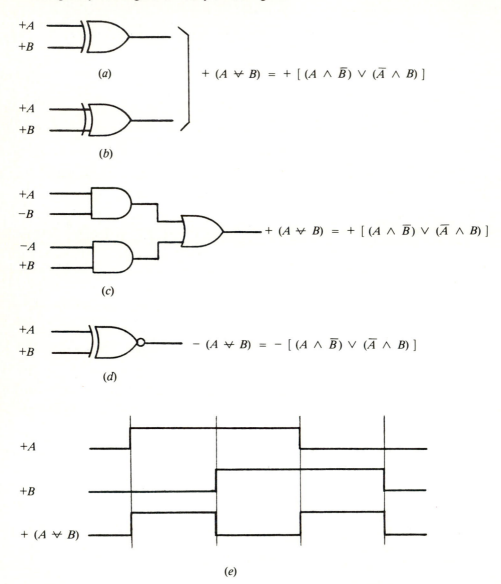

Figure 1.13 Logic symbols and waveforms for the EXCLUSIVE-OR function.

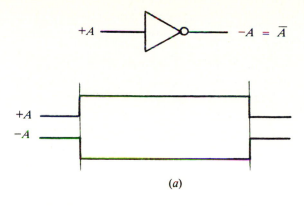

(a)

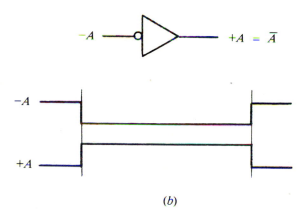

(b)

Figure 1.14 Logic symbols and waveforms for the NOT function.

We will assume that only active plus signals are available. Fig. 1.16(*a*) shows that the NOT function can be generated using a single NOR gate. The NOR gate can also be represented as a negative AND-inverter, as shown in the second symbol of Fig. 1.16(*a*). The output of the first NOR gate in Fig. 1.16(*b*) produces an OR function that is active negative. If the positive level is required, then the signal $-(A \lor B)$ is inverted. The inversion can be accomplished by means of the single NOR gate of Fig. 1.16(*a*), which is the NOT function. Therefore, the signal $-(A \lor B)$ is inverted by passing it through a NOT circuit to generate $+(A \lor B)$. The AND function can be generated using the method of Fig. 1.16(*c*). The NAND gate can be shown to be functionally complete in a similar manner.

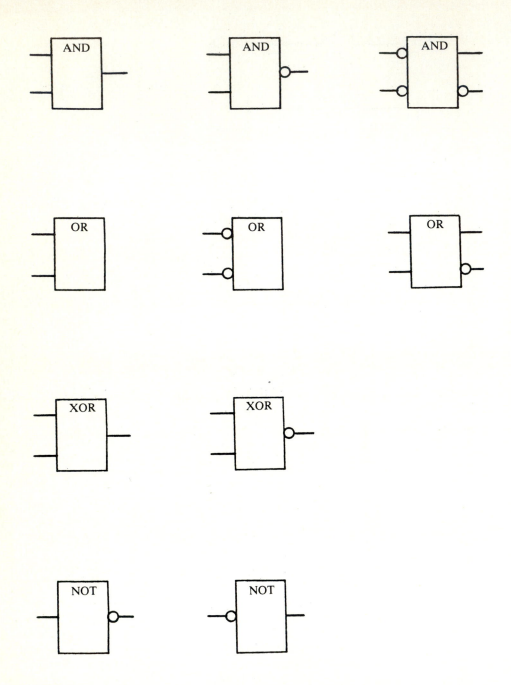

Figure 1.15 Alternate method of drawing symbols for the AND, OR, EXCLUSIVE-OR, and NOT functions.

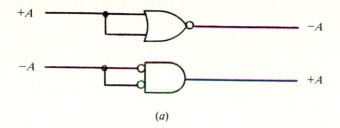

(a)

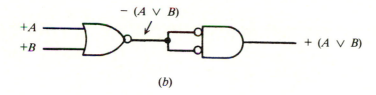

(b)

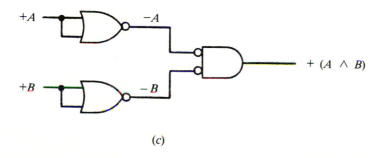

(c)

Figure 1.16 Interconnection of NOR gates to produce other functions: (a) NOT, (b) OR, and (c) AND.

Half adder A *half adder* is a combinational circuit that performs the addition of two binary bits and produces two outputs—a sum bit and a carry-out bit. The half adder does not accommodate a carry-in bit. The truth table for a half adder is shown in Table 1.10. The equations for the sum and carry-out can be obtained directly from the truth table as

$$s_i = (\bar{a}_i b_i) \vee (a_i \bar{b}_i) \tag{1.60}$$

$$= a_i \veebar b_i$$

$$c_i = a_i b_i \tag{1.61}$$

Table 1.10 Truth table for half adder

a_i	b_i	s_i	c_i
0	0	0	0
0	1	1	0
1	0	1	0
1	1	0	1

The logic diagram for the implementation of a half adder using the sum of products of Eq. 1.60 is shown in Fig. 1.17(a). If only active plus signals are available for the two operand bits, then the circuit of Fig. 1.17(b) can be used to achieve the same result.

Full adder A *full adder* is a combinational circuit that computes the sum of two operand bits plus a carry-in bit. The carry-in signal represents the carry-out of the previous lower-order bit position. The full adder produces two outputs: a sum bit and a carry-out bit. The truth table for the full adder is shown in Table 1.11. The carry-in bit is specified as c_{i-1}. The equations for the sum and carry-out can be obtained directly from the truth table as

$$s_i = \bar{a}_i \, \bar{b}_i \, c_{i-1} \vee \bar{a}_i \, b_i \, \bar{c}_{i-1} \vee a_i \, \bar{b}_i \, \bar{c}_{i-1} \vee a_i \, b_i \, c_{i-1}$$

$$= a_i \veebar b_i \veebar c_{i-1} \tag{1.62}$$

$$c_i = \bar{a}_i \, b_i \, c_{i-1} \vee a_i \, \bar{b}_i \, c_{i-1} \vee a_i \, b_i \, \bar{c}_{i-1} \vee a_i \, b_i \, c_{i-1}$$

$$= a_i \, b_i \vee a_i \, c_{i-1} \vee b_i \, c_{i-1} \tag{1.63}$$

The design of the full adder can be implemented using the sum of products as specified in Eqs. 1.62 and 1.63 (see Fig. 2.1). The full adder can also be designed using two half adders, as shown in Fig. 1.18. For high-speed addition, the sum-of-products implementation is preferred.

Code conversion Conversion from binary-coded decimal (BCD) form to binary form and the reverse conversion are common in most digital computers. The numerical data supplied to a computer may be presented in BCD, where each digit consists of four bits. The most common BCD code is 8, 4, 2, 1. If the computer has no decimal arithmetic unit, then the information must be converted to binary. The computation is then performed in binary, and the binary results are converted to decimal. The two-way conversion could be accomplished using combinational logic, but the number of gates required would be prohibitive due to the

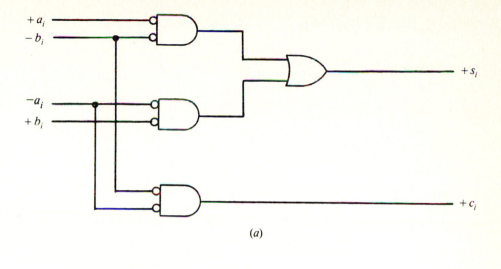

(a)

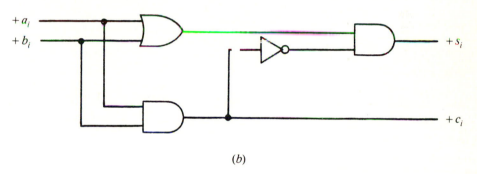

(b)

Figure 1.17 Two methods for implementing a half adder.

**Table 1.11 Truth table for
full adder.**

a_i	b_i	c_{i-1}	s_i	c_i
0	0	0	0	0
0	0	1	1	0
0	1	0	1	0
0	1	1	0	1
1	0	0	1	0
1	0	1	0	1
1	1	0	0	1
1	1	1	1	1

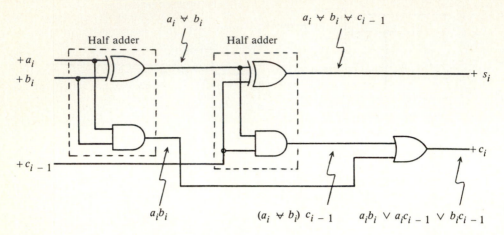

Figure 1.18 Implementation of full adder using two half adders.

large number of possible decimal numbers.

The conversion from decimal to binary can be done by repeated divide-by-2 operations. Each decimal digit is encoded in binary (8, 4, 2, 1), but the complete decimal number is not. The paper-and-pencil method for converting from BCD to binary form is illustrated in Table 1.12 for 22_{10}. The BCD number 22 is divided by 2 and yields a quotient of 11_{10} and a remainder of 0. The quotient is divided by 2 and gives a new quotient of 5 and a remainder of 1. This process is repeated until the quotient becomes 0. The coefficients of the binary number are obtained

**Table 1.12 Paper-and-pencil method
for decimal-to-binary conversion**

Quotient	Remainder
$\dfrac{22}{2} = 11$	0 (LSB)
$\dfrac{11}{2} = 5$	1
$\dfrac{5}{2} = 2$	1
$\dfrac{2}{2} = 1$	0
$\dfrac{1}{2} = 0$	1

from the remainders, with the first remainder corresponding to the least significant (or low-order) bit. Thus, the equivalent binary number for BCD 22 is 1 0 1 1 0.

Division by 2 can be performed in hardware by shifting all BCD digits one bit position to the right and saving the low-order bit that is shifted out. The bit that is shifted out becomes the remainder. All BCD digits may require adjustment after the shift. For example, after the first shift of BCD 22 in step 1 of Table 1.13, the low-order bit position of the tens decade contains a 1. This bit provides a value of 10_{10} before shifting. Since a right shift represents a division by 2, the shifted bit should carry a value of 5 into the units decade. However, after the second right shift (step 2), the shifted bit produces a value of 8, because it is placed in the high-order bit position of the units decade. Thus, a substraction of 3 is required to adjust the BCD number in the units position.

Table 1.13 Example of BCD decade adjustment during BCD-to-binary conversion

Step	Tens	Units	Binary bits
	0 0 1 0	0 0 1 0	
1. SR1*	0 0 0 1	0 0 0 1	0
2. SR1	0 0 0 0	1 0 0 0	1 0
3. Adjust (subtract 3)	0 0 0 0	0 1 0 1	

*SR1 = Shift right one bit position.

The procedure for converting BCD to binary form is as follows:

1. Shift the BCD number one bit position to the right and save the remainder.
2. If the high-order bit of any decade is a 1 after shifting, then subtract 3 from the decade.

Perform steps 1 and 2 n times until the binary number has been formed, where n is the number of bits in the binary number.

The hardware required to convert BCD to binary form is shown in Fig. 1.19. Register A contains m BCD digits and is initially loaded from a data bus. Register B accumulates n binary bits as these are shifted out of register A during the divide-by-2 operation.

Registers A and B are shifted one bit position to the right in concatenation, and the BCD digits in register A are then checked to determine if their value is greater than or equal to 1 0 0 0_2 (8_{10}). Only the high-order bit in each decade needs to be checked. Any digit that is greater than or equal to 8 is adjusted by subtracting 3 from the digit. There are m four-bit binary adders, one for each BCD digit. The adjusted digits are reloaded into their respective locations in register A. The process is performed n times under the control of a sequence counter to generate an n-bit binary number in register B. An example of BCD-to-binary conversion is given in Table 1.14.

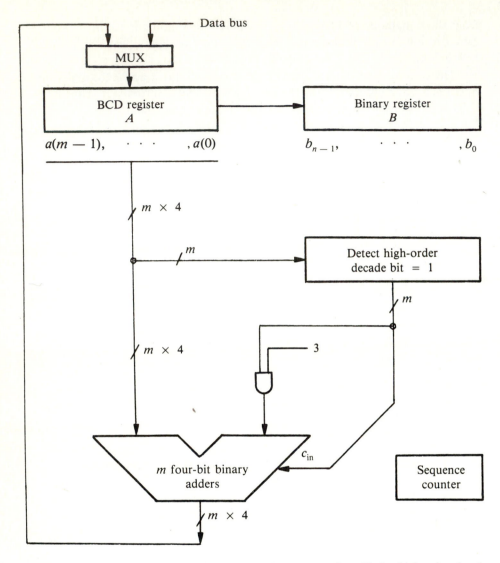

Figure 1.19 Hardware organization for BCD-to-binary conversion. If the high-order decade bit = 1, then c_{in} = 1. (Refer to Sec. 2.3 for a description of fixed-point subtraction.)

The conversion from binary to BCD form can be done by repeated multiply-by-2 operations. The multiplication by 2 is accomplished by a left-shift operation followed by an adjustment of the BCD digit, if necessary. For example, a left shift of BCD 1 0 0 1 (9_{10}) yields 1 0 0 1 0, which is 18 in binary but only 12 in BCD. Adding 0 1 1 0 (6_{10}) to the left-shifted BCD digit produces 1 1 0 0 0, which is the required value of 18. Instead of adding 6 after the shift, the same result can be obtained by adding 3 before the shift, since a left shift multiplies any number by 2. BCD digits in the range 0–4 will not require an adjustment after a

Table 1.14 Example of BCD-to-binary conversion:
$(143)_{10}$ = $(0\ 0\ 0\ 1\quad 0\ 1\ 0\ 0\quad 0\ 0\ 1\ 1)_{BCD}$ = $(1\ 0\ 0\ 0\ 1\ 1\ 1\ 1)_2$

	Register A			Register B
	10^2	10^1	10^0	$2^7, \cdots, 2^0$
Operation	$a(2)$	$a(1)$	$a(0)$	$b_7, \cdots, b_0$
Initialize	0 0 0 1	0 1 0 0	0 0 1 1	0 0 0 0 0 0 0 0
SR1*	0 0 0 0	1 0 1 0	0 0 0 1	1
$a(1)\ -\ 3$	0 0 0 0	0 1 1 1	0 0 0 1	1
SR1	0 0 0 0	0 0 1 1	1 0 0 0	1 1
$a(0)\ -\ 3$	0 0 0 0	0 0 1 1	0 1 0 1	1 1
SR1	0 0 0 0	0 0 0 1	1 0 1 0	1 1 1
$a(0)\ -\ 3$	0 0 0 0	0 0 0 1	0 1 1 1	1 1 1
SR1	0 0 0 0	0 0 0 0	1 0 1 1	1 1 1 1
$a(0)\ -\ 3$	0 0 0 0	0 0 0 0	1 0 0 0	1 1 1 1
SR1	0 0 0 0	0 0 0 0	0 1 0 0	0 1 1 1 1
SR1	0 0 0 0	0 0 0 0	0 0 1 0	0 0 1 1 1 1
SR1	0 0 0 0	0 0 0 0	0 0 0 1	0 0 0 1 1 1 1
SR1	0 0 0 0	0 0 0 0	0 0 0 0	1 0 0 0 1 1 1 1

*SR1 = Shift right one bit position.

left shift, because the new number will be in the range 0–8, which can still be contained in a four-bit BCD digit. However, if the number to be shifted is in the range 5–9, then an adjustment is necessary after a left shift, because the new range will be 10–18, which requires two BCD digits. Thus, if the BCD digit to be shifted has a value of 5–9, then 3 is added to the digit and the digit is shifted left one bit position.

The hardware required to convert binary to BCD form is shown in Fig. 1.20. Register B contains n binary bits and is initially loaded from a data bus. The BCD number is formed in register A, which is initialized to 0. The adjustment is performed before each shift by inspecting each BCD digit. If a digit requires adjustment, then 3 is added to the digit and the sum is reloaded into the appropriate position in register A. Then registers A and B are shifted left one bit position in concatenation. The process is performed n times under the control of a sequence counter until all n bits have been shifted out of register B. An example of binary-to-BCD conversion is given in Table 1.15.

Code conversion can also be accomplished by means of a read-only memory (ROM). A ROM can implement any combinational logic circuit. The code to be converted is applied to the address lines of the ROM, and the converted code is available at the outputs. The ROM is constructed from a truth table that lists the relationship between the two codes.

Figure 1.21 shows three BCD-to-binary conversion techniques using ROMs. The first uses a single ROM with five inputs and five outputs. Two BCD digits in the range 0 0 0 0 0 0 0 0 to 0 0 1 1 1 0 0 1 are converted to the equivalent binary values. Note that the low-order bit of the units decade bypasses the ROM, because this bit is equal to the low-order bit of the converted binary

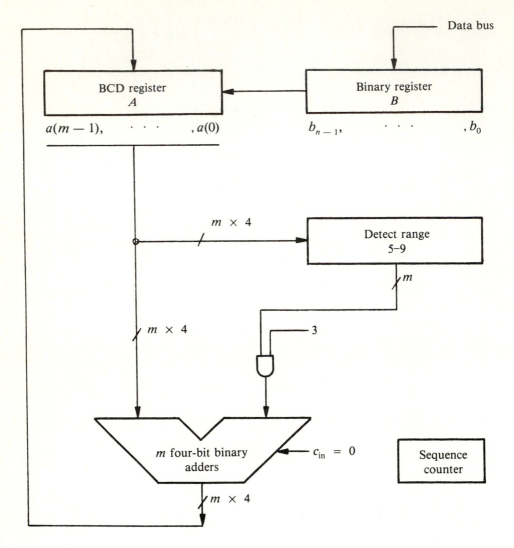

Figure 1.20 Hardware organization for binary-to-BCD conversion.

number. The five input lines can specify 32 addresses. However, every even-odd pair of addresses specify the same converted binary code with the exception of the low-order bit. The low-order bit will be 0 for an even address and 1 for an odd address. Thus, only 20 of the input address lines have significance for BCD; the remaining 12 input combinations can specify an output of all 0s.

Figure 1.21(*b*) shows a conversion technique for two BCD digits. The ROM is addressed by seven bits of the two digits, and the output produces six binary bits to which the low-order bit is right-concatenated. In most computers it is desirable to have a minimum number of different logic circuit part numbers; it is especially desirable in VLSI, since the cost of fabrication is very high, particularly for small quantities. Thus, the ROM of Fig. 1.21(a) can be used in a cascaded manner to produce the same results as the ROM of Fig. 1.21(b), as shown in Fig. 1.21(c). The conversion operation using cascaded ROMs is slower, however, because the two ROMs are connected in series such that the lower ROM cannot be addressed until the outputs from the first ROM are available.

Figure 1.22 shows three binary-to-BCD conversion techniques using ROMs. The first technique uses a single five-input, six-output ROM to convert a six-bit binary number to a two-digit BCD number in the range 0 0 0 0 0 0 0 0 to 0 1 1 0 0 0 1 1. The second converts a seven-input binary number to a two-digit BCD number in the range 0 0 0 0 0 0 0 0 to 1 0 0 1 1 0 0 1. The third uses cascaded ROMs to generate a three-digit BCD number in the range 0 0 0 0 0 0 0 0 0 0 0 0 to 0 0 1 0 0 1 0 1 0 1 0 1 from eight binary inputs.

Table 1.15 Example of binary-to-BCD conversion:
$(143)_{10} = (1\ 0\ 0\ 0\ 1\ 1\ 1\ 1)_2 = (0\ 0\ 0\ 1\ \ 0\ 1\ 0\ 0\ \ 0\ 0\ 1\ 1)_{BCD}$

	Register A			Register B	
	10^2	10^1	10^0	$2^7,$ $\cdots$	$, 2^0$
Operation	$a(2)$	$a(1)$	$a(0)$	$b_7,$ $\cdots$	$; b_0$
Initialize	0 0 0 0	0 0 0 0	0 0 0 0	1 0 0 0 1 1 1 1	
SL1*			0 0 0 1	0 0 0 1 1 1 1	
SL1			0 0 1 0	0 0 1 1 1 1	
SL1			0 1 0 0	0 1 1 1 1	
SL1			1 0 0 0	1 1 1 1	
$a(0) + 3$			1 0 1 1	1 1 1 1	
SL1		0 0 0 1	0 1 1 1	1 1 1	
$a(0) + 3$		0 0 0 1	1 0 1 0	1 1 1	
SLI		0 0 1 1	0 1 0 1	1 1	
$a(0) + 3$		0 0 1 1	1 0 0 0	1 1	
SL1		0 1 1 1	0 0 0 1	1	
$a(1) + 3$		1 0 1 0	0 0 0 1	1	
SL1	0 0 0 1	0 1 0 0	0 0 1 1	0 0 0 0 0 0 0 0	

*SL1 = Shift left one bit position.

Comparator A *comparator* is a combinational logic circuit that determines the relative magnitude of two numbers A and B. There are three outputs from the comparator that indicate

$$A < B \quad A = B \quad A > B$$

A circuit that compares 2 two-bit binary numbers can be designed directly from Karnaugh maps. Three maps are required, one each for $A < B$, $A = B$, and $A > B$. Figure 1.23 shows the three maps with the A and B operands represented

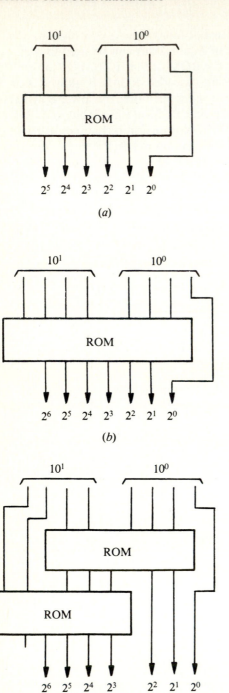

Figure 1.21 BCD-to-binary conversion using ROMs.

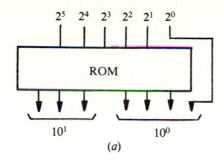

(a)

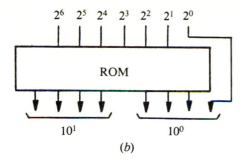

(b)

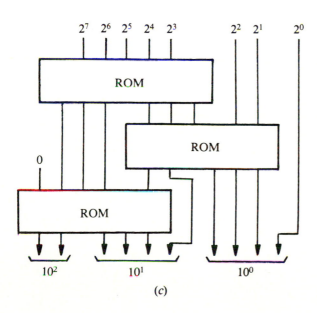

(c)

Figure 1.22 Binary-to-BCD conversion using ROMs.

by the rows and columns, respectively, where

$$A = a_1a_0$$
$$B = b_1b_0$$

There are four variables involved, two for the number A and two for the number B, with a_0 and b_0 being the low-order bits.

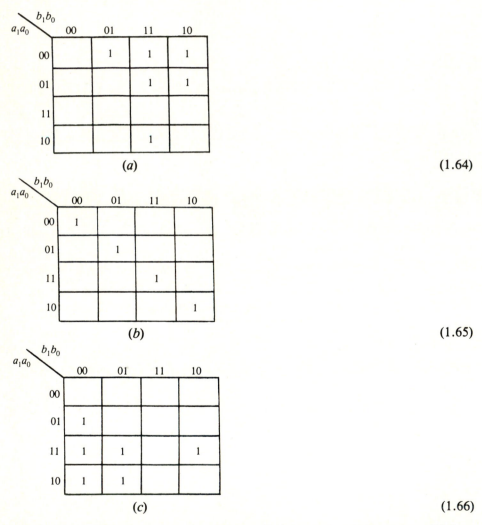

$$(1.64)$$

$$(1.65)$$

$$(1.66)$$

Figure 1.23 Karnaugh maps for two-bit comparator circuit.   (a) $(A < B) = \bar{a}_1b_1 \vee \bar{a}_0b_1b_0 \vee \bar{a}_1\bar{a}_0b_0$; (b) $(A = B) = \bar{a}_1\bar{a}_0\bar{b}_1\bar{b}_0 \vee \bar{a}_1a_0\bar{b}_1b_0 \vee a_1a_0b_1b_0 \vee a_1\bar{a}_0b_1\bar{b}_0$; and (c) $(A > B) = a_1\bar{b}_1 \vee a_1a_0\bar{b}_0 \vee a_0\bar{b}_1\bar{b}_0$.

Equation 1.64 states that A will be less than B

if $\quad b_1 = 1$ and $a_1 = 0$
or if $\quad b_1 = b_0 = 1$ and $a_0 = 0 \qquad$ regardless of the value of a_1
or if $\quad b_0 = 1$ and $a_1 = a_0 = 0 \qquad$ regardless of the value of b_1

Equation 1.64 can be rearranged such that

$$(A < B) = \bar{a}_1 b_1 \lor \bar{a}_0 b_1 b_0 \lor \bar{a}_1 \bar{a}_0 b_0$$

$$= \bar{a}_1 b_0 \lor \bar{a}_0 b_0 \, (b_1 \lor \bar{a}_1) \tag{1.67}$$

The parenthesized expression in the last line of Eq. 1.67 can be expanded to

$$a_1 b_1 \lor \bar{a}_1 \bar{b}_1$$

because both a_1 and b_1 can be 1 or 0 for Eq. 1.67 to be true; that is, A will be less than B for either

	2^1	2^0		2^1	2^0
$A =$	1	0	or	0	0
$B =$	1	1		0	1

Thus, Eq. 1.67 can be rewritten as

$$(A < B) = \bar{a}_1 b_0 \lor \bar{a}_0 b_0 \, (b_1 \lor \bar{a}_1)$$

$$= \bar{a}_1 b_0 \lor \bar{a}_0 b_0 \, (a_1 b_1 \lor \bar{a}_1 \bar{b}_1)$$

$$= \bar{a}_1 b_0 \lor \bar{a}_0 b_0 \, \overline{(a_1 \veebar b_1)} \tag{1.68}$$

The form of Eq. 1.68 will be useful when comparing two numbers containing more than two bits per number.

The equations of Fig. 1.23 can be easily expanded to three-bit operands. For example, the equation for $A < B$, where

$$A = a_2 a_1 a_0$$

$$B = b_2 b_1 b_0$$

is

$$(A < B) = \bar{a}_2 b_2 \lor \bar{a}_1 b_1 \, \overline{(a_2 \veebar b_2)} \lor \bar{a}_0 b_0 \, \overline{(a_2 \veebar b_2)} \, \overline{(a_1 \veebar b_1)} \tag{1.69}$$

In a similar manner,

$$(A = B) = (\overline{a_2 \not\vee b_2})(\overline{a_1 \not\vee b_1})(\overline{a_0 \not\vee b_0}) \qquad (1.70)$$

and

$$(A > B) = a_2\overline{b_2} \vee a_1\overline{b_1}(\overline{a_2 \not\vee b_2}) \vee a_0\overline{b_0}(\overline{a_2 \not\vee b_2})(\overline{a_1 \not\vee b_1}) \qquad (1.71)$$

For n-bit operands, where

$$A = a_{n-1} a_{n-2} \cdots a_1 a_0$$

$$B = b_{n-1} b_{n-2} \cdots b_1 b_0$$

the three boolean functions become

$$
\begin{aligned}
(A < B) = \quad & \overline{a}_{n-1}b_{n-1} \vee \overline{a}_{n-2}b_{n-2}(\overline{a_{n-1} \not\vee b_{n-1}}) \\
& \vee \overline{a}_{n-3}b_{n-3}(\overline{a_{n-1} \not\vee b_{n-1}})(\overline{a_{n-2} \not\vee b_{n-2}}) \\
& \vee \cdots \vee \overline{a}_1b_1(\overline{a_{n-1} \not\vee b_{n-1}}) \cdots (\overline{a_2 \not\vee b_2}) \\
& \vee \overline{a}_0b_0(\overline{a_{n-1} \not\vee b_{n-1}}) \cdots (\overline{a_2 \not\vee b_2})(\overline{a_1 \not\vee b_1}) \qquad (1.72)
\end{aligned}
$$

$$(A = B) = (\overline{a_{n-1} \not\vee b_{n-1}})(\overline{a_{n-2} \not\vee b_{n-2}}) \cdots (\overline{a_1 \not\vee b_1})(\overline{a_0 \not\vee b_0}) \qquad (1.73)$$

$$
\begin{aligned}
(A > B) = \quad & a_{n-1}\overline{b}_{n-1} \vee a_{n-2}\overline{b}_{n-2}(\overline{a_{n-1} \not\vee b_{n-1}}) \\
& \vee a_{n-3}\overline{b}_{n-3}(\overline{a_{n-1} \not\vee b_{n-1}})(\overline{a_{n-2} \not\vee b_{n-2}}) \\
& \vee \cdots \vee a_1\overline{b}_1(\overline{a_{n-1} \not\vee b_{n-1}}) \cdots (\overline{a_2 \not\vee b_2}) \\
& \vee a_0\overline{b}_0(\overline{a_{n-1} \not\vee b_{n-1}}) \cdots (\overline{a_2 \not\vee b_2})(\overline{a_1 \not\vee b_1}) \qquad (1.74)
\end{aligned}
$$

The logic diagram for comparing two *n*-bit binary numbers is shown in Fig. 1.24 and is designed directly from Eqs. 1.72 to 1.74.

Decoders and encoders A *decoder* is a combinational logic circuit that translates *n* binary bits into *m* output bits, where $m \leqslant 2^n$. A decoder requires more than one input signal (bit) to produce an active output signal and is constructed with AND gates. For example, a 3-to-8 decoder and corresponding truth table are shown in Fig. 1.25. The logic diagram uses bundled inputs, as described in Sec. 1.3.2. The three inputs *A*, *B*, and *C* represent a binary number consisting of three bits. The three inputs are converted into eight outputs, only one of which is active (plus) at any time; that is, the outputs are mutually exclusive. The remaining seven output signals are inactive (minus). The decoder of Fig. 1.25 is also referred

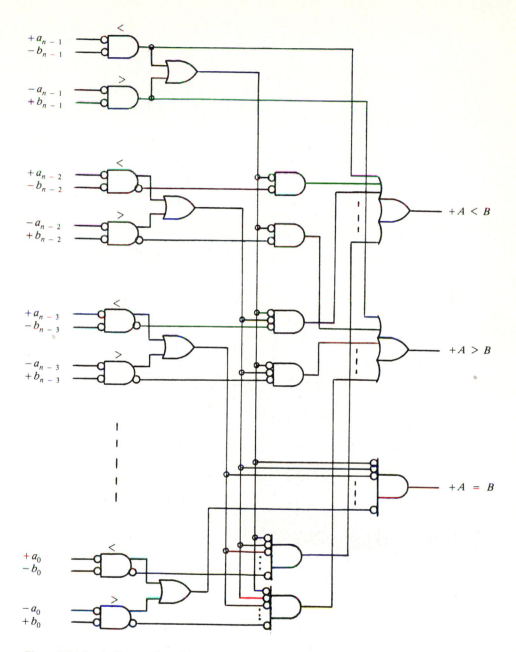

Figure 1.24 Logic diagram for *n*-bit magnitude comparator.

to as of *1-of-8 decoder*, because only one of the eight output lines is active at any given time (allowing time for gate propagation delay and wire delay between gates).

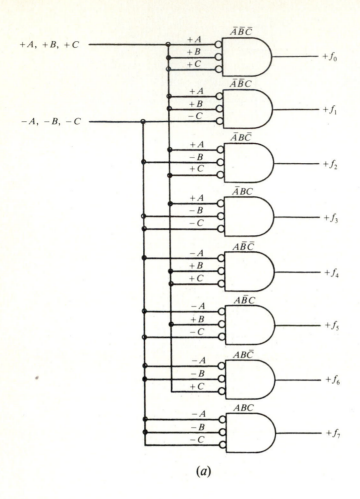

(a)

A	B	C	f_0	f_1	f_2	f_3	f_4	f_5	f_6	f_7
0	0	0	1	0	0	0	0	0	0	0
0	0	1	0	1	0	0	0	0	0	0
0	1	0	0	0	1	0	0	0	0	0
0	1	1	0	0	0	1	0	0	0	0
1	0	0	0	0	0	0	1	0	0	0
1	0	1	0	0	0	0	0	1	0	0
1	1	0	0	0	0	0	0	0	1	0
1	1	1	0	0	0	0	0	0	0	1

(b)

Figure 1.25 (a) Logic diagram for 3-to-8 decoder; (b) truth table for 3-to-8 decoder.

An *enable input* may also be incorporated into the design of the decoder. This requires that each of the eight AND gates has a fourth input, which is used to enable the output of the gate. The enable inputs of all AND gates are connected together such that a minus level on the enable line will allow the decoded inputs to be transferred to the outputs. Other common decoders are 2-to-4 and 4-to-16, and are constructed in a manner similar to the 3-to-8 decoder of Fig. 1.25.

An *encoder* is a combinational logic circuit that has m input signals and generates a binary code of n output signals, where $m \leqslant 2^n$. Each input to the encoder may produce more than one output. Figure 1.26 shows an 8-to-3 encoder constructed with OR gates and the corresponding truth table. Eight inputs are encoded to generate the appropriate binary outputs. The inputs must be mutually exclusive to prevent errors from appearing in the output. Although there are 2^8 possible input combinations, only eight of these combinations are valid.

If the outputs are to be enabled, then the gating occurs on the output of the OR gates, as shown in Fig. 1.26. Other common encoders are 4-to-2 and 16-to-4, and these are constructed in a manner similar to the 8-to-3 encoder.

Multiplexers A *multiplexer* is a combinational logic circuit that selects one of 2^n input signals and connects it to a common output signal. The selection of the input signals is determined by a set of n input selection lines. The selection lines are decoded to select only one of the 2^n input data signals, which is then directed to the common output. The boolean equation for the output function of an 8-to-1 multiplexer is given in Eq. 1.75, and the logic diagram is shown in Fig. 1.27.

$$f_8 = D_0 \bar{S}_2 \bar{S}_1 \bar{S}_0 \lor D_1 \bar{S}_2 \bar{S}_1 S_0 \lor D_2 \bar{S}_2 S_1 \bar{S}_0$$

$$\lor D_3 \bar{S}_2 S_1 S_0 \lor D_4 S_2 \bar{S}_1 \bar{S}_0 \lor D_5 S_2 \bar{S}_1 S_0$$

$$\lor D_6 S_2 S_1 \bar{S}_0 \lor D_7 S_2 S_1 S_0 \tag{1.75}$$

The equations for other common multiplexers are given below, and the logic diagrams are similar in construction to the 8-to-1 multiplexer of Fig. 1.27. An additional input may be added to each AND gate to permit the output function to be enabled or disabled, as shown in Fig. 1.27.

The equation for a 2-to-1 multiplexer is

$$f_2 = D_0 \bar{S}_0 \lor D_1 S_0 \tag{1.76}$$

The equation for a 4-to-1 multiplexer is

$$f_4 = D_0 \bar{S}_1 \bar{S}_0 \lor D_1 \bar{S}_1 S_0 \lor D_2 S_1 \bar{S}_0 \lor D_3 S_1 S_0 \tag{1.77}$$

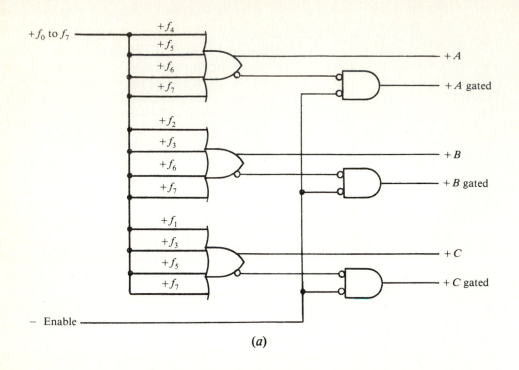

(a)

f_0	f_1	f_2	f_3	f_4	f_5	f_6	f_7	A	B	C
1	0	0	0	0	0	0	0	0	0	0
0	1	0	0	0	0	0	0	0	0	1
0	0	1	0	0	0	0	0	0	1	0
0	0	0	1	0	0	0	0	0	1	1
0	0	0	0	1	0	0	0	1	0	0
0	0	0	0	0	1	0	0	1	0	1
0	0	0	0	0	0	1	0	1	1	0
0	0	0	0	0	0	0	1	1	1	1

(b)

Figure 1.26 (a) Logic diagram for 8-to-3 encoder; (b) truth table for 8-to-3 encoder.

1.2.4 Sequential Logic

A sequential circuit consists of combinational logic and storage elements. The state of the storage elements depends upon the preceding inputs and the preceding states of the elements. The output signals of a sequential circuit are a function of

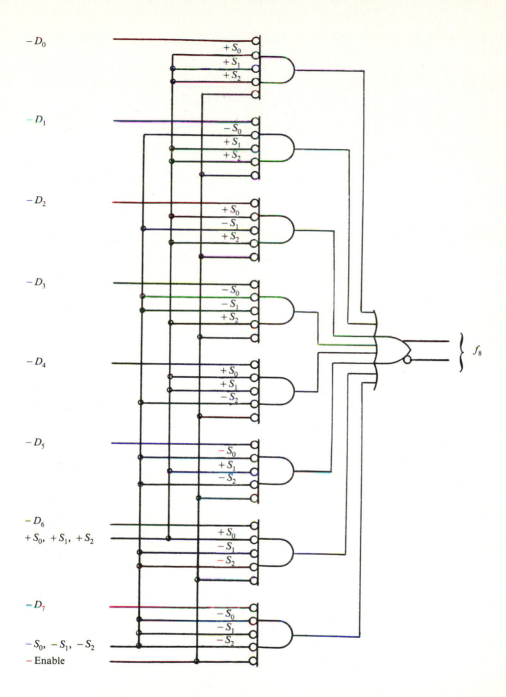

Figure 1.27 Logic diagram for 8-to-1 multiplexer. The select lines have the following binary weights: $S_0 = 1$, $S_1 = 2$, and $S_2 = 4$.

both the present inputs and the present internal states. A sequential circuit can assume a finite number of internal states and may, therefore, be regarded as a finite-state machine. The synthesis of finite-state machines is discussed in more detail later in this section. The block diagram of a sequential circuit, shown in Fig. 1.28, consists of two parts: combinational logic and delays. The circuit is called *sequential*, because operations are performed in sequence.

In general, there are two types of sequential circuits: synchronous and asynchronous. *Synchronous* sequential circuits respond to signals only at discrete intervals of time; that is, clock pulses control the operation of the circuit. Clock pulses are synchronization signals provided by a clock. *Asynchronous* sequential circuits are not clocked, but respond to input signals and storage element outputs without a regular or predictable time relationship to specified events. Most computers use synchronous sequential circuits, because this permits the operation of the system to be more predictable.

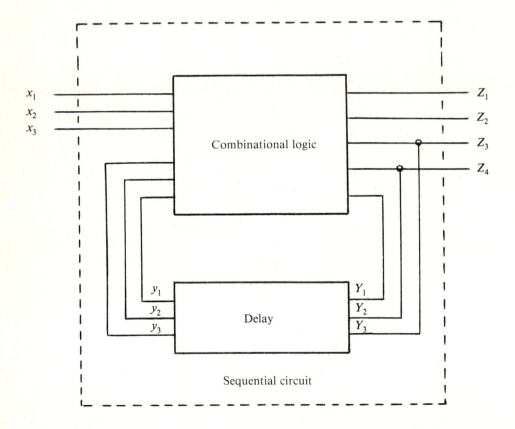

Figure 1.28 Block diagram of a sequential circuit.

Latches and flip-flops A *flip-flop* is a logic circuit that is capable of assuming either one of two stable states at a given time. Flip-flops are the storage elements that are used in a clocked sequential circuit, and are binary cells capable of storing one bit of information. A flip-flop has two outputs: one for the normal (or true) state and one for the complemented (or false) state. Other common names for flip-flops are *latches* and *triggers*.

Latch (RS flip-flop) The simplest sequential logic circuit is shown in Figs. 1.29 and 1.30, which illustrate latches (*RS* flip-flops) constructed from NAND gates and NOR gates, respectively. For now, refer to Fig. 1.29 for the following discussion. The top gate of the latch is a NAND gate, but it is drawn as a negative-input OR gate (dual of NAND) because the function of this gate is the OR operation; that is, the latch will be set (Q = plus) if the set input is minus or the feedback path ② is minus. Feedback path ② will be minus (resulting in the circuit being latched) if feedback path ① and the reset input are plus; that is, no reset pulse is applied to the circuit.

A 1 is used in the next-state truth tables to indicate the active state of a variable or function, even though the active state may be plus or minus. For example, the set input to the latch of Fig. 1.29 is active minus, whereas the set input to the latch of Fig. 1.30 is active plus.

In the truth table of Fig. 1.29(*b*), a situation is indicated that is not allowed, that is, an active (1) set pulse and an active (1) reset pulse applied simultaneously. This indicates an attempt to set and reset the latch at the same time, an operation that should not occur. When this happens, both outputs will be at the more positive voltage level.

When the set input becomes minus in the absence of a reset pulse, then the circuit is latched (or set). The set pulse can then be removed and the latch will remain in the set condition by means of feedback path ② . Any further application of the set pulse will have no affect on the state of the latch. The latch is reset in the absence of a set pulse by changing the reset line to its more negative voltage. The latch of Fig. 1.30 operates in an identical manner, except that the active voltage levels are reversed.

Clocked RS flip-flop The *RS* flip-flop responds to changes at the inputs whenever they occur. The input signals can be controlled, however, by ANDing the inputs with a clock pulse. A clocked *RS* flip-flop is shown in Fig. 1.31 and consists of a NOR latch and two AND gates. The outputs of the two input AND gates remain at the minus voltage level whenever the clock pulse is inactive (plus). This permits the state of the flip-flop to remain unchanged. Thus, the flip-flop can change states only when a clock pulse occurs. The flip-flop will be set when both the set and clock inputs are minus, with the reset input at the plus level. The reset condition occurs when both the reset and clock inputs are minus and the set input is plus. The truth table is the same as in Fig. 1.30(*b*), with the assumption that the *S* and *R* entries are gated with the clock input. The logic equation for an

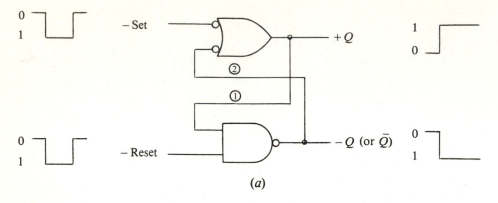

(a)

Present state	Present inputs		Next state
Q_t	S	R	Q_{t+1}
0	0	0	0
0	1	0	1
0	0	1	0
0	1	1	Not allowed
1	0	0	1
1	1	0	1
1	0	1	0
1	1	1	Not allowed

1 = active (or set) state.
0 = inactive (or reset) state.

(b)

Figure 1.29 Basic flip-flop (or latch) using NAND gates. (a) Logic diagram; (b) truth table.

RS flip-flop is

$$Q_{t+1} = S\bar{R} \vee Q_t \bar{S}\bar{R} \tag{1.78}$$

D flip-flop The *D* flip-flop can be implemented from a clocked *RS* flip-flop and an inverter, as shown in the logic diagram of Fig. 1.32. The inverter reduces the number of data inputs from two to one. The data (*D*) input goes directly to the set input and the complement of *D* goes to the reset input. When *D* is minus, the occurrence of a clock pulse will cause the flip-flop to be set ($-Q$ is minus), unless it is already set. Likewise, when *D* is plus, the clock pulse will reset the flip-flop ($-Q$ is plus). Thus, the next state of the flip-flop is the same as the state of the *D* input and is independent of the present state of the flip-flop.

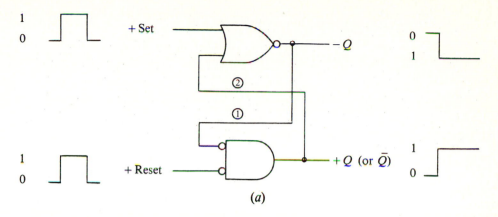

(a)

Present state	Present inputs		Next state
Q_t	S	R	Q_{t+1}
0	0	0	0
0	1	0	1
0	0	1	0
0	1	1	Not allowed
1	0	0	1
1	1	0	1
1	0	1	0
1	1	1	Not allowed

1 = active (or set) state.
0 = inactive (or reset) state.

(b)

Figure 1.30 Basic flip-flop (or latch) using NOR gates. (a) Logic diagram; (b) truth table.

A necessary requirement for correct operation of the flip-flop is that the D input state remains constant during the duration of the clock pulse. If the D input changes state while the clock pulse is minus, then the next state of the flip-flop will be the same as the final state of the D input before the clock pulse became inactive, or the next state will be indeterminate. The logic equation for the D flip-flop is

$$Q_{t+1} = D \qquad (1.79)$$

The problem associated with data changing state during a clock pulse can be resolved by using the master-slave D flip-flop shown in Fig. 1.33. The method of operation is called *edge-triggering*, because the state of the D input is transferred to the outputs at the leading (negative) edge of the clock pulse.

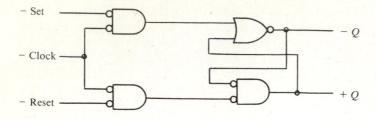

Figure 1.31 Clocked *RS* flip-flop.

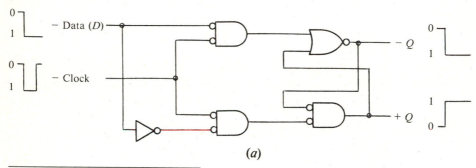

(*a*)

Present state	Present input	Next state
Q_t	D	Q_{t+1}
0	0	0
0	1	1
1	0	0
1	1	1

1 = active (or set) state.
0 = inactive (or reset) state.

(*b*)

Figure 1.32 Clocked *D* flip-flop. (*a*) Logic diagram; (*b*) truth table.

For the following description of the operation of the flip-flop, refer to Fig. 1.33. If the clock is inactive (plus), the outputs of gates 1 and 4 will be minus, thus maintaining the current state of the flip-flop. Any change in the *D* input during this time will result in a change in the outputs of gates 1, 2, and 3. For example, if *D* becomes minus (active), then the output of gate 2 becomes plus and the outputs of gates 1 and 3 becomes minus. The occurrence of a clock pulse will then cause the output of gate 4 to set the slave latch, causing the output of the flip-flop to become minus. Gate 6 is enabled from the output of gate 1 and the feedback from gate 5. Similarly, the slave latch is reset to a logical 0 ($-Q$ = high) when the *D* input is plus (inactive) at the leading edge of the clock pulse.

The time immediately preceding and following the leading edge of the clock pulse is critical for correct operation of the flip-flop. The D input must not change during the interval represented by the summation of the setup time and the hold time. The setup time is the duration that the D input must be stable

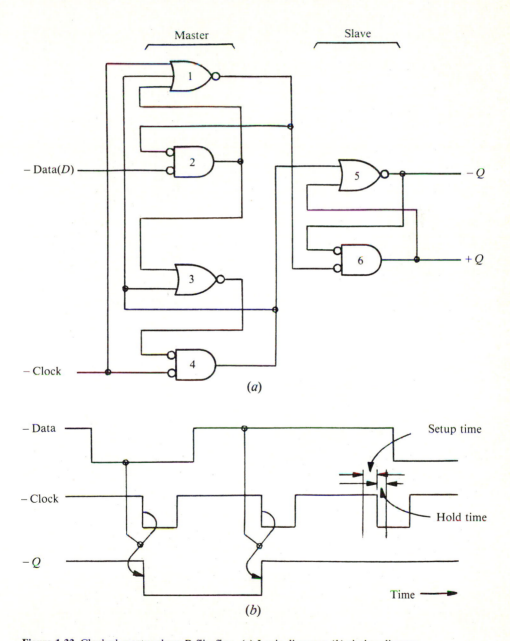

Figure 1.33 Clocked master-slave D flip-flop. (a) Logic diagram; (b) timing diagram.

before the clock pulse occurs. This allows time for the state of the D input to propagate through gates 2 and 3. The hold time is the duration that the D input must remain stable after the clock pulse has become inactive. The hold time for the D master-slave flip-flop is 0.

JK flip-flop The JK flip-flop is similar in operation to the RS flip-flop except that the two inputs are allowed to be active at the same time. The function of the J and K inputs is the same as that of the S and R inputs, respectively; that is, J sets the flip-flop and K resets (clears) it. When inputs J and K are active simultaneously, the flip-flop changes state (toggles) at the next clock pulse regardless of the present state.

The JK flip-flop can be designed without master-slave stages, but then proper operation cannot be guaranteed, because of feedback paths from the outputs to the inputs. If there are not separate master and slaves stages, the circuit will oscillate when both J and K are active. The implementation of a clocked master-slave JK flip-flop is shown in Fig. 1.34. A reset input (not shown) is normally applied to gates 4 and 8 to initialize the flip-flop to a known state. The information applied to the J and K inputs is transmitted to the master stage at the leading edge of the clock pulse. The information is retained in the master stage until the trailing edge of the clock pulse, at which time the information is transferred to the slave stage. When the clock is inactive, the J and K inputs are prevented from affecting the master flip-flop. When the clock is active, the inverted clock signal prevents the output of the master flip-flop from affecting the state of the slave flip-flop. The logic equation for the JK flip-flop is

$$Q_{t+1} = \overline{Q}_t J \vee Q_t \overline{K} \tag{1.80}$$

The JK flip-flop can also be drawn as in Fig. 1.35. This implementation requires one less gate, but the operation is essentially the same.

Registers Registers are used to store binary information in a digital system. An n-bit register consists of n flip-flops and can store n bits of information, one bit in each flip-flop. Any of the flip-flops previously described in this section can be used to construct a register. Data can be loaded into a register either in parallel or in series. Parallel loading is faster, because all flip-flops receive new information during one clock pulse. During a serial load operation, each flip-flop receives new data from the flip-flop to the immediate left or right depending on the direction of loading. The end flip-flop receives its data from an external source.

Flip-flops may also be interconnected to form a shift register. A right-shift register is one in which the output of each flip-flop is connected to the input of the flip-flop to the immediate right. A common clock pulse is applied to all flip-flops simultaneously. The only external data input is to the input of the leftmost flip-flop. There is always an output from the rightmost stage; however, the other stages may not have their outputs made available to the rest of the system. All bits

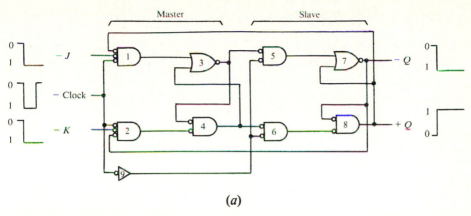

(a)

Present state	Present inputs		Next state
Q_t	J	K	Q_{t+1}
0	0	0	0
0	0	1	0
0	1	0	1
0	1	1	1
1	0	0	1
1	0	1	0
1	1	0	1
1	1	1	0

1 = active (or set) state.
0 = inactive (or reset) state.

(b)

Figure 1.34 Clocked master-slave *JK* flip-flop. (*a*) Logic diagram; (*b*) truth table.

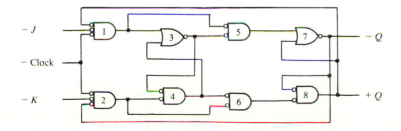

Figure 1.35 Clocked master-slave *JK* flip-flop using eight NOR gates.

are shifted right one bit position during each clock pulse. Figure 1.36 shows the contents of an eight-bit shift register after four successive right-shift operations. The register is initially parallel-loaded with 0 1 1 0 1 0 1 1. The serial input is 0 1 1 0. Two shift registers are shown in Fig. 1.37; one is implemented with master-slave D flip-flops and one with master-slave JK flip-flops.

Synchronous logic design This section will present two types of synchronous sequential circuits. The first consists of a network of flip-flops and a single external clock signal that is applied to the network. The second consists of a sequential network that has a clock signal and additional inputs. In general, the sequence of both flip-flop states and output states depends on the input sequence that is applied to the network. Thus, during each clock cycle, the next-state function produces a new state that depends on the present state and the present inputs.

Counters are one of the simplest types of sequential circuits that require only one input. The single input is a clock pulse. A counter is constructed from two or more flip-flops that change states in a prescribed sequence upon the application of a series of clock pulses. The sequence of states in a counter may generate a binary count, a BCD count, or any other sequence of states. Counters are used for counting the number of occurrences of an event and for generating timing sequences.

Two counters are presented in this section—a binary counter and a BCD counter, both of which are synchronous counters. Synchronous counter operation is characterized by simultaneous state changes for all flip-flops having input conditions that cause the flip-flop to change state. An n-bit binary counter consists of n flip-flops and has a counting range from 0 to $2^n - 1$. For example, the state diagram for a three-bit binary counter is shown in Fig. 1.38. This is a modulo-8 counter that repeats the binary sequence by returning to 0 0 0 after reaching a count of 1 1 1. The arrows indicate the state sequence. The outputs of a counter are the outputs of the flip-flops, and thus the state of the counter is determined from the present state of the individual flip-flops. For example, if the state of the flip-flops is $A = 1$, $B = 0$, and $C = 1$, then the state of the counter is 1 0 1, where C is the low-order flip-flop.

JK flip-flops will be used in the design of a modulo-8 binary counter. The next-state truth table is shown in Table 1.16. A_t indicates the present state of the A flip-flop, and A_{t+1} is the required next state of the A flip-flop. The states of flip-flops B and C are similarly defined. J_A and K_A are the states of the J and K inputs, respectively, for flip-flop A that are necessary to take A from state A_t to state A_{t+1}. The J and K inputs for flip-flops B and C are similarly defined.

Flip-flop A is used in the following discussion, but the same rationale applies to flip-flops B and C. If $A_t = 0$ and $A_{t+1} = 0$, then J_A must equal 0, because the next state of flip-flop A is 0 and $J_A = 1$ would tend to set the flip-flop to 1. The state of K_A can be 0 or 1, because if $K_A = 0$, then we have

$$J_A = 0 \quad \text{and} \quad K_A = 0$$

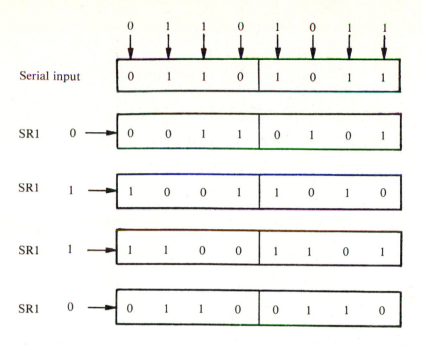

Figure 1.36 Contents of an eight-bit register during four successive right shifts. SR1 = Shift right one bit position.

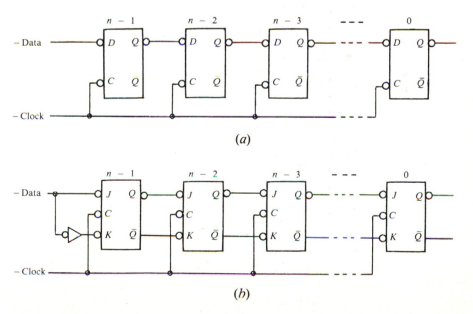

Figure 1.37 Shift-right shift register implemented with (*a*) master-slave *D* flip-flops and (*b*) master-slave *JK* flip-flops.

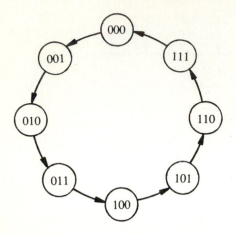

Figure 1.38 State transition diagram for a modulo-8 binary counter.

and the flip-flop will not change state. Also, if $K_A = 1$, then we have

$$J_A = 0 \quad \text{and} \quad K_A = 1$$

and the flip-flop will be reset. However, the flip-flop is already reset; thus, $K = \text{x (don't care)}$.

When $A_t = 0$ and $A_{t+1} = 1$, then J_A must equal 1, because the next state of flip-flop A is 1 and $J_A = 1$ will set the flip-flop to 1. The K input, however, can be 0 or 1. If $K_A = 0$, then we have

$$J_A = 1 \quad \text{and} \quad K_A = 0$$

and the flip-flop will be set to 1. Also, if $K_A = 1$, then we have

$$J_A = 1 \quad \text{and} \quad K_A = 1$$

Table 1.16 Truth table for a modulo-8 binary counter

Present state			Present inputs						Next state		
A_t	B_t	C_t	J_A	K_A	J_B	K_B	J_C	K_C	A_{t+1}	B_{t+1}	C_{t+1}
0	0	0	0	x	0	x	1	x	0	0	1
0	0	1	0	x	1	x	x	1	0	1	0
0	1	0	0	x	x	0	1	x	0	1	1
0	1	1	1	x	x	1	x	1	1	0	0
1	0	0	x	0	0	x	1	x	1	0	1
1	0	1	x	0	1	x	x	1	1	1	0
1	1	0	x	0	x	0	1	x	1	1	1
1	1	1	x	1	x	1	x	1	0	0	0

and the flip-flop will toggle (change states) from 0 to 1. Thus, $K_A = x$.

When $A_t = 1$ and $A_{t+1} = 0$, then K_A must equal 1. This will cause the flip-flop to be reset. J_A, however, can be 0 or 1. If $J_A = 0$, then

$$J_A = 0 \quad \text{and} \quad K_A = 1$$

and A will be reset to 0. If $J_A = 1$, then

$$J_A = 1 \quad \text{and} \quad K_A = 1$$

and the state of A will toggle from 1 to 0. Thus, $J_A = x$.

If $A_t = 1$ and $A_{t+1} = 1$, then K_A must be 0, because the flip-flop must not be reset. J_A, however, can be 0 or 1. If $J_A = 0$, then

$$J_A = 0 \quad \text{and} \quad K_A = 0$$

and the flip-flop will not change state. If $J_A = 1$, then

$$J_A = 1 \quad \text{and} \quad K_A = 0$$

which is the set condition for the flip-flop. The above requirements for J_A and K_A are summarized in Table 1.17 for a general flip-flop Q.

Table 1.17 Next-state table for a *JK* flip-flop

Present state	Present inputs		Next state
Q_t	J_Q	K_Q	Q_{t+1}
0	0	x	0
0	1	x	1
1	x	1	0
1	x	0	1

The next step in the design process is to construct Karnaugh maps that represent the *JK* input excitations for flip-flops A, B, and C. The information contained in Table 1.16 will be used for this purpose. The Karnaugh maps for the *JK* input equations for a modulo-8 binary counter are shown in Fig. 1.39. When

$$A_t = 0 \quad B_t = 0 \quad C_t = 0$$

then $J_A = 0$ and $K_A = x$ (Table 1.16). This information is transferred directly to the J_A and K_A maps; that is, the 0 0 0 entries for J_A and K_A are 0 and x, respectively. Likewise, when

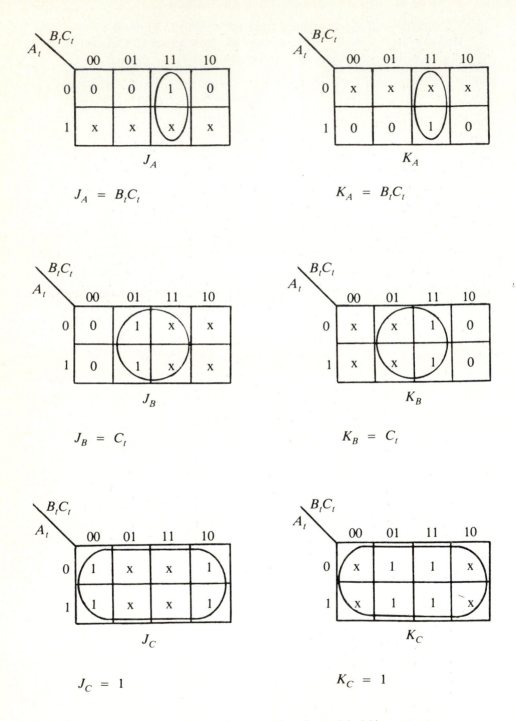

Figure 1.39 Karnaugh maps for J and K input equations for modulo-8 binary counter.

$$A_t = 0 \qquad B_t = 1 \qquad C_t = 1$$

then the 0 1 1 entries for J_A and K_A are 1 and x, respectively. The remaining entries in the maps are completed in a similar manner. The J and K input equations are shown beneath the corresponding maps. The logic diagram for the modulo-8 counter is shown in Fig. 1.40 and is designed directly from the J and K input equations.

Each decade of a BCD counter requires four flip-flops. The next-state truth table for a single decade is shown in Table 1.18. The design of a decade follows the same procedure as the design of the modulo-8 binary counter. The design of an n-digit BCD counter is constructed from n four-bit binary counters having a counting sequence of 0 0 0 0 to 1 0 0 1 and then back to 0 0 0 0 for each decade. The logic diagram for a three-digit BCD counter is shown in Fig. 1.41. Note that, with the exception of the units decade, the clock pulse is transmitted to each decade only when the previous lower-order decade has reached a state of 1 0 0 1. Since the counter is designed with JK master-slave flip-flops, the outputs of each decade will not change state until the trailing edge of the clock pulse, thus assuring that the next higher-order decade receives a clock pulse of full duration.

The sequential networks that have been considered thus far have had no inputs other than a clock pulse. We will now consider sequential machines that have additional inputs. The sequential machines presented next are abstract models of logic circuits found within digital computers. The model of this type of sequential machine requires two functions—one that changes the contents of the storage elements (flip-flops) of the network by the application of input sequences and clock pulses, and one that generates an output. This type of network is often referred to as a *finite-state machine*. Figure 1.42 illustrates this definition. The input sequence is represented by x, and s_t is the state of the machine that is fed back

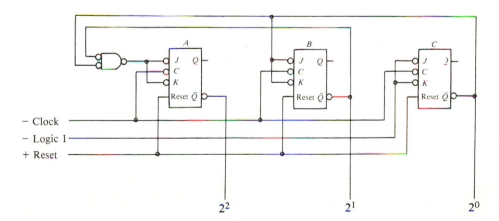

Figure 1.40 Logic diagram for modulo-8 binary counter using JK flip-flops.

Table 1.18 Truth table for one decade of a BCD counter

A_t	B_t	C_t	D_t	J_A	K_A	J_B	K_B	J_C	K_C	J_D	K_D	A_{t+1}	B_{t+1}	C_{t+1}	D_{t+1}
0	0	0	0	0	x	0	x	0	x	1	x	0	0	0	1
0	0	0	1	0	x	0	x	1	x	x	1	0	0	1	0
0	0	1	0	0	x	0	x	x	0	1	x	0	0	1	1
0	0	1	1	0	x	1	x	x	1	x	1	0	1	0	0
0	1	0	0	0	x	x	0	0	x	1	x	0	1	0	1
0	1	0	1	0	x	x	0	1	x	x	1	0	1	1	0
0	1	1	0	0	x	x	0	x	0	1	x	0	1	1	1
0	1	1	1	1	x	x	1	x	1	x	1	1	0	0	0
1	0	0	0	x	0	0	x	0	x	1	x	1	0	0	1
1	0	0	1	x	1	0	x	0	x	x	1	0	0	0	0

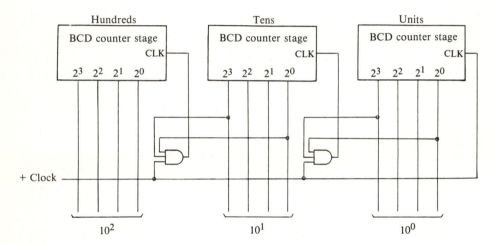

Figure 1.41 Three-stage BCD counter.

to the input. During each clock cycle, the next-state function produces a new state s_{t+1} that depends on the present state s_t and the present input. Also, during each cycle, the output function maps the present state into an output state.

The operation of a finite-state machine can be specified by its present inputs, the next-state function, and the output function. For example, the state graph and state table of Fig. 1.43 describe a finite-state machine that produces a 1 output whenever the preceding four inputs form the sequence 1 1 1 0. The symbol

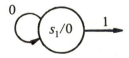

defines state 1 with the output $Z = 0$. If the next input is 0, then the machine remains in state 1. If the next input is 1, then the machine proceeds to the next state s_2. Thus, each input is associated with a transformation of states. The states s_1, s_2, . . . , s_5 remember the number of symbols of the sequence 1 1 1 0 that have

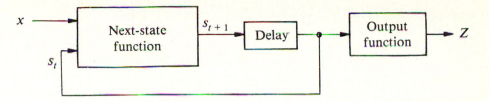

Figure 1.42 Model of finite-state machine.

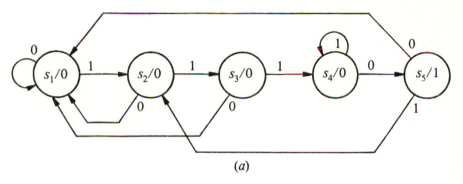

(a)

Present state s_t	Next state s_{t+1}		Present output Z
	$x = 0$	$x = 1$	
s_1	s_1	s_2	0
s_2	s_1	s_3	0
s_3	s_1	s_4	0
s_4	s_5	s_4	0
s_5	s_1	s_2	1

(b)

Figure 1.43 (a) State graph and (b) state table for the next-state and output functions for a machine to detect the input sequence 1 1 1 0.

been received thus far. State s_1 corresponds to no symbol having been received; that is, s_1 is the initial state in which the machine begins to detect the input sequence. State s_2 corresponds to having received the initial 1, s_3 occurs after the sequence 1 1 has been received, and so forth.

The machine is initialized to start in state s_1. When the correct input sequence occurs, the machine advances successively through states s_2, s_3, s_4, and s_5, with the output being 0 for all states except s_5, where the output is 1. If the input sequence is not 1 1 1 0, then the machine does not advance sequentially through the states, as is evidenced by the feedback loops. At each input, the machine proceeds to a state that indicates how much of the sequence 1 1 1 0 has been received. For example, if a 1 is received in state 4, the machine remains in state 4 until a 0 is received, which takes the machine to state 5. Also, if a 0 is received in state 3, then the input sequence of 1s has been discontinued and the machine returns to s_1.

Different machines may produce identical output sequences for the same input sequence. Thus, the operation of the machines may be indistinguishable even though the designs are different. Therefore, it is necessary to identify and eliminate unnecessary states. Two states are equivalent if it is impossible to distinguish them by observing the input and output sequences. For example, the three-state machine of Fig. 1.44 can be reduced to two states. By observing only

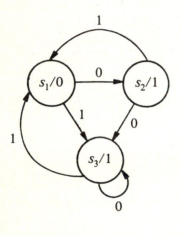

Present state s_t	Next state s_{t+1}		Present output Z
	$x = 0$	$x = 1$	
s_1	s_2	s_3	0
s_2	s_3	s_1	1
s_3	s_3	s_1	1

(a)

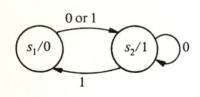

Present state s_t	Next state s_{t+1}		Present output Z
	$x = 0$	$x = 1$	
s_1	s_2	s_2	0
s_2	s_2	s_1	1

(b)

Figure 1.44 (a) A sequential machine; (b) an equivalent reduced machine.

the input and output sequences of the machine, an observer would be unable to distinguish state s_2 from s_3. Therefore, every occurrence of s_3 in Fig. 1.44(a) can be replaced by s_2, thus forming the equivalent machine in which s_3 has been eliminated [Fig. 1.44(b)]. This has been a simple example; however, the same procedure can be used to simplify machines with many states.

Asynchronous logic design The sequential circuits presented previously can be categorized as clocked sequential (or clocked synchronous) networks, in which a change of state occurs only in response to a clock pulse. This causes all flip-flops to change state simultaneously, because they are synchronized by a common clock pulse. In some situations, however, the inputs may change state at random times, thus making the circuit unsuitable for synchronization (the output signals may be required before the next clock pulse occurs). In these cases, an asynchronous design is more appropriate for the network.

In this section we will consider the synthesis of asynchronous sequential circuits; that is, the design of unclocked sequential circuits. A flip-flop is a clocked circuit; however, the internal structure operates in an asynchronous manner. Time is an element in sequential circuits. Thus, the outputs are a function not only of present inputs but also of past circuit states. The design of asynchronous circuits is more difficult than that of synchronous circuits because of timing problems associated with circuit path delays.

The input states to the circuit are represented by x_i, the output states by Z_i. The states of the storage elements (internal states) are represented by y_i, their corresponding input excitations by Y_i. Thus, the next state of an internal state will be the same as its present excitation. The internal states are the feedback paths of an asynchronous sequential circuit.

Flow tables are used in the design of asynchronous circuits. A flow table describes the operation of a sequential circuit and is similar to a Karnaugh map, because each entry is defined by a unique combination of variables. The variables consist of the inputs x_i and internal states y_i, where the inputs define the columns and the internal states define the rows. Every possible circuit state is represented in the flow table. Some states may be stable, some may be unstable, and some may be don't-care conditions.

When synthesizing asynchronous sequential circuits, the circuit operation is completely described in the flow table. The flow table is then simplified, if necessary, and transformed into Karnaugh maps from which the circuit can be designed. The steps in the synthesis procedure are as follows:

1. Construct a primitive flow table from the word description of the problem.
2. Reduce the primitive flow table by eliminating all redundant states.
3. Construct a merger diagram so that rows in the primitive flow table can be merged.
4. This produces a merged flow table.
5. An internal state excitation map (Y map) is obtained from the merged flow table.
6. An output map (Z map) is obtained from the merged flow table in conjunction with the primitive flow table.
7. The sequential circuit is designed from the internal state excitation map and the output map. Circuit hazards must be detected and eliminated.

Each step in the above procedure will now be defined and illustrated in Example 1.5.

Example 1.5 A circuit is to be designed that will propagate oscillator pulses through the circuit only if the oscillator pulse is initially inactive when an oscillator-enable signal is asserted. This permits oscillator pulses of full duration to be obtained regardless of when the enable signal is made active (minus). The timing diagram for this circuit is shown in Fig. 1.45.

The primitive flow table is shown in Fig. 1.46. Each stable state (circled entry) is assigned a separate row. A state is stable when the next state will be the same as the present state, that is, $Y = y$. A state is unstable (uncircled entries) when the next state will not be the same as the present state, that is $Y \neq y$. The state numbers in the flow table are chosen to correspond to the sequence of events. Only one input can change state at a time.

The primitive flow table can be developed by first considering the sequence that will produce an output of 1 ($Z = 1$), that is, a sequence that will cause an oscillator pulse to be propagated. If the circuit is in stable state ① ($x_1 \ x_2 = 0 \ 0$) and the inputs change to 1 0, then the circuit proceeds to stable state ②, where $Z = 0$. If the inputs change to 1 1, the oscillator pulse will be propagated and $Z = 1$. The dashed lines in the squares indicate conditions that are assumed will never occur. Thus, the dashed entry in row 3 of column 0 1 specifies that the enable signal will never be made inactive while the oscillator pulse is active . As long as the enable is active, the pulses will continue to be propagated, as illustrated by the sequence below.

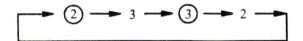

If an oscillator pulse occurs while the enable is inactive ($x_1 \ x_2 = 0 \ 1$), the circuit proceeds to stable state ④, where $Z = 0$, then returns to ① when the inputs change from 0 1 to 0 0. The remainder of the primitive flow table is completed according to the specifications of Example 1.5.

In constructing the primitive flow table, it is possible to introduce redundant states, thus producing more stable states than required. If two states are equivalent, then one state can be eliminated, thus reducing the number of rows in the primitive flow table.

Two stable states are equivalent if:

1. They have the same input states; that is, they are in the same column.
2. They have the same output states.
3. For each possible change of input states, there is a transition from the two stable states to the same state or to equivalent states.

There are no equivalent states in Fig. 1.46. The only two stable states with the same inputs are ③ and ⑤ , but the output states are different.

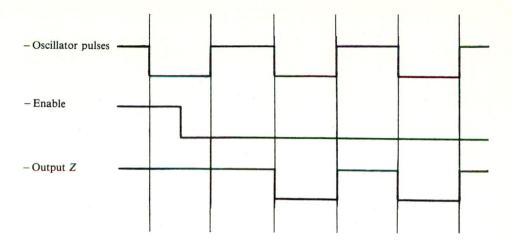

Figure 1.45 Timing diagram for Example 1.5.

x_1 = enable
x_2 = oscillator pulse
Z = output

$x_1 x_2$

	00	01	11	10	Z
	①	4	—	2	0
	1	—	3	②	0
	—	—	③	2	1
	1	④	5	—	0
	—	—	⑤	2	0

Figure 1.46 Primitive flow table for Example 1.5.

The next step is to merge the rows of the primitive flow table, which will produce a merged flow table. Merging reduces the number of rows in the flow table
by placing more than one stable state in the same row, but does not reduce the
number of stable states. Merging will reduce the number of internal states y_i required, thus producing a simpler circuit with fewer logic gates.

The rules for merging are as follows:

1. Two or more rows can merge if the state numbers in each column are the same, or if there is a state number and a dash in the same column, or two dashes in the same column.
2. All state numbers in the rows to be merged are written in the respective columns of the merged row. If a state is circled in one of the merging rows, then it is also circled in the merged row.

The output states do not affect the merging and are not used in the merged flow table.

In order to simplify the merging process and obtain an optimum merger, a merger diagram is used. The merger diagram is constructed by arranging the stable-state numbers in a circular fashion, as shown in Fig. 1.47. A line is then drawn between any pair of states that can be merged according to the preceding merger rules. The construction of the merger diagram is facilitated by starting at the top of the reduced primitive flow table and comparing row 1 with rows 2–5, in sequence, for possible mergers. Using this process, rows 1 and 2 can be merged, because there is no conflict of states. Also, rows 1 and 3, 1 and 4, and 1 and 5 can be merged. Row 2 can be merged only with row 3, because there is a conflict of states in column $x_1\ x_2\ =\ 1\ 1$ for rows 4 and 5. The remaining mergers are completed in a similar manner.

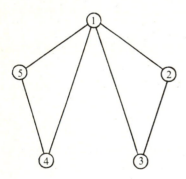

Figure 1.47 Merger diagram for Example 1.5.

Since rows 1, 2, and 3 of the merger diagram are connected, then each row can merge with the other two rows; that is, rows 1, 2, and 3 can merge into a single row. The same is true for rows 1, 4, and 5. Thus, two possible mergers can be obtained as shown below.

$$1\ 2\ 3\ /\ 4\ 5$$
$$1\ 4\ 5\ /\ 2\ 3$$

When there is more than one possibility for a minimum-row merger, all possibilities should be considered, because one method may result in a minimum number of logic gates. For this example, we will use the merger indicated by 1 2 3 / 4 5.

The merged flow table is obtained directly from the merger diagram and is illustrated in Fig. 1.48. When assigning internal states to the rows of a merged flow table, the row-to-row transitions must be considered. If there is a transition between two rows, then the internal states for the two rows must differ in only one variable. If the rows differ in more than one variable, then the result is a race condition. If the resulting stable state is the desired stable state, then this is called a *noncritical race*. When it is possible for the circuit action to terminate in two or more stable states, depending on the order in which the internal states change, then this is a *critical race* condition. The behavior of a circuit with a critical race is unpredictable, and this condition must be avoided. In order to avoid critical races, an internal state assignment must be found such that only one internal state variable changes during each transition. The merged flow table of Fig. 1.48 has no race conditions.

x_1 = enable
x_2 = oscillator pulse
y = internal state

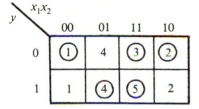

Figure 1.48 Merged flow table for Example 1.5.

When constructing the internal state excitation map (Y map), it is convenient to assign the entries for the stable states first. Each map entry that corresponds to a stable state will have the same value as the internal state value assigned to that row. Thus, the entries for stable states ①, ③, and ② will be 0, corresponding to $y = 0$, as shown in Fig. 1.49. Each map entry corresponding to an unstable state will be the same as the next internal state resulting from a transition. In this example, unstable state 4 will contain the value of 1. In a similar manner, the row corresponding to $y = 1$ contains the entries 0 1 1 0 for the four columns. The internal state excitation equation is

$$Y = \overline{x}_1 x_2 \lor y x_2 \tag{1.81}$$

The output map (Z map) is obtained from the merged flow table and the reduced primitive flow table. The output value for each stable state is obtained from the primitive flow table, and the location of that state on the output map is

x_1 = enable
x_2 = oscillator pulse
y = internal state

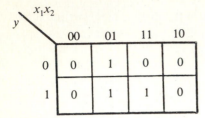

Figure 1.49 Internal state excitation map (Y map) for Example 1.5.

obtained from the merged flow table. A partially completed output map that lists only the stable state outputs is shown in Fig. 1.50 for this example. An output of 1 occurs only for stable state ③ , as shown in the primitive flow table of Fig. 1.46. All other stable states have outputs equal to 0. The state-to-state transitions are identified in the primitive flow table, and this information is used to assign values to the unstable output states.

x_1 = enable
x_2 = oscillator pulse
y = internal state

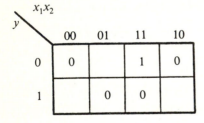

Figure 1.50 Output map (Z map) for Example 1.5 showing circuit output for stable states only.

The rules for assigning values to the unstable output states are as follows:

1. If the states of the initial and final output stable states are the same during a transition, then this same value is assigned to all unstable states that are encountered in the transition. This eliminates transient changes in the output state.
2. The values of unstable states that are not defined by rule 1 are optional. This gives the designer the flexibility to provide a faster or slower change in output states and also to reduce circuit complexity, if possible.

The completed output map for Example 1.5 is shown in Fig. 1.51, and the output equation is

$$Z = x_1 x_2 \bar{y} \qquad (1.82)$$

The logic diagram is designed directly from the Y and Z equations (Eqs. 1.81 and 1.82 respectively), and is shown in Fig. 1.52.

x_1 = enable
x_2 = oscillator pulse
y = internal state

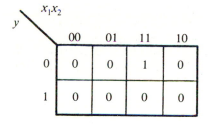

Figure 1.51 Output map (Z map) for Example 1.5.

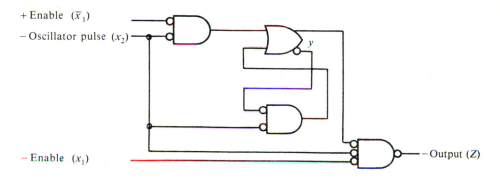

Figure 1.52 Logic diagram for Example 1.5.

A final topic in this review section on logic design is hazards. Hazards can occur in both combinational and sequential circuits and are caused by different gate delays and wire delays in the circuit. Assume that a logic circuit is to be designed using the following equation:

$$Z = x_1 x_2 \vee \bar{x}_1 x_3 \qquad (1.83)$$

The Karnaugh map and logic diagram are shown in Fig. 1.53. Let x_1 switch from

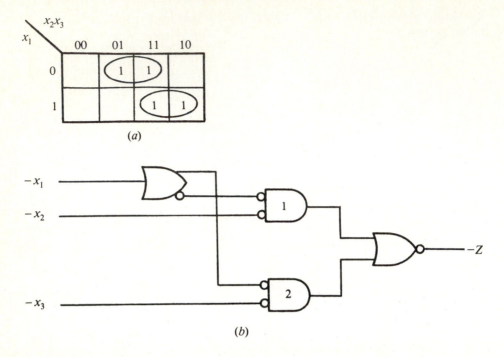

(a)

(b)

Figure 1.53 (a) Output map and (b) logic diagram for Eq. 1.83.

active to inactive, that is, change from a minus level to a more positive level, with x_2 and x_3 both being active minus. Then the output of gate 1 will become minus and the output of gate 2 will become plus, thus maintaining the output Z at the required state. If, however, the propagation delay of gate 2 is longer than that of gate 1, then the outputs of gates 1 and 2 will both be minus momentarily, causing a transient positive pulse at the Z output of the circuit. The output Z will regain its correct active minus state when the output of gate 2 becomes plus.

Recall that two entries in a Karnaugh map are said to be adjacent if they differ by only one variable, which is uncomplemented in one square and complemented in the other. The same analogy can be extended to groups of entries, in which each group contains adjacent squares. A hazard can exist when an input change causes a transition between two states that are not in the same group. Thus, in Fig. 1.53(a), a hazard can exist between x_1 x_2 x_3 = 0 1 1 and x_1 x_2 x_3 = 1 1 1 when x_1 changes state. The hazard can be eliminated by forming one more group of adjacent squares as shown in Fig. 1.54(a). This third grouping connects the other two groups, and the hazard is eliminated, because the logic gate corresponding to the term x_2 x_3 maintains the circuit output in the active state while x_1 is changing state. The boolean equation for hazard-free operation of this circuit is

$$Z = x_1 x_2 \vee \bar{x}_1 x_3 \vee x_2 x_3 \qquad (1.84)$$

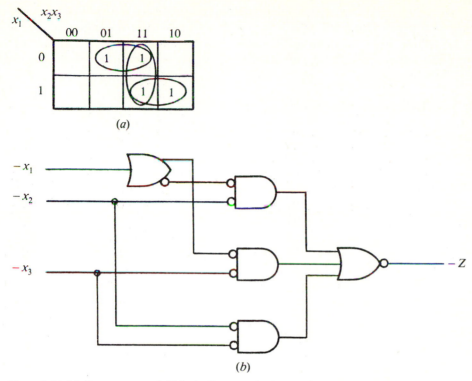

Figure 1.54 (*a*) Output map and (*b*) logic diagram with hazard eliminated for Eq. 1.84.

This section on logic design has been presented as a review of basic analysis and synthesis techniques for combinational and sequential circuits. It was not intended to replace a good book on logic design, because much more could have been written on the subject than has been presented in this text.

Many of the logic circuits presented in this section are used in arithmetic processors either as functional units or in the application of control techniques for arithmetic operations. Boolean algebra has been introduced and provides the basic mathematical tools to analyze and design certain classes of switching networks. A discussion of flip-flops was included, because flip-flops are used extensively in arithmetic processor design either as individual storage elements or in groups to form registers and counters. Also, in most digital system design, there is at least one situation that requires a knowledge of minimization techniques and asynchronous circuit design.

1.3 VERY LARGE SCALE INTEGRATION TECHNOLOGY

Very large scale integration (VLSI) has become so dense that a single chip may contain more than 100,000 logic gates. A typical example of a VLSI product is a microprocessor. Current 32-bit microprocessor architectures, together with appropriate support chips, consist of more than 100,000 transistors. For example, the two-chip processing unit of the Intel 432 computer represents a total of 160,000 transistor placements. And VLSI technology is expanding at such a rapid rate that single chips consisting of 200,000 to 300,000 logic gates will become commonplace.

As chip densities increase, the methods in which digital systems are structured and the requirements for system design capabilities change. Also affected is the design of computational algorithms and the tradeoffs between hardware and software to optimize performance with a minimum amount of hardware cost. Algorithm design will be a major area of research during the coming decades. New tools are being developed to aid the design engineer in developing a new VLSI product in the shortest time with the greatest assurance of error-free operation. Computer-aided design (CAD) systems and design automation (DA) techniques, such as automatic placement and routing of gate interconnections, logic gate terminal and load checking, test pattern generation, and logic simulation have achieved prominence as essential tools for VLSI system design.

As a result of increased chip density and the corresponding increase in speed achieved by the close proximity of related logic gates, modular building blocks for logic systems are becoming more functional. This permits the system designer to organize system-level functions as functional blocks. For example, modular iterative cellular arrays for high-speed multipliers and dividers are ideally suited to VLSI technology; the designs of these are described in detail in this book.

A major concern in VLSI chip design is the long turnaround time for implementing changes to the hardware. The correction of design errors and changes due to design modifications may take several weeks to obtain a new updated chip. The need for an excellent logic simulator is paramount for VLSI system design. However, even with an excellent simulation program, the checking provided for the chip design is only as good as the input test patterns. If the test patterns are not comprehensive, then the logic design will not be fully tested, possibly resulting in some faults being undetected. It is for this reason that programmable finite-state machines are being implemented as part of the control for functional logic blocks. This permits reconfiguration of certain functions in which errors have been detected, so that prototype system testing can continue.

1.3.1 VLSI Chip Fabrication

Today's integrated circuits (ICs) are fabricated on silicon wafers. The series of steps by which a geometric pattern, or set of patterns, is transformed into a functional logic system is called a *wafer fabrication process*. A typical fabrication process for an integrated circuit consists of superimposing layers of conducting, insulating, and transistor-forming materials. Wafer fabrication is an extremely exacting production process. Dimensions are controlled to a few parts per million. The process steps construct the circuits either as junction transistors (bipolar) or field-effect devices [metal-oxide semiconductor (MOS)]. Bipolar technology is most familiar to logic designers as transistor-transistor logic (TTL) or emitter-coupled logic (ECL). Bipolar circuits utilize *npn* bipolar junction transistors and are usually faster than corresponding MOS circuits. However, bipolar circuits are usually less dense and more expensive and dissipate more power than their MOS counterparts.

Transistor-transistor logic, one of the most popular logic families, is finding wide use in VLSI gate arrays. The technology provides a balance between high speed and low power. To achieve a higher speed, a Schottky barrier diode is connected between the base and collector terminals of the output transistor. This prevents the transistor from saturating, thus allowing switching speeds to approach those of ECL technology.

Emitter-coupled logic is a nonsaturating logic family. Its voltage swings are small (typically 800 mV; that is, -0.9 V to -1.7 V), making it the fastest logic family. An alternate name for this technology is *current-mode logic*, because the output states change when the current is switched. Although power dissipation is high, gate propagation delays of 350 ps can be realized. The VLSI gate arrays using ECL technology are finding wide use in high-speed processors and storage subsystems.

1.3.2 VLSI Design Methodologies

There are two principal design methodologies using VLSI technology: mask-programmable design and custom design. The mask-programmable approach consists of a cellular array of gates, as shown in Fig. 1.55. This gate-array technology offers the advantage of lower cost over custom designs, because only the last few steps in the fabrication process are customized (the interconnection of gates). The uncommitted components (transistors, resistors, etc.) in each cell can be interconnected to form some basic primitive function, such as an AND gate or an OR gate. The designer is also usually provided with a library of macro functions that interconnect the components of a cell into larger, more complex functions, such as flip-flops and multiplexers.

In the custom approach, the designer has a library of available cells to perform the desired logical function. The designer places selected cells on the display screen of an interactive graphics display terminal and routes the interconnections. The library consists of primitive functions (AND, OR) and macro functions (multiplexers, sum of products, flip-flops, *n*-bit registers, etc.). Each primitive or macro function is contained in an assigned number of array sites. Thus, the number of array sites required for a logic function depends on the number and size of the primitives and macros utilized in the design. For example, a two-input AND gate may require only 0.125 array sites, whereas a *D* flip-flop may require 0.5 array sites. A typical customized chip may have more than 8000 array sites, as shown in Fig. 1.56.

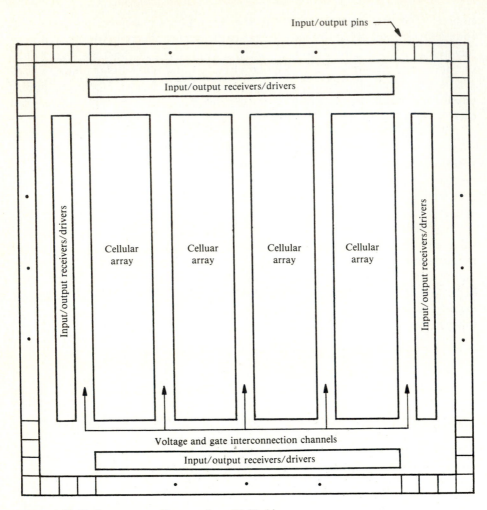

Figure 1.55 Mask-programmable array for a VLSI chip.

The designer also has the option of creating a personal macro library from the set of primitives. An example of a typical design sequence for a sum-of-products macro creation is given below.

1. The designer selects a two-input AND gate from the circuit library primitives by entering the appropriate command into the system via a keyboard.
2. When the two-input gate appears on the display screen, it is moved to the required position on the screen by means of an *xy* coordinate control mechanism.
3. Steps 1 and 2 are repeated until all of the necessary gate types have been called from the library and assembled on the screen.
4. The interconnection between gates is then accomplished using the *xy* coordi-

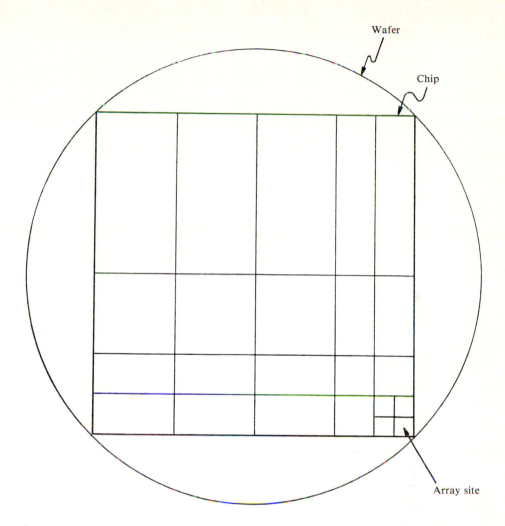

Figure 1.56 Array site organization for customized VLSI chip. There are 128 array sites for primitive or macro logic functions.

nate control mechanism to produce the sum-of-products logic function, as shown in Fig. 1.57(a).

5. A symbol is then created [Fig. 1.57(b)] that represents the sum-of-products logic diagram. This symbol becomes the designer's macro function that can be used repeatedly whenever a $[(A \wedge B) \vee (C \wedge D)]$ sum of products is required.

A further refinement can be realized by "bundling" the four input nets so that they appear as one wide line on the logic diagram. Bundling has the advantage of reducing clutter on logic diagrams by combining a number of related nets into one bundled net. Figure 1.57(c) shows an example of bundled nets.

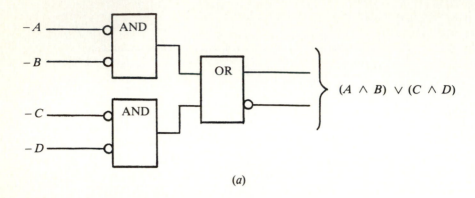

(a)

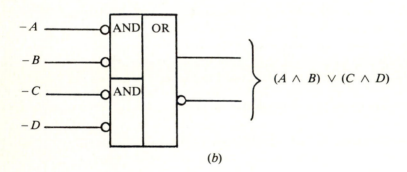

(b)

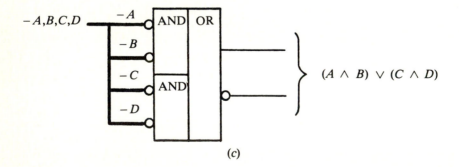

(c)

Figure 1.57 (a) Sum of products using logic primitives; (b) sum-of-products logic macro; and (c) sum-of-products logic macro with bundling.

The concept of macro creation can be carried to several levels. For example, macros can be combined with other macros to form new macros, as in the case of designing an iterative cellular multiplier array. A full adder (defined in Sec. 2.2.2) can be designed with logic primitives using the five steps listed above. The logic macro symbol for the full adder is then created, as shown in Fig. 1.58(*a*). The full-adder macro is then used to create a larger macro consisting of full adders and AND gate primitives to perform array multiplication on 2 two-bit operands, as illustrated in Fig. 1.58(*b*). A logic macro symbol is then created to represent the 2 × 2 multiplier array with bundled inputs and outputs, as shown in Fig. 1.58(*c*). This is a hierarchical approach to logic systems design, in which the top-most symbol of the hierarchical tree is expanded downward through logic macro expansion techniques until the lowest level of logic primitives is reached. Interconnect checking, gate loading, and simulation can then be performed at this lowest level.

1.3.3 Placement and Routing

Wire delays on VLSI chips become increasingly important as circuit density and speed increase. In small-scale integration (SSI) and medium-scale integration (MSI), wire delays were negligible because of the slow gate propagation delays (typically, 3 ns for TTL). In VLSI ECL technology, however, with gate propagation delays of 350 ps, the delay caused by the interconnecting wire between logic gates is a major contributing factor in the overall speed of the system. The wire delay may be equal to the gate propagation delay.

In very high speed processors, where the machine cycle time is 10 ns or less, the wire delay can account for half the delay in propagating signals through combinational logic. Figure 1.59 shows a typical register-to-register transfer path through combinational logic (for example, a high-speed fixed-point adder). If the machine cycle time is 8 ns, then only seven levels of logic are permitted in the combinational logic. This is one reason why efficient placement algorithms are essential for high-speed VLSI design. The placement algorithm (which is part of the design automation programming package) places the primitive and macro logic circuits as close as possible to other related circuits so that the wire length between circuits is as short as possible. It may be necessary to override the placement program and manually place some functions so that the flow of logic through a chip may be optimized.

A routing program connects the logic gates on a chip so that the wire path (net) between gates is optimized for the shortest distance. The routing program should always be able to find a solution, if one exists. There should be no undesirable routes; that is, the router should not include too many turns in the path or make the path too long. Another constraint is that future routes should not be blocked by an existing route.

Figure 1.60(*a*) illustrates a typical logic diagram that has a net connecting one output terminal to four input terminals (or loads). The placement of the gates in an array site may cause the terminals to be distributed as shown in Fig. 1.60(*b*).

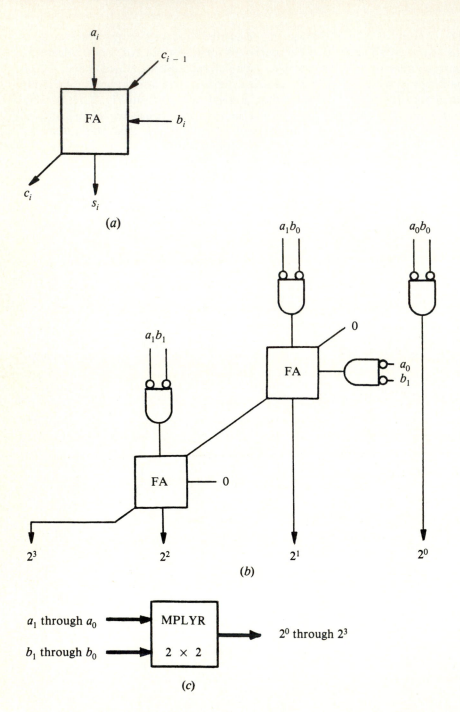

Figure 1.58 (*a*) Full-adder logic macro; (*b*) a 2 × 2 multiplier array using the full-adder macro and logic primitives; (*c*) a 2 ×2 multiplier array logic macro.

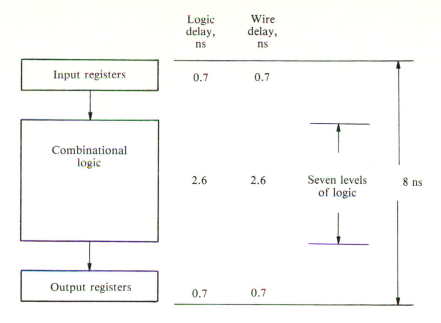

	Logic delay, ns	Wire delay, ns		
Input registers	0.7	0.7		
Combinational logic	2.6	2.6	Seven levels of logic	8 ns
Output registers	0.7	0.7		

Figure 1.59 Register-to-register transfer path through combinational logic.

The net can be broken down into pin pairs, such as *AB, BC, CD,* and *DE.* Separating the nets into distinct pin pairs as shown in Fig. 1.60(*c*), we can assign source *s* and target *t* pins. There may be many routes between a given pin pair *st.* One such route is shown in Fig. 1.61(*a*). Other possible routes are shown in Fig. 1.61(*b*).

A backtracking technique is sometimes used to find routing paths between different sets of pin pairs. The backtracking algorithm separates the net into pin pairs 1 through *n*, where *n* is the total number of pin pairs. The routing program searches for a feasible route between pin pairs in ascending numerical order starting with pin pair 1. If the router fails to find a feasible route for the *i*th pin pair, then the program backtracks to the previous (*i* − 1) pin pair and searches for a different route for that pin pair. If the new route for the (*i* − 1) pin pair results in a feasible route for the *i*th pin pair, then the routing program continues and attempts to find an optimum route between pins of the (*i* + 1) pin pair. If, however, a feasible route for the (*i* − 1) pin pair is not found, then further backtracking is needed. Upon termination of the routing program, it is known whether or not a routing solution was obtained for the chip under consideration.

1.3.4 Simulation

Design verification is essential in permitting the advantages of VLSI to be realized. With VLSI technology, it is no longer possible to place an oscilloscope probe on a logic terminal. Thus, logic simulation is a prerequisite to chip fabrication.

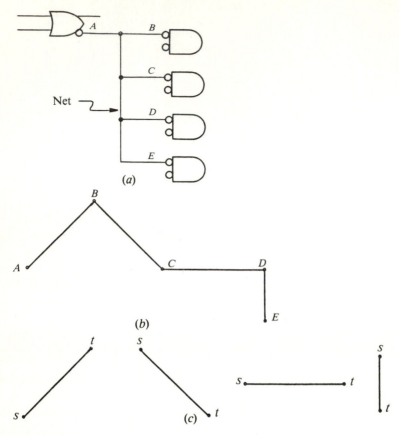

Figure 1.60 (*a*) A typical net between logic gates; (*b*) the net in (*a*) after physical placement of gates in an array site; and (*c*) the net in (*b*) after separation in distinct pin pairs.

The logic functionality of a design can be checked as well as ensuring that timing constraints are met. Also, the progress of the design verification status can be monitored to ensure that a predetermined goal has been met before committing the design to hardware. The main goal of a logic simulation system is to test for logical correctness as well as for timing and signal propagation characteristics. This will establish an orderly design process that includes testing repeatability and test data integrity not only for the initial design but also for any subsequent design modifications.

Logic simulation is the process of constructing and evaluating a model of a functional logic circuit on a digital computer. There are two main applications for a logic simulation program: the evaluation of a new design and the analysis of faults. The first provides information relating to the logical operation of the system, including race, hazard, and oscillatory conditions. The second provides information relating to what faults are detected by a particular input pattern and how the circuit operates for specific fault conditions. Besides being cost-effective,

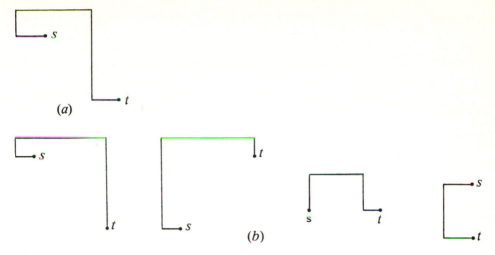

Figure 1.61 Constituent line segments for routing between different pin pairs. (*a*) A five-segment route between a pin pair; and (*b*) typical routing for different types of pin pairs.

the simulation program must be able to produce a close correspondence between predicted timing as calculated by the simulator and actual timing as realized by the hardware.

Input information to a logic simulator usually consists of the following:

1. A description of the circuit to be simulated
2. Input test patterns to be simulated
3. Initialization states for flip-flops, registers, etc.
4. Output signals or internal states to be monitored

The circuit description consists of the topology or interconnection of the logic circuit and the logic elements (primitives or macros). The specification of delay parameters, both for logic elements and interconnecting wire, should also be included.

There are two generally accepted ways of describing an input sequence that is to be simulated. The first way is to apply a sequence of input vectors in real time. Each vector is specified at the input terminals at a different time. This permits the application of clock pulses and other time-varying stimuli, if required. Otherwise, the inputs are static. The second way is to specify the input vectors by means of a high-level language.

The basic structure of a logic simulation system has four modules:

1. A preprocessor module
2. A structure module
3. A simulation module
4. An output module

The preprocessor module reads in the circuit description by the user and replaces it with an equivalent circuit consisting only of logic primitives. All macro functions are expanded to logic primitives. The structure module describes the topology or interconnection of the logic circuit as well as provides information pertaining to logic block function and delay. The simulation module performs the actual simulation of the logic circuits and quantifies the operation in terms of units of delay, for example, 1 ns. A logic element does not need to be simulated unless at least one of its inputs changes state. The output module produces an abundance of information. It can generate output vectors of 1s and 0s that indicate the logical operation of the circuit being simulated. Waveforms may also be provided that signify the time-varying operation of the circuit. Most output formats are extremely flexible, thereby permitting conformity to whatever documentation standards are appropriate.

1.3.5 The Future of VLSI Technology

Much higher chip densities will be attained in the coming years. Building blocks, such as library macros, will be more complex and will achieve much more functionality. More specialized computer-aided design systems will be available that have been designed specifically for the VLSI era. Such a system will support a hierarchical approach to system design and will be used principally for custom VLSI.

Research in placement and routing algorithms will continue to achieve success in this important field. Automatic placement algorithms based on heuristics are currently being studied both in the United States and abroad and will be incorporated into a hierarchical system layout. As commercial processor speeds increase beyond the 20 million instructions per second (MIPS) range, routing programs, such as those based on an enumeration technique that sequentially produces alternate paths for pin pairs, will become much faster.

Logic simulation, which is inherently a slow process, will continue to be refined. Timing verification will become more important as circuit geometries shrink and processor speeds increase. For example, timing verification validates path delays to make certain that they are neither too long nor too short. Clock pulse widths are also checked to verify that the pulse duration is within a prescribed range. Logic simulation facilitates accurate, faithful modeling of network timing.

PROBLEMS

1.1 Consider the hexadecimal integer 4A3CB. Rewrite the number in binary and octal.

1.2 State the differences or similarities between the following:
- (*a*) Real arithmetic versus machine arithmetic
- (*b*) Fixed-point versus floating-point number representation
- (*c*) Fixed-point integer versus fixed-point fraction arithmetic

(*d*) Single-precision versus double-precision arithmetic operations

(*e*) Normalized versus unnormalized floating-point operations

1.3 Represent each of the following numbers in sign magnitude, diminished-radix complement, and radix complement for radix 2 and 10: $+136$, -136.

1.4 Represent each of the decimal values $+54$, -28, $+127$, and -113 in the following binary formats for $r = 2$ and $n = 8$:

(*a*) Sign magnitude

(*b*) Diminished-radix complement

(*c*) Radix complement

1.5 Convert the following octal numbers to hexadecimal: 6536_8, 52257_8.

1.6 Calculate the value of the following binary string and give your answer in decimal and hexadecimal: 0 1 0 0 1 1 0 1. 1 0 1 1.

1.7 Give the decimal equivalent of 0 1 1 0 1 1. 1 1 1_2, 44.3_8, and $2D.C_{16}$.

1.8 Convert the following decimal numbers to binary numbers with 16-bit operands: $+36.0625$, $+48.5625$, $+127.0156$.

1.9 Convert decimal $+130.21875$ to octal and hexadecimal representation.

1.10 What are the main uses for fixed-point, decimal, and floating-point number representations? Generally describe the format of each.

1.11 Name and describe the three conventional ways to represent positive and negative numbers in a positional number system. Describe them for radix 2.

1.12 What is the range of positive and negative numbers in radix 2 for

(*a*) Sign magnitude?

(*b*) Diminished-radix complement?

(*c*) Radix complement?

1.13 Why is radix complement more desirable for a fixed-point binary adder than diminished-radix complement?

1.14 Prove algebraically that $A \wedge 0 = 0$, using the axioms of Sec. 1.2.1.

1.15 Prove algebraically that $A \wedge A = A$, using the axioms and theorems of Sec. 1.2.1.

1.16 Prove algebraically that $A \wedge (A \vee B) = A$, using the axioms and theorems of Sec. 1.2.1.

1.17 Prove algebraically that $A \wedge (\bar{A} \vee B) = A \wedge B$, using the axioms and theorems of Sec. 1.2.1.

1.18 Prove DeMorgan's law $\overline{(A \wedge B)} = \bar{A} \vee \bar{B}$ algebraically, using the axioms and theorems of Sec. 1.2.1.

1.19 Use truth tables to show that the associative laws are true for three variables A, B, and C.

1.20 Obtain the sum-of-products boolean equation for the function f, which is represented by the following Karnaugh map:

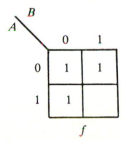

1.21 Obtain the sum-of-products boolean equation for the function f, which is represented by the following Karnaugh map:

BC

A \	00	01	11	10
0	1			1
1	1		1	1

f

1.22 Obtain the sum-of-products boolean equation for the function f, which is represented by the following Karnaugh map:

CD

AB \	00	01	11	10
00	1			1
01		1	1	1
11		1	1	1
10	1			1

f

1.23 Obtain a Karnaugh map for the boolean equation
$$f(A, B, C) = \bar{A}B \vee \bar{A}\bar{B}C \vee \bar{A}BC \vee ABC$$

1.24 Simplify the function of prob. 1.23.

1.25 Obtain a Karnaugh map for the boolean equation
$$f(A, B, C, D) = ABD \vee A\bar{B}C$$

1.26 Expand the function of prob. 1.25 into a sum of minterms and then simplify the function algebraically by using the axioms and theorms of Sec. 1.2.1.

1.27 Use algebraic manipulation to minimize the following function:
$$f(A, B, C) = AB \vee AC \vee A\bar{B}C \vee \bar{A}BC \vee \bar{A}B$$

1.28 Minimize the function of prob. 127 by using a Karnaugh map.

1.29 Use algebraic manipulation to minimize the following function:
$$f(A, B, C) = \bar{A}\bar{B}\bar{C} \vee \bar{A}\bar{B}C \vee \bar{A}BC \vee A\bar{B}C$$

1.30 Minimize the function of prob. 1.29 by using a Karnaugh map.

1.31. Design a logic circuit that will produce an output of 1 whenever a four-bit binary number is equal to or greater than 7_{10}. Use a clocked RS flip-flop.

1.32 Repeat prob. 1.31 using a clocked D flip-flop.

1.33 Repeat prob. 1.31 using a JK flip-flop.

1.34 Construct a state graph and state table for a synchronous finite-state machine that will produce an output of 1 when the machine has received three consecutive 0s. The output is to be 0 otherwise.

1.35 Construct a state graph and state table for a synchronous finite-state machine that will operate as follows: The machine will accept 5-, 10-, or 25-cent coins and will produce an output of 1 when the total accumulated amount equals 25 cents. The machine will also be capable of giving change of 5, 10, 15, or 20 cents.

1.36 Construct a state graph and state table for a synchronous finite-state machine that will produce an output of 1 when the machine receives the sequence 1 0 1 0 1. There must be five symbols in each correct sequence; that is, two correct consecutive sequences are 1 0 1 0 1 1 0 1 0 1.

1.37 Design an asynchronous two-output logic circuit that operates according to the following timing diagram:

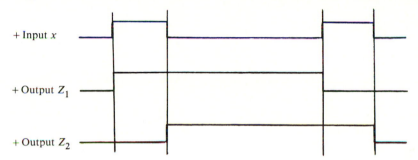

1.38 Design an asynchronous logic circuit that operates according to the following timing diagram:

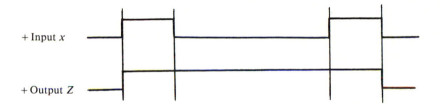

1.39 Design an asynchronous logic circuit that disables a sequence of oscillator pulses, but allows the last oscillator pulse to be full width before the sequence of pulses is disabled.

TWO

FIXED-POINT ADDITION AND SUBTRACTION

2.1 INTRODUCTION

Fixed-point numbers are treated here as signed or unsigned integers. In an unsigned fixed-point number, all bits are used to express the absolute value of the number. In signed fixed-point numbers, the leftmost bit represents the sign, which is followed by the field representing the integer's magnitude. Positive numbers are represented in 2s complement notation in simple positional binary notation with the sign bit set to 0. Negative numbers are represented in 2s complement notation with the sign bit set to 1. Specifically, a negative number is represented by the 2s complement of the corresponding positive number. The 2s complement of a number is obtained by inverting each of the binary digits and adding a 1 to the low-order bit position. For example, $+19$ and -19 are represented below for eight-bit operands.

$$+19 = 0\ 0\ 0\ 1\ 0\ 0\ 1\ 1$$
$$-19 = 1\ 1\ 1\ 0\ 1\ 1\ 0\ 1$$

This type of number representation can be considered the low-order portion of a number in which the sign bit may be extended indefinitely to the left. When the number is positive, all bits to the left of the most significant 1 in the number are 0s. When the number is negative, all bits to the left of the most significant 0 in the number are 1s. Therefore, when an operand must have its sign extended to the left, the expansion is achieved by setting the extended bits equal to the high-order bit of the operand. The maximum positive number consists of an integer field of 1s and a sign bit of 0. The maximum negative number consists of an integer field of 0s and a sign bit of 1. This is a negative number with the maximum absolute value.

Numbers in the above form do not have to be regarded as integers only. The radix point may be assumed to be in any fixed position in the number. Wherever it is assumed to be, it is fixed by the programmer, who has the responsibility of specifying its position and keeping track of it. The radix (or binary) point is usually assumed to be immediately to the right of the low-order bit position. This number representation in computers is thus called either *integer* or *fixed-point format*. In an actual computer, the radix point is implicit; that is, it does not occupy a physical location in storage.

In a fixed-point machine, the arithmetic algorithms remain the same, regardless of where the radix point is assumed to be in any given number. The processor treats all numbers as strings of digits for the purpose of performing arithmetic. This is illustrated for the multiplication of two decimal numbers as shown below.

$$125 \times 60 = 07500 \qquad \text{computed result}$$
$$125. \times 60. = 07500. \qquad \text{integers}$$
$$.125 \times .60 = .07500 \qquad \text{fractions}$$

In the example, the product is interpreted as either an integer or a fraction, depending on where the radix point is assumed to lie in the multiplicand and multiplier. Keeping track of the radix point is not always a trivial matter. The necessity of always knowing the location of the radix point is a major drawback of the fixed-point format. Thus, when using fixed-point arithmetic, most programmers treat the operands as either integers or fractions with the radix point to the right or left of the number, respectively. This greatly simplifies the programs, but restricts the range of numbers that can be represented. For example, it is impossible to represent the number 13,000 in a four-bit fixed-point machine. However, if the number is scaled by 1000, then it becomes 13, which can be represented by a four-bit binary number. In a fixed-point processor, scaling must be done by the programmer; in a floating-point processor, it is done automatically.

A signed-radix number must be either positive or negative, but not both. Consider the following number with radix r,

$$A = (a_{n-1} \; a_{n-2} \cdots a_1 \; a_0)_r$$

where the sign bit a_{n-1} assumes the value

$$a_{n-1} = \begin{cases} 0 & \text{if } A \geqslant 0 \\ r-1 & \text{if } A < 0 \end{cases}$$

Thus, for radix 2, the sign bit $a_{n-1} = 0$ or 1. The remaining digits in A specify either the true magnitude (when $a_{n-1} = 0$) or one of two complemented magnitudes (when $a_{n-1} = 1$). When $a_{n-1} = 1$, this text will use the 2s complement notation. As mentioned previously, there are two commonly accepted conventions for fixed-point number representations. The two conventions are interchangeable. Every n-digit integer can be considered as a fraction multiplied by a constant r^n. For example, the integer portion of the number

$$\overset{n}{\overbrace{0 \ 1 \ 0 \ 0}}. 1 \ 1_2$$

can be considered as the fraction .0100 multiplied by 2^4; that is,

$$2^{-2} \times 2^4 = .25 \times 16 = 4$$

Also, every k-digit fraction can be considered as an integer multiplied by a constant r^{-k}. For example, the fraction portion of the number

$$0 \ 1 \ 0 \ 0 . \overset{k}{\overbrace{1 \ 1}}_2$$

can be considered as the integer 11_2 multiplied by 2^{-2}; that is,

$$3 \times 2^{-2} = 3 \times .25 = .75$$

which is correct because

$$.11_2 = 1 \times 2^{-1} + 1 \times 2^{-2}$$
$$= .50 + .25$$
$$= .75$$

This illustrates the ease of converting between integers and fractions.

Therefore, the two most commonly chosen positions for the radix point are the extreme left or the extreme right of the magnitude portion of the number. In the former case, the radix point is positioned between sign digit a_{n-1} and most-significant-magnitude digit a_{n-2}. This makes any fraction always less than 1. In the latter case, the radix point is located to the immediate right of least significant digit a_0, which makes the magnitude of the number always an integer. The two conventions are essentially equivalent, and this text will assume the integer convention unless otherwise noted. The fixed-radix point is self-implied; that is, there is no need to mark it explicitly.

For positive fixed-point numbers, the sign bit $a_{n-1} = 0$ and the remaining digits $a_{n-2} \cdots a_1 \ a_0$ contain the magnitude. The magnitude of the number

$$A = (a_{n-1} \ a_{n-2} \cdots a_1 \ a_0)_r$$

can be denoted as

$$|A| = (a_{n-2} \ a_{n-3} \cdots a_1 \ a_0)_r$$

This is for $a_{n-1} = 0$; that is, $A \geq 0$. Therefore, a positive fixed-point number can be represented as

$$A = (0 \; a_{n-2} \; a_{n-3} \; \cdots \; a_1 \; a_0)_r \tag{2.1}$$

and its magnitude has the value

$$|A| = \sum_{i=0}^{n-1} a_i r^i$$

When $r = 2$, this is the familiar sum of n binary digits for $a_{n-1} = 0$. For example, for $n = 6$, the magnitude of $A = 0\ 1\ 1\ 0\ 0\ 1$ is

$$i = \frac{5\ 4\ 3\ 2\ 1\ 0}{0\ 1\ 1\ 0\ 0\ 1}$$

and may be evaluated as follows:

$$|A| = \sum_{i=0}^{n-1} a_i r^i$$

$$= 1 \times 2^0 + 0 \times 2^1 + 0 \times 2^2 + 1 \times 2^3 + 1 \times 2^4$$

$$= 1 + 8 + 16$$

$$= 25$$

For negative fixed-point numbers, $a_{n-1} = 1$ and the number is represented by the 2s complement notation. Let $(\bar{A})_{+1}$ be the negative version of a positive number A, which is defined by Eq. 2.1. Then $(\bar{A})_{+1}$ has a sign digit with the value $r - 1$. The r's complement representation is

$$(\bar{A})_{+1} = \left\{ [(r - 1) \; \bar{a}_{n-2} \; \bar{a}_{n-3} \; \cdots \; \bar{a}_1 \; \bar{a}_0] + 1 \right\}_r$$

In this notation $(\bar{A})_{+1} = r^n - A$. For $r = 2$, $n = 6$, and A and $(\bar{A})_{+1}$ defined as

		$n-1$	$n-2$	$\cdots$		1	0	
A	$=$	0	1	1	0	0	1	$(+25)$
$(\bar{A})_{+1}$	$=$	1	0	0	1	1	1	(-25)

then

$$(\bar{A})_{+1} = r^n - A$$
$$= 2^6 - 25$$
$$= 64 - 25$$
$$= 39 \qquad \text{unsigned value}$$

with $a_{n-1} = r - 1 = 2 - 1 = 1$.

The range of integers associated with the fixed-point representation is determined by the number of bits n that are used. The upper bound is determined by the largest positive integer contained in an n-bit number including the sign position. The binary bit pattern for this upper bound is $(0\ 1\ 1\ \cdots\ 1)_2$, which is equal to $2^{n-1} - 1$ in decimal. The lower bound is determined by the most negative integer contained in an n-bit number, including the sign position. In 2s complement notation the most negative number is

$$(1\ 0\ 0\ 0\ \cdots\ 0\ 0)_2 = -2^{n-1}$$

Overflow occurs when a positive number exceeds the upper bound. Similarly, underflow occurs when a negative number exceeds the lower bound. For 2s complement notation, there is a unique 0 vector of $(0\ 0\ \cdots\ 0)_2$.

2.2 ADDITION

2.2.1 Introduction

The operands of addition are the *addend* and the *augend*. The addend is added to the augend to form a sum. In most computers, the augmented operand (the augend) is replaced by the sum, whereas the addend is unchanged. High-speed adders are essential not only for addition but also for subtraction, multiplication, and division. The speed of a digital arithmetic processor depends heavily on the speed of the adder used in the system. Only the two-operand parallel-adder class is presented here, although there are a number of excellent multioperand adder designs available using the carry-save technique. Carry-save adders save the carry propagation until all additions are completed and then take a final cycle to complete the carry propagation for all additions. The basic carry-save adder is attractive for its low hardware requirement, but the extra cycle required may be too slow for some higher-performance machines.

The rules for binary addition are as follows:

+	0	1
0	0	1
1	1	0*

*$1 + 1 = 0$ with a carry-out into the next column on the left; that is,

$$
\begin{array}{r}
1 \\
+)\quad 1 \\
\hline
10
\end{array}
$$

The sum of $1 + 1$ requires the two-bit vector 1 0 to represent the value 2. Using the above rules, the sum of 0 1 and 1 1 would be calculated as

	2^2	2^1	2^0
Augend (1_{10})		0	1
Addend (3_{10})		1	1
Carry from column 2^0		$\boxed{1}\ \leftarrow$	0
Carry from column 2^1	$\boxed{1}\ \leftarrow$	0	
Sum (4_{10})	1	0	0

The sum is 0 0 and the carry-out is 1.

These examples extend to the addition of multibit vectors, and the operation is analogous to the usual paper-and-pencil computation with decimal numbers. Bit pairs are added starting from the low-order (right) end of the bit vectors, and carries are propagated toward the high-order (left) end. If

$$
A = a_{n-1}\, a_{n-2} \cdots a_1\, a_0
$$

and

$$
B = b_{n-1}\, b_{n-2} \cdots b_1\, b_0
$$

are two binary numbers (vectors) to be added, then an n-bit addition can be performed in the time it takes the carry signal to reach the $n - 1$ position, added to the delay to generate the $n - 1$ sum bit. The carry propagation can be speeded up in two ways. The first—and most obvious—way is to use a faster logic circuit technology. The second way is to generate carries by means of lookahead logic that does not rely on the carry signal being rippled from stage to stage of the adder. Carry lookahead will be presented in Sec. 2.2.3.

The most widely used number representation is 2s complement, which will be used for the design of adders in this chapter. There is no inherent difficulty in modifying adder designs so that they can be applied to 1s complement representation. Sign-magnitude adders are significantly different when operating on negative numbers.

The addition process takes place as described above; however, the operands may be positive or negative. If operand A is negative, then its magnitude is $2^n - |A|$. There are three cases to consider:

1. Both operands are positive, that is, $A \geqslant 0$ and $B \geqslant 0$. The result is $|A| + |B|$, which represents the positive number $A + B$.
2. The operands have different signs. If $A \geqslant 0$, $B < 0$, and $|A| > |B|$, then the sum is $|A| + (2^n - |B|)$. There will be a carry-out, which is dicarded and indicative of a positive sum. If $|A| < |B|$, then the sum is again $|A| + (2^n - |B|)$. In this case, there is no carry-out indicating a negative number. Similarly, when $A < 0$ and $B \geqslant 0$, a carry-out indicates a positive number, while absence of a carry-out indicates a negative sum.
3. Both operands are negative. Then the sum is

$$2^n - |A| + 2^n - |B| = 2^{n+1} - (|A| + |B|)$$

A carry-out indicates a negative number.

When the sum does not fall within the representable range of numbers in the machine, then an arithmetic overflow has occurred. Thus, a valid sum is

$$(\text{positive number})_{\text{max}} \geqslant \text{sum} \geqslant (\text{negative number})_{\text{max}}$$

The maximum positive number consists of an integer field of 1s and a sign bit of 0, whereas the maximum negative number (the negative number with the greatest absolute value) consists of an integer field of 0s and a sign bit of 1. Overflow is possible only when both operands have the same sign. An overflow cannot occur during addition if one number is positive and the other is negative, since adding a positive number to a negative number produces a number (either positive or negative) that is smaller than the larger of the two original numbers.

Overflow An overflow can be detected in two ways. First, an overflow has occurred whenever the sign of the sum does not agree with the signs of the operands and the signs of the operands are the same. In an n-bit adder, overflow can be defined as

$$\text{Overflow} = a_{n-1} b_{n-1} \bar{s}_{n-1} \vee \bar{a}_{n-1} \bar{b}_{n-1} s_{n-1} \tag{2.2}$$

Secondly, if the carry-out of the high-order numeric (magnitude) position of the sum and the carry-out of the sign position of the sum agree, the sum is satisfactory; if they disagree, an overflow has occurred. Thus,

$$\text{Overflow} = c_{n-1} \veebar c_{n-2} \tag{2.3}$$

A parallel adder adds the two operands, including the sign bits. An overflow from the magnitude part will tend to change the sign of the sum.

To see how this happens, consider first the case in which both operands are positive, that is, $a_{n-1} = b_{n-1} = 0$. The sum should also be positive, making

$s_{n-1} = 0$. If there is a carry-out of the magnitude part, $c_{n-2} = 1$. Because $a_{n-1} = 0$ and $b_{n-1} = 0$, $s_{n-1} = 1$ and $c_{n-1} = 0$. Thus, $c_{n-1} \neq c_{n-2}$ and an overflow occurs. When the two operands are negative, $a_{n-1} = b_{n-1} = 1$. The sum should also be negative, making $s_{n-1} = 1$. If there is no overflow from the magnitude part, $c_{n-2} = 1$ and since

$$a_{n-1} + b_{n-1} + c_{n-2} = 11$$

$c_{n-1} = 1$ also and the sum is negative, as required. Note that a 0 for negative numbers corresponds to a 1 for positive numbers. However, if $c_{n-2} = 0$ (an overflow), then

$$a_{n-1} + b_{n-1} + c_{n-2} = 10$$

making $c_{n-1} = 1$. The result is an incorrect positive number where $c_{n-1} \neq c_{n-2}$. These results can be summarized in Table 2.1. From the preceding discussion, it can be concluded that an overflow occurs if the two operands are positive and the sum is negative, or if the two operands are negative and the sum is positive; that is, an overflow produces an erroneous sign reversal.

Table 2.1 Overflow detection for 1s and 2s complement

a_{n-1}	b_{n-1}	s_{n-1}	c_{n-1}	c_{n-2}	Overflow
0	0	0	0	0	0
0	0	1	0	1	1
1	1	0	1	0	1
1	1	1	1	1	0

2.2.2 Ripple-Carry Addition

The emphasis of this text is on high-speed arithmetic, and a ripple adder is not normally used in such cases. However, in situations in which a minimum amount of hardware is required and speed is not critical, then a ripple adder can prove advantageous. A parallel ripple adder that adds two n-bit operands requires n full adders. A *full adder* is a combinational circuit that has three inputs: an augend a_i, an addend b_i, and a carry-in c_{i-1}. There are two outputs: a sum s_i and a carry-out c_i. (A *half adder* is a combinational circuit that has two inputs: an augend a_i and an addend b_i. There are two outputs: a sum s_i and a carry-out c_i.)

The truth table for the sum and carry-out functions for adding two equally weighted bits a_i and b_i in vectors

$$A = a_{n-1} \, a_{n-2} \cdots a_1 \, a_0$$

and

$$B = b_{n-1}\, b_{n-2} \cdots b_1\, b_0$$

is shown in Table 2.2. Note that each stage of the addition algorithm must be able to accommodate carry-in bit c_{i-1} from the immediately preceding low-order stage. The carry out of the ith stage is designated c_i. The sum and carry equations for the full adder are

$$
\begin{aligned}
s_i &= \bar{a}_i\bar{b}_ic_{i-1} \lor \bar{a}_ib_i\bar{c}_{i-1} \lor a_i\bar{b}_i\bar{c}_{i-1} \lor a_ib_ic_{i-1} \\
&= c_{i-1}\,(a_i \veebar b_i) \lor c_{i-1}(\overline{a_i \veebar b_i}) \\
&= a_i \veebar b_i \veebar c_{i-1}
\end{aligned}
\tag{2.4}
$$

$$
\begin{aligned}
c_i &= \bar{a}_ib_ic_{i-1} \lor a_i\bar{b}_ic_{i-1} \lor a_ib_i\bar{c}_{i-1} \lor a_ib_ic_{i-1} \\
&= \bar{a}_ib_ic_{i-1} \lor a_i\bar{b}_ic_{i-1} \lor a_ib_i \\
&= a_ib_i \lor a_ic_{i-1} \lor b_ic_{i-1}
\end{aligned}
\tag{2.5}
$$

Table 2.2 Truth table for binary addition

a_i	b_i	Carry-in c_{i-1}	Sum s_i	Carry-out c_i
0	0	0	0	0
0	0	1	1	0
0	1	0	1	0
0	1	1	0	1
1	0	0	1	0
1	0	1	0	1
1	1	0	0	1
1	1	1	1	1

It may appear initially that the sum $a_i \veebar b_i \veebar c_{i-1}$ requires less logic than the sum of product terms, but since the only available logic primitive in VLSI is an AND/OR logic gate for the design of the full adder, the logic for the sum of products requires fewer gates and fewer levels of delay. The logic diagram and symbol for a full adder are given in Figure 2.1.

Hardware organization The n bits of two n-bit operands are presented in parallel to n full adders. Since the carries propagate, or ripple, through this organization, the configuration is called an *n-bit ripple-carry adder*. The organization of the adder is shown in Fig. 2.2. The full adders are connected in such a way that the carry-out for adder i is the carry-in for adder $i + 1$, for $0 \leqslant i \leqslant n - 2$. The carry-in of adder$_0$ is usually connected to a logical 0 for addition, and the carry-out of adder$_{n-1}$ can be used for overflow detection. Because a carry can be propagated from c_0 to the last sum and carry outputs of adder $_{n-1}$, the worst-case delay is n full-adder levels.

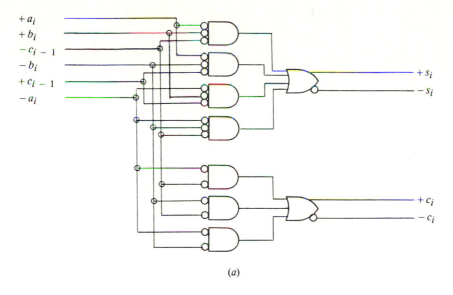

$+a_i$
$+b_i$
$-c_{i-1}$
$-b_i$
$+c_{i-1}$
$-a_i$

$+s_i$
$-s_i$

$+c_i$
$-c_i$

(a)

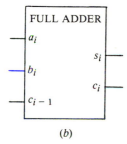

(b)

Figure 2.1 Full adder: (a) logic, (b) symbol.

The n-bit ripple-carry adder described in this section may have too much delay in developing its outputs $c_{n-1}, s_{n-1}, \ldots, s_1,$ and s_0. Whether the delay associated with this organization is acceptable depends on the speed of other processor components, main storage, and the application of the computer system in which the adder is used.

2.2.3 Carry Lookahead Addition

The limitation in the sequential method of forming the carries in the ripple adder arises from specifying c_i as a specific function of c_{i-1}. It will be shown in this section that a carry does not have to depend explicitly on the preceding one, but can be expressed as a function of the relevant augend and addend bits and some lower-order carry. A considerable increase in speed can be realized as a result of this approach.

Restating Eq. 2.5 we have

$$c_i = \bar{a}_i b_i c_{i-1} \vee a_i \bar{b}_i c_{i-1} \vee a_i b_i$$
$$= a_i b_i \vee (a_i \not\vee b_i) c_{i-1} \tag{2.6}$$

This states that a carry will be obtained whenever $a_i = b_i = 1$, whenever $a_i = 1$ and $b_i = 0$ with $c_{i-1} = 1$, or whenever $a_i = 0$ and $b_i = 1$ with $c_{i-1} = 1$. However, a different approach can be taken that requires less logic and fewer levels of delay. Using the Karnaugh map below,

a_i \ $b_i\, c_{i-1}$	0 0	0 1	1 1	1 0
0			1	
1		1	1	1

Equation 2.6 can be simplified to

$$c_i = a_i b_i \vee a_i c_{i-1} \vee b_i c_{i-1}$$
$$= a_i b_i \vee (a_i \vee b_i) c_{i-1} \tag{2.7}$$

Equation 2.7 states that a carry will be obtained whenever $a_i = b_i = 1$ and also whenever either $a_i = 1$ or $b_i = 1$ or both a_i and $b_i = 1$, all with $c_{i-1} = 1$. The second term of Eq. 2.7 is more encompassing than the second term of Eq. 2.6, because it includes the case where both a_i and b_i are 1. This is redundant, because the first term of Eq. 2.7 will also produce a carry when both a_i and b_i are 1, but this redundancy results not only in fewer levels of logic (higher speed) but also in fewer logic gates. This happens because $a_i \vee b_i$ requires only one level of logic, whereas $a_i \not\vee b_i$ requires two levels of logic. Therefore, c_i, as indicated by Eq. 2.7, will be used to specify the carry rather than Eq. 2.6.

Generate and propagate functions A technique will now be described to increase the speed of the carry propagation in a parallel adder. The carries entering all the bit positions of the adder can be generated simultaneously by *a carry lookahead (CLA) generator*. This results in a constant addition time independent of the length of the adder. However, due to the limited number of inputs in current VLSI technology, adders with a large number of elements (for example, 64) may require two or three levels of carry lookahead. This will be discussed in more detail later.

Let A and B be the augend and addend inputs, respectively, to an n-bit adder, where

$$A = a_{n-1} a_{n-2} \cdots a_1 a_0$$

and

$$B = b_{n-1} b_{n-2} \cdots b_1 b_0$$

The sign bits are a_{n-1} and b_{n-1}; c_{i-1} is the carry input to the ith bit position. The carry input to the low-order bit position is c_{-1}. Also, s_i and c_i are the sum and carry outputs, respectively, of the ith stage. Two auxiliary functions are now defined.

$$\text{Generate} \quad G_i = a_i b_i$$
$$\text{Propagate} \quad P_i = a_i \vee b_i$$

The carry generate function G_i reflects the condition where a carry is generated at the ith stage. The carry propagate function P_i is true when the ith stage will pass (or propagate) the incoming carry c_{i-1} to the next higher stage $i + 1$. Equation 2.7 can now be restated as

$$c_i = a_i b_i \vee (a_i \vee b_i) c_{i-1}$$
$$= G_i \vee P_i c_{i-1} \tag{2.8}$$

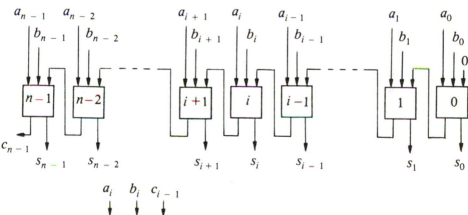

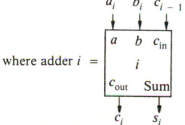

where adder $i =$

Figure 2.2 Organization for an n-bit ripple adder.

This equation indicates that the generate G_i and propagate P_i functions for any carry c_i for $i = n - 1, n - 2, \ldots, 1, 0$ can be obtained independently and in parallel when the operand inputs are applied to the n-bit adder.

The recursive Eq. 2.8 can be applied repeatedly to obtain the following set of carry equations in terms of the variables G_i, P_i, and c_{-1}.

$$
\begin{aligned}
c_0 &= G_0 \vee P_0 c_{-1} \\
c_1 &= G_1 \vee P_1 c_0 \\
    &= G_1 \vee P_1 (G_0 \vee P_0 c_{-1}) \\
    &= G_1 \vee P_1 G_0 \vee P_1 P_0 c_{-1} \\
c_2 &= G_2 \vee P_2 c_1 \\
    &= G_2 \vee P_2 (G_1 \vee P_1 G_0 \vee P_1 P_0 c_{-1}) \\
    &= G_2 \vee P_2 G_1 \vee P_2 P_1 G_0 \vee P_2 P_1 P_0 c_{-1}
\end{aligned}
\tag{2.9}
$$

$$
\begin{aligned}
c_i &= G_i \vee P_i c_{i-1} \\
    &= G_i \vee P_i G_{i-1} \vee P_i P_{i-1} G_{i-2} \vee \cdots \\
    &\quad \vee P_i P_{i-1} P_{i-2} \cdots P_1 G_0 \vee \cdots \\
    &\quad \vee P_i P_{i-1} P_{i-2} \cdots P_1 P_0 c_{-1}
\end{aligned}
$$

$$
\begin{aligned}
c_{n-1} &= G_{n-1} \vee P_{n-1} G_{n-2} \vee P_{n-1} P_{n-2} G_{n-3} \\
        &\quad \vee \cdots \vee P_{n-1} P_{n-2} \cdots P_1 G_0 \\
        &\quad \vee \cdots \vee P_{n-1} P_{n-2} \cdots P_1 P_0 c_{-1}
\end{aligned}
$$

Equation 2.9 can be stated concisely as

$$
c_i = G_i \vee \sum_{j=0}^{i-1} \left(\prod_{k=j+1}^{i} P_k \right) G_j \vee \prod_{k=0}^{i} P_k c_{-1}
\tag{2.10}
$$

Each of the carries is now a three-level expression in terms of augend, addend, and c_{-1}. The three levels for c_i are shown in Fig. 2.3. This makes the addition of two n-bit numbers extremely fast. The sum is generated with two delays and the carries are generated with three delays, giving a maximum delay for any n-bit adder of only five delays. An adder that uses this technique for producing carries simultaneously is called a *carry lookahead adder*, because a carry can be predicted before its corresponding sum bit has been obtained.

Group generate and propagate There is, however, a major problem. As n becomes large, the number of inputs to the high-order gates in the carry generation logic also becomes large. From Eq. 2.9, it can be seen that the final carry c_{n-1} requires an AND gate of $n+1$ inputs. For a 64-bit adder, no current technology can supply a gate with that number of inputs. The problem can be solved by partitioning the adder into four-bit groups. The logic diagram for a four-bit carry lookahead adder is shown in Fig. 2.4 This also shows the generate and propagate functions for the four-bit group. The group generate and group propagate signals are required so that a group carry can be produced as a carry-in to the next higher-order group.

For long operands, group generate and group propagate are necessary to maintain high performance during addition. In the four-bit adder of Fig. 2.4, each adder stage is considered a unit, with its individual carry being sent to the next higher-order adder stage. At the next higher level of carry lookahead, each group of four adders is considered a unit, with its individual group carry being sent to the next higher-order group. Additional auxiliary functions are defined for a group as

Group generate $\qquad GG_j = G_{i+3} \lor P_{i+3}G_{i+2} \lor P_{i+3}P_{i+2}G_{i+1}$
$$\lor P_{i+3}P_{i+2}P_{i+1}G_i$$

Group propagate $\qquad GP_j = P_{i+3}P_{i+2}P_{i+1}P_i \qquad\qquad (2.11)$

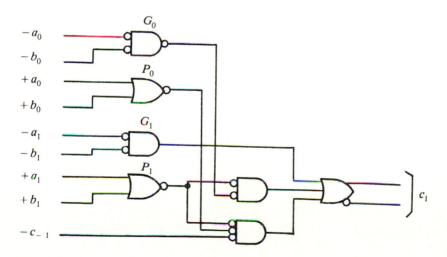

Figure 2.3 Logic diagram for carry bit c_1.

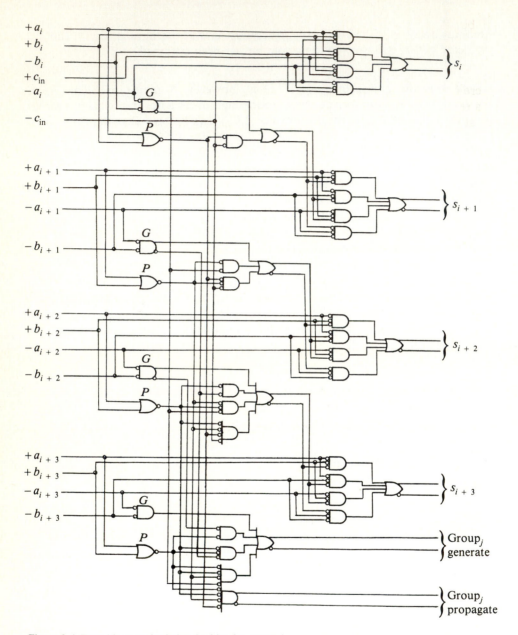

Figure 2.4 Four-bit carry lookahead adder for group j.

The variable GG_j corresponds to the condition that the carry generated out of the most significant $(i + 3)$ position of the group originated within the group itself. The variable GP_j is true if a carry-in to the group is propagated through the group, resulting in a carry-out of the group. Therefore, the carry-out of group j

can be written as

$$\text{Group carry} \qquad GC_j = GG_j \lor GP_j \, GC_{j-1} \qquad\qquad (2.12)$$

where GC_{j-1} is the carry-in to the group. Equation 2.12 permits the utilization of a technology with far fewer fan-in requirements than was previously needed, but at the expense of added delay. Figure 2.5 shows the block diagram of a four-

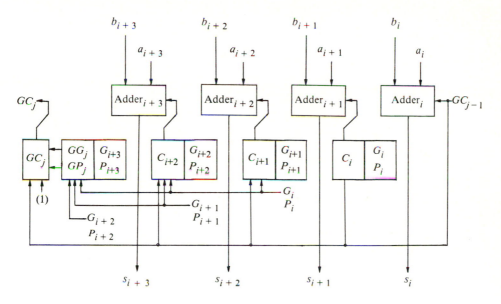

(1) Group generate and group propagate from lower-order groups

Figure 2.5 Block diagram of four-bit group$_j$.

bit group. Each adder stage has its own generate, propagate, and carry functions, and the group contains the group generate, group propagate, and group carry functions.

Section generate and propagate The fan-in limitations of current technology may still require additional levels of CLA above that provided by a group. In this case, the groups are partitioned into sections, with each section consisting of four groups. For a 64-bit adder, there would be four sections with four groups per section and four bits per group. A typical section is shown in Fig. 2.6. If section $_k$ is the low-order section, then the two lines labeled SC_{k-1} and c_{-1} in Fig. 2.6 merge to become one line and connect to the GC blocks and the SC block.

The recursive Eq. 2.12 can now be applied repeatedly to obtain the following set of group carry equations in terms of the variables GC_j, GP_j, and GC_{j-1} for section$_k$.

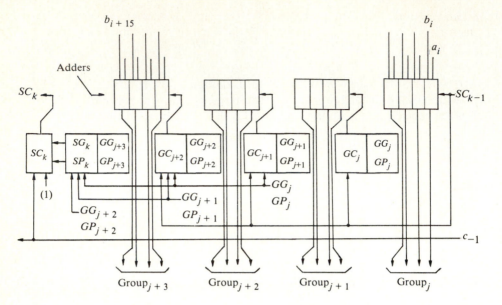

(1) Section generate and section propagate from lower-order sections

Figure 2.6 Block diagram of four-group section$_k$.

$$
\begin{aligned}
GC_j \;\; &= \; GG_j \vee GP_j GC_{j-1} \\
GC_{j+1} &= \; GG_{j+1} \vee GP_{j+1} GG_j \vee GP_{j+1} GP_j GC_{j-1} \\
GC_{j+2} &= \; GG_{j+2} \vee GP_{j+2} GG_{j+1} \vee GP_{j+2} GP_{j+1} GG_j \\
&\quad \vee GP_{j+2} GP_{j+1} GP_j GC_{j-1} \\
GC_{j+3} &= \; GG_{j+3} \vee GP_{j+3} GG_{j+2} \vee GP_{j+3} GP_{j+2} GG_{j+1} \\
&\quad \vee GP_{j+3} GP_{j+2} GP_{j+1} GG_j \\
&\quad \vee GP_{j+3} GP_{j+2} GP_{j+1} GP_j GC_{j-1} \\
&= \; SC_k \hspace{6cm} (2.13)
\end{aligned}
$$

It should be noted that if section$_k$ is the low-order section, then $GC_{j-1} = c_{-1}$. Also, if section$_k$ is not the low-order section, then $GC_{j-1} = SC_{k-1}$, where SC_{k-1} is the carry-out of the next lower-order section. The carry-out of the high-order group in a section, that is, GC_{j+3}, is also the carry-out of the section; thus, GC_{j+3} can be written as SC_k. The logic diagram for group carry generation, section generate, and section propagate is illustrated in Fig. 2.7. GC_{j+3} (SC_k) is not shown on the diagram because the section carries will be generated individually from the generate and propagate functions of all sections.

Since the organization of the adder now contains sections, additional functions must be defined for section generate and section propagate. These are

$$\text{Section generate} \quad SG_k = GG_{j+3} \lor GP_{j+3}GG_{j+2}$$
$$\lor GP_{j+3}GP_{j+2}GG_{j+1}$$
$$\lor GP_{j+3}GP_{j+2}GP_{j+1}GG_j$$
$$\text{Section propagate} \quad SP_k = GP_{j+3}GP_{j+2}GP_{j+1}GP_j \qquad (2.14)$$

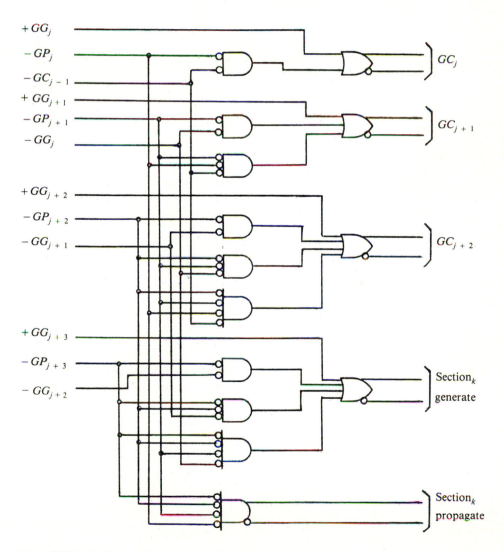

Figure 2.7 Logic diagram for group carry generation.

The variable SG_k corresponds to the condition that the carry-out generated from the most significant position of the section (the $j + 3$ group) originated within the section itself. The variable SP_k is true if a carry-in to the section is propagated through the section, resulting in a carry-out of the section. Therefore, the carry-out of section$_k$ can be written as

$$\text{Section carry} \quad SC_k = SG_k \vee SP_k \, SC_{k-1} \tag{2.15}$$

where SC_{k-1} is the carry-in to the section. Equation 2.15 permits the utilization of present technology for carry generation, but at the expense of additional delays resulting from a higher level of carry lookahead.

The recursive Eq. 2.15 can be applied repeatedly to obtain the following set of section carry equations in terms of the variables SG_k, SP_k, and SC_{k-1} for the complete adder.

$$
\begin{aligned}
SC_k &= SG_k \vee SP_k \, SC_{k-1} \\
SC_{k+1} &= SG_{k+1} \vee SP_{k+1} SG_k \vee SP_{k+1} SP_k SC_{k-1} \\
SC_{k+2} &= SG_{k+2} \vee SP_{k+2} SG_{k+1} \vee SP_{k+2} SP_{k+1} SG_k \\
&\quad \vee SP_{k+2} SP_{k+1} SP_k SC_{k-1} \\
SC_{k+3} &= SG_{k+3} \vee SP_{k+3} SG_{k+2} \vee SP_{k+3} \, SP_{k+2} SG_{k+1} \\
&\quad \vee SP_{k+3} SP_{k+2} SP_{k+1} SG_k \\
&\quad \vee SP_{k+3} SP_{k+2} SP_{k+1} \, SP_k SC_{k-1} \\
&= c_{n-1} \tag{2.16}
\end{aligned}
$$

The statements made previously for groups also apply to sections; that is, if section$_k$ is the low-order section, then $SC_{k-1} = c_{-1}$. The carry-out of the high-order group, that is, SC_{k+3}, is also the carry-out of the adder; thus, SC_{k+3} can also be written as c_{n-1}.

Hardware organization The block diagram for a 64-bit adder is shown in Fig. 2.8, which includes section generate, section propagate, section carry, and the carry-out (c_{n-1}) of the adder. The logic diagram for the implementation of section carries is shown in Fig. 2.9. Consider each section as an individual unit. If section$_k$ propagates a carry signal, then the carry-out of section$_k$ is a function of c_{-1}. If section$_{k+1}$ and section$_k$ both propagate, then the carry-out of section$_{k+1}$ is a function of c_{-1}. The same is true for the remaining sections; that is, if section$_{k+3}$, section$_{k+2}$, section$_{k+1}$, and section$_k$ all propagate, then the carry-out of the adder is a function of c_{-1}. This situation occurs when every stage of the adder propagates, such as when augend A and addend B are

$$
\begin{aligned}
A &= 1\ 0\ 1\ 0\ 1\ 0\ 1\ 0\ 1\ 0 \cdots 1\ 0 \\
B &= 0\ 1\ 0\ 1\ 0\ 1\ 0\ 1\ 0\ 1 \cdots 0\ 1
\end{aligned}
$$

It is for this reason that the carry used for section carry generation in Fig. 2.9 is c_{-1} and not SC_{k-1}, as might otherwise be expected. Since c_{-1} is normally 0 for addition of positive operands, then 0 would be propagated through all the stages of the adder. However, when subtraction is the operation being performed, then $c_{-1} = 1$.

If a parallel adder with less hardware and lower speed is required, then one or more levels of carry lookahead can be eliminated. This would permit partial carry lookahead with the remaining carries propagating in a ripple mode. Carry lookahead is not advantageous for adders of length $\leqslant 4$, because a four-stage ripple adder is almost as fast and requires less hardware. For adders of greater length ($n > 16$), multilevel carry lookahead is usually desirable. A 64-bit adder using three levels of generate/propagate would encounter the following number of logic gate delays:

$$
\begin{array}{rcl}
G, P &=& 1\ \triangle \\
GG, GP &=& 2\ \triangle \\
SG, SP &=& 2\ \triangle \\
SC &=& 2\ \triangle \\
GC &=& 2\ \triangle \\
C &=& 2\ \triangle \\
\mathrm{Sum} &=& 2\ \triangle \\
\hline
&& 13\ \triangle
\end{array}
$$

where $\triangle$ is the gate propagation delay for the technology being used.

The objective of the work presented in this section is to design a large-operand (64-bit) adder with the highest possible speed using present technology. To this end there has been developed carry lookahead logic within individual groups, within individual sections (between groups), and between sections. Each four-bit adder slice is as shown in Fig. 2.4; the carry generation logic between groups is shown in Fig. 2.7; and the carry generation logic between sections is in Fig. 2.9. This completes the design of a 64-bit adder, the organization of which is illustrated in Fig. 2.8.

2.2.4 Carry-Select Addition

The last type of fixed-point arithmetic adder is the carry-select adder. It is not as fast as the carry lookahead adder and requires considerably more hardware, but it has an interesting design concept that is worthwhile presenting.

The carry-select principle requires two identical parallel adders that are partitioned into four-bit groups. Each group consists of the same design as that shown in Fig. 2.4, with the exception that a group carry is also produced. The group carry is

$$C_j = G_j \vee P_j C_{in}$$

Hardware organization In the carry-select adder, two sums are generated simultaneously, as shown in Fig. 2.10. One sum assumes that the carry-in to the group is 0; the other sum assumes that the carry-in to the group is 1. Subsequently, the predicted group carry is used to select one of the two sums. The carry-out of $group_0$, with an assumed carry-in $= 0$, is written as $C_0(0)$. Similarly, the carry-out of $group_0$, with an assumed carry-in $= 1$, is written as $C_0(1)$. $C_0(0)$ may be considered as the generate function G_0 for $group_0$, while $C_0(1)$ may be considered the propagate function for $group_0$. The equations for the group carries of Fig. 2.10 are

$$
\begin{aligned}
GC_0 &= G_0 \vee P_0 C_{-1} \\
&= C_0(0) \vee C_0(1)C_{-1}
\end{aligned}
$$

$$
\begin{aligned}
GC_1 &= G_1 \vee P_1 G_0 \vee P_1 P_0 C_{-1} \\
&= C_1(0) \vee C_1(1)C_0(0) \vee C_1(1)C_0(1)C_{-1}
\end{aligned}
$$

$$
\begin{aligned}
GC_2 &= G_2 \vee P_2 G_1 \vee P_2 P_1 G_0 \vee P_2 P_1 P_0 C_{-1} \\
&= C_2(0) \vee C_2(1)C_1(0) \vee C_2(1)C_1(1)C_0(0) \\
&\quad \vee C_2(1)C_1(1)C_0(1)C_{-1}
\end{aligned}
$$

$$
\begin{aligned}
GC_3 &= G_3 \vee P_3 G_2 \vee P_3 P_2 G_1 \vee P_3 P_2 P_1 G_0 \\
&\quad \vee P_3 P_2 P_1 P_0 C_{-1} \\
&= C_3(0) \vee C_3(1)C_2(0) \vee C_3(1)C_2(1)C_1(0) \\
&\quad \vee C_3(1)C_2(1)C_1(1)C_0(0) \\
&\quad \vee C_3(1)C_2(1)C_1(1)C_0(1)C_{-1}
\end{aligned}
\tag{2.17}
$$

It can be seen that the group carries for a carry-select adder are generated in a manner similar to those for the CLA adder. However, the complexity of the group carry logic increases rapidly when more high-order groups are added to increase the total adder length. This complexity can be decreased, with a subsequent increase in delay, by partitioning a long adder into sections, with four groups per section, similar to the CLA adder. In this case, the carry-in to $section_1$ would be the same as the carry-out of $group_3$; that is,

$$SC_0 = GC_3$$

Let the $group_0$ adder with carry-in $= 0$ be designated as the $group_0(0)$ adder. Similarly, the $group_0$ adder with carry-in $= 1$ will be denoted as the $group_0(1)$

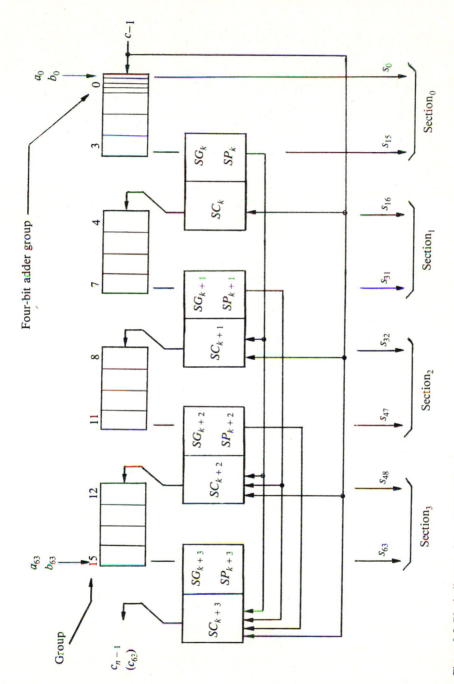

Figure 2.8 Block diagram for a 64-bit adder.

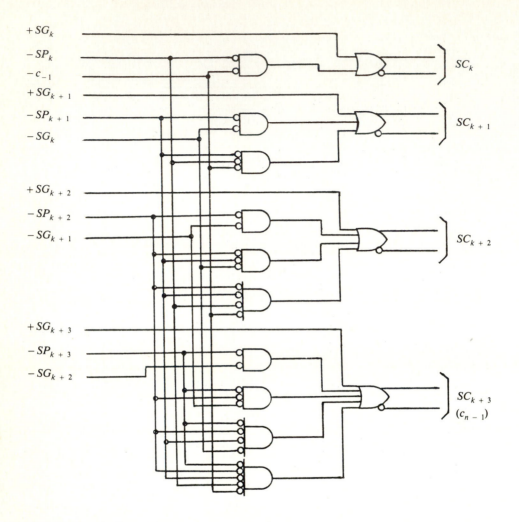

Figure 2.9 Logic diagram for section carry generation.

adder. A carry-out of the $group_0$ adder combination will occur if the $group_0(0)$ adder produces a carry on the $C_0(0)$ line or if the $group_0(1)$ adder produces a carry on the $C_0(1)$ line. A logic 1 on the $C_0(0)$ line indicates that a carry was generated within the $group_0(0)$ adder. A logic 1 on the $C_0(1)$ line indicates that a carry was generated within or propagated through the $group_0(1)$ adder only if $C_{-1} = 1$. The carry-in to the $group_0(1)$ adder was assumed to be 1; therefore, in order to use the $C_0(1)$ line, C_{-1} must be equal to 1. This is evidenced by the GC_0 equation of Eq. 2.17. The OR of the carries produced by the $group_0$ adder combination selects the sum output from either the $group_1(0)$ adder or the $group_1(1)$ adder. If $GC_0 = 1$, then the $group_1(1)$ sum is selected, because the $group_1(1)$ adder assumed that the carry-in was equal to 1. Otherwise, the $group_1(0)$ sum is selected. The

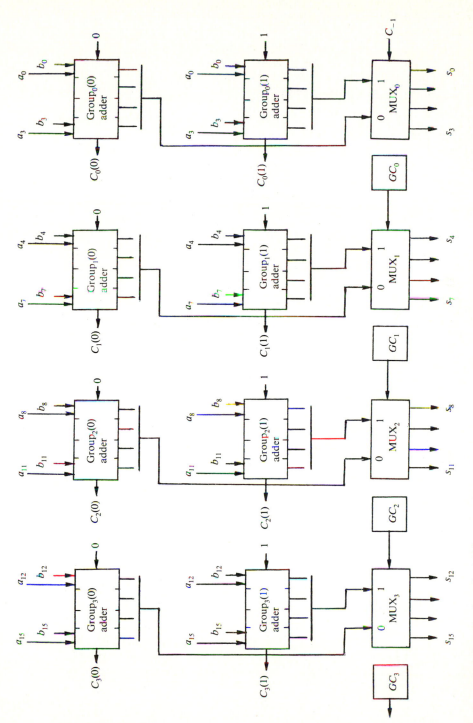

Figure 2.10 Organization of a 16-bit carry-select adder.

operation of the higher-order groups is executed in a similar manner. The logic diagram for a typical group carry and multiplexer is shown in Fig. 2.11. The logic to select s_{11}, s_{10}, s_9, and s_8 was chosen for this example.

2.2.5 Conditional-Sum Addition

Conditional-sum addition is similar to carry-select addition, except that the conditional-sum technique initially considers individual columns of augend-addend bits rather than partitioned groups of operand bits. Both the carry-select and conditional-sum methods overcome the carry propagation delay by generating conditional sums and carries based on assumed carry-ins. The carries select the correct sum from two conditional sums that were produced by adding augend and addend bits with an assumed carry-in equal to 0 and 1.

Let the augend and addend be represented by A and B, respectively, where,

$$A = a_{n-1} \, a_{n-2} \cdots a_1 \, a_0$$

$$B = b_{n-1} \, b_{n-2} \cdots b_1 \, b_0$$

Each pair of augend-addend bits (a_i, b_i) are added simultaneously and independently to produce conditional sums and conditional carries. Figure 2.12 illustrates conditional-sum addition for 2 eight-bit operands. The steps represent successive time intervals during which conditional sums and carries are computed.

During step 1, two sum-and-carry pairs are calculated: one pair with an assumed carry-in of 0 to the ith column, and the second pair with an assumed carry-in of 1. For $i = 0$, however, only a carry-in of 0 is assumed. The first row $s_i(0)$ of step 1 contains the conditional sums assuming carry-in $= 0$; that is, $c_{-1} = 0$. The second row $c_i(0)$ contains the conditional carries assuming $c_{-1} = 0$. The third row $s_i(1)$ and fourth row $c_i(1)$ contain the conditional sums and carries, respectively, assuming $c_{-1} = 1$.

During step 2, conditional sums and carries are generated simultaneously for pairs of operand bits, that is, for $i = 0$ and 1, $i = 2$ and 3, ..., $i = 6$ and 7 for an assumed carry-in of 0 and 1. During step 3, conditional sums and carries are generated simultaneously for four-bit segments, that is, for $i = 0, 1, 2, 3$ and $i = 4, 5, 6, 7$. During step 4, the sums and final carry are no longer conditional, and represent the final sum of $A + B$.

Refer to Fig. 2.12 for the following discussion. The sum in the location labeled ② assumes a carry-in of 0. Since the carry-out of location ① was a 0, then

$$\begin{bmatrix} 1 & 1 \\ 0 & \end{bmatrix}$$

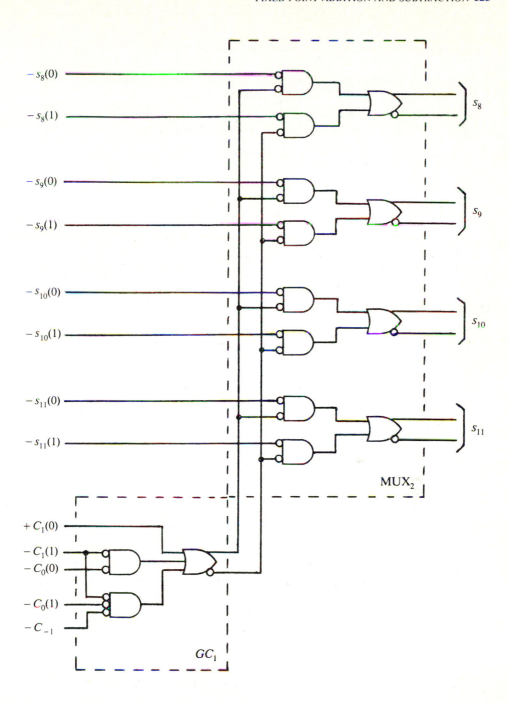

Figure 2.11 Selection of sums s_8, s_9, s_{10}, and s_{11}.

becomes the entry for ⑤ together with the sum bits from ①, which also assumed a carry-in of 0. The sum in location ③ assumes a carry-in of 0. Since the carry-out of ② was 0, then the sum bits in ③ become the low-order two bits (0 0) of ⑥. The sum in location ④ assumes a carry-in of 1, and since the carry-out of ③ was a 1, then the sum bits in ④ become the high-order two bits (1 0) of ⑥. The sum and carry bits in the remaining locations are obtained by a similar process. The arrows indicate the progression through individual columns, groups-of-two columns, and groups-of-four columns based upon the assumed carry-in and the actual carry-in.

2.3 SUBTRACTION

2.3.1 Introduction

This section will consider the machine subtraction of integers (fixed-point numbers). In subtraction, the subtrahend is subtracted from the minuend according to the rules shown in Table 2.3.

Table 2.3 Rules for binary subtraction

−	0	1
0	0	1*
1	1	0

*Indicates a borrow from the minuend in the next column on the left.

An example will illustrate these rules.

	2^3	2^2	2^1	2^0
		borrow		
Minuend (5_{10})	0	1	0	1
Subtrahend (3_{10}) −)	0	0	1	1
Difference (2_{10})	0	0	1	0

	i	7	6	5	4	3	2	1	0	Assumed carry-in c_{-1}
Step	a_i	0	1	0	1	1	0	0	1	
	b_i	0	0	1	1	0	1	0	1	
1	$s_i(0)$	0	1	1	0	1	1	0	0	0
	$c_i(0)$	0	0	0	1	0	0	0	1	
	$s_i(1)$	1	0	0	1	0	0	1		1
	$c_i(1)$	0	1	1	1	1	1	0		
2	$s_i(0)$	0	1	0	0	1	1	1	0	0
	$c_i(0)$	0		1		0		0		
	$s_i(1)$	1	0	0	1	0	0			1
	$c_i(1)$	0			1	1				
3	$s_i(0)$	1	0	0	0	1	1	1	0	0
	$c_i(0)$	0				0				
	$s_i(1)$	1	0	0	1					1
	$c_i(1)$	0								
4	S	1	0	0	0	1	1	1	0	
	C	0								

Figure 2.12 Example of conditional-sum addition: $A(89_{10}) + B(53_{10}) = S(142_{10})$.

The borrow from the minuend of the third column from the right results in that column changing from

1   0

to

0   0

This is the paper-and-pencil approach to binary subtraction and is not easily applied to machine subtraction. The method that is used in most digital processors is to add the 2s complement of the subtrahend to the minuend.

The $(r - 1)$'s complement of an n-digit, radix r integer B is defined as

$$\overline{B} = (r^n - 1) - B \tag{2.18}$$

The r's complement of an n-digit, radix r integer B is defined as

$$(\overline{B})_{+1} = r^n - B$$
$$= \overline{B} + 1 \tag{2.19}$$

That is, the r's complement is simply the $(r - 1)$'s complement plus 1. When using the r's complement in subtracting the n-digit integers

$$A = a_{n-1} \, a_{n-2} \cdots a_1 \, a_0$$

and

$$B = b_{n-1} \, b_{n-2} \cdots b_1 \, b_0$$

the difference can be written as

$$D = A - B$$
$$= A - r^n + r^n - B$$
$$= A - r^n + (r^n - B)$$
$$= A - r^n + (\overline{B})_{+1} \tag{2.20}$$

Using Eq. 2.20, subtraction can be performed by first forming the r's complement of B and then adding this value to A, both of which are straightforward operations. In fact, the 1 that must be added to form the r's complement of B can be combined with the addition of A to save time.

An example using Eq. 2.20 is shown below. The integer $0\ 0\ 0\ 1\ 1$ ($+3$) is subtracted from the integer $0\ 0\ 1\ 0\ 1$ ($+5$).

$$A = 0\ 0\ 1\ 0\ 1$$
$$B = 0\ 0\ 0\ 1\ 1$$

$$
\begin{array}{rcl}
A - B = & 0\ 0\ 1\ 0\ 1 & \qquad\qquad 0\ 0\ 1\ 0\ 1 \\
& -)\ 0\ 0\ 0\ 1\ 1 & \longrightarrow \qquad +)\ 1\ 1\ 1\ 0\ 1 \\
\hline
& & \qquad\qquad 0\ 0\ 0\ 1\ 0
\end{array}
$$

From Eq. 2.20, for $n = 5$ and $r = 2$,

$$D = A - r^n + (\bar{B})_{+1}$$
$$= 5 - 2^5 + 29$$
$$= 2$$

Let A and B be two r's complemented integers. The subtraction of A and B follows the following procedure.

1. Construct the $(r - 1)$'s complement of B. This is obtained by inverting the digits of B such that $b_i \rightarrow \bar{b}_i$; that is, 0s become 1s and 1s become 0s. Add digit by digit starting from the least significant pair $a_0 \bar{b}_0$ and proceed left, adding each pair in turn, up to and including the sign digits. A carry-in of 1 is assumed for the low-order bit position.
2. Compare the carry-out of the $n - 2$ position with the carry-out of the $n - 1$ (sign) position. If the two carries agree (both 1 or 0), then the result is in correct r's complement form, and the carry-out of the sign position is ignored. If the two carries differ, then an addition overflow has occurred and the result is invalid.

There are three cases to consider when subtracting two integers.

1. A is positive and B is initially negative; that is,

$$(\bar{B})_{+1} = \left\{ [(r - 1) \, \bar{b}_{n-2} \, \bar{b}_{n-3} \cdots \bar{b}_1 \bar{b}_0] + 1 \right\}_r$$

which is the r's complement of B. After B has been r's-complemented, both A and B are positive such that

$$A = a_{n-1} \, a_{n-2} \cdots a_1 \, a_0$$

and

$$B = b_{n-1} \, b_{n-2} \cdots b_1 \, b_0$$

with $a_{n-1} = b_{n-1} = 0$. Then the result is

$$D = A + B = s_{n-1} \cdots s_1 s_0$$

In this case, no carry-out will be generated from the sign position, and the resulting sum will be positive ($s_{n-1} = 0$) and in correct notation if $A + B < r^{n-1}$. This implies that no carry will enter the sign position. An addition overflow will take place if $A + B \geq r^{n-1}$. For example, assuming $n = 5$,

$$A = \quad 0\ 0\ 1\ 0\ 1 \quad (+5) \qquad\qquad 0\ 0\ 1\ 0\ 1$$

$$\text{becomes}$$

$$(\bar{B})_{+1} = \ -)\ \underline{1\ 1\ 1\ 0\ 1}\ \ (-3) \qquad\qquad +)\ \underline{0\ 0\ 0\ 1\ 1}$$

$$0\ 1\ 0\ 0\ 0 \quad (+8)$$

2. A is negative and B is initially positive. After B has been r's-complemented, both A and B will be negative such that

$$(\bar{A})_{+1} = a_{n-1}\, a_{n-2} \cdot\cdot\cdot a_1\, a_0$$

and

$$(\bar{B})_{+1} = b_{n-1}\, b_{n-2} \cdot\cdot\cdot b_1\, b_0$$

with $a_{n-1} = b_{n-1} = 1$.

Let $(\bar{A})_{+1} = r^n - A$ and $(\bar{B})_{+1} = r^n - B$ from Eq. 2.19. Then the result is

$$D = (r^n - A) + (r^n - B)$$
$$= 2r^n - (A + B) \qquad\qquad (2.21)$$

Since $a_{n-1} = b_{n-1} = 1$, there will always be a carry-out of the sign position. If there is no overflow, the result is negative and the carry-out of the sign position can be ignored (this is equivalent to a 0 carry-out of the sign position for positive numbers). Ignoring the carry-out of the sign position is equivalent to dividing the result by r^n and retaining the remainder. For example, for $n = 5$ and $r = 2$,

$$
\begin{array}{ll}
\quad\ 1\ 1\ 0\ 1\ 1 & (-5) \\
+)\ \ \underline{1\ 1\ 1\ 0\ 1} & (-3) \\
1\ 1\ 1\ 0\ 0\ 0 & (-8)
\end{array}
$$

$$\Updownarrow$$

$$1\ 1\ 1\ 0\ 0\ 0 \div \underbrace{1\ 0\ 0\ 0\ 0\ 0}_{2^5} = 1\ 1\ 0\ 0\ 0$$

Thus, from Eq. 2.21,

$$\frac{D}{r^n} = \frac{2r^n - (A + B)}{r^n}$$

$$= 2 - \frac{A + B}{r^n}$$

$$= 1 + \frac{[r^n - (A + B)]}{r^n}$$

Therefore, the result is in the correct form $r^n - (A + B)$ and will be valid if $A + B < r^{n-1}$. An addition overflow will occur if $A + B \geq r^{n-1}$. For example, for $n = 5$ and $r = 2$,

$$
\begin{array}{rlcr}
A = & 1\ 1\ 0\ 0\ 0 & (-8) & 1\ 1\ 0\ 0\ 0 \\
B = -) & 0\ 0\ 1\ 0\ 1 & (+5) & +)\ 1\ 1\ 0\ 1\ 1 \\
\hline
& & & 1\ 0\ 0\ 1\ 1\,(-13)
\end{array}
$$

3. A is positive and B is initially positive, or A is negative and B is initially negative. In either case, the signs of A and B will be opposite after r's complementation and no overflow will occur.

$$
\begin{array}{cccc}
(a) & A & & A \qquad \text{or} \\
    & -)\ B & \longrightarrow & +)\ (\bar{B})_{+1} \\
    & \rule{1.2cm}{0.4pt} & & \rule{1.2cm}{0.4pt}
\end{array}
$$

$$
\begin{array}{cccc}
(b) & (\bar{A})_{+1} & & (\bar{A})_{+1} \\
    & -)\ (\bar{B})_{+1} & \longrightarrow & +)\ B \\
    & \rule{1.2cm}{0.4pt} & & \rule{1.2cm}{0.4pt}
\end{array}
$$

In case (a), the result D will be the sum of $A + (\bar{B})_{+1}$, that is

$$D = A + (\bar{B})_{+1}$$
$$= A + (r^n - B)$$
$$= r^n + (A - B) \qquad (2.22)$$

If $B > A$, then the result will be negative and in the correct form. Assuming that $n = 5$ and $r = 2$,

$$
\begin{array}{rlcrl}
A = & 0\ 0\ 1\ 0\ 1 & (+5) & 0\ 0\ 1\ 0\ 1 & (+5) \\
B = -) & 0\ 1\ 0\ 0\ 0 & (+8) & +)\ 1\ 1\ 0\ 0\ 0 & (-8) \\
\hline
& & & \underbrace{1\ 1\ 1\ 0\ 1} & (-3) \\
\end{array}
$$

Unsigned binary value $= 29$ ⟶ ↑

The result D is calculated from Eq. 2.22 as

$$
\begin{aligned}
D &= r^n + (A - B) \\
&= 2^5 + (5 - 8) \\
&= 32 - 3 \\
&= 29
\end{aligned}
$$

If $B < A$, then the result will be positive and also in the correct form. For $n = 5$ and $r = 2$,

$$
\begin{array}{llll}
A = & 0\ 1\ 0\ 0\ 0 & (+8) & \quad\quad +)\ 0\ 1\ 0\ 0\ 0 \quad (+8) \\
B = & -)\ 0\ 0\ 1\ 0\ 1 & (+5) & \longrightarrow \quad +)\ 1\ 1\ 0\ 1\ 1 \quad (-5) \\
& & & \underline{\quad\quad\quad\quad\quad\quad} \\
& & & 1\ 0\ 0\ 0\ 1\ 1 \quad (+3)
\end{array}
$$

Unsigned binary value $= 35$

The result D is calculated from Eq. 2.22 as

$$
\begin{aligned}
D &= r^n + (A - B) \\
&= 2^5 + (8 - 5) \\
&= 32 + 3 \\
&= 35
\end{aligned}
$$

In case (b), the result D will be the sum of $(\bar{A})_{+1} + 1$; that is,

$$
\begin{aligned}
D &= (\bar{A})_{+1} + B \\
&= (r^n - A) + B \\
&= r^n - (A - B) \tag{2.23}
\end{aligned}
$$

If $B > A$, then the result will be positive and in the correct form. If $B < A$, then the result will be negative and in the correct form.

The logical simplicity and speed of performing subtraction of signed numbers in 2s complement notation is the reason that this number representation is so widely used in the arithmetic processors of most modern digital computers. It might seem that 1s complement representation would be equally as good. However, although complementation is easier, the result that is obtained after the add operation is not always correct. In 1s complement notation, the final carry-out c_{n-1} cannot be ignored. If $c_{n-1} = 1$, then it must be added to the result to make it correct; if $c_{n-1} = 0$, then the result as obtained is correct. Therefore, 1s complement subtraction may require an extra add cycle to obtain the correct result.

2.3.2 Ripple and Carry Lookahead Subtraction

Once the principles of fixed-point addition are understood, fixed-point subtraction is relatively easy and straightforward. Implementation is simple, consisting
only of the logic required to perform 2s complementation on the subtrahend according to the rules outlined in Sec. 2.3.1. It is desirable to have the subtractor
perform the function of addition as well; there is no advantage in having a
separate adder and subtractor. Therefore, the adders of Sec. 2.2 will be used in
the design of subtractors. They will be modified so that they can accomplish subtraction while still maintaining the ability to add.

   Each digit of the subtrahend must be inverted with a corresponding carry-
in $= 1$ to the low-order adder stage. An inverter could be used to invert each
subtrahend digit, but this would not permit the noninverted operand to be used
for addition. The logic that is used to invert the subtrahend should also allow the
noninverted operand to be applied to the adder inputs. The EXCLUSIVE-OR
function will accomplish this. The EXCLUSIVE-OR function for two variables is
defined as

$$p \veebar q = (p \wedge \bar{q}) \vee (\bar{p} \wedge q)$$

which states that $p \veebar q = 1$ if and only if $p \neq q$. The truth table for the
EXCLUSIVE-OR operation is shown in Table 2.4. Note that when $p = 1$, q is
inverted; that is, for $p = 1$ and $q = 0$, the output of the EXCLUSIVE-OR circuit is 1. When $p = 0$, q is noninverted. Thus, a variable such as p can be used to
control the version of the operand that is applied to the adder inputs. Specifically,
when $p = 0$, an add operation is to be performed, and when $p = 1$, a subtract
operation is to be performed. The logic diagram for the EXCLUSIVE-OR circuit
and its symbol is shown in Fig. 2.13.

**Table 2.4 Rules for
EXCLUSIVE-OR
operation**

		q	
$\veebar$		0	1
p	0	0	1
	1	1	0

Hardware organization Let A and B be the minuend and subtrahend, respectively, where

$$A = a_{n-1} \, a_{n-2} \cdots a_1 a_0$$

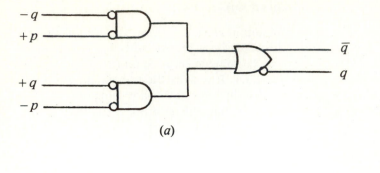

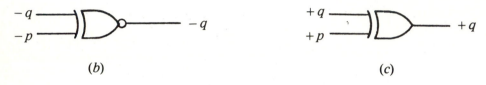

Figure 2.13 EXCLUSIVE-OR, (a) logic diagram, (b) and (c) logic symbol.

and

$$B = b_{n-1} \; b_{n-2} \cdots b_1 \; b_0$$

The n-ripple adder of Fig. 2.2, modified to perform subtraction, is shown in Fig. 2.14. Note that during a subtraction, a 1 is forced into the carry-in of the low-order adder stage. Once the subtrahend has been negated by 2s complementation, the addition is carried out as described in Sec. 2.2.2.

The carry lookahead adder of Sec. 2.2.3 is redrawn in Fig. 2.15, with the modifications necessary to permit both addition and subtraction. The four-bit group 0 was chosen for this illustration. Once the subtrahend has been 2s complemented, high-speed addition takes place, using full carry lookahead as described in Sec. 2.2.3. The 2s complementation does not change the operation of either adder. The effect of complementation is to apply a different operand to the adder inputs. Setting $c_{-1} = 1$ completes the complementation.

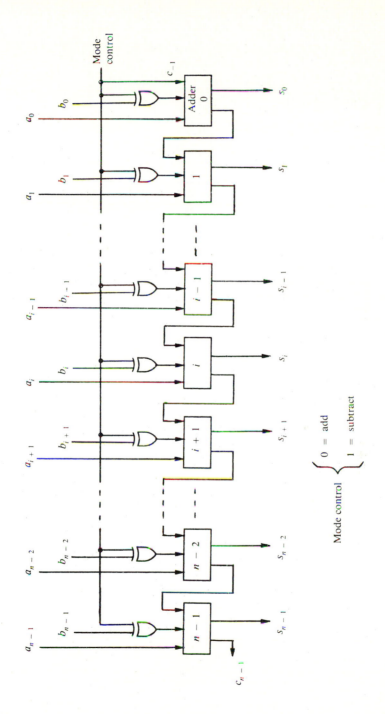

Figure 2.14 Organization for an *n*-bit ripple adder/subtractor.

133

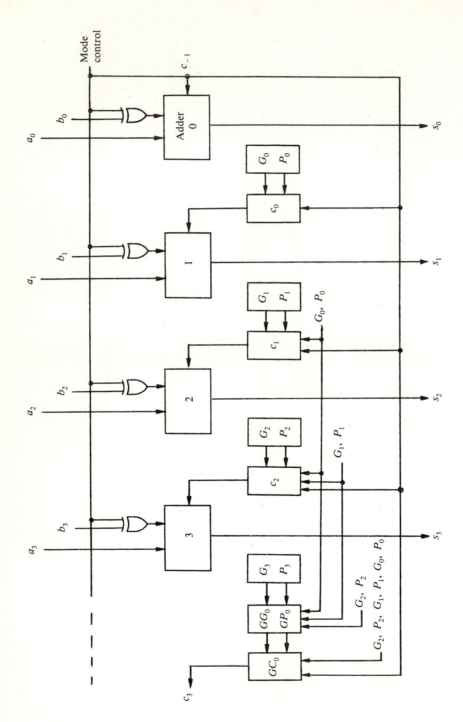

Figure 2.15 Block diagram of a four-bit group carry lookahead adder/subtractor. Mode control: 0 = add, 1 = subtract.

PROBLEMS

2.1 Given eight-bit registers and radix 2, convert the decimal numbers $+15$, $+96$, -26, and -127 into
(a) Sign magnitude
(b) Diminished-radix complement
(c) Radix complement
Then perform the following operations in 2s complement and indicate whether or not overflow occurs.

$$(+15) + (+96)$$
$$(-26) + (+96)$$
$$(+15) - (-127)$$
$$(+96) + (-127)$$

2.2 Write the sum and carry equations for the two high-order stages of a six-bit carry lookahead adder in which the six bits are one group, that is, the stages with outputs s_{i+4} and s_{i+5}. Be sure to include the group generate and group propagate equations for the six-bit adder. Write the carry equations as a sum-of-products expansion in terms of the generate and propagate functions.

2.3 Design and draw a complete 18-bit carry lookahead adder using the six-bit adder of prob. 2.2. The 18-bit adder is to have three groups of six-bits/group. Draw the six-bit adder as a single block with the appropriate inputs and outputs. Use group carry lookahead between groups to increase the speed of the adder. Assume that both levels (plus and minus) are available from the group generate and group propagate functions of the six-bit adder. Use ECL technology.

2.4 Let A and B be two signed fixed-point binary integers in 2s complement representation, where $A = 1\ 0\ 1\ 1\ 0\ 0\ 0\ 1$ and $B = 1\ 1\ 1\ 0\ 0\ 1\ 0\ 0$.
Find

$$A + B$$
$$A - B$$
$$A + \bar{B} + 1$$
$$\bar{A} + 1 + B$$
$$A - (\bar{B} + 1)$$
$$\bar{A} + 1 - B$$
$$\bar{A} + 1 + \bar{B} + 1$$
$$\bar{A} + 1 - (\bar{B} + 1)$$

where $\bar{A}$ and $\bar{B}$ are the 1s complement of A and B, respectively.

2.5 List all the combinations of addition and subtraction for two signed operands A and B. Indicate which combinations are "true addition" and which are "true subtraction."

2.6 Given a 16-bit CLA adder with four groups of four bits per group, calculate the number of gate delays to generate the high-order sum bit and the high-order carry-out.

2.7 Perform the arithmetic operations below with fixed-point numbers in 2s complement representation, where $n = 7$. In each case, indicate if there is an overflow.

$$(+35) + (+42)$$
$$(-63) - (+63)$$
$$(-31) + (-34)$$
$$(-31) - (+33)$$

2.8 The following binary numbers are signed eight-bit values in 2s complement representation. Perform the indicated operations and indicate whether or not overflow occurs.

(a)   0 1 1 0 0 1 0 0   (b)   1 1 0 0 0 0 0 0
    +) 0 0 0 1 1 0 1 1   +) 1 0 1 1 1 1 1 1

(c)   1 0 0 1 1 1 0 0   (d)   0 0 1 1 1 0 0 1
    −) 0 0 0 1 1 1 0 1   −) 1 0 1 1 1 0 0 0

2.9 Perform the operation of subtraction on the following 2s complement numbers:

(a)   0 1 0 1 1.0 1 0 1   (b)   0 0 0 1 1 1.0 1 1 0
    −) 0 0 1 1 0.1 1 0 0   −) 1 1 0 0 1 1.0 0 1 1

2.10 Write the group carry equations for each four-bit group of a 16-bit carry-select adder. Write the equations using generate and propagate functions. Also write them in expanded form without generate and propagate functions.

2.11 For $n = 8$, let A and B be two signed fixed-point binary integers in 2s complement representation, where

$A = 0 1 1 0 1 1 0 1$
$B = 1 1 0 0 1 1 1 1$

Find $A + \bar{B} + 1 + B$, where $\bar{B}$ is the 1s complement.

2.12 Perform the arithmetic operations below with fixed-point binary numbers in 2s complement representation, where $n = 8$. In each case, indicate if there is an overflow. Check the answers for (a), (b), (c), and (d) by converting the operands to decimal sign-magnitude representation.

(a)   0 1 0 0 0 0 0 0   (b)   0 0 1 1 0 1 1 0
    +) 0 1 0 0 0 0 0 0   +) 1 1 1 0 0 0 1 1

(c)   1 0 0 1 1 0 0 0   (d)   0 0 1 1 0 1 1 0
    −) 0 0 1 0 0 0 1 0   −) 1 1 1 0 0 0 1 1

(e) $+64_{10}$ (f) -63_{10}
    +) $+63_{10}$ −) $+66_{10}$

2.13 Write the equations for two ways to detect overflow in fixed-point addition assuming radix complementation for $r = 2$.

2.14 Perform the arithmetic operations below with fixed-point binary numbers in 2s complement representation, where $n = 8$. In each case, indicate if there is an overflow.

(a) $(+35) + (+42)$ (b) $(-62) - (+67)$
(c) $(-31) + (-34)$ (d) $(-31) - (+33)$

2.15 Repeat prob. 2.14, where $n = 7$.

2.16 The fixed-point binary numbers below are in 2s complement notation. Perform the indicated arithmetic operations and leave the results in 2s complement form.

(a) 1 1 1 0 0 0 0 0 + 1 1 0 1 1 1 0 1
(b) 1 1 1 1 0 0 0 1 + 0 0 1 1 1 0 1 1
(c) 0 0 0 0 1 1 1 1 + 1 1 1 0 0 1 0 0
(d) 0 0 1 1 1 1 1 1 + 0 0 0 0 1 1 1 1
(e) 1 0 0 0 0 1 1 1 − 1 1 1 0 0 1 1 0
(f) 1 1 1 0 0 0 0 1 − 1 1 1 1 0 0 0 0
(g) 0 0 1 1 1 1 1 0 − 1 1 1 0 1 1 1 1
(h) 0 0 0 1 0 0 1 1 − 0 1 0 1 1 1 0 0

THREE

FIXED-POINT MULTIPLICATION

3.1 INTRODUCTION

Multiplication of two fixed-point binary operands will now be considered. A hardware multiply/divide unit has become a standard feature in most digital computers. Arithmetic processors for high-speed multiplication based on various add-shift methods will be presented in this section. This includes multiple-bit scanning and multiplier recoding techniques. Also included will be two hardware array multipliers and a table lookup method.

Multiplication can be defined as repeated addition. The number to be added is the multiplicand, the number of times that it is added is the multiplier, and the result is the product. Each step of the addition generates a partial product. In most computers, the operands usually contain the same number of bits. When the operands are interpreted as integers, as in fixed-point arithmetic, the product is usually twice the length of the operands in order to preserve the information content. This repeated addition method that is suggested by the arithmetic definition is so slow that it is almost always replaced by an algorithm that makes use of positional number representation.

By the multiplication of two n-digit binary numbers

$$A = a_{n-1} a_{n-2} \cdots a_0$$

and

$$B = b_{n-1} b_{n-2} \cdots b_0$$

is meant the generation of $2n$ product digits $P = p_{2n-1} p_{2n-2} \cdots p_0$. Multiplication of two fixed-point binary numbers in sign-magnitude representation is done with paper and pencil by a process of successive add and shift operations. This process is best illustrated by means of a numerical example, as shown below.

$$
\begin{array}{rr}
\text{Multiplicand } A = & 1\ 0\ 1\ 1 \\
\text{Multiplier } B = & \times)\ 1\ 0\ 0\ 1 \\
\hline
& 1\ 0\ 1\ 1 \\
\text{Partial} & 0\ 0\ 0\ 0 \\
\text{product} & 0\ 0\ 0\ 0 \\
\text{bits} & 1\ 0\ 1\ 1 \\
\hline
\text{Product } P = & 0\ 1\ 1\ 0\ 0\ 0\ 1\ 1
\end{array}
$$

The process consists of looking at successive bits of the multiplier, least-significant bit first. If the multiplier bit is a 1, the multiplicand is copied; otherwise, 0s are inserted. The numbers copied in successive lines are shifted left one position from the previous number. Finally, the numbers are added and their sum forms the product. The sign of the product is determined from the signs of the multiplicand and multiplier. If these are the same, the sign of the product is plus. If they are different, the sign of the product is minus.

Machine multiplication schemes usually begin with a step that is quite similar to this paper-and-pencil method. An array of partial product digits can be formed in parallel at the beginning of the process or as needed from the two operands. A straightforward way of accomplishing this add-shift operation is to make n passes through an adder, since there are n partial product numbers to be summed. This is a time-consuming process and a number of other schemes are available that are much faster and not much more expensive.

In 2s complement notation, the sign bit is treated in the same way as the other operand bits. Some machines that use this complement notation convert to and from sign-magnitude notation at the start and end of multiplication. This appears to be more attractive, since the hardware for the multiply algorithms would be required to work only with positive operands. The sign of the result is determined separately. Time is lost, however, due to the extra recomplementation cycles.

Four situations arise, as shown below:

Sign of multiplicand	+	−	+	−
Sign of multiplier	+	−	−	+
Sign of product	+	+	−	−

As long as the multiplier is positive, there is no problem in obtaining the correct answer, even when the sign of the multiplicand is negative. The sign of the multiplicand must be extended for each partial product that is produced from a 1 bit in the multiplier, as shown below.

$$
\begin{array}{r}
1\ 0\ 0\ 1 \quad (-7) \\
\times)\ 0\ 0\ 1\ 0 \quad (+2) \\
\hline
\end{array}
$$

```
0 0 0 0 0 0 0 0
1 1 1 1 0 0 1
0 0 0 0 0 0
0 0 0 0 0
```
$$
\overline{1\ 1\ 1\ 1\ 0\ 0\ 1\ 0 \quad (-14)}
$$

It is only when the multiplier is negative that a problem arises.

$$
\begin{array}{r}
0\ 1\ 1\ 1 \quad (+7) \\
\times)\ 1\ 1\ 1\ 0 \quad (-2) \\
\hline
\end{array}
$$

```
      0 0 0 0
    0 1 1 1
  0 1 1 1
0 1 1 1
```
$$
\overline{1\ 1\ 0\ 0\ 0\ 1\ 0 \quad (-30)}
$$

This is true regardless of the sign of the multiplicand, because the binary value of the multiplier is not the absolute value. In this situation, if the multiply hardware cannot operate with a negative multiplier, then the multiplier must be 2s-complemented, the multiplication operation performed, and the sign adjusted.

In computers, 2s complement is widely used since negative numbers are already in a form in which subtraction can be replaced by addition. Section 3.2 will discuss algorithms and hardware that operate on 2s complement numbers, where negative multipliers are complemented before the actual multiply operation.

3.2 SEQUENTIAL ADD-SHIFT MULTIPLICATION

Many computers that require hardware multiplication implement it by a sequential digital circuit consisting of registers, a shift register, and an adder. This method uses either a hardware control sequencer or a microcode control sequencer. The hardware sequencer is obviously faster, but requires more logic. The most common approach is to have a microprogram control the multiply function during each cycle of the add-shift operation. The circuit performs multiplication by using a single adder n times to implement the addition being performed on the n rows of partial products.

When using a negative multiplier, the multiplication of two binary operands is complicated because the function of the multiplier bits is not always the same during the generation of the partial products. When the multiplier is positive the bits are treated the same as in the sign-magnitude representation. When it is negative, any low-order 0s and the first 1 bit are treated the same as a positive multiplier, but the remaining higher-order bits have an opposite effect because they are complemented. It is possible to design a multiplication algorithm that operates with 2s complement numbers directly—and this is done in a later section—but a simple way to solve this complication is to use an algorithm that 2s complements a negative multiplier and multiplicand before the operation. Thus, only positive numbers would be multiplied. The positive product thus obtained would be complemented only if the product was to be negative. The correct sign can be determined from the signs of the operands. If the signs of the operands are the same (either positive or negative), then the sign of the product is positive. If the signs of the operands are different, then the sign of the product is negative.

The multiplier, however, must always be positive. A convenient procedure is to change only the multiplier to a positive number, leaving the multiplicand either positive or negative. Then, depending upon the signs of the initial operands, it may then be necessary to complement the product. An alternative approach is to complement both the multiplier and the multiplicand when the multiplier is negative. This is equivalent to multiplying both operands by -1, which does not change the product or the sign, but makes the multiplier positive. If the multiplier and multiplicand are both positive, then no complementation is required. If the multiplier is positive and the multiplicand is negative, then no complementation is required and the product will be negative in 2s complement form. If a negative multiplicand is added to a negative partial product and both are in 2s complement notation, then the result will be a negative partial product that is also in 2s complement notation. Therefore, it makes no difference whether the multiplicand is positive or negative. In the first case, positive partial products are formed; in the second case, negative partial products are formed.

Examples will now be presented to illustrate the add-shift algorithm for positive and negative multiplicands. Assume two n-bit operands

$$A = a_{n-1} a_{n-2} \cdots a_0$$

and

$$B = b_{n-1} b_{n-2} \cdots b_0$$

are used, where A is a positive multiplicand and B is a positive multiplier. The multiplication algorithm is shown in Fig. 3.1 for $n = 4$. The multiplicand is in an n-bit register, and the multiplier and the product share a $2n$-bit shift register. The multiplier is at the least-significant digit end, and the product, initially at 0, is at the most-significant end. Note that the control to determine whether or not to add the multiplicand to the partial product depends only on the rightmost bit of the multiplier at any one time.

During the first cycle, when the least-significant bit of the multiplier is 0, the shift register is shifted right one bit position and the sign of the multiplicand is

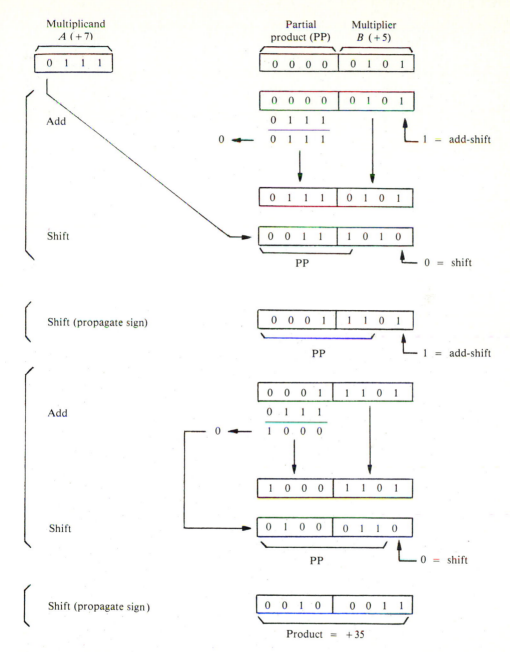

Figure 3.1 Multiplication in 2s complement with positive multiplicand and positive multiplier.

placed in the leftmost bit position. When the least-significant bit is 1, the multiplicand is added to the n most-significant bits and then the register is shifted right one bit position. The n most-significant bits of the register are replaced with the

$n + 1$ bits resulting from the addition (n bits) to which the sign of the multiplicand is left-concatenated. If A is negative, then a carry-out is generated after the first such process and it corresponds to the most-significant bit of the accumulated partial product. If A is positive, then a 0 will be placed in the most-significant bit position. The above procedure is repeated once for each of the n bits of the multiplier, and results in the desired product. A hardware or software counter is required to determine the number of add-shift cycles. If a count-down counter is used, then the counter is initialized to the number of bits in the multiplier.

Now assume that A is a negative multiplicand and B is a positive multiplier. The desired result, which is a negative number, should be in the 2s complement representation of $A \times B$. The sign of the multiplicand should be extended to the left when it is added to the subproduct array, that is, to represent negative A as $2^{2n} - |A|$ instead of $2^n - |A|$. This results in a product in the form of

$$(2^{2n} - |A|) \times B = 2^{2n} \times B - |A \times B|$$

which is shown in the example below for $n = 4$. Since the carry is discarded, the correct representation is obtained in the low-order $2n$ bits.

$$
\begin{array}{r}
1\ 0\ 0\ 1 \quad (-7) \\
\times)\ 0\ 1\ 0\ 1 \quad (+5) \\
\hline
1\ 1\ 1\ 1\ 1\ 0\ 0\ 1 \\
0\ 0\ 0\ 0\ 0\ 0\ 0\ 0 \\
1\ 1\ 1\ 1\ 1\ 0\ 0\ 1 \\
0\ 0\ 0\ 0\ 0\ 0\ 0\ 0 \\
\hline
1\ 0\ 0\ 1\ 1\ 0\ 1\ 1\ 1\ 0\ 1 \quad (-35)
\end{array}
$$

$2n$ bits

It appears that a $2n$-bit adder is required, since the multiplicand has doubled in length. However, an n-bit adder and a $2n$-bit shift register are sufficient, as demonstrated in Fig. 3.2 Whenever the multiplier is negative, it can be 2s-complemented with the multiplicand and the above algorithm used to produce the desired 2s complement product.

When multiplication is implemented in a digital computer, a single adder is provided for the summation of two binary numbers and the partial products are successively accumulated in a register. Also, instead of shifting the multiplicand to the left, as in the paper-and-pencil method, the partial product is shifted to the right, which results in leaving the partial product and the multiplicand in the required relative positions. When the least-significant bit in the multiplier is 0, there is no need to add all 0s to the partial product, since this will not alter its value; the partial product can be simply shifted right one bit position. However, shifting the partial product right may require more control logic than adding all 0s to the par-

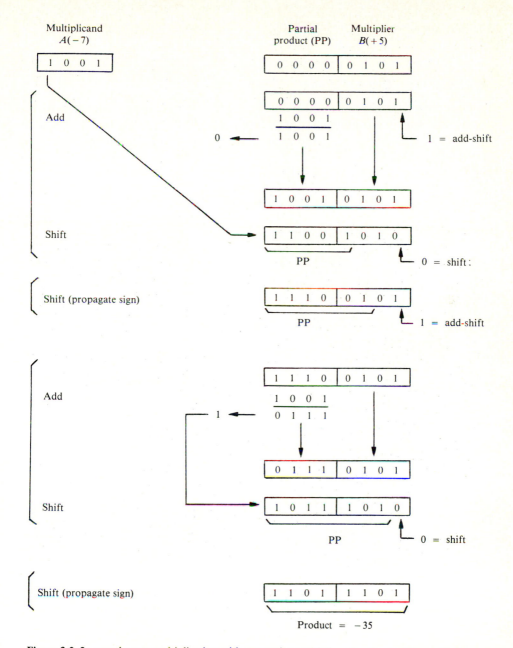

Figure 3.2 2s complement multiplication with a negative multiplicand and a positive multiplier.

tial product. An *n*-bit 0 vector can be obtained by ANDing each bit of the multiplicand with the least-significant bit (b_0) of the multiplier. When $b_0 = 0$, this produces the required 0 vector to be added to the previous partial product.

This permits every cycle to be identical; that is, every cycle consists of an add-shift operation.

3.2.1 Hardware Organization

The hardware for multiplication consists of the functional units shown in Fig. 3.3. Three n-bit parallel-load registers are required: multiplicand register A; register D, which contains the high-order n bits of the partial product; and multiplier register B. A carry register (1 bit) is also needed to store the carry-out from the adder. An n-bit parallel adder, which typically employs carry lookahead, is required to generate partial product $i + 1$ from the multiplicand and partial product i. The multiplicand and multiplier are initially loaded into registers A and B, respectively. The initial contents of register D should be 0, corresponding to a 0 initial partial product, and carry bit C is set to the sign of the multiplicand. Alternatively,

$$C = a_{n-1} \veebar b_{n-1}$$

A sequence counter is also provided to keep track of the number of add-shift cycles and to recognize the completion of multiplication.

The following operations take place during each add-shift cycle. The least-significant multiplier bit b_0 determines whether or not the multiplicand is added to the partial product. If $b_0 = 1$, then the multiplicand in A is added to the present partial product in D. If $b_0 = 0$, then 0s are added to the partial product in D. In both cases, the sum output of the adder

$$S = s_{n-1} \, s_{n-2} \cdots s_1 \, s_0$$

is loaded in register D, the carry-out bit is loaded into flip-flop C, and registers C, D, and B, treated as one unit, are shifted right one bit position in concatenation. The sequence counter is decreased by 1 and its new value is checked. If it is not equal to 0, then the process is repeated and a new partial product is formed. The partial product grows in length by one bit per cycle from the initial vector of n 0s in register D. It was mentioned previously that the sum output of the adder was loaded into register D and then registers C, D, and B were shifted. The same result would be obtained by placing a right shifter at the output of the adder (which also shifts the remaining bits in the multiplier and bit C) and then loading registers D and B. The design of registers D and B would then be less complex, because now they would be required to only store information, not to store and shift.

The preceding sequence of operations will now be restated more formally. An auxiliary vector V is defined as

$$V = A \wedge b_0$$

where $\wedge$ is the AND function. The auxiliary vector V is obtained by ANDing each of the n outputs of register A with the current least-significant bit b_0 of register B such that

$$V = \begin{cases} A & \text{if } b_0 = 1 \\ \Phi & \text{if } b_0 = 0 \end{cases}$$

Φ refers to a 0 vector of n bits. The adder performs the following addition during each counter cycle with $C_{in} = 0$.

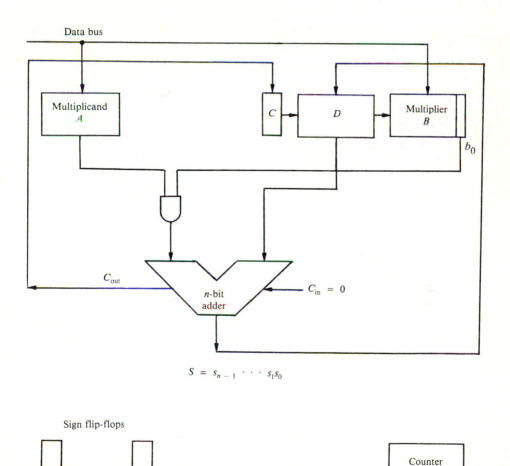

$$S = s_{n-1} \cdots s_1 s_0$$

Figure 3.3 Basic hardware for fixed-point add-shift multiplication

$$C_{\text{out}} \cdot S \leftarrow D + (A \wedge b_0)$$

where the center dot ($\cdot$) is concatenation and the plus sign ($+$) is addition. A possible $C_{\text{out}} = 1$ may be generated by this addition. The following right-shift operation is performed after sum S has been loaded into register D and indicates the placement of the sum bits in registers D and B at the end of the cycle.

$$D \cdot B \leftarrow C_{\text{out}} \cdot s_{n-1} \cdots s_1 s_0 \cdot b_{n-1} \cdots b_1$$

This means that the adder outputs $C_{\text{out}} \cdot s_{n-1} \cdots s_1$ reside in register D positions $n - 1$ to 0, respectively; that s_0 has been shifted into b_{n-1}; and that b_0 has been shifted out of the right end of register B. Note that the carry-out from the adder is the leftmost bit of the new partial product and that it must be stored in flip-flop C to be shifted right with the contents of registers D and B.

The preceding procedure illustrates that during each cycle of the counter (each add-shift cycle), either a copy of multiplicand A or a 0 vector is added to the upper n bits of the partial product depending upon whether the current least-significant multiplier bit b_0 is 1 or 0. The shifting of each successive partial product to the right is equivalent to the left shift performed in the paper-and-pencil method in which the multiplier bits are entered in fixed columns. This process is repeated n times until all multiplier bits have been examined, one at a time. At the end of the computation, the n-bit multiplier will have been shifted out of the right end of register B. After n cycles, the high-order half of the product is held in register D and the low-order half is in register B.

3.2.2 Logical Design of Multiplier

The design of register A is shown in Fig. 3.4. This is a simple design in which the only property required by the register is that of storing the multiplicand. The waveforms for the clock, set, and reset signals are shown below. The operation of the register is similar to that of a register designed with D flip-flops; that is, the leading edge of the clock sets the register to the contents of the input data regardless of the previous state of the register. The leading edge of the clock pulse

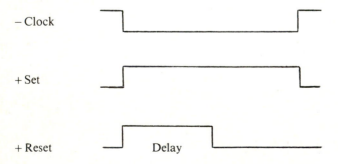

$-$ Clock

$+$ Set

$+$ Reset   Delay

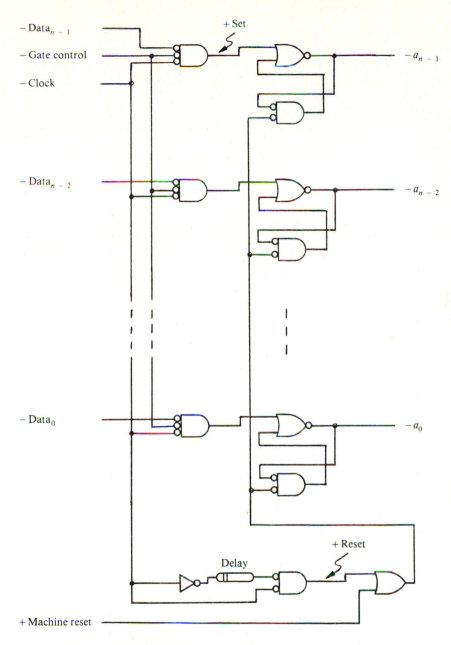

Figure 3.4 Multiplicand register A.

gates the data bits (1 or 0) into the OR gate of each latch. After one delay of the clock occurs, a reset pulse is applied to the AND gates of each latch. This pulse resets the register to 0, except for those elements in which a 1 bit appears on the input data bus.

The design of registers D and B is different, because they must not only store information but must also execute a right shift. Each element in the registers consists of a *JK* master-slave flip-flop, as shown in Fig. 3.5. A master-slave flip-flop is utilized to guarantee that the outputs will not change state during a shift operation until the clock pulse becomes inactive.

The logic diagram for registers C, D, and B is shown in Fig. 3.6. This illustrates the parallel-load capability and the concatenated right-shift function of the three registers. The design process for the count-down counter is shown in Fig. 3.7 (for simplicity, only the four low-order elements are shown), and the logic diagram is illustrated in Fig. 3.8. This counter design requires that the counter be reset before being loaded. This should not be a cause for concern in most designs. However, an alternative approach is shown in Fig. 3.9, in which a prior reset is not required. This typical counter element uses the same clock pulse for both load and count functions. Note also that the output of each stage of the counter is propagated serially to each of the higher-order stages. There is more than enough time for this propagation to take place in this type of add-shift multiply operation, because the propagation of the flip-flop outputs has most of the cycle time to stabilize. If a faster propagation time is required, then simply use the method shown in Fig. 3.10. Alternatively, a count-up counter could be used to count up from 0 to n, where n is the number of bits in the multiplier. The adder is a carry lookahead design, which was described in Sec. 2.2.3.

3.3 BOOTH ALGORITHM

This section will describe the Booth algorithm, which is a powerful direct algorithm for signed-number multiplication. It generates a $2n$-bit product and treats both positive and negative numbers uniformly. Section 3.4 will describe the hardware associated with a multiplication speedup technique that is derived from the Booth algorithm.

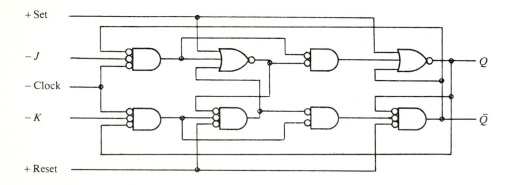

Figure 3.5 *JK* master-slave flip-flop used in registers C, D, and B.

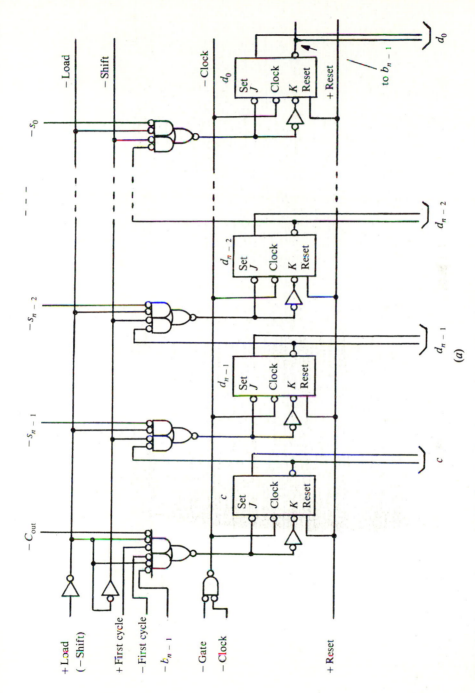

Figure 3.6 (*a*) Logic diagram for flip-flop *C* and register *D*; (*b*) logic diagram for register *B*.

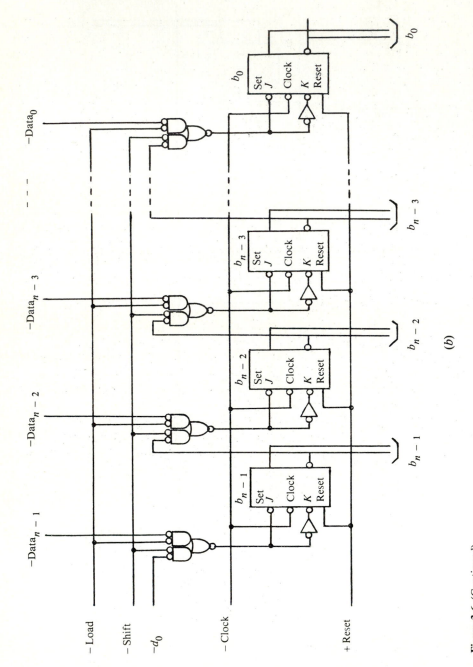

Figure 3.6 (Continued)

150

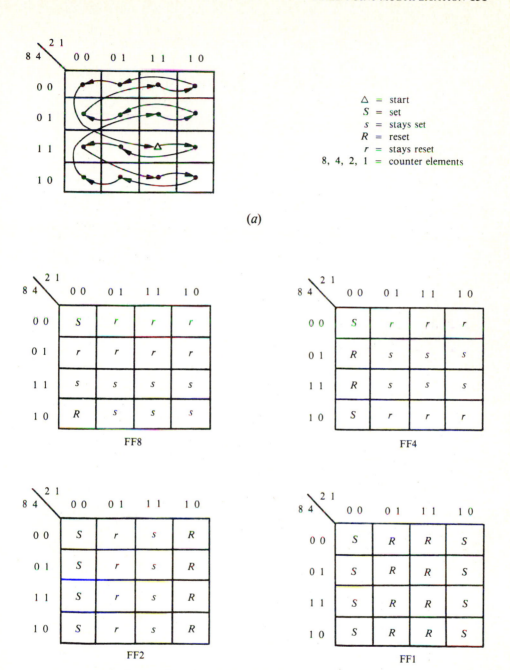

Figure 3.7 Synthesis of count-down counter (15–0). (*a*) Transition diagram; (*b*) next-state maps; (*c*) excitation maps for counter elements 8 and 4; and (*d*) excitation maps for counter elements 2 and 1.

8 4 \ 2 1	0 0	0 1	1 1	1 0
0 0	1	0	0	0
0 1	0	0	0	0
1 1	x	x	x	x
1 0	x	x	x	x

J8

$$J8 = \overline{4} \wedge \overline{2} \wedge \overline{1}$$

8 4 \ 2 1	0 0	0 1	1 1	1 0
0 0	x	x	x	x
0 1	x	x	x	x
1 1	0	0	0	0
1 0	1	0	0	0

K8

$$K8 = \overline{4} \wedge \overline{2} \wedge \overline{1}$$

8 4 \ 2 1	0 0	0 1	1 1	1 0
0 0	1	0	0	0
0 1	x	x	x	x
1 1	x	x	x	x
1 0	1	0	0	0

J4

$$J4 = \overline{2} \wedge \overline{1}$$

8 4 \ 2 1	0 0	0 1	1 1	1 0
0 0	x	x	x	x
0 1	1	0	0	0
1 1	1	0	0	0
1 0	x	x	x	x

K4

$$K4 = \overline{2} \wedge \overline{1}$$

(c)

Figure 3.7 (Continued)

In the standard add-shift method, each multiplier bit generates one multiple of the multiplicand to be added to the partial product. When the multiplier becomes large, this means that a large number of multiplicands have to be added. The execution time of a multiply instruction is determined mainly by the number of additions to be performed. Therefore, it is desirable to reduce the number of additions. A bit-scanning method is now presented that will reduce the number of multiplicand multiples. This is based on the fact that the execution time can be reduced by shifting across a string of 0s in a recoded version of the multiplier. This process is often referred to as *skipping over 0s* and can be generalized to shifts of variable lengths if strings of 0s can be detected. The greater the number of 0s in the multiplier, the faster the operation. Consider a string of k consecutive 1s in the multiplier as shown below.

$$\cdots, i + k, i + k - 1, i + k - 2, \cdots, i, i - 1, \cdots$$
$$\cdots, \quad 0 \quad, \quad 1 \quad, \quad 1 \quad, \cdots, 1, \quad 0 \quad, \cdots$$
$$\underbrace{\qquad\qquad\qquad\qquad\qquad}_{k \text{ consecutive 1s}}$$

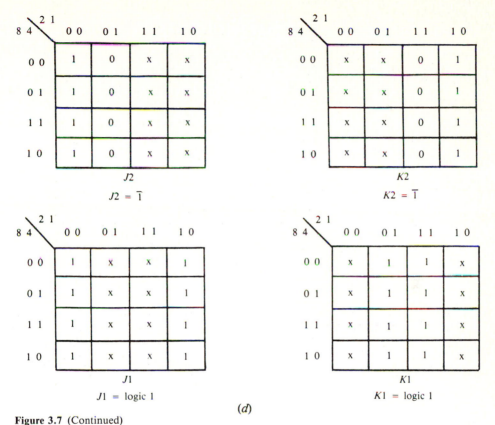

Figure 3.7 (Continued)

By using the following property of binary strings

$$2^{i+k} - 2^i = 2^{i+k-1} + 2^{i+k-2} + \cdots + 2^{i+1} + 2^i$$

the k consecutive 1s can be replaced by the following string

$$\cdots, i+k+1, i+k, i+k-1, \cdots, i+1, i, i-1, \cdots$$

$$\cdots, \quad 0 \quad, \quad 1 \quad, \quad 0 \quad, \cdots, \quad 0 \quad, -1, \quad 0 \quad, \cdots$$

$$\underbrace{}_{k-1 \text{ consecutive 0s}}$$

$$\uparrow \qquad\qquad\qquad\qquad\qquad \uparrow$$

Addition $\qquad\qquad\qquad\qquad$ Subtraction $\qquad\qquad$ (3.1)

The procedure is easier to understand if two dummy digits $b_n = b_{-1} = 0$ are attached to both ends of an n-digit binary multiplier vector B, where

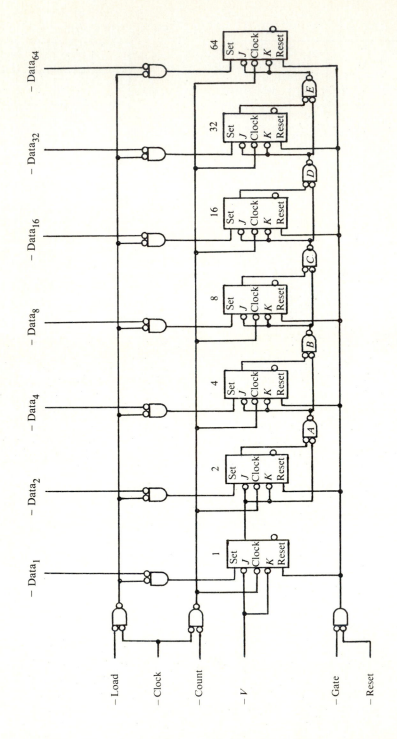

Figure 3.8 Parallel-load count-down counter. When the output of any AND gate (*A*, *B*, *C*, *D*, or *E*) is low, the next higher-order flip-flop will change state at the next clock pulse. For example, the output of AND gate *B* can be labeled: " – change state of FF8."

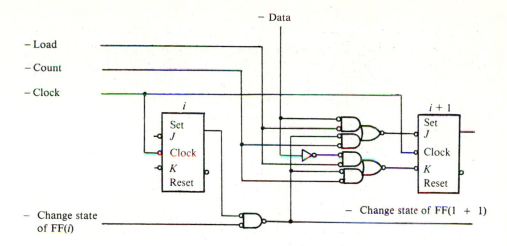

Figure 3.9 Parallel load, using the same pulse for load/count.

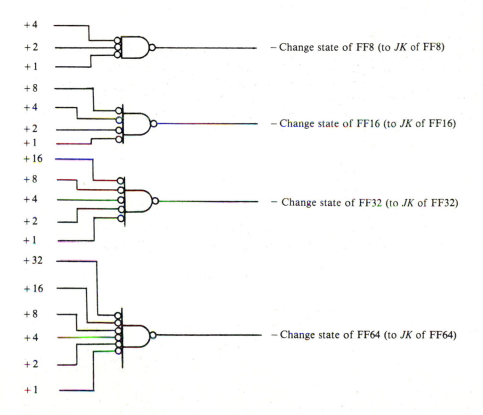

Figure 3.10 Logic for fast propagation of counter states.

$$B = b_{n-1} \, b_{n-2} \cdots b_1 \, b_0$$

This will be more apparent when negative multipliers are discussed.

Consider a multiplication example in which a positive multiplier has a single block of 1s with at least one 0 at each end, for example, 0 0 1 1 1 1 0. The product could be derived by adding four appropriately shifted versions of the multiplicands as in the standard procedure. However, the number of additions can be reduced by observing that a multiplier in this form can be regarded as the difference of two numbers as follows:

$$
\begin{array}{ll}
0\;1\;0\;0\;0\;0\;0 & (32) \\
-)\;0\;0\;0\;0\;0\;1\;0 & (\;2) \\
\hline
0\;0\;1\;1\;1\;1\;0 & (30)
\end{array}
$$

This was shown in Eq. 3.1 and indicates that the product can be generated by one addition and one subtraction, that is, by adding 32 and subtracting 2. In particular, in the above example, adding 2^5 times the multiplicand and subtracting 2^1 times the multiplicand gives the desired result.

In the standard representation, the multiplier can be written as

$$0 \quad 0 +1 +1 +1 +1 \quad 0$$

and the recoded multiplier written as

$$0 +1 \quad 0 \quad 0 \quad 0 -1 \quad 0$$

Note that -1 times the left-shifted multiplicand occurs at 0 to 1 boundaries and $+1$ times the left-shifted multiplicand occurs at 1 to 0 boundaries as the multiplier is scanned from right to left. Figure 3.11 illustrates the two methods. This procedure can be extended to any number of blocks of 1s in a multiplier, including the case in which a single 1 is considered a block.

Before showing an example of how the Booth technique can be applied to a negative multiplier, some properties will be given for negative number representation in 2s complement form. Let

$$B = 1 \, b_{n-2} \, b_{n-3} \cdots b_1 \, b_0$$

be an n-bit negative number with a value given by

$$V(B) = -2^{n-1} + b_{n-2} \, 2^{n-2} + b_{n-3} \, 2^{n-3} + \cdots + b_1 2^1 + b_0 2^0$$

$$(3.2)$$

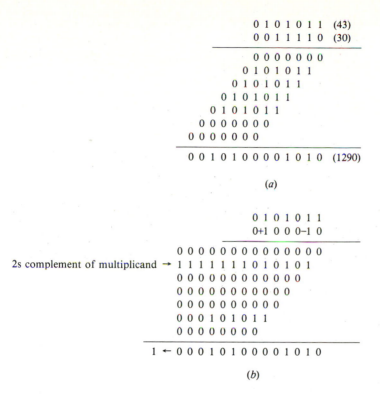

```
              0 1 0 1 0 1 1  (43)
              0 0 1 1 1 1 0  (30)
          ─────────────────
            0 0 0 0 0 0 0
          0 1 0 1 0 1 1
        0 1 0 1 0 1 1
      0 1 0 1 0 1 1
    0 1 0 1 0 1 1
  0 0 0 0 0 0 0
0 0 0 0 0 0 0
─────────────────────────────
0 0 1 0 1 0 0 0 0 1 0 1 0  (1290)
```

(a)

```
                                    0 1 0 1 0 1 1
                                    0+1 0 0 0−1 0
                              ─────────────────────
                              0 0 0 0 0 0 0 0 0 0 0 0 0 0
2s complement of multiplicand →   1 1 1 1 1 1 1 0 1 0 1 0 1
                              0 0 0 0 0 0 0 0 0 0 0 0
                              0 0 0 0 0 0 0 0 0 0 0
                              0 0 0 0 0 0 0 0 0
                              0 0 0 1 0 1 0 1 1
                              0 0 0 0 0 0 0 0
                          ──────────────────────────────
                        1 ← 0 0 0 1 0 1 0 0 0 0 0 1 0 1 0
```

(b)

Figure 3.11 Two multiplication methods: (a) normal, (b) with Booth recoding.

This can be verified from the following examples.

$$V\,(1\;0\;0\;1\;1) = -2^4 + 0 + 0 + 2^1 + 2^0 = -13$$
$$V\,(1\;1\;1\;0\;0) = -2^4 + 2^3 + 2^2 + 0 + 0 = -4$$

If B is a multiplier and has no 0s, then $B = 1\;1\;\cdots\;1\;1$ and the value of B is $V(B) = -1$, which is correct for 2s complement representation. Applying the Booth technique for recoding the multiplier and letting dummy bit $b_{-1} = 0$, B is interpreted as $0\;0\;\cdots\;0 - 1$. This is obtained from the 0 to 1 boundary at the right end of the multiplier. The product is then computed as the negative of the multiplicand, which is correct. However, if B has at least one 0 and the left-most 0 is in position b_k, then B has the form $1\;1\;\cdots\;1\;0\;b_{k-1}$ $b_{k-2}\;\cdots\;b_1 b_0$. After recoding the rightmost $k + 1$ bits $(0\;b_{k-1}\;b_{k-2}\;\cdots\;b_1 b_0)$ and using this vector to add the appropriately shifted multiplicands, a correct partial product up to this point is obtained. In other words, $0\;b_{k-1}\;b_{k-2}\;\cdots\;b_1 b_0$ times the multiplicand has been correctly calculated according to the previous interpretation. It remains to compute

$1_{n-1} 1_{n-2} \cdots 1_{k+1}$ times the multiplicand portion of the multiplication and add the partial product thus obtained to the previous partial product to obtain the product. This can be accomplished by using the method established in Eq. 3.2 on the vector $1_{n-1} 1_{n-2} \cdots 1_{k+1}$ to obtain

$$(-2^{n-1} + 2^{n-2} + \cdots + 2^{k+1}) \times \text{multiplicand} \qquad (3.3)$$

But, it was previously shown that a vector $(1 \ 1 \ \cdots \ 1 \ 1)$ had the value -1, that is, -2^0. Therefore, Eq. 3.3 reduces to

$$-2^{k+1} \times \text{multiplicand} \qquad (3.4)$$

which is exactly what happens when crossing a 0 to 1 boundary with a 1 in the kth position. That is, a multiplier vector of the form

$$\underbrace{1 \ 1 \ 1 \ 1 \ 1 \ 1}_{\displaystyle 0 \ 0 \ 0 \ 0 \ 0 \ 1} 0 \ b_{k-1} \ b_{k-2} \cdots b_1 \ b_0$$

has the $k + 1$ low-order bits recoded as previously shown and the high-order string of 1s simply recoded as -1 with a string of 0s to the left. The sign extension of vector B is nothing more than a string of 1s for a negative number. Thus, the Booth recoded multiplier algorithm works equally well for both positive and negative numbers. Figure 3.12 shows Booth multiplication with a negative multiplier.

```
0 1 0 1 1  (+11)              0 1 0 1 1
1 1 0 1 0  ( -6)              0-1+1-1 0
                   _____
                   0 0 0 0 0 0 0 0 0 0
                   1 1 1 1 1 0 1 0 1
                   0 0 0 0 1 0 1 1
                   1 1 1 0 1 0 1
                   0 0 0 0 0 0
                   _____
                   1 1 1 1 0 1 1 1 1 1 0  (-66)
```

Figure 3.12 Booth multiplication with a negative multiplier.

The transformation that takes

$$0 \ 1 \ 1 \cdots 1 \ 1 \ 0 \qquad \text{into} \qquad +1 \ 0 \ 0 \cdots 0 \ -1 \ 0$$

is often referred to as the technique of skipping over 1s. The reasoning is that in cases in which the multiplier has its 1s grouped into a few blocks, only a few versions of the multiplicand need to be added to generate the product. If only a few additions are required, the multiplication process becomes much faster. In the worst-case situation when the multiplier is of the form 0 1 0 1 · · · 0 1 0 1 or 1 0 1 0 · · · 1 0 1 0 (alternating 1s and 0s), there is no skipping. In fact, more additions are required than if the algorithm was not used. Table 3.1 shows a worst-case multiplier, a normal multiplier, and a good multiplier—each with its corresponding recoded vector. The recoding technique for multipliers is summarized in Table 3.2.

Table 3.1 Booth recoded multipliers

Worst case	0	1	0	1	0	1	0	1	0	1	0	1	0	1	0	1
Normal	1	1	0	0	1	0	0	1	1	0	0	1	1	1	1	0
Good	0	0	0	0	1	1	1	1	1	0	0	0	0	1	1	1

Worst case	+1	−1	+1	−1	+1	−1	+1	−1	+1	−1	+1	−1	+1	−1	+1	−1
Normal	0	−1	0	+1	−1	0	+1	0	−1	0	+1	0	0	0	−1	0
Good	0	0	0	+1	0	0	0	0	−1	0	0	0	+1	0	0	−1

The Booth algorithm achieves two purposes. First, it uniformly transforms both positive and negative n-bit multipliers into a form that selects appropriate versions of n-bit multiplicands, which are added to the shifted partial products to produce a $2n$-bit product in the 2s complement number representation. Secondly, it increases the speed of the multiply operation when the multiplier has blocks of 1s. This is particularly true when the multiplier has long strings of 1s or 0s in the high-order part, indicating a small absolute-valued number. Since the speed of the multiply operation depends on the bit configuration of the multiplier, the efficiency of the Booth algorithm is obviously data-dependent.

Table 3.2 Booth multiplier recoding table

Multiplier		Version of multiplicand
Bit i	Bit $i - 1$	determined by bit i
0	0	0 × multiplicand
0	1	+1 × multiplicand
1	0	−1 × multiplicand
1	1	0 × multiplicand

3.4 BIT-PAIR RECODING

Section 3.3 discussed the Booth algorithm, which increases the speed of a multiply operation by skipping over 1s in the multiplier. The amount of increase in speed depended upon the bit configuration of the multiplier. In this section, a multiplication speedup technique will be described that guarantees that an n-bit multiplier will generate at most $n/2$ partial products. It can multiply two 2s complement numbers directly without regard for the signs of the two numbers. In other words, there is no need for precomplementing the multiplier or postcomplementing the product. The product is in the 2s complement number representation. This represents a multiplication speed increase of almost a factor of 2 over the standard add-shift method.

The new technique is derived from the Booth technique. Recall the example in Sec. 3.3 of a multiplication operation in which a positive multiplier had a single block of 1s (0 0 1 1 1 1 0). The product could be obtained by adding four appropriately shifted versions of the multiplicand as in the standard procedure, or the number of operations could be reduced by observing that the multiplier in this form could be regarded as the difference of two numbers as shown below.

$$2^6 \ 2^5 \ 2^4 \ 2^3 \ 2^2 \ 2^1 \ 2^0$$

$$
\begin{array}{r}
0 \ 1 \ 0 \ 0 \ 0 \ 0 \ 0 \quad (32) \\
-) \ 0 \ 0 \ 0 \ 0 \ 0 \ 1 \ 0 \quad (\ 2) \\
\hline
\text{Multiplier} \quad 0 \ 0 \ 1 \ 1 \ 1 \ 1 \ 0 \quad (30)
\end{array}
$$

This indicates that the number 0 0 1 1 1 1 0 (30) has the same value as

$$2^5 - 2^1 = 32 - 2 = 30$$

This is true for any number of contiguous 1s, including the case in which there is a single 1 with 0s on either side. This is an extremely important concept, because the entire technique of bit-pair recoding revolves around this method of regarding a string of 1s as the difference of two numbers. This string property is restated below.

$$2^{i+k} - 2^i = 2^{i+k-1} + 2^{i+k-2} + \cdots + 2^{i+1} + 2^i \quad (3.5)$$

where k is the number of consecutive 1s and i is the position of the rightmost 1 in the string of 1s under consideration. In the above multiplier example, $k = 4$ and $i = 1$ (2^1) such that Eq. 3.5 yields

$$2^{1+4} - 2^1 = 2^{1+4-1} + 2^{1+4-2} + 2^{1+4-3} + 2^{1+4-4}$$
$$2^5 - 2^1 = 2^4 + 2^3 + 2^2 + 2^1$$
$$30 = 30$$

Note that the rightmost term of the first line is actually $2^1 = 2^i$, which is the rightmost entry in Eq. 3.5

Consider two more examples

$$2^4 \quad 2^3 \quad 2^2 \quad 2^1 \quad 2^0$$

$$0 \quad 0 \quad 1 \quad 0 \quad 0$$

which, using Eq. 3.5, yields

$$2^{i+k} - 2^i = 2^{2+1} - 2^2 = 8 - 4 = 4$$

and

$$2^4 \quad 2^3 \quad 2^2 \quad 2^1 \quad 2^0$$

$$0 \quad 0 \quad 1 \quad 1 \quad 0$$

which, using Eq. 3.5, yields

$$2^{i+k} - 2^i = 2^{1+2} - 2^1 = 8 - 2 = 6$$

Return to the multiplier on p.160 and scan it from right to left, bit by bit. In going from 0 (2^0) to 1 (2^1), we saw previously that this resulted in subtracting the value of the 1 in that position, in this case $- 2^1$. Scanning from 1 (2^1) to 1 (2^2) resulted in no change, that is, neither addition nor subtraction. The same is true in scanning from 1 (2^2) to 1 (2^3), and from 1 (2^3) to 1 (2^4). However, in going from 1 (2^4) to 0 (2^5), we saw that this resulted in an addition of 2^5. There is no change in scanning from 0 (2^5) to 0 (2^6). The results of scanning this multiplier are as follows: 2^1 was subtracted and 2^5 was added.

The same results can be obtained by looking at pairs of bits in the multiplier in conjunction with the bit that is to the right of the bit pair being considered, as shown below.

$$2^6 \quad 2^5 \quad 2^4 \quad 2^3 \quad 2^2 \quad 2^1 \quad 2^0$$

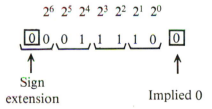

Sign
extension

Implied 0

That is, bit pair 2^1, 2^0 is examined with an implied 0 to the right of the low-order bit; bit pair 2^3, 2^2 is examined with bit 2^1; bit pair 2^5, 2^4 is examined with bit 2^3; and bit-pair 2^7, 2^6 is examined with bit 2^5. Bit 2^7 is simply the sign extension of the multiplier. Scanning the bit pairs from right to left and using the rightmost bit of each pair as the column reference for the partial product placement (because it is the center bit of the three bits being examined), we obtain the following additions and subtractions on the multiplicand:

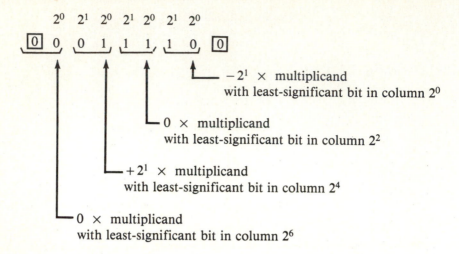

Only binary weights 2^1, 2^0 are used, because each bit pair is examined independently of other bit pairs.

Since each bit pair is examined concurrently with the high-order bit of the next lower pair, there are a total of eight possible versions of the multiplicand. This is shown in Table 3.3.

Consider the following bit combination, which is a string of one 1; that is, it is both the beginning and end of a string.

$$2^1 \quad 2^0$$
$$0 \quad 1 \quad 0$$

$-2^0 \times$ multiplicand $\quad \} \quad (+2^1 - 2^0) \times$ multiplicand

$+2^1 \times$ multiplicand $\quad \} \quad = +1 \times$ multiplicand

The beginning of the string specifies that $-2^0 \times$ multiplicand is added to the partial product; the end of the string specifies that $+2^1$ is to be added. The net result of this string is that $+1 \times$ multiplicand is added to the partial product starting at the appropriate column. Similarly,

$$2^1 \quad 2^0$$
$$1 \quad 0 \quad 1$$

$+2^0 \times$ multiplicand $\quad \} \quad (-2^1 + 2^0) \times$ multiplicand

$-2^1 \times$ multiplicand $\quad \} \quad = -1 \times$ multiplicand

Table 3.3 Multiplier bit-pair recoding

Multiplier bit-pair		Multiplier bit on the right	Multiplicand multiples	
2^1	2^0			
$i + 1$	i	$i - 1$	to be added	Explanation
0	0	0	$0 \times$ multiplicand	No string
0	0	1	$+1 \times$ multiplicand	End of string
0	1	0	$+1 \times$ multiplicand	Single 1 $(+2 - 1)$
0	1	1	$+2 \times$ multiplicand	End of string
1	0	0	$-2 \times$ multiplicand	Beginning of string
1	0	1	$-1 \times$ multiplicand	End/beginning of string $(+1 - 2)$
1	1	0	$-1 \times$ multiplicand	Beginning of string
1	1	1	$0 \times$ multiplicand	String of 1s

Note that $-2 \times$ multiplicand is actually the 2s complement of the multiplicand with an equivalent left shift of one bit position. This multiplies the 2s complement by two. Also, $+2 \times$ multiplicand is the multiplicand shifted left one bit position, which is equivalent to multiplying by 2.

Figure 3.13 shows an example of the normal, Booth, and bit-pair recoding multiplication techniques. Six additional examples are shown in Fig. 3.14 using different combinations of positive and negative multiplicands and multipliers, and using different versions of the multiplicands depicted in Table 3.3.

3.4.1 Hardware Organization

Two hardware implementations using bit-pair recoding will now be presented. One implementation uses the basic components found in the sequential add-shift technique of Sec. 3.2, with some added hardware for bit-pair recoding and shift control. The other uses a planar array to implement 2s complement multiplication combinationally.

3.4.2 Sequential Add-Shift

Figure 3.15 shows three examples of the hardware algorithm that will be used for the add-shift method. An $(n + 1)$-bit adder is required to allow for the case where $\pm 2 \times$ multiplicand is entered into the adder. In this case, the multiplicand is offset one bit to the left when it is entered into the adder and a 0 is forced in the low-order multiplicand position. When the partial product is shifted two bit positions to the right, the sign is extended to the left.

Different versions of the multiplicand are added to the new partial product during each add-shift cycle. The equations determining the version of the multiplicand to be used are described below. These equations are derived directly from the bit-pair recoding table of Table 3.3.

```
        0 0 0 0 1 1  (+3)
    ×) 0 1 1 1 0 1  (+29)
    ─────────────────
        0 0 0 0 1 1
        0 0 0 0 0 0
      0 0 0 0 1 1
    0 0 0 0 1 1
  0 0 0 0 1 1
0 0 0 0 0 0
────────────────────────
0 0 0 0 1 0 1 0 1 1 1  (+87)
```

(*a*)

```
                0 0 0 0 1 1
          ×) +1 0 0–1 0 1
────────────────────────────
0 0 0 0 0 0 0 0 0 0 1 1
0 0 0 0 0 0 0 0 0 0 0
1 1 1 1 1 1 1 1 0 1      ←  2s complement
0 0 0 0 0 0 0 0 0            of multiplicand
0 0 0 0 0 0 0 0
0 0 0 0 1 1
────────────────────────────
0 0 0 0 1 0 1 0 1 1 1  (+87)
```

(*b*)

M = multiplicand

```
                0   0   0   0   1   1
          ×) 0 .1   1   1   0   1   0
             ‿‿‿    ‿‿‿    ‿‿‿
            +2×M  −1×M  +1×M

     0   0   0   0   0   0   0   0   0   0   1   1
     1   1   1   1   1   1   1   1   1   0   1
     0   0   0   0   0   1   1   0
────────────────────────────────────────────────
 1 ← 0   0   0   0   0   1   0   1   0   1   1   1  (+87)
```

(*c*)

Figure 3.13 Multiplication techniques: (*a*) normal, (*b*) Booth, and (*c*) bit-pair recoding requiring only *n*/2 partial products.

Example 1

$$
\begin{array}{r}
1\ 1\ 1\ 1\ 0\ 1 \quad (-3)\\
\times)\ \underbrace{0\ 1,}\ \underbrace{1\ 1,}\ \underbrace{0\ 1}\ \boxed{0} \quad (+29)\\
\hline
+2\ \ -1\ \ +1
\end{array}
$$

1 1 1 1 1 1 1 1 1 1 0 1

2s complement of multiplicand ⟶ 0 0 0 0 0 0 0 0 1 1

1 1 1 1 1 0 1 0

1 ← 1 1 1 1 1 0 1 0 1 0 0 1   (−87)

Example 2

$$
\begin{array}{r}
1\ 1\ 1\ 1\ 0\ 1 \quad (-3)\\
\times)\ \underbrace{1\ 0,}\ \underbrace{0\ 0,}\ \underbrace{1\ 1}\ \boxed{0} \quad (-29)\\
\hline
-2\ \ +1\ \ -1
\end{array}
$$

0 0 0 0 0 0 0 0 0 0 1 1

1 1 1 1 1 1 1 1 0 1

Shifted 2s complement ⟶ 0 0 0 0 0 1 1 0

1 ← 0 0 0 0 0 1 0 1 0 1 1 1   (+87)

Example 3

Sign extension ⟶

$$
\begin{array}{r}
0\ 0\ 1\ 1\ 0 \quad (+6)\\
\times)\ \boxed{1}\ \underbrace{1\ 0,}\ \underbrace{0\ 1\ 0}\ \boxed{0} \quad (-14)\\
\hline
-1\ \ +1\ \ -2
\end{array}
$$

1 1 1 1 1 1 0 1 0 0

0 0 0 0 0 1 1 0

1 1 1 0 1 0

1 ← 1 1 1 0 1 0 1 1 0 0   (−84)

(*a*)

Figure 3.14 Multiplication examples using bit-pair recoding.

Example 4

$$
\begin{array}{r}
0\ 1\ 1\ 0\ 1\ 1 \qquad (+27)\\
\boxed{1}\ 1\ 0\ 0\ 0\ 1\ 0\ \boxed{0} \qquad (-30)\\
\hline
-2\ \ +1\ \ -2\\
\end{array}
$$

$$
\begin{array}{r}
1\ 1\ 1\ 1\ 1\ 1\ 0\ 0\ 1\ 0\ 1\ 0\\
0\ 0\ 0\ 0\ 0\ 1\ 1\ 0\ 1\ 1\\
1\ 1\ 0\ 0\ 1\ 0\ 1\ 0\\
\hline
1\ \leftarrow\ 1\ 1\ 0\ 0\ 1\ 1\ 0\ 1\ 0\ 1\ 1\ 0 \qquad (-810)
\end{array}
$$

Example 5

$$
\begin{array}{r}
0\ 0\ 0\ 1\ 1 \qquad (+3)\\
\boxed{1}\ 1\ 0\ 0\ 1\ 1\ \boxed{0} \qquad (-13)\\
\hline
-1\ \ +1\ \ -1\\
\end{array}
$$

$$
\begin{array}{r}
1\ 1\ 1\ 1\ 1\ 1\ 1\ 1\ 0\ 1\\
0\ 0\ 0\ 0\ 0\ 0\ 1\ 1\\
1\ 1\ 1\ 1\ 0\ 1\\
\hline
1\ \leftarrow\ 1\ 1\ 1\ 1\ 0\ 1\ 1\ 0\ 0\ 1 \qquad (-39)
\end{array}
$$

Example 6

$$
\begin{array}{r}
0\ 0\ 0\ 1\ 0\ 1 \qquad (+5)\\
1\ 0\ 0\ 1\ 1\ 0\ \boxed{0} \qquad (-26)\\
\hline
-2\ \ +2\ \ -2\\
\end{array}
$$

$$
\begin{array}{r}
1\ 1\ 1\ 1\ 1\ 1\ 1\ 1\ 0\ 1\ 1\ 0\\
0\ 0\ 0\ 0\ 0\ 0\ 1\ 0\ 1\ 0\\
1\ 1\ 1\ 1\ 0\ 1\ 1\ 0\\
\hline
1\ \leftarrow\ 1\ 1\ 1\ 1\ 0\ 1\ 1\ 1\ 1\ 1\ 1\ 0 \qquad (-130)
\end{array}
$$

(*b*)

Figure 3.14 (Continued)

	n	n−1	·	·	·	1	0							
	0	0	0	0	0	0	0							
+1 × multiplicand	1	1	1	1	1	0	1							
	1	1	1	1	1	0	1							
SR2	1	1	1	1	1	1	1	0	1					Partial product 0 (PP0)
−1 × multiplicand	0	0	0	0	0	1	1							
	0	0	0	0	0	1	0							
SR2	0	0	0	0	0	0	0	1	0	0	1			PP1
+2 × multiplicand	1	1	1	1	0	1	0							
	1	1	1	1	0	1	0							
SR2		1	1	1	1	1	0	1	0	1	0	0	1	PP2
Product		1	1	1	1	1	0	1	0	1	0	0	1	(−87)

SR2 = shift right two bit positions

(a)

	n	n−1	·	·	·	1	0							
	0	0	0	0	0	0	0							
−2 × multiplicand	1	0	0	1	0	1	0							
	1	0	0	1	0	1	0							
SR2	1	1	1	0	0	1	0	1	0					PP0
+1 × multiplicand	0	0	1	1	0	1	1							
	0	0	0	1	1	0	1							
SR2	0	0	0	0	0	1	1	0	1	1	0			PP1
−2 × multiplicand	1	0	0	1	0	1	0							
	1	0	0	1	1	0	1							
SR2		1	1	0	0	1	1	0	1	0	1	1	0	PP2
Product		1	1	0	0	1	1	0	1	0	1	1	0	(−810)

(b)

Figure 3.15 Hardware add-shift algorithm for bit-pair recoding for (a) Example 1 of Fig. 3.14(a); (b) Example 4 of Fig. 3.14(b); and (c) Example 6 of Fig. 3.14(b). For ±2 × the multiplicand, the multiplicand is offset one bit to the left when entered into the adder and a 0 is forced in the low-order bit position.

	n	n−1	·	·	·	1	0							
	0	0	0	0	0	0	0							
−2 × multiplicand	1	1	1	0	1	1	0							
	1	1	1	0	1	1	0							
SR2	1	1	1	1	1	0	1	1	0					*PP*0
+2 × multiplicand	0	0	0	1	0	1	0							
	0	0	0	0	1	1	1							
SR2	0	0	0	0	0	0	1	1	1	1	0			*PP*1
−2 × multiplicand	1	1	1	0	1	1	0							
	1	1	1	0	1	1	1							
SR2	1	1	1	1	0	1	1	1	1	1	1	0		*PP*2
Product	1	1	1	1	0	1	1	1	1	1	1	0		(−130)

(c)

Figure 3.15 (Continued)

(0) Do not add the multiplicand to the partial product (add 0s instead). Then shift two bit positions to the right.

$$(\overline{i+1})\,(\bar{i})\,(\overline{i-1}) \quad \lor \quad (i+1)\,(i)\,(i-1)$$

(+1) Add the multiplicand to the partial product. Then shift two bit positions to the right.

$$(\overline{i+1})\,(\bar{i})\,(i-1) \quad \lor \quad (\overline{i+1})\,(i)\,(\overline{i-1}) = (\overline{i+1})\,[(i) \; \veebar \; (i-1)]$$

(−1) Add the 2s complement of the multiplicand to the partial product. Then shift two bit positions to the right.

$$(i+1)\,(\bar{i})\,(i-1) \quad \lor \quad (i+1)\,(i)\,(\overline{i-1}) = (i+1)\,[(i) \; \veebar \; (i-1)]$$

(+2) Add two times the multiplicand to the partial product. (Offset this row of summands one bit position to the left.) Then shift two bit positions to the right.

$$(\overline{i+1})\,(i)\,(i-1)$$

(−2) Add two times the 2s complement of the multiplicand to the partial product. (Offset this row of summands one bit position to the left.) Then shift two bit positions to the right.

$$(i+1)\,(\bar{i})\,(\overline{i-1})$$

The logic diagrams for the preceding equations are shown in Fig. 3.16.

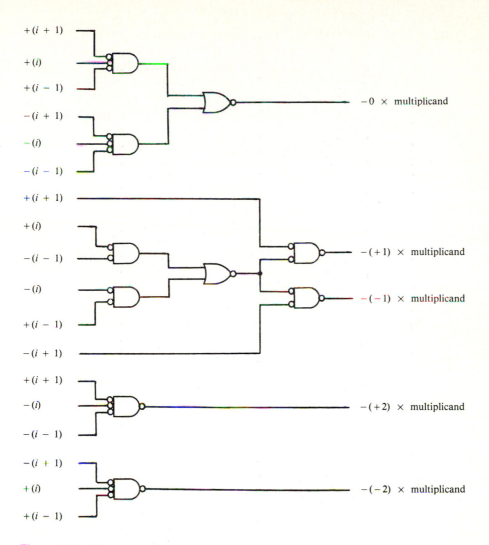

Figure 3.16 Logic diagrams to select appropriate versions of the multiplicand.

The hardware organization to implement the bit-pair recoding technique for sequential add-shift multiplication is shown in Fig. 3.17. This is essentially the same hardware that was used in the normal add-shift technique described in Sec. 3.2, with the exception that three bits are now employed in the multiplier to decode the version of the multiplicand that is to be used and a multiplexer is employed to selectively gate the different versions to the adder. Four $(n + 1)$-bit parallel-load registers are required—multiplier register B; register D, which contains the high-order n bits of the partial product; multiplicand register A; and register C, which contains the 2s complement of the multiplicand. A 5-to-1 multiplexer gates a logic 0 to the adder, the multiplicand, two times the multiplicand, the 2s complement of the multiplicand, or two times the 2s complement of the multiplicand. The decoder is illustrated by the logic diagrams in Fig. 3.16, in which the five exclusive outputs select one of the multiplicand versions for the adder. An $(n + 1)$-bit parallel adder with carry lookahead is required to generate the partial products from the sum of the multiplicand and the previous partial product. The adder is of the type previously described and requires $n + 1$ bits instead of n bits, because ± 2 times the multiplicand shifts the multiplicand version one bit to the left. A counter is also needed to determine when the multiply operation is complete.

The multiplier, the multiplicand, and the 2s complement of the multiplicand are initially loaded into registers B, A, and C, respectively. When registers A and C are loaded, the sign bit is extended to the left one bit position; that is, $a_n = a_{n-1}$ and $c_n = c_{n-1}$. Bit position b_{-1} of register B should be initialized to 0 and the initial contents of D should be 0, corresponding to an initial partial product of 0.

The following operations take place during each add-shift cycle. The sequence can best be understood by referring to Fig. 3.18 during the discussion that follows. This figure depicts the sequence that takes place during the multiply operation of multiplicand 1 1 1 1 0 1 (-3) and multiplier 0 1 1 1 0 1 ($+29$). Multiplier bits b_1, b_0, and b_{-1} are decoded to select the $+1$ version of the multiplicand to be added to the partial product. The sum output of the adder

$$S = s_n s_{n-1} \cdot \cdot \cdot s_1 s_0$$

is loaded into register D positions $d_n d_{n-1} \cdot \cdot \cdot d_1 d_0$. Registers D and B are then shifted two bit positions to the right. There is a uniform two-bit right shift per step. Bit positions $d_n d_{n-1} \cdot \cdot \cdot d_1 d_0 b_{n-1} b_{n-2}$ contain partial product 0 (PP0). The new contents of $b_1 b_0 b_{-1}$ are now decoded to again select a particular version of the multiplicand to be added to partial product 0. In this case, -1 times the multiplicand is selected. The sum output of the adder is again loaded into register D, and a double right shift takes place as before. Partial product 1 is located in $d_n d_{n-1} \cdot \cdot \cdot d_1 d_0 b_{n-1} \cdot \cdot \cdot b_2$. Finally, $b_1 b_0 b_{-1}$ select $+2$ times the multiplicand, which is added to partial product 1 and loaded into register D. The contents of D and B are shifted two bit positions to the right, and the final product is contained in $d_{n-1} \cdot \cdot \cdot d_1 d_0 b_{n-1} \cdot \cdot \cdot b_1 b_0$. Thus, after n cycles ($n = 3$ in this example), the high-order half of the product is held in register D and the low-order half is in register B, with the multiplier having been shifted out of the right end of register B.

The design of registers A and C is shown in Fig. 3.19. Note that the contents of bits n and $n - 1$ are identical; bit n is simply the sign extension. The $n + 1$ bits of A and C correspond to the $n + 1$ bits of the adder. The logic diagram for register D is contained in Fig. 3.20. Each element in register D as well as in register B consists of a JK master-slave flip-flop.

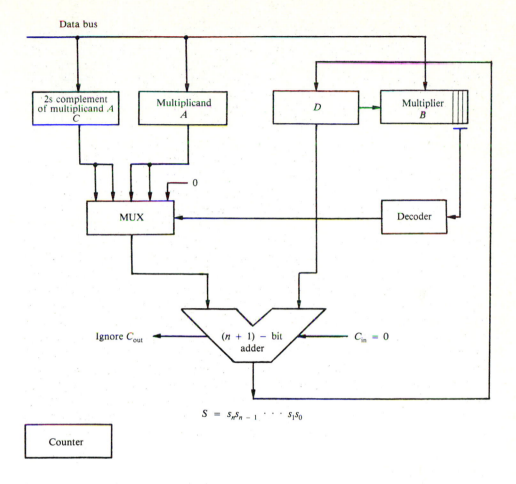

Figure 3.17 Hardware organization for bit-pair recoding multiplication.

Register D bit positions $d_n d_{n-1} \cdots d_1 d_0$ are loaded from the adder outputs $s_n s_{n-1} \cdots s_1 s_0$, respectively. During a shift operation, the sign is maintained in position d_n according to the following function

$$d_n \cdot d_{n-1} \cdot d_{n-2} \leftarrow d_n$$
$$d_{i-2} \leftarrow d_i$$

where the center dot ($\cdot$) indicates concatenation. Multiplier register B is illustrated in Fig. 3.21 and shows the b_{-1} position initialized to 0 during a load operation to generate the implied 0 as previously mentioned.

Recall that the $b_1 b_0 b_{-1}$ positions are used to select a version of the multiplicand to be added to the partial product. In order to make registers D and B more

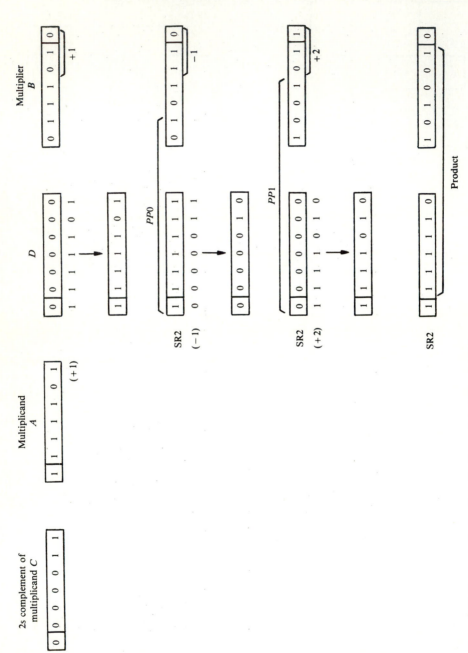

Figure 3.18 Sequence of operations for Example 1 of Fig. 3.14(a)

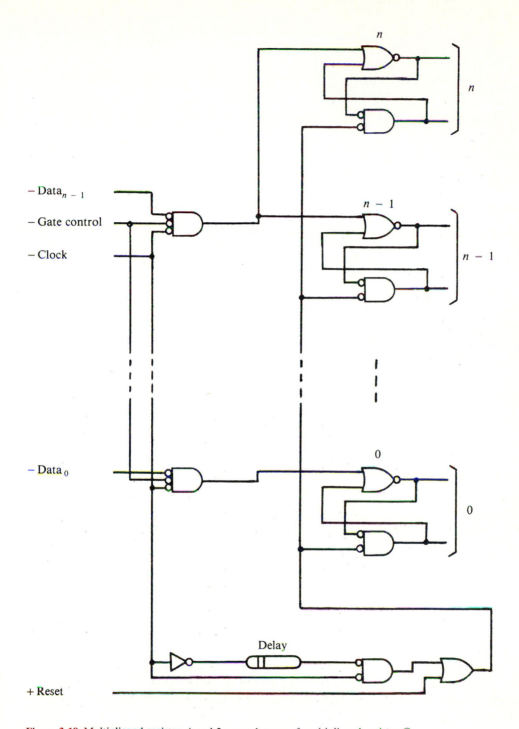

Figure 3.19 Multiplicand register A and 2s complement of multiplicand register C.

general purpose, they were designed to execute one shift per clock pulse. Therefore, two clock pulses are required during each cycle to execute a double-right shift. If the duration of the add-shift cycle time does not permit two clock pulses for shifting, then the input gating to flip-flop i can be easily modified so that, instead of accepting the output from the flip-flop $i + 1$, it accepts the output from flip-flop $i + 2$, as in Fig. 3.22. Finally the organization of the multiplexer function is shown in Fig. 3.23. One of the five inputs to each multiplexer is selected by the decoder of Fig. 3.16 to be added to the corresponding partial product bit. Note that during a $\pm 2 \times$ multiplicand operation, the multiplicand bits are shifted one bit position to the left before being added to the partial product. This completes the description of multiplication using bit-pair recoding as applied to sequential add-shift hardware.

3.4.3 Planar Array

A method will now be described that uses the bit-pair recoding technique in a planar array to implement 2s complement multiplication combinationally. The module that will be used is shown in Fig. 3.24. Each element of the array consists of this module. One of the input vectors entering the top is the four-bit slice $pp_{k + 3} \, pp_{k + 2} \, pp_{k + 1} \, pp_k$ of the incoming partial product (initially all 0s). The other input vector from the top is the four-bit slice $a_{j + 3} \, a_{j + 2} \, a_{j + 1} \, a_j$, which represents the multiplicand. It is assumed that the multiplicand is available in noninverted and inverted form. The five outputs from the decoder of Fig. 3.16 select one of the five inputs to the multiplexer, which gates the appropriate version of the multiplicand to the adder, where it is added to the incoming partial product. This is the same multiplexer with the same inputs that was used in the add-shift method previously described in this section. The $+2$ and -2 inputs to the rightmost multiplexer$_j$ come from $+1$ and -1 inputs, respectively, of the leftmost multiplexer$_{j + 3}$ in the module$_{i - 1}$ to the right of the one under consideration. If the module being considered is the rightmost module in a row, then $+2$ and -2 inputs contain logic 0. Similarly $+1$ and -1 inputs to multiplexer$_{j + 3}$ also connect to $+2$ and -2 inputs, respectively, of multiplexer$_j$ in module$_{i + 1}$. If the module being considered is the leftmost module in a row, then these inputs connect only to multiplexer$_{j + 3}$.

The carry-in to adder$_j$ is the OR of the group carry-out of module$_{i - 1}$ (logic 0 if module$_i$ is the rightmost module in a row), and a logic 1 when $-1 \times$ multiplicand is selected. Logic 1 is added to the inverted multiplicand to form the 2s complement. The carry-in to adder$_{j + 1}$ is the OR of the carry-out of the jth position, and logic 1 when $-2 \times$ multiplicand is selected. Logic 1 is added to the left-shifted inverted multiplicand to form two times the 2s complement. The functions used to produce a carry in Fig. 3.24 are defined as follows:

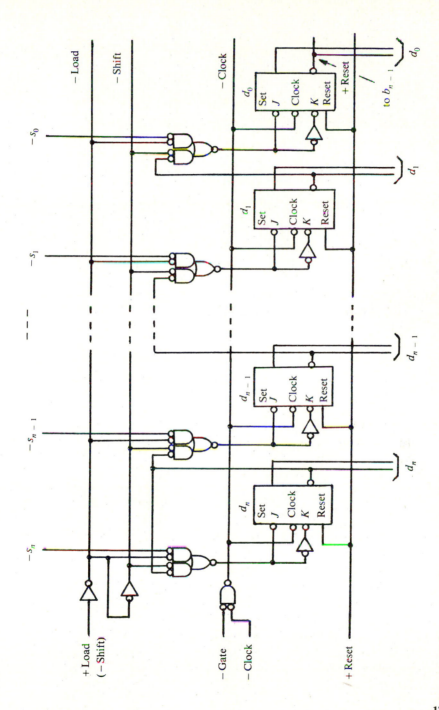

Figure 3.20 Logic diagram for register D.

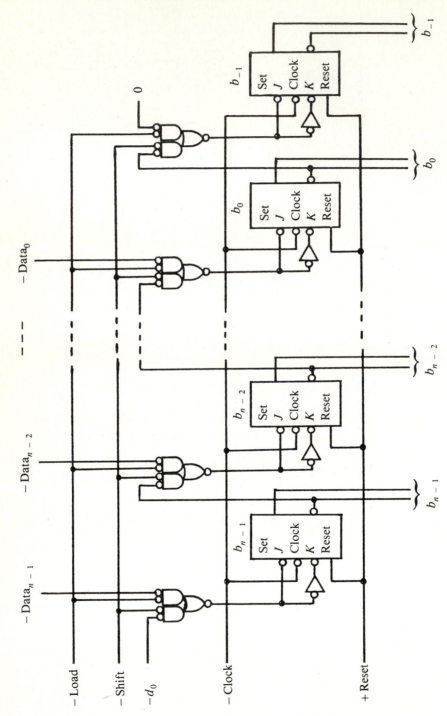

Figure 3.21 Logic diagram for multiplier *B*.

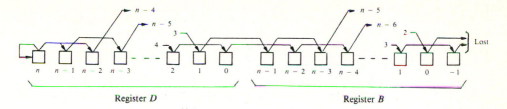

Register D   Register B

Figure 3.22 Double-shift sequence for registers D and B.

$$G = \text{generate}$$
$$P = \text{propagate}$$
$$C = \text{carry}$$
$$GG = \text{group generate}$$
$$GP = \text{group propagate}$$
$$GC = \text{group carry}$$

The four-bit adder in each module uses carry lookahead and is illustrated in Fig. 3.25. Also, since signed numbers are being handled, the leftmost module in a row must implement a partial product sign extension. This is necessary to provide inputs to the left pair of partial product inputs for the module directly below it in the next row.

The array structure for multiplying a seven-bit multiplicand by a six-bit multiplier is shown in Fig. 3.26. Although eight positions are available for the multiplicand, only seven bits are permitted, because the multiplicand must be shifted left one bit position during an operation involving ± 2 times the multiplicand. The operation of this design follows that of the add-shift method, except that the alignment is now accomplished by the placement of the modules rather than by the shifting of the partial products. All of the multiplier bit pairs (including $i - 1$) are decoded simultaneously and select the appropriate version of the multiplicand to be added to the shifted partial product at each level of the array. The interconnection of module$_{1,1}$ and module$_{1,2}$ in the first row is shown in Fig. 3.27. Note that pp_7 is extended two bit positions to the left and connects to partial product positions pp_8 and pp_9 of module $_{2,1}$ in the next row.

An example will now be given to illustrate the operation of the 7×6 multiplier hardware. Consider multiplicand 1 1 1 1 1 1 0 1 and multiplier 0 1 1 1 0 1. The operation of the hardware is identical to the calculations that take place in Fig. 3.28. The organization of the array, with the appropriate inputs for this example, is shown in Fig. 3.29. This illustrates the sequence that takes place at each level of the array. Only the true version of the multiplicand is shown as inputs to the three levels of the array, although the 1s complement is also available. The selection of the appropriate multiplicand version then takes place

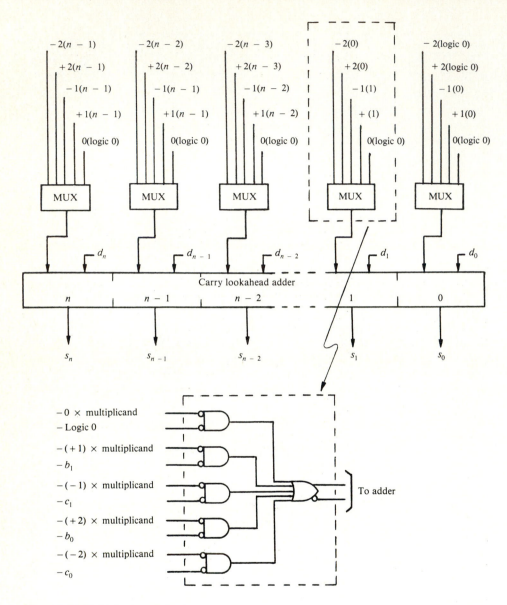

Figure 3.23 Multiplexer organization.

within the module. The multiplier bit pairs are decoded to select appropriate versions of the multiplicand to be added to the partial product that has been shifted two places to the right. The algorithms and hardware presented in this section are intended for high-speed 2s complement multiplication and can be expanded to any size $m \times n$ multiplier arrays.

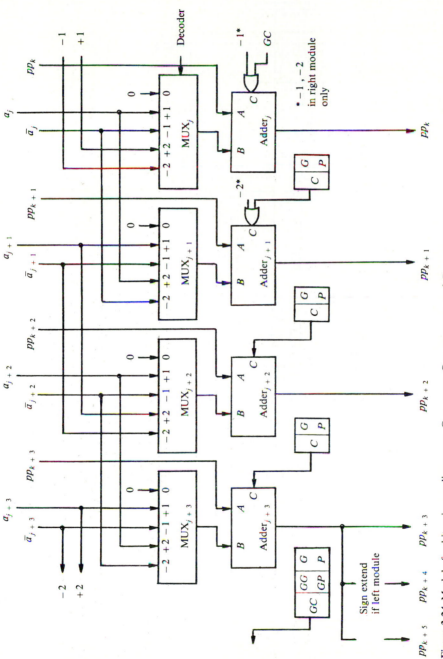

Figure 3.24 Module for bit-pair recoding array. C = carry, G = generate, and P = propagate.

179

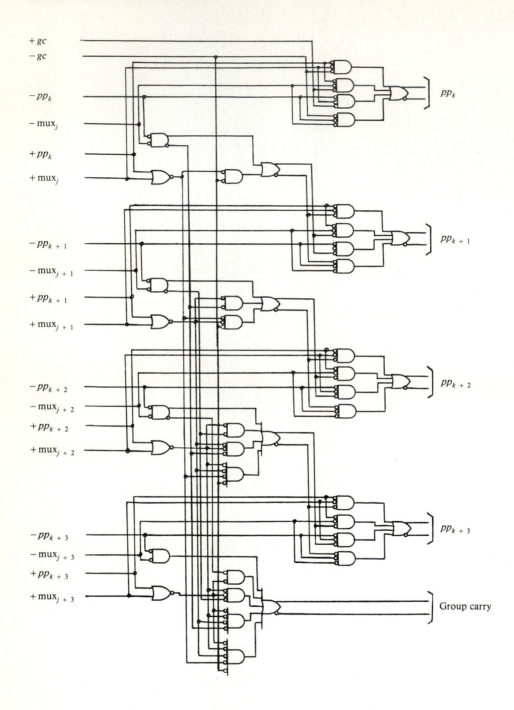

Figure 3.25 Four-bit carry lookahead adder.

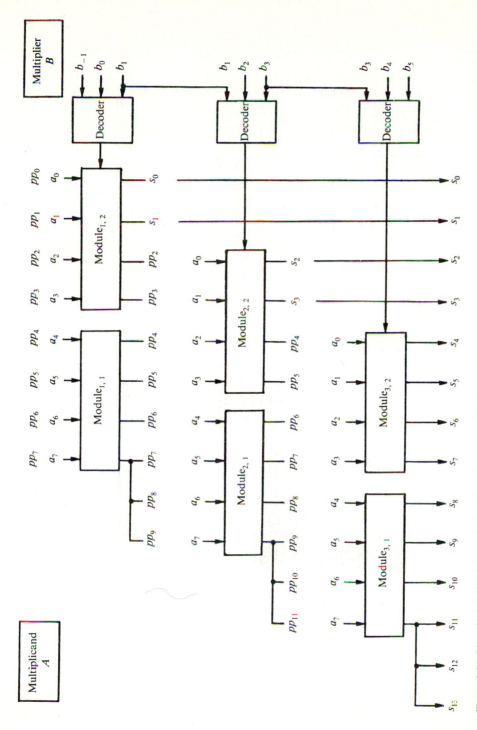

Figure 3.26 Bit-pair recoding array structure for a 7 × 6 multiplier circuit.

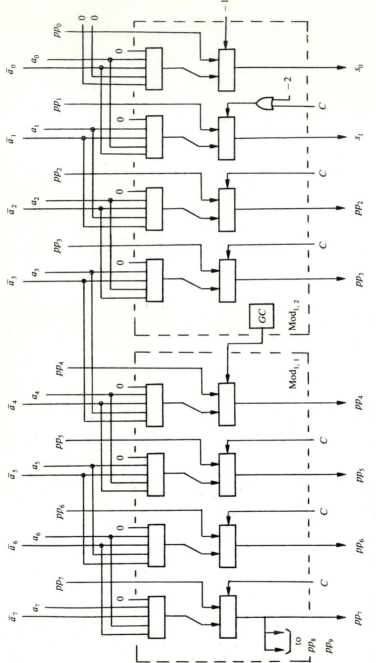

Figure 3.27 Interconnection of module$_{1,1}$ and module$_{1,2}$.

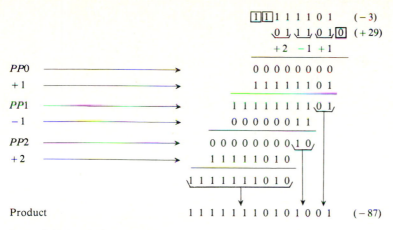

Figure 3.28 Multiplication example.

3.5 MODULAR ARRAY MULTIPLICATION AND WALLACE TREES

Computers have always multiplied slowly regardless of whether a software subroutine or a hardware/software approach was used. The first approach requires complicated programming; the second also requires programming, but usually in the form of microprogramming for a multistep sequential design. In the next two sections, a third approach will be presented—one-step combinational planar array multipliers. Because very little software is required, the resulting multiplication takes place at a very high speed. The speed depends upon technology, but even low-speed logic families can produce a multiplication unit of very high speed compared to other methods. This section demonstrates the modular network realization of large-scale multiplication arrays using basic multiply modules.

The usual paper-and-pencil algorithm for multiplication of binary numbers is shown in Fig. 3.30 assuming four-bit operands. The product of two n-digit numbers can be accommodated in $2n$ digits, so that the product in this example fits into eight bits as shown. In the binary system, multiplication of the multiplicand by a 1 bit in the multiplier simply copies the multiplicand. If the multiplier bit is 1, the multiplicand is entered in the appropriately shifted position to be added with other shifted multiplicands to form the product. If the multiplier bit is 0, then 0s are entered as in the second row of the example.

A more general example of multiplication using positive four-bit binary operands is shown in Fig. 3.31. Each bit in the multiplicand is multiplied by the low-order bit b_0 of the multiplier. In binary multiplication, this operation can be considered to be an AND function resulting in the first partial product of the form

$$a_3b_0 \quad a_2b_0 \quad a_1b_0 \quad a_0b_0$$

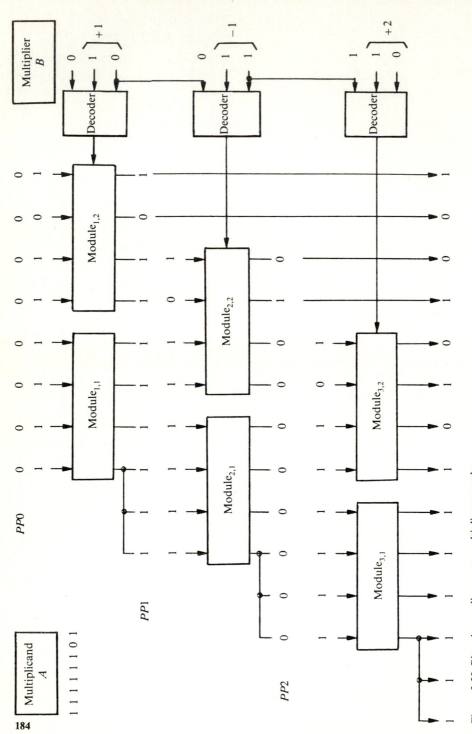

Figure 3.29 Bit-pair recoding array multiplier example.

Each bit in the multiplicand is then multiplied by the next low-order bit b_1 of the multiplier, and the resulting partial product is shifted one bit position to the left. This procedure is repeated for each bit in the multiplier. Each column in the partial product array is then added, proceeding from right to left, to produce the product. Any carry-out of a column sum is added to the sum of the next appropriate column to the left. A carry may be added to the next column to the left, as in the case of 10 or 11, or it may be added to the second column on the left, as in the case of 100 or 101.

```
      1 1 0 0   (12) Multiplicand A
   ×) 1 1 0 1   (13) Muliplier B
   ─────────
      1 1 0 0
      0 0 0 0
    1 1 0 0
  1 1 0 0
  ─────────────
  1 0 0 1 1 1 0 0   (156) Product P
```

Figure 3.30 Multiplication algorithm.

				a_3	a_2	a_1	a_0
			×)	b_3	b_2	b_1	b_0
Partial product 0				a_3b_0	a_2b_0	a_1b_0	a_0b_0
Partial product 1			a_3b_1	a_2b_1	a_1b_1	a_0b_1	
Partial product 2		a_3b_2	a_2b_2	a_1b_2	a_0b_2		
Partial product 3	a_3b_3	a_2b_3	a_1b_3	a_0b_3			
Product	2^7	2^6	2^5	2^4	2^3	2^2	2^1	2^0

Figure 3.31 General multiply algorithm for four-bit operands.

The above method can be used for operands of any length. An example of multiplication using eight-bit operands is shown in Fig. 3.32. In this case, there are more entries in the partial product array, but the same rules for binary addition still apply. The carry-out of a column may result from a sum of 1000, which will add a 1 to the third column to the left of the column that produced the carry.

The operation can be modularized in sections of four-bit operands using *nonadditive multiply modules* (NMMs). It is possible to implement positive-operand binary multiplication in a purely combinational two-dimension logic array. Modular combinational logic arrays perform fast multiplication on small or medium-length operands. The array multiply modules perform local multiplication (summation of shifted multiplicands) independent of the results of other multiply modules.

Partial product array

								a_7	a_6	a_5	a_4	a_3	a_2	a_1	a_0
							$\times)$	b_7	b_6	b_5	b_4	b_3	b_2	b_1	b_0
								a_7b_0	a_6b_0	a_5b_0	a_4b_0	a_3b_0	a_2b_0	a_1b_0	a_0b_0
							a_7b_1	a_6b_1	a_5b_1	a_4b_1	a_3b_1	a_2b_1	a_1b_1	a_0b_1	
						a_7b_2	a_6b_2	a_5b_2	a_4b_2	a_3b_2	a_2b_2	a_1b_2	a_0b_2		
					a_7b_3	a_6b_3	a_5b_3	a_4b_3	a_3b_3	a_2b_3	a_1b_3	a_0b_3			
				a_7b_4	a_6b_4	a_5b_4	a_4b_4	a_3b_4	a_2b_4	a_1b_4	a_0b_4				
			a_7b_5	a_6b_5	a_5b_5	a_4b_5	a_3b_5	a_2b_5	a_1b_5	a_0b_5					
		a_7b_6	a_6b_6	a_5b_6	a_4b_6	a_3b_6	a_2b_6	a_1b_6	a_0b_6						
	a_7b_7	a_6b_7	a_5b_7	a_4b_7	a_3b_7	a_2b_7	a_1b_7	a_0b_7							
2^{15}	2^{14}	2^{13}	2^{12}	2^{11}	2^{10}	2^9	2^8	2^7	2^6	2^5	2^4	2^3	2^2	2^1	2^0

Figure 3.32 General multiply algorithm for eight-bit operands.

Figure 3.33 shows the previous eight-bit operand multiplication example that is now sectioned into four multiply modules. The multiplication, shifting, and addition for each module is the same as was shown for the example in Fig. 3.31. The 4×4 multiply modules are used to produce the local partial products, called subproducts, of eight bits each. The subproduct for the upper-right multiply module of Fig. 3.33 will be

$$2^7 \ 2^6 \ 2^5 \ 2^4 \ 2^3 \ 2^2 \ 2^1 \ 2^0$$

as shown in Fig. 3.31. In order to generate all the subproducts simultaneously, the input operands (multiplicand and multiplier) must be decomposed into four-bit slices. The 16-bit product can be written as

$$
\begin{aligned}
P &= A \times B \\
&= (A_H \cdot A_L) \times (B_H \cdot B_L) \\
&= A_H \times B_H + A_H \times B_L + A_L \times B_H + A_L \times B_L \\
&= P_{HH} + P_{HL} + P_{LH} + P_{LL}
\end{aligned}
$$

where

$$
\begin{aligned}
A &= A_H \cdot A_L \\
B &= B_H \cdot B_L
\end{aligned}
$$

and the subscripts identify the high-order and low-order four bits in each eight-bit operand as shown below

$$
\begin{array}{cc}
a_7 \ a_6 \ a_5 \ a_4 & a_3 \ a_2 \ a_1 \ a_0 \\
\text{High order} & \text{Low order}
\end{array}
$$

The center dot ($\cdot$) refers to concatenation. The resulting product is the sum of 4 eight-bit subproducts shifted four bits apart. The multiplication to obtain the 4 eight-bit subproducts is shown in Fig. 3.34.

Each of the four subproducts must be added to produce the final product. Each weighted bit in a subproduct must be added to the bits of the other subproducts that have the same weight. That is, all bits with weight 2^4 are added together, all bits with weight 2^7 are added together, etc. The weighted bits of each subproduct are shown in Fig. 3.35. Columns 2^{15}, 2^{14}, 2^{13}, 2^{12} and columns 2^3, 2^2, 2^1, 2^0 contain only one entry, while columns 2^{11}, 2^{10}, 2^9, 2^8 and columns 2^7, 2^6, 2^5, 2^4 contain three entries. Columns 2^3–2^0 can be used directly in the formation of the product. Columns 2^{11}–2^4 must each be added in a three-input, two-output carry-save adder. A carry-save adder is one that does not propagate the carry to the following stage. Instead, it saves the carry propagation until all the additions are completed.

A final level of summation then takes place after the summation of the sub-products. This summation adds the carry generated by one column of the sub-product array to the sum generated by the next higher-order column.

3.5.1 Four × Four Multiplier Design

Next, the logic for a 4 × 4 multiplier will be discussed. The design for this device, shown in Fig. 3.36, is called a nonadditive multiply module. It duplicates the operation of the paper-and-pencil method for multiplying 2 four-bit operands to produce an eight-bit product. A typical cell in the NMM is shown in Fig. 3.37, while the gate-level design of a full adder used in the NMM appears in Fig. 3.38.

The logical operation of the NMM exactly follows the calculation of the operation matrix shown in Fig. 3.31. That is,

a_0 is ANDed with b_0 (a_0 b_0) to produce the subproduct bit 2^0.
a_1 b_0 is added to a_0 b_1 to produce 2^1.
a_2 b_0 is added to a_1 b_1. This sum is added to a_0 b_2 together with the carry-out of column 2^1 to produce subproduct bit 2^2.

The operation of the remaining elements in the NMM is similar to the above description and produces the subproduct 2^7–2^0.

3.5.2 Hardware Organization

The design of a multiplier to perform high-speed multiplication of 2 eight-bit operands will now be presented. The block diagram is shown in Fig. 3.39. Four NMMs are used to form the four subproducts, as previously discussed. Some of the subproducts are sent to bit-slice versions of the carry-save adder. These bit-slice adders, known as *Wallace trees*, will be used to sum the subproducts that were independently generated by the NMMs. A k-input Wallace tree is a bit-slice summing circuit, which produces the sum of k bit-slice inputs—for example, all of the 2^5 subproducts shown in Fig. 3.35. Since there are three subproducts, each containing 2^5, a three-input Wallace tree is required, as shown in Fig. 3.39. Figure 3.40 presents two Wallace trees, one with three inputs and another with five inputs. The three-input Wallace tree is nothing but a 3-to-2 carry-save full adder with two outputs representing the binary sum of the three input bits. The five-input Wallace tree adds five bit-slice inputs to yield a three-bit sum output. Figure 3.41 presents a Wallace tree that adds seven bit-slice inputs to yield a three-bit sum output.

Referring again to Fig. 3.39, the alignment of the subproducts is accomplished by inputting them to the appropriate Wallace tree. The column alignments are important to ensure the correctness of the result in the form of two vectors: the sum vector and the carry vector. The sum and carry outputs from each Wallace

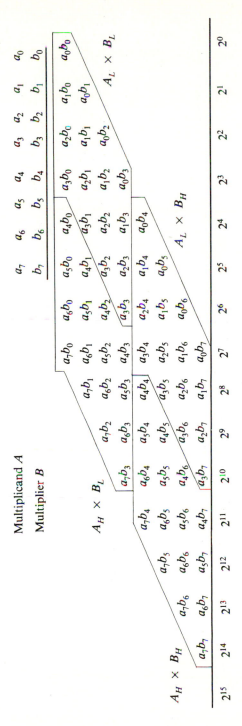

Figure 3.33 General multiply algorithm for eight-bit operands using multiply modules.

189

$P_{LL} = A_L \times B_L$

2^7	2^6	2^5	2^4	2^3	2^2	2^1	2^0
				a_3	a_2	a_1	a_0
				b_3	b_2	b_1	b_0
				a_3b_0	a_2b_0	a_1b_0	a_0b_0
			a_3b_1	a_2b_1	a_1b_1	a_0b_1	
		a_3b_2	a_2b_2	a_1b_2	a_0b_2		
	a_3b_3	a_2b_3	a_1b_3	a_0b_3			

$P_{LH} = A_L \times B_H$

2^{11}	2^{10}	2^9	2^8	2^7	2^6	2^5	2^4
				a_3	a_2	a_1	a_0
				b_7	b_6	b_5	b_4
				a_3b_4	a_2b_4	a_1b_4	a_0b_4
			a_3b_5	a_2b_5	a_1b_5	a_0b_5	
		a_3b_6	a_2b_6	a_1b_6	a_0b_6		
	a_3b_7	a_2b_7	a_1b_7	a_0b_7			

(a)

$P_{HL} = A_H \times B_L$

2^{11}	2^{10}	2^9	2^8	2^7	2^6	2^5	2^4
				a_7	a_6	a_5	a_4
				b_3	b_2	b_1	b_0
				a_7b_0	a_6b_0	a_5b_0	a_4b_0
			a_7b_1	a_6b_1	a_5b_1	a_4b_1	
		a_7b_2	a_6b_2	a_5b_2	a_4b_2		
	a_7b_3	a_6b_3	a_5b_3	a_4b_3			

$P_{HH} = A_H \times B_H$

2^{15}	2^{14}	2^{13}	2^{12}	2^{11}	2^{10}	2^9	2^8
				a_7	a_6	a_5	a_4
				b_7	b_6	b_5	b_4
				a_7b_4	a_6b_4	a_5b_4	a_4b_4
			a_7b_5	a_6b_5	a_5b_5	a_4b_5	
		a_7b_6	a_6b_6	a_5b_6	a_4b_6		
	a_7b_7	a_6b_7	a_5b_7	a_4b_7			

(b)

Figure 3.34 Subproduct weighted bits for (a) P_{LL} and P_{LH}, and (b) P_{HL} and P_{HH}.

$A_L \times B_L$

$A_L \times B_H$

$A_H \times B_L$

$A_H \times B_H$

2^{15}	2^{14}	2^{13}	2^{12}	2^{11}	2^{10}	2^9	2^8	2^7	2^6	2^5	2^4	2^3	2^2	2^1	2^0
								2^7	2^6	2^5	2^4	2^3	2^2	2^1	2^0
				2^{11}	2^{10}	2^9	2^8	2^7	2^6	2^5	2^4				
				2^{11}	2^{10}	2^9	2^8	2^7	2^6	2^5	2^4				
2^{15}	2^{14}	2^{13}	2^{12}	2^{11}	2^{10}	2^9	2^8								

2^{15}	2^{14}	2^{13}	2^{12}	2^{11}	2^{10}	2^9	2^8	2^7	2^6	2^5	2^4	2^3	2^2	2^1	2^0
2^{15}	2^{14}	2^{13}	2^{12}	2^{11}	2^{10}	2^9	2^8	2^7	2^6	2^5					

2^{15}	2^{14}	2^{13}	2^{12}	2^{11}	2^{10}	2^9	2^8	2^7	2^6	2^5	2^4	2^3	2^2	2^1	2^0

Figure 3.35 Summation of weighted subproduct bits. The arrows indicate carry-out of position 2^i into position 2^{i+1}.

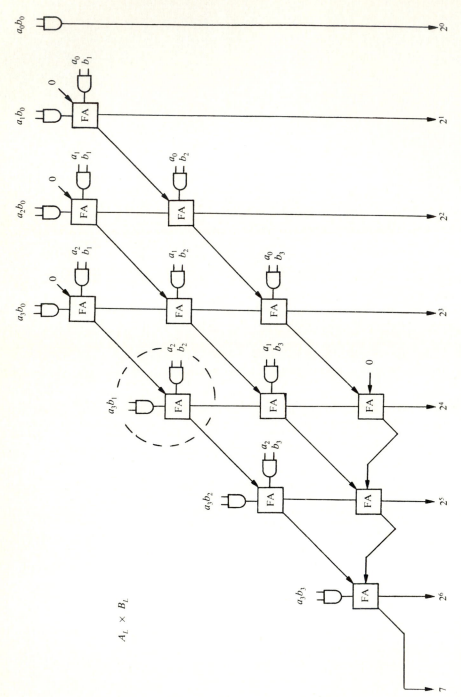

Figure 3.36 A 4 × 4 NMM.

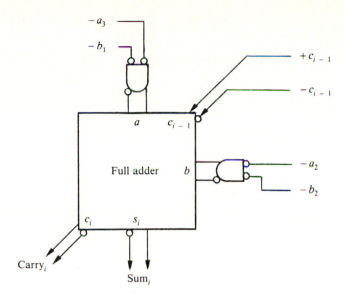

Figure 3.37 Typical NMM array cell.

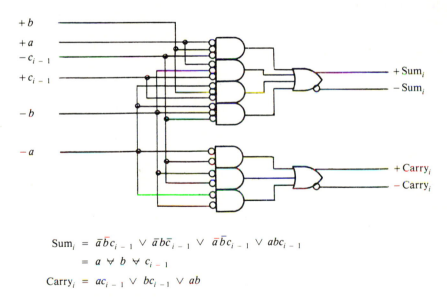

$$\text{Sum}_i = \bar{a}\bar{b}c_{i-1} \vee \bar{a}b\bar{c}_{i-1} \vee a\bar{b}c_{i-1} \vee abc_{i-1}$$
$$= a \veebar b \veebar c_{i-1}$$
$$\text{Carry}_i = ac_{i-1} \vee bc_{i-1} \vee ab$$

Figure 3.38 Full-adder logic diagram.

tree are sent to a conventional binary adder with carry lookahead, which merges the two vectors into the final product. The carry-out of Wallace tree W_i is added to the sum output of W_{i+1}. Note that the least-significant slices, corresponding to $P_{LL} = A_L \times B_L$, need not go through the carry lookahead (CLA) adder.

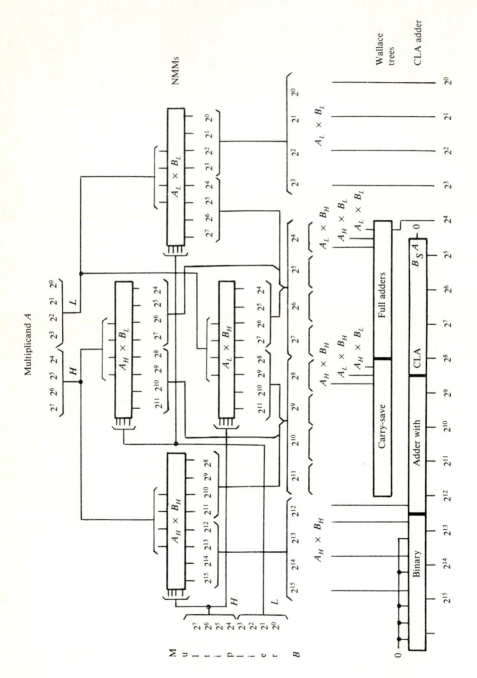

Figure 3.39 An 8 × 8 array multiplier.

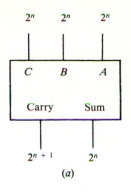

(a)

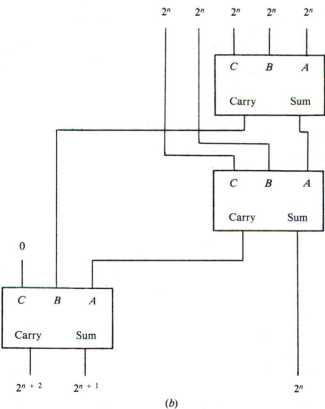

(b)

Figure 3.40 Bit-slice Wallace trees built with carry-save full adders: (a) three-bit-slice W_3 and (b) five-bit-slice W_5.

The output of the adder then becomes the final 16-bit product. A more detailed logic diagram for the 8 $\times$ 8 multiplier is presented in Fig. 3.42.

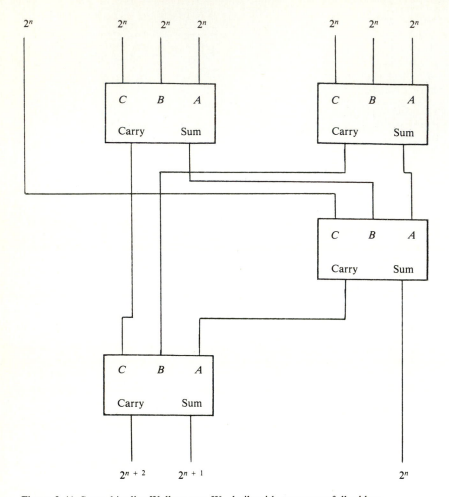

Figure 3.41 Seven-bit-slice Wallace tree W_7, built with carry-save full adders.

Figure 3.43 illustrates the modular arrangement of NMMs for 2 eight-bit operands. It is now easy to see how the subproducts line up. W_3 is a three-input Wallace tree, of which there are a total of eight. The three inputs are, for example, the three 2^4 outputs from NMMs $A_H \times B_L$, $A_L \times B_L$, and $A_L \times B_H$.

Figure 3.44 shows the modular arrangement for array multiplication networks ranging in size from 4×4 to 32×32, that is, from 4-bit operands to 32-bit operands. Each rectangle represents an eight-bit subproduct divided into high and low four-bit slices. All slices are added in a columnwise fashion by Wallace trees of odd-numbered inputs. For an 8×8 multiplication network, only three-input trees are required. For a 16×16 network, Wallace trees of sizes 3, 5, 7, 7, 5, 3 are required; for a 32×32 network, trees with up to 15 in-

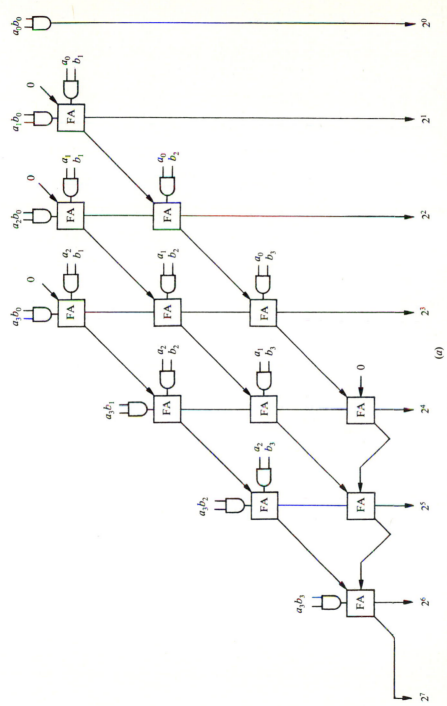

Figure 3.42 (*a*) A 4×4 NMM $A_L \times B_L$; (*b*) a 4×4 NMM $A_L \times B_H$; (*c*) a 4×4 NMM $A_H \times B_L$; (*d*) a 4×4 NMM $A_H \times B_H$; and (*e*) Wallace trees and CLA adder.

197

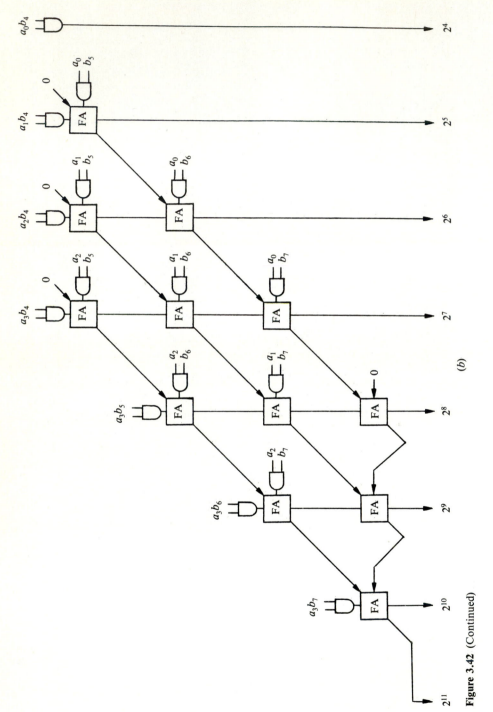

Figure 3.42 (Continued)

(b)

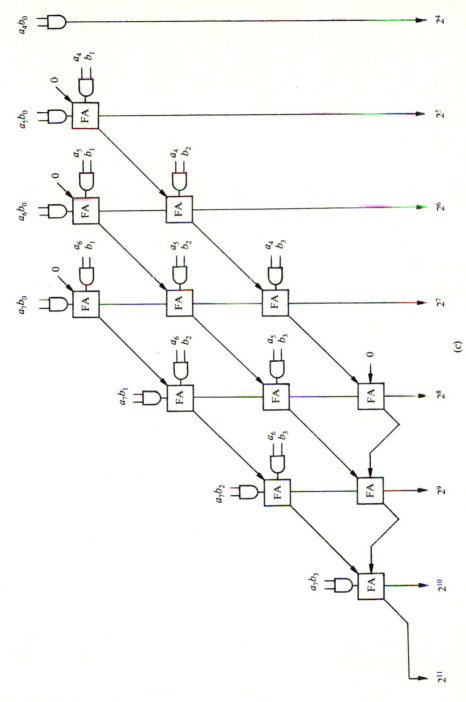

Figure 3.42 (Continued)

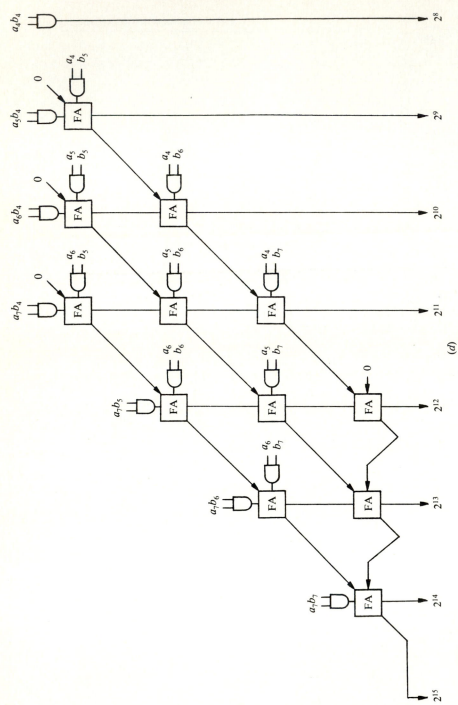

Figure 3.42 (Continued)

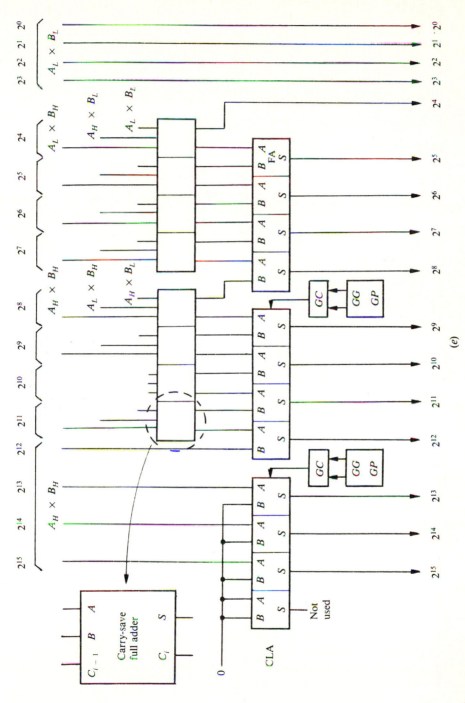

Figure 3.42 (Continued)

201

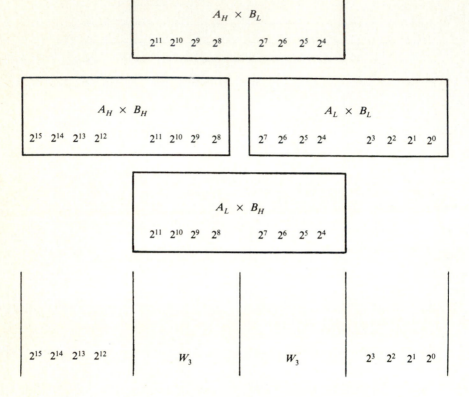

Figure 3.43 Modular arrangement for 2 eight-bit operands.

puts are required. Note that the 2 four-bit slices at both ends do not require Wallace trees. All unused inputs to a Wallace tree must be connected to a logical 0.

When using five-input Wallace trees, as in the case of a 16 $\times$ 16 array, additional three-input trees must also be used, which in turn connect to a CLA adder. In the example below, 3 five-input trees and 3 three-input trees are used to generate a six-bit sum. The logic for this example is shown in Fig. 3.45.

$$
\begin{array}{cccccc}
& & & 2^{n+2} & 2^{n+1} & 2^{n} \\
& & & 2^{n+2} & 2^{n+1} & 2^{n} \\
& & & 2^{n+2} & 2^{n+1} & 2^{n} \\
& & & 2^{n+2} & 2^{n+1} & 2^{n} \\
& & & 2^{n+2} & 2^{n+1} & 2^{n} \\
\hline
2^{n+5} & 2^{n+4} & 2^{n+3} & 2^{n+2} & 2^{n+1} & 2^{n}
\end{array}
$$

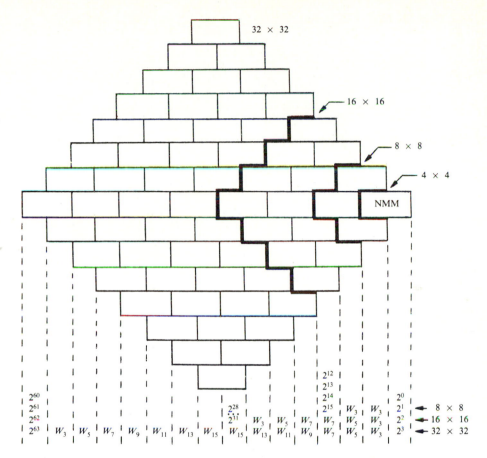

Figure 3.44 Array arrangement for multipliers ranging in size from 4 × 4 to 32 × 32.

The multiplier presented in this section is for positive operands only. If 2s complementation is required, then either of the two logic representations illustrated in Fig. 3.46 can be used.

3.6 2S COMPLEMENT ARRAY MULTIPLICATION

An array multiplier that performs multiplication of 2s complement numbers will be described next. This method significantly speeds the multiplication process by eliminating the slow 2s complementing operation and the final addition. The mathematical properties associated with such direct 2s complement multiplication will be described first.

Thus far, 2s complement numbers have been treated as positional numbers (the binary weight depends upon the position of the bit in the vector) with an unweighted sign and positively weighted coefficients. Another approach is to

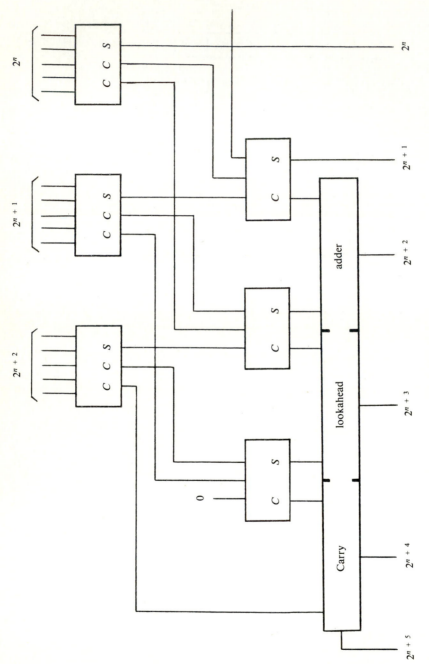

Figure 3.45 Summation circuit using five-input and three-input Wallace trees.

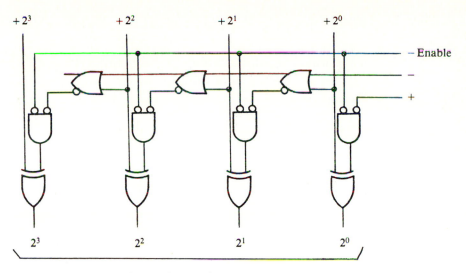

2s complemented outputs

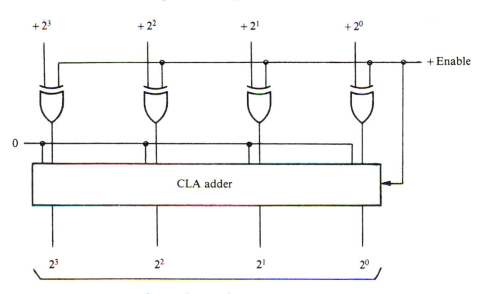

2s complemented outputs

Figure 3.46 2s complement circuits.

evaluate 2s complement numbers as positional numbers with a negatively weighted sign bit and positively weighted coefficients. Consider a 2s complement number

$$N = (a_{n-1} \, a_{n-2} \, \cdots \, a_1 \, a_0)_2$$

where a_{n-1} is the designated sign bit. The value of N can be represented as follows depending on the sign.

$$N = + \sum_{i=0}^{n-2} a_i 2^i \qquad \text{if } a_{n-1} = 0 \text{ (positive)} \qquad (3.6)$$

$$N = - \left[1 + \sum_{i=0}^{n-2} (1 - a_i) \, 2^i \right] \quad \text{if } a_{n-1} = 1 \text{ (negative)} \qquad (3.7)$$

Equation 3.7 indicates that the decimal value of a negative number can be found by inverting the bits, adding 1, and then making the sign negative. The same results can be obtained by attaching a negative weighting factor of -2^{n-1} to the sign bit a_{n-1}. This has the effect of making the value of the high-order bit (the sign bit) negative and then adding to this number the positively weighted value for all 1 bits. For example, the value of

$$1\ 0\ 1\ 0 = -1 \times 2^3 + 0 \times 2^2 + 1 \times 2^1 + 0 \times 2^0$$
$$= -8 + 2$$
$$= -6$$

This is indeed the 2s complement of 6 (0 1 1 0). The two positional representations in Eqs. 3.6 and 3.7 can be combined into the following form:

$$N = -a_{n-1} \, 2^{n-1} + \sum_{i=0}^{n-2} a_i 2^i \qquad (3.8)$$

Equation 3.8 can best be illustrated by numerical examples, such as $+6 = 0\ 1\ 1\ 0$ and $-5 = 1\ 0\ 1\ 1$ for $n = 4$.

$$0\ 1\ 1\ 0 = -0 \times 2^3 + 1 \times 2^2 + 1 \times 2^1 + 0 \times 2^0$$
$$= 4 + 2$$
$$= 6$$

$$1\ 0\ 1\ 1 = -1 \times 2^3 + 0 \times 2^2 + 1 \times 2^1 + 1 \times 2^0$$
$$= -8 + 2 + 1$$
$$= -5$$

An algorithm for direct 2s complement array multiplication has been proposed by Baugh and Wooley. The principal advantage of this algorithm is that the signs of all the summands are positive, thus allowing the array to be constructed entirely with conventional full adders. Each of the partial product terms $a_i b_j$ is called a *summand*. In Fig. 3.47, $a_1 b_0$, $a_0 b_0$, $a_1 b_1$, and $a_0 b_1$ are all summands. The uniform structure of this design is very attractive for large-scale-integration technology.

$$
\begin{array}{cc}
a_1 & a_0 \\
b_1 & b_0 \\
\hline
a_1 b_0 & a_0 b_0 \\
a_1 b_1 \quad a_0 b_1 & \\
\hline
2^2 \quad 2^1 & 2^0
\end{array}
$$

Figure 3.47 Multiplication showing summands in the partial product.

Consider two 2s complement integer operands, an m-bit multiplicand

$$A = (a_{m-1} \, a_{m-2} \cdot \cdot \cdot a_1 \, a_0)_2$$

and an n-bit multiplier

$$B = (b_{n-1} \, b_{n-2} \cdot \cdot \cdot b_1 \, b_0)_2$$

The values for A and B can be written by Eq. 3.8 as

$$A = -a_{m-1} 2^{m-1} + \sum_{i=0}^{m-2} a_i 2^i \tag{3.9}$$

$$B = -b_{n-1} 2^{n-1} + \sum_{i=0}^{n-2} b_i 2^i \tag{3.10}$$

The value of the product P is

$$P = A \times B = (p_{m+n-1} \, p_{m+n-2} \cdot \cdot \cdot p_1 \, p_0)_2$$

Since the product of two operands with m and n bits has $m + n$ terms, and the low-order bit is designated p_0, then the high-order bit must be designated p_{m+n-1} as shown. The product can be written in 2s complement notation in terms of the coefficient product of a_is and b_js with the appropriate weighting factor 2^k as follows:

$$P = -p_{m+n-1} 2^{m+n-1} + \sum_{i=0}^{m+n-2} p_i 2^i = A \times B$$

$$= \left(-a_{m-1} 2^{m-1} + \sum_{i=0}^{m-2} a_i 2^i\right)\left(-b_{n-1} 2^{n-1} + \sum_{i=0}^{n-2} b_i 2^i\right)$$

$$= a_{m-1} b_{n-1} 2^{m+n-2} + \sum_{i=0}^{m-2} \sum_{j=0}^{n-2} a_i b_j 2^{i+j}$$

$$- a_{m-1} 2^{m-1} \sum_{i=0}^{n-2} b_i 2^i - b_{n-1} 2^{n-1} \sum_{i=0}^{m-2} a_i 2^i$$

$$= a_{m-1} b_{n-1} 2^{m+n-2} + \sum_{i=0}^{m-2} \sum_{j=0}^{n-2} a_i b_j 2^{i+j}$$

$$- \sum_{i=0}^{n-2} a_{m-1} b_i 2^{m-1+i} - \sum_{i=0}^{m-2} a_i b_{n-1} 2^{n-1+i} \qquad (3.11)$$

In Eq. 3.11, the signs of the summands for the third and fourth entries are negative. That is, the signs for the summands $a_{m-1} b_i$ for $i = 0, \ldots, n - 2$ and $a_i b_{n-1}$ for $i = 0, \ldots, m - 2$ are all negative. It is desirable to have all signs positive, since this will permit straightforward addition of all summands in each column of the partial product array. There will be no need to perform subtraction for the negative summands as a separate step in the summing process. In other words, we want to add the negation of the negative summands while still maintaining a mathematically correct equation for the product.

At this point it will be advantageous to put Eq. 3.8 in a different form to help generate a subproduct array with all positive summands. Equation 3.8 is reproduced below.

$$N = -a_{n-1} 2^{n-1} + \sum_{i=0}^{n-2} a_i 2^i$$

Multiplying both sides by -1, we obtain

$$-N = a_{n-1} 2^{n-1} - \sum_{i=0}^{n-2} a_i 2^i$$

$$= a_{n-1} 2^{n-1} + (2^{n-1} - 2^{n-1}) - \sum_{i=0}^{n-2} a_i 2^i$$

The terms in parentheses do not alter the equation and will be useful later. Continuing,

$$-N = a_{n-1}2^{n-1} + 2^{n-1} - 2^{n-1} - \sum_{i=0}^{n-2} a_i 2^i$$

$$= a_{n-1}2^{n-1} - 2^{n-1} + 2^{n-1} - \sum_{i=0}^{n-2} a_i 2_i$$

$$= (a_{n-1} - 1) 2^{n-1} + 2^{n-1} - \sum_{i=0}^{n-2} a_i 2^i$$

$$= -(1 - a_{n-1}) 2^{n-1} + 2^{n-1} - \sum_{i=0}^{n-2} a_i 2^i$$

$$= -(1 - a_{n-1}) 2^{n-1} + \left(1 + \sum_{i=0}^{n-2} 2^i\right) - \sum_{i=0}^{n-2} a_i 2^i$$

The middle term equates $2^{n-1} = 1 + \sum_{i=0}^{n-2} 2^i$. This is true since the value of any

bit in a binary vector is equal to the sum of all low-order bits plus 1. For example, for $n = 6$

2^{n-1}	2^{n-2}	.	.	.	2^1	2^0
1	1		1	1	1	1

where

$$2^{n-1} = 32 = (1) + \sum_{i=0}^{n-2} 2^i$$

$$= (1) + 1 + 2 + 4 + 8 + 16 = 32$$

Continuing,

$$-N = -(1 - a_{n-1}) 2^{n-1} + \sum_{i=0}^{n-2} 2^i - \sum_{i=0}^{n-2} a_i 2^i + 1$$

$$= -(1 - a_{n-1}) 2^{n-1} + \left[\sum_{i=0}^{n-2} (1 - a_i) 2^i\right] + 1 \qquad (3.12)$$

which is the 2s complement of the original.

Remembering that the purpose of the preceding derivation was to change the negatively signed summands of the third and fourth entries in Eq. 3.11 to positively signed summands, we now proceed to do this using Eq. 3.12. The third entry in Eq. 3.11 is

$$\sum_{i=0}^{n-2} a_{m-1} b_i 2^{m-1+i} = 2^{m-1} \sum_{i=0}^{n-2} a_{m-1} b_i 2^i$$

$$= 2^{m-1} \left(-0 \times 2^n + 0 \times 2^{n-1} + \sum_{i=0}^{n-2} a_{m-1} b_i 2^i \right) \quad (3.13)$$

The terms -0×2^n and $+0 \times 2^{n-1}$ do not change the equation and will be useful later in simplification. Use Eq. 3.12 to change Eq. 3.13 so that the subtraction of Eq. 3.13 in the subproduct array can be replaced by the addition of its 2s complement. Equation 3.13 then becomes

$$2^{m-1} \left(-1 \times 2^n + 1 \times 2^{n-1} + 1 + \sum_{i=0}^{n-2} \bar{a}_{m-1} \bar{b}_i 2^i \right) \quad (3.14)$$

This follows from Eq. 3.12 because $1 - 0 = 1$ and $1 - 1 = 0$. $1 - a_{m-1} = \bar{a}_{m-1}$, where a_{m-1} is either 1 or 0. Equation 3.14 has the value

$$0 \quad \text{for } a_{m-1} = 0 \text{ when substituted in Eq. 3.13}$$

$$2^{m-1} \left(-2^n + 2^{n-1} + 1 + \sum_{i=0}^{n-2} \bar{b}_i 2^i \right) \text{ for } a_{m-1} = 1$$

when substituted in Eq. 3.13. $\quad (3.15)$

From Eq. 3.15, Eq. 3.14 can be rewritten as

$$2^{m-1} \left(-2^n + 2^{n-1} + \bar{a}_{m-1} 2^{n-1} + a_{m-1} + \sum_{i=0}^{n-2} a_{m-1} \bar{b}_i 2^i \right) \quad (3.16)$$

This can be verified by substituting $a_{m-1} = 0$ and $a_{m-1} = 1$ to obtain the results shown in Eq. 3.15.

Similarly, the subtraction of the fourth term in Eq. 3.11 can be replaced by the addition of

$$2^{n-1} \left(-2^m + 2^{m-1} + \bar{b}_{n-1} 2^{m-1} + b_{n-1} + \sum_{i=0}^{m-2} \bar{a}_i b_{n-1} 2^i \right)$$

$$(3.17)$$

Thus, the complete equation to generate the product of two $m \times n$ (multiplicand $\times$ multiplier) operands is

$$P = a_{m-1}b_{n-1}2^{m+n-2} + \sum_{i=0}^{m-2} \sum_{j=0}^{n-2} a_i b_j 2^{i+j}$$

$$+ 2^{m-1}\left(-2^n + 2^{n-1} + \bar{a}_{m-1}2^{n-1} + a_{m-1} + \sum_{i=0}^{n-2} a_{m-1}\bar{b}_i 2^i\right)$$

$$+ 2^{n-1}\left(-2^m + 2^{m-1} + \bar{b}_{n-1}2^{m-1} + b_{n-1} + \sum_{i=0}^{m-2} \bar{a}_i b_{n-1} 2^i\right)$$

$$(3.18)$$

The above calculations may seem tedious, but they are necessary in order to understand the design of the Baugh-Wooley 2s complement array multiplier, for it is designed directly from Eq. 3.18.

3.6.1 Hardware Organization

The design of a 2s complement array multiplier will now be presented. For convenience, a 5×5 array will be used; that is, both the multiplicand and the multiplier have 5 bits, where $m = n = 5$. Using Eq. 3.18 and letting $m = n = 5$, the first term becomes

$$a_4 b_4 2^8$$

The second term is expanded to

$a_0 b_0 2^0$	$a_0 b_1 2^1$	$a_0 b_2 2^2$	$a_0 b_3 2^3$
$a_1 b_0 2^1$	$a_1 b_1 2^2$	$a_1 b_2 2^3$	$a_1 b_3 2^4$
$a_2 b_0 2^2$	$a_2 b_1 2^3$	$a_2 b_2 2^4$	$a_2 b_3 2^5$
$a_3 b_0 2^3$	$a_3 b_1 2^4$	$a_3 b_2 2^5$	$a_3 b_3 2^6$

Substituting $m = n = 5$ into the third term produces

$$2^8$$
$$\bar{a}_4 2^8$$
$$a_4 2^4$$
$$a_4 \bar{b}_0 2^4$$
$$a_4 \bar{b}_1 2^5$$
$$a_4 \bar{b}_2 2^6$$
$$a_4 \bar{b}_3 2^7$$

Substituting $m = n = 5$ into the fourth term produces

$$2^8$$
$$\bar{b}_4 2^8$$
$$b_4 2^4$$
$$\bar{a}_0 b_4 2^4$$
$$\bar{a}_1 b_4 2^5$$
$$\bar{a}_2 b_4 2^6$$
$$\bar{a}_3 b_4 2^7$$

Each of the above summands has a weighting factor of 2^k, where $k = 0$, $1, \ldots, 8$. Combining summands with the same weighting factor and placing them in the same column yields the subproduct array (summand matrix) of Fig. 3.48. The summands in each column are added and, together with the carries generated by the columns, produce the final product.

The logic diagram for a 5×5 2s complement array multiplier is shown in Fig. 3.49. The full adder is the same as that which was used in Sec. 3.5. Both true and inverted operand bits are assumed to be available. Note that the logic was designed directly from the summand matrix of Fig. 3.48, which in turn was obtained directly from the terms of Eq. 3.18.

The 5×5 matrix can be expanded to a 32×32 (or any size) matrix by simply using Eq. 3.18, where $m = n = 32$. From this, generate the summand matrix and then the logic diagram. The final row of full adders in Fig. 3.49 could be replaced by a CLA adder. In this design, the carry is generated in a ripple fashion and the inclusion of a CLA adder would greatly speed the multiplication time, especially for large operands. The multiplication time for two 16-bit operands and two 32-bit operands would be $46 \, \Delta$ and $78 \, \Delta$, respectively, where Δ is the gate propagation time for the technology being used.

					$a_4\bar{b}_0$	$a_3 b_0$	$a_2 b_0$	$a_1 b_0$	$a_0 b_0$
				$a_4\bar{b}_1$	$a_3 b_1$	$a_2 b_1$	$a_1 b_1$	$a_0 b_1$	
			$a_4\bar{b}_2$	$a_3 b_2$	$a_2 b_2$	$a_1 b_2$	$a_0 b_2$		
		$a_4\bar{b}_3$	$a_3 b_3$	$a_2 b_3$	$a_1 b_3$	$a_0 b_3$			
	$a_4 b_4$	$\bar{a}_3 b_4$	$\bar{a}_2 b_4$	$\bar{a}_1 b_4$	$\bar{a}_0 b_4$				
	$\bar{a}_4$				a_4				
1	$\bar{b}_4$				b_4				

Product	2^9	2^8	2^7	2^6	2^5	2^4	2^3	2^2	2^1	2^0

Figure 3.48 Summand matrix $m = n = 5$.

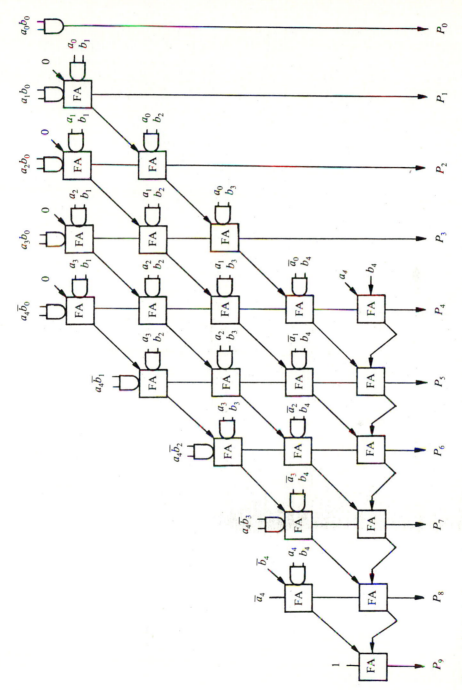

Figure 3.49 Logic diagram for a 5 × 5 2s complement array multiplier.

213

3.7 TABLE LOOKUP MULTIPLICATION

The method of multiplication presented in this section uses random access memory (RAM) for a local storage that contains different versions of the multiplicand. The multiply operation is faster than the standard add-shift technique, but not as fast as the array multipliers. Two approaches will be discussed. The first shifts the partial product three bit positions to the right after the add operation. The second shifts the partial product four bit positions to the right after the add operation, which is faster but requires more hardware. Both are variations of the standard add-shift method that shifts the partial product only one position to the right. These approaches are faster than the standard approach, but additional overhead cycles are required to load the different versions of the multiplicand into local store.

3.7.1 Three-Bit Shift

The organization of the first approach is shown in Fig. 3.50. Assume two n-bit operands multiplicand A and multiplier B, where

$$A = a_{n-1} \, a_{n-2} \cdots a_1 \, a_0$$

and

$$B = b_{n-1} \, b_{n-2} \cdots b_1 \, b_0$$

The microcode loads the multiplier from the data bus into the n-bit B register, which is also a shift register with the ability to shift three bit positions to the right. It is similar in design to the shift registers presented in Sec. 3.2. The RAM contains eight words of $n + 3$ bits per word and is loaded from either the data bus or the shifter. A word length of $n + 3$ bits is required, because the highest entry in the RAM is the multiplicand $\times$ 7 or, in other words, the multiplicand $\times$ 1 1 1 (or a product of $n + 3$ bits). The accumulator must be of sufficient length to accommodate the RAM entries ($n + 3$ bits), the multiplier (n bits), and any sign extension bits for the multiplier such that the number of bits in the multiplier is divisible by 3. For an eight-bit multiplier, the accumulator must be $[(8 + 3) + (8) + 1]$ bits wide. The adder must be the same width as the accumulator and can be any parallel implementation, preferably the CLA adder described in Sec. 2.2.3. The shifter is simply a string of multiplexers capable of shifting the sum outputs

$$S = s_{m-1} \, s_{m-2} \cdots s_1 \, s_0$$

three bit positions to the right. However, the design of the shifter is made more general than this and can accommodate a 0 shift; a right shift of one, two, three,

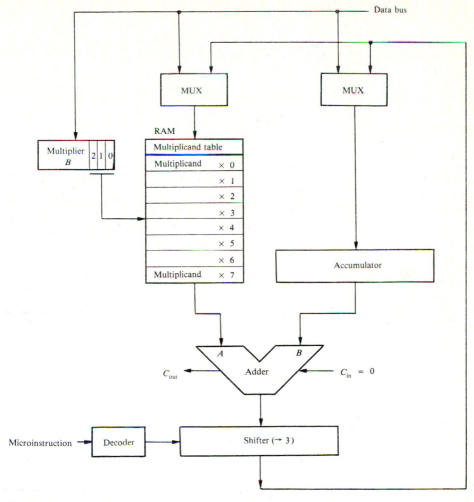

Figure 3.50 Organization for add-shift (three) multiplication.

or four positions; and a left shift of one, two, three, or four positions. These added features, although not needed for this design, will be useful in subsequent sections.

The operation of the multiply unit is controlled by a microprogram and is now described for 2 eight-bit operands. RAM location 0 is loaded with all 0s. The multiplicand is loaded into accumulator (ACC) positions 16–9, with positions 19–17 and 8–0 containing 0s.

	19		17	16				9	8								0
ACC	0	0	0		Multiplicand					0	0	0	0	0	0	0	0	0

Accumulator positions 19–0 connect to the B input positions 19–0 of the adder. RAM outputs 10–0 connect to the A input positions 19–9 of the adder, with adder A inputs 8–0 connected to a logic 0. Bit 0 of the RAM outputs is the low-order bit. The connections are shown in Fig. 3.51.

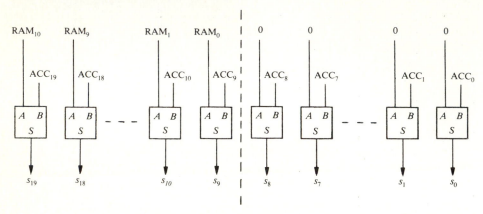

Figure 3.51 Interconnections between RAM, accumulator, and adder.

RAM location$_0$ is added to the contents of ACC$_{19-9}$ and stored in RAM location$_1$. The contents of RAM location$_1$ now contain the multiplicand. RAM location$_1$ is added to the contents of ACC$_{19-9}$ and stored in RAM location$_2$, the contents of which now contain the multiplicand $\times$ 2. The above procedure continues according to the operation

$$\text{RAM loc}_{i+1} \leftarrow \text{RAM loc}_i + \text{ACC}_{19-9}$$

until RAM locations 0–7 have been loaded with multiplicand $\times$ 0 to multiplicand $\times$ 7, respectively. The accumulator is reset to 0 and the multiplier is loaded into register B. With the overhead cycles now complete, the multiply calculation can begin.

The low-order three bits of the multiplier, $b_2 b_1 b_0$, are applied to the RAM address lines. Three bits were chosen to address the RAM, because this requires that only eight RAM locations be used, thus necessitating eight cycles to load the RAM. If the four low-order bits of the multiplier were used to address 16 storage locations, this would require 16 cycles to load storage and thus would increase the time for a multiply operation. Two multiplier bits addressing four storage locations does not offer any appreciable advantage over other add-shift methods, especially for small operands.

The contents of the RAM location addressed by the three low-order multiplier bits is added to the contents of the accumulator (initially all 0s). The adder performs the following addition with a 0 carry-in during each cycle:

$$S \leftarrow \text{RAM loc}_{b_2 b_1 b_0} \cdot \text{logic } 0_{8-0} + \text{ACC}_{19-0}$$

where the center dot ($\cdot$) represents concatenation and the plus sign ($+$) is addition. The following right-shift operation is performed immediately after sum S is formed at the outputs of the adder.

$$S_{i-3} \leftarrow S_i$$

The sum is shifted three bit positions to the right with the sign extended to the left such that

$$S_{18} \cdot S_{17} \cdot S_{16} \leftarrow S_{19}$$

and the shifted sum is loaded into the accumulator, according to the following operation:

$$\text{ACC}_{19\text{-}0} \leftarrow \text{SHFT}_{19\text{-}17} \text{ (sign extend)} \cdot \text{SHFT}_{16\text{-}0}$$

Sum bits $s_2 s_1 s_0$ are discarded during the shift.

The multiplier in register B is shifted three bit positions to the right and the above procedure repeats until all 3-tuples of the multiplier have been expended. In the case of eight-bit operands, register B requires one additional bit b_n for sign extension. This allows the number of bits in the multiplier to be divisible by 3; that is, there are three 3-tuples.

Two multiplication examples, using the method described in this section, are illustrated in Fig. 3.52. Figure 3.52(a) depicts a positive product while Fig. 3.52(b) shows a negative product. The carry-out of the adder is not used. With no overflow occurring, a carry-out is simply the sign extension for a negative number, and the number is already contained in the low-order $2n$ bits of the accumulator. The decoder and shifter logic for a typical shift element are shown in Fig. 3.53.

3.7.2 Four-Bit Shift

The second method of multiplication using table lookup is similar in concept to the bit-pair recoding scheme presented earlier. The main difference is that four bits are examined instead of two. Recall that a string of 1s could be interpreted as a subtraction followed by an addition at some higher value in the positional number system. The same is true in four-bit-pair recoding. The multiplier is partitioned into four-bit segments, and each segment is examined to determine the version of the multiplicand to be used. This results in either an addition of the multiplicand version or a subtraction followed subsequently by an addition. The goal is to be able to shift four bits at a time and still require only eight versions of the multiplicand in RAM instead of the 16 versions normally required when shifting four bits. This will reduce the multiply time beyond that of the previous method by maintaining the advantage of only eight entries in RAM, together with a further speedup by shifting the multiplier four bits instead of three. As it turns out, nine entries are required, as will be apparent later.

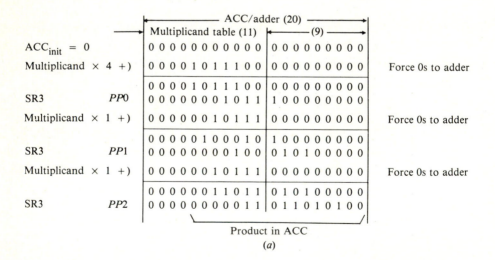

$$
\begin{array}{r}
0\;0\;0\;1\;0\;1\;1\;1 \quad (+23)\\
\boxed{0}\;0\;1\;0\;0\;1\;1\;0\;0\; \quad (+76)\\
\hline
0\;0\;0\;0\;0\;0\;0\;0\;0\;0\;0\;0\;0\;0\;0\;0\\
0\;0\;0\;0\;0\;0\;0\;0\;0\;0\;0\;0\;0\;0\;0\;0\\
0\;0\;0\;0\;0\;0\;0\;0\;1\;0\;1\;1\;1\\
0\;0\;0\;0\;0\;0\;0\;0\;1\;0\;1\;1\;1\\
0\;0\;0\;0\;0\;0\;0\;0\;0\;0\;0\\
0\;0\;0\;0\;0\;0\;0\;0\;0\;0\\
0\;0\;0\;0\;0\;1\;0\;1\;1\;1\\
0\;0\;0\;0\;0\;0\;0\;0\;0\\
\hline
0\;0\;0\;0\;0\;1\;1\;0\;1\;1\;0\;1\;0\;1\;0\;0 \quad (+1748)
\end{array}
$$

Multiplicand $\times$ 1 = 0 0 0 | 0 0 0 1 0 1 1 1

Multiplicand $\times$ 4 = 0 0 0 | 0 1 0 1 1 1 0 0

		ACC/adder (20)	
		Multiplicand table (11)	(9)
ACC_{init} = 0		0 0 0 0 0 0 0 0 0 0 0	0 0 0 0 0 0 0 0 0
Multiplicand $\times$ 4 +)		0 0 0 0 1 0 1 1 1 0 0	0 0 0 0 0 0 0 0 0	Force 0s to adder
		0 0 0 0 1 0 1 1 1 0 0	0 0 0 0 0 0 0 0 0	
SR3	PP0	0 0 0 0 0 0 0 1 0 1 1	1 0 0 0 0 0 0 0 0	
Multiplicand $\times$ 1 +)		0 0 0 0 0 0 1 0 1 1 1	0 0 0 0 0 0 0 0 0	Force 0s to adder
		0 0 0 0 0 1 0 0 0 1 0	1 0 0 0 0 0 0 0 0	
SR3	PP1	0 0 0 0 0 0 0 0 1 0 0	0 1 0 1 0 0 0 0 0	
Multiplicand $\times$ 1 +)		0 0 0 0 0 0 1 0 1 1 1	0 0 0 0 0 0 0 0 0	Force 0s to adder
		0 0 0 0 0 0 1 1 0 1 1	0 1 0 1 0 0 0 0 0	
SR3	PP2	0 0 0 0 0 0 0 0 0 1 1	0 1 1 0 1 0 1 0 0	

Product in ACC

(*a*)

Figure 3.52 Add-shift-three multiplication examples.

```
                    1 0 0 0 0 1 1 1   (−121)
                 [0] 0 1, 0 1 0, 0 1 1  (+83)
          ─────────────────────────────
          1 1 1 1 1 1 1 1 1 0 0 0 0 1 1 1
          1 1 1 1 1 1 1 1 0 0 0 0 1 1 1
          0 0 0 0 0 0 0 0 0 0 0 0 0 0
          0 0 0 0 0 0 0 0 0 0 0 0 0
          1 1 1 1 1 0 0 0 0 1 1 1
          0 0 0 0 0 0 0 0 0 0 0
          1 1 1 0 0 0 0 1 1 1
          0 0 0 0 0 0 0 0 0
     ─────────────────────────────────
     1 1 1 1 0 1 1 0 0 0 1 1 0 0 0 1 0 1  (−10043)
```

```
Multiplicand × 1 = 1 1 1|1 0 0 0 0 1 1 1
Multiplicand × 2 = 1 1 1|0 0 0 0 1 1 1 0
Multiplicand × 3 = 1 1 0|1 0 0 1 0 1 0 1
```

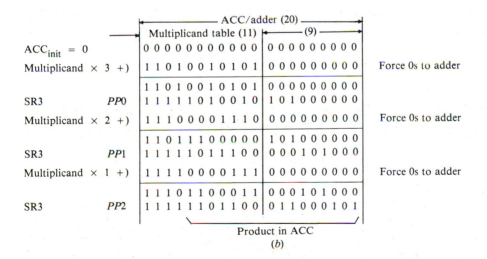

Product in ACC

(b)

Figure 3.52 (Continued)

8	4	2	1	
0	0	0	0	No shift
0	0	0	1	Shift right 1
0	0	1	0	Shift right 2
0	0	1	1	Shift right 3
0	1	0	0	Shift right 4
0	1	0	0	
0	1	1	0	
0	1	1	1	
1	0	0	0	
1	0	0	1	Shift left 1
1	0	1	0	Shift left 2
1	0	1	1	Shift left 3
1	1	0	0	Shift left 4
1	1	0	1	
1	1	1	0	
1	1	1	1	

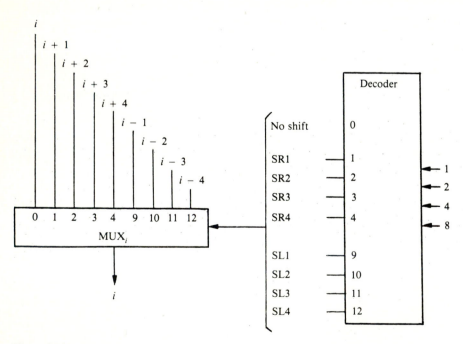

Figure 3.53 Decoder and typical shift element.

Consider the following 2 four-bit segments.

2^7	2^6	2^5	2^4	2^3	2^2	2^1	2^0
	$i + 1$				i		
0	0	0	0	1	1	0	0

The value of segment i is 12. This means that 12 times the multiplicand should be added to the partial product. But this would require more than nine entries in RAM. If, instead, four times the multiplicand were subtracted from the partial product, this would be contained within the eight entries and the adder would become a subtractor. By subtracting four times the multiplicand, this puts the resultant partial product a distance 16 lower than what it should be. Therefore, 16 must be added back to the partial product, indicating that a 1 should be placed in bit postion 2^4. The two segments would be effectively changed, as shown below.

2^7	2^6	2^5	2^4	2^3	2^2	2^1	2^0
	$i + 1$				i		
0	0	0	1	1	1	0	0

The multiplier bits are not physically changed, but the multiplicand versions in RAM are selected based upon the following rules.

1. If the high-order bit of the segment under consideration is a 0, then select the appropriate multiplicand version from the RAM and add this to the partial product.
2. If the high-order bit of the segment under consideration is a 1, then a multiplicand version n is subtracted from the partial product such that

$$\left| \text{Segment}_i + n \right| = 16$$

The binary string 0 0 0 1 is then added to segment $i + 1$ to change its effective value.

In step 2 above, there is no hardware addition; a pointer selects the appropriate version of the multiplicand in RAM. Referring to the original segments $i + 1 = 0\ 0\ 0\ 0$ and $i = 1\ 1\ 0\ 0$, segment i causes a pointer to select multiplicand $\times$ 4 from the RAM. This is subtracted from the partial product and a SUBTRACT flip-flop is set to 1. The $i + 1$ segment (0 0 0 0) of the multiplier is then examined. This would normally select multiplicand $\times$ 0, but since the SUBTRACT flip-flop is set, multiplicand $\times$ 1 is selected instead, and this is added to the appropriately shifted partial product. The multiplier is scanned from right to left and each four-bit segment is examined in turn, after which the appropriate addition or subtraction takes place based upon the preceding rules.

The architecture for the four-bit-pair recoding scheme is shown in Fig. 3.54. The multiplicand table is a RAM that is loaded from either the data bus or the sum output of the adder. The three high-order bits allow for the maximum version of the multiplicand, which is the multiplicand $\times$ 8. Register D, a shift register that contains the partial product, is initially reset to all 0s. It is configured as follows:

$$d_{n+2} \cdot d_{n+1} \cdot d_n \cdot d_{n-1} \cdots \cdots d_1 \cdot d_0$$

The multiplier register B is also a shift register into which the partial product from register D is shifted as the multiplier is shifted out. It is configured as follows:

$$b_{n+3} \cdot b_{n+2} \cdot b_{n+1} \cdot b_n \cdot b_{n-1} \cdots \cdots b_1 \cdot b_0$$

The high-order four bits are initialized to 0 0 0 0 when the multiplier is loaded. The reason for this will be discussed when a worked example is executed. The last-operation (last-op) flip-flop is set from b_3 near the end of each add-shift cycle. The add/subtract control store (ASCS) ROM selects the appropriate version of the multiplicand, contingent upon the current multiplier bits $b_3 b_2 b_1 b_0$ and the state of the last-op flip-flop.

The contents of the ASCS ROM are shown in Table 3.4. If the current four-bit segment ranges from 0 0 0 0 to 0 1 1 1 and the previous operation was an add, then the appropriate multiplicand table entry will be selected and the contents will be added to the partial product. The same sequence will occur if the last operation was a subtract and the current four-bit segment is in the range 0 0 0 0 to 0 1 1 1. However, a different multiplicand version will be selected. If the current four-bit segment ranges from 1 0 0 0 to 1 1 1 1 and the previous operation was an add, then the appropriate version of the multiplicand will be subtracted from the partial product. The same is true if the last operation was a subtract and the current four-bit sequence ranges from 1 0 0 0 to 1 1 1 1, except that a different version of the multiplicand will be subtracted. The ASCS ROM address bits are

2^4	2^3	2^2	2^1	2^0
Last op FF	b_3	b_2	b_1	b_0

and the outputs are $2^3\ 2^2\ 2^1\ 2^0$, which are applied to the address inputs of the multiplicand table RAM.

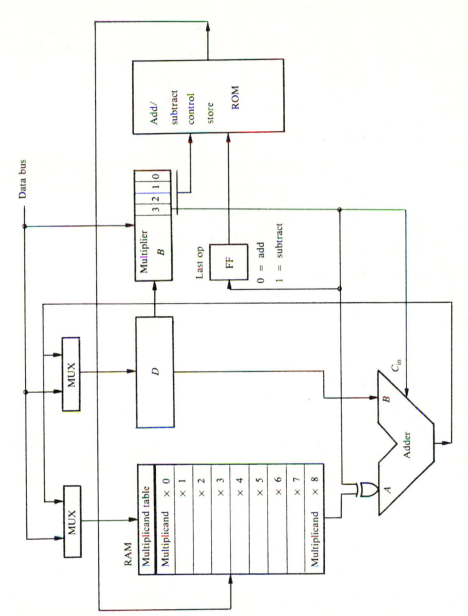

Figure 3.54 Organization for four-bit-pair multiplication.

Table 3.4 Add/subtract control ROM

ROM address	Last op	Four-bit segment	Multiplicand table entry (hex)	Present op
0 0 0 0 0		0 0 0 0	0	
0 0 0 0 1		0 0 0 1	1	
0 0 0 1 0		0 0 1 0	2	
0 0 0 1 1		0 0 1 1	3	Add
0 0 1 0 0		0 1 0 0	4	
0 0 1 0 1	Add	0 1 0 1	5	
0 0 1 1 0		0 1 1 0	6	
0 0 1 1 1		0 1 1 1	7	
0 1 0 0 0	(FF = 0)	1 0 0 0	8	
0 1 0 0 1		1 0 0 1	7	
0 1 0 1 0		1 0 1 0	6	
0 1 0 1 1		1 0 1 1	5	Subtract
0 1 1 0 0		1 1 0 0	4	
0 1 1 0 1		1 1 0 1	3	
0 1 1 1 0		1 1 1 0	2	
0 1 1 1 1		1 1 1 1	1	
1 0 0 0 0		0 0 0 0	1	
1 0 0 0 1		0 0 0 1	2	
1 0 0 1 0		0 0 1 0	3	
1 0 0 1 1		0 0 1 1	4	Add
1 0 1 0 0		0 1 0 0	5	
1 0 1 0 1	Subtract	0 1 0 1	6	
1 0 1 1 0		0 1 1 0	7	
1 0 1 1 1		0 1 1 1	8	
1 1 0 0 0	(FF = 1)	1 0 0 0	7	
1 1 0 0 1		1 0 0 1	6	
1 1 0 1 0		1 0 1 0	5	
1 1 0 1 1		1 0 1 1	4	Subtract
1 1 1 0 0		1 1 0 0	3	
1 1 1 0 1		1 1 0 1	2	
1 1 1 1 0		1 1 1 0	1	
1 1 1 1 1		1 1 1 1	0	

It is now appropriate to consider examples that illustrate how contiguous segments work together to produce various versions of the multiplicand that are added to or subtracted from the previous partial product. Figure 3.55 contains a number of different segment combinations that illustrate this principle.

The operation of the four-bit-pair multiplication technique is easily understood by the application of a worked example. Refer to the hardware organization of Fig. 3.54 while studying the example described below. Figure 3.56 shows the multiplication of two 16-bit operands. The multiplier is assumed to be positive; it is either initially positive or the 2s complement of a negative multiplier. The hardware algorithm for the same two operands, as established by the organization of the four-bit-pair technique, is shown in Fig. 3.57. Multiplier

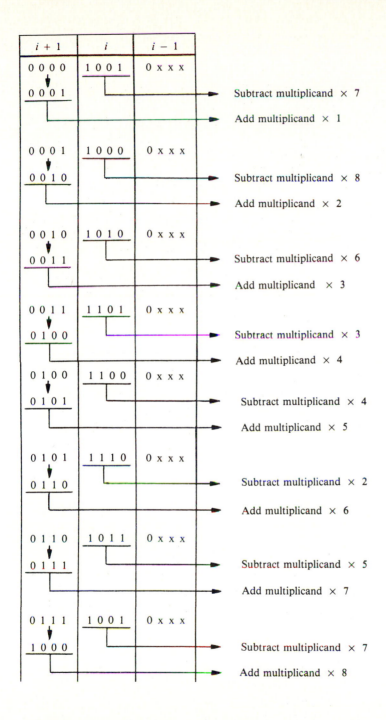

Figure 3.55 Examples for selecting multiplicand table entries; x = don't care.

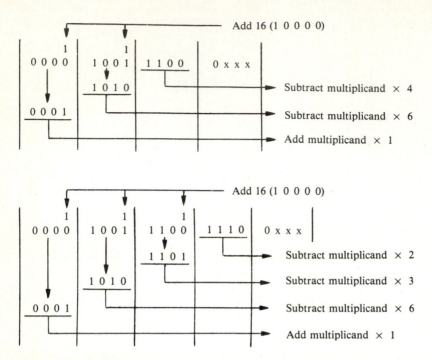

Figure 3.55 (Continued)

register B must contain a leftmost segment$_{m-1}$ of 0 0 0 0. This is to ensure that a final addition will take place in the event that segment$_{m-2}$ caused a subtraction.

The multiplicand table location 0 is reset to all 0s, and the multiplicand is loaded into location 1 and register D. The contents of location 1 are added to the contents of register D and the sum is stored in location 2. Location 2 now contains the multiplicand $\times$ 2. Multiplicand table location 2 is now added to the contents of register D and the sum is stored in location 3, which now contains the multiplicand $\times$ 3. This procedure repeats until locations 0–8 have been loaded with multiplicand $\times$ 0 to multiplicand $\times$ 8, respectively, as illustrated in Fig. 3.54. The microcode loads each multiplicand table location according to the following operation:

$$\text{Location}_{i+1} \leftarrow \text{location}_i + (d_{n+2} \cdots d_1 d_0)$$

Register D and the last-op flip-flop (FF) are then reset to 0 and the multiplier is loaded into register B.

The four low-order bits of the multiplier, $b_3 b_2 b_1 b_0$, together with the state of the last-op FF, are applied to the address inputs of the ASCS ROM. Since the first segment (0 0 1 0) of the multiplier is in the range 0 0 0 0 to 0 1 1 1 and

Multiplicand	0 0 0 0 0 0 0 0 0 0 0 1 0 1 0 0 (+20)
Multiplier	×) 0 1 1 0 1 1 0 1 0 1 0 1 0 0 1 0 (+27,986)

```
0 0 0 0 0 0 0 0 0 0 0 0 0 0 0 0 0 0 0 0 0 0 0 0 0 0 0 0 0 0 0 0
0 . . . . . . . . . . . . . . . . . . . . . . . . . 0 0 1 0 1 0 0
0 . . . . . . . . . . . . . . . . . . . . . . . . . 0 0 0 0 0 0 0
0 . . . . . . . . . . . . . . . . . . . . . . . 0 0 0 0 0 0 0
0 . . . . . . . . . . . . . . . . . . . . 0 0 1 0 1 0 0
0 . . . . . . . . . . . . . . . . . . . 0 0 0 0 0 0 0
0 . . . . . . . . . . . . . . . . . 0 0 1 0 1 0 0
0 . . . . . . . . . . . . . . . . 0 0 0 0 0 0 0
0 . . . . . . . . . . . . . . . 0 0 1 0 1 0 0
0 . . . . . . . . . . . . . . 0 0 0 0 0 0 0
0 . . . . . . . . . . . . 0 0 1 0 1 0 0
0 . . . . . . . . . . . 0 0 1 0 1 0 0
0 . . . . . . . . . . 0 0 0 0 0 0 0
0 . . . . . . . . . 0 0 1 0 1 0 0
0 . . . . . . . . 0 0 1 0 1 0 0
0 0 0 0 0 0 0 0 0 0 0 0 0 0 0 0 0
```

0 0 0 0 0 0 0 0 0 0 0 0 1 0 0 0 1 0 0 0 1 0 1 0 0 1 1 0 1 0 0 0 (+ 559,720)

Figure 3.56 Paper-and-pencil calculation for multiplying two 16-bit operands.

last-op FF $= 0$, location 2 (multiplicand $\times$ 2) in the multiplicand table is added to the initial partial product PP of all 0s. The sum outputs of the adder

$$S = s_{n+2} \, s_{n+1} \, s_n \, s_{n-1} \, \cdots \, s_1 \, s_0$$

are loaded into register D locations

$$d_{n+2} \, d_{n+1} \, d_n \, d_{n-1} \, \cdots \, d_1 \, d_0$$

respectively. The three high-order bits, $s_{n+2} \, s_{n+1} \, s_n$, of the adder are needed to allow for the $(n+3)$-bit product that resides in the multiplicand table. Registers D and B are then shifted right four bit positions in concatenation such that

$$d_{n+1} \cdot d_n \cdot d_{n-1} \cdot d_{n-2} \leftarrow d_{n+2}$$
$$d_{i-4} \leftarrow d_i$$
$$b_{n+3} \leftarrow d_3$$
$$b_{n+2} \leftarrow d_2$$
$$b_{i-4} \leftarrow b_i$$

and last-op FF is reset.

The next four-bit segment (0 1 0 1), which is now in positions $b_3 b_2 b_1 b_0$ of register B, together with last-op FF $= 0$, is applied to the address inputs of the ASCS ROM, and location 5 (multiplicand $\times$ 5) of the multiplicand table is add-

+Multiplicand × 2	0000 0000 0000 0000 0000 0000 0000 0010 1000 1000				
PP0	0000 0000 0010 1000 1000				1 0 0 0
SR4	0000 0000 0000 0010 1000				
+Multiplicand × 5	0000 0000 0110 0110 0100 0000 0000 0110 0110 0110				
PP1	0000 0000 0110 0110 0110			0 1 1 0 1 0 0 0	
SR4	1111 1111 1100 0100				
−Multiplicand × 3	1111 1111 1100 1010 0100				
PP2	1111 1111 1100 1010	1 0 1 0 0 1 1 0 1 0 0 0			
SR4	0000 0000 1000 1100				
+Multiplicand × 7	0000 0000 1000 1000 1000 0000 0000 1000 1000 1010 0110 1000				
PP3	0000 0000 1000 1000 1000				
SR4	0000 0000 0000 0000				
Multiplicand × 0	0000 0000 0000 1000 0000 0000 0000 0000				
PP4	0000 0000 0000 0000 1000 1000 1010 0110 1000				
SR4					

Product = +559,720

Figure 3.57 Hardware algorithm for four-bit-pair multiplication technique.

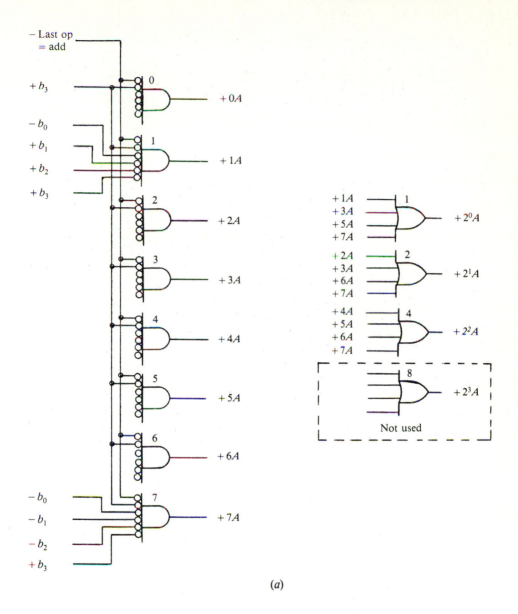

(a)

Figure 3.58 Logic diagram for ASCS ROM. $(a) + b_3 \Rightarrow$ segment $= 0\ 0\ 0\ 0$ to $0\ 1\ 1\ 1\ \Rightarrow$ add. Inputs b_3, b_2, b_1, b_0 increase in a binary manner from $0\ 0\ 0\ 0$ to $0\ 1\ 1\ 1$ for AND gates 0–7, respectively. $(b) - b_3 \Rightarrow$ segment $= 1\ 0\ 0\ 0$ to $1\ 1\ 1\ 1 \Rightarrow$ subtract. $(c) + b_3 \Rightarrow$ segment $= 0\ 0\ 0\ 0$ to $0\ 1\ 1\ 1 \Rightarrow$ add. $(d) - b_3 \Rightarrow$ segment $= 1\ 0\ 0\ 0$ to $1\ 1\ 1\ 1 \Rightarrow$ subtract. (e) Logic diagram includes last-op FF.

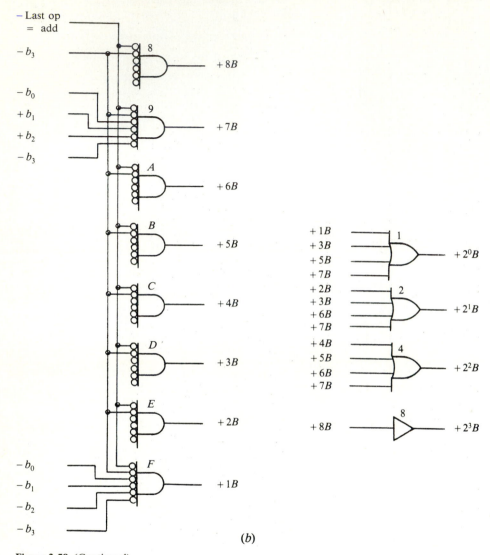

(b)

Figure 3.58 (Continued)

ed to the shifted partial product. The adder sum is loaded into register D and registers D and B are again shifted four bit positions to the right. Last-op FF is reset.

The next four-bit segment (1 1 0 1) of the multiplier subtracts three times the multiplicand from the partial product (the actual operation is to add the 2s complement of multiplicand $\times$ 3). The sum is loaded into register D and shifted right. Last-op FF is set to 1. The final segment of the multiplier causes seven times the multiplicand to be added to the partial product. The sum is loaded into register D and shifted right. Last-op FF is reset to 0. The left 0s segment of the

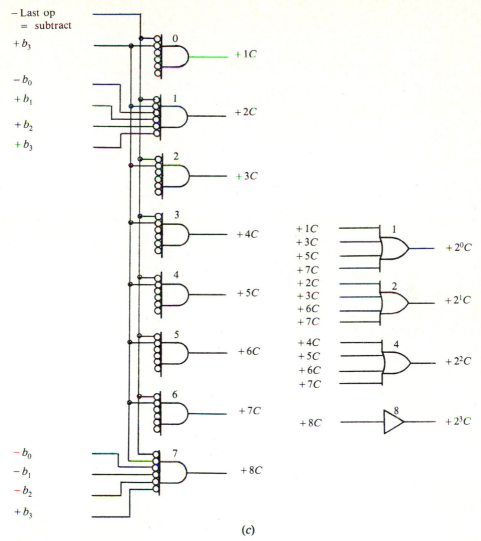

(c)

Figure 3.58 (Continued)

multiplier simply adds 0 to the partial product. After the right shift takes place, the final 32-bit product is in positions

$$d_{n-5} \cdot d_{n-4} \cdots \cdots d_1 \cdot d_0 \cdot b_{n+3} \cdot b_{n+2} \cdots \cdots b_1 \cdot b_0$$

If the access time for the ASCS ROM is not fast enough for the performance requirements of the processor, then the ROM can be replaced by the hardware illustrated in Fig. 3.58. This appears to be a substantial amount of logic to replace one ROM, but the designs in this text are based upon LSI and VLSI technology, so that the required logic may use only a small part of one chip. A further in-

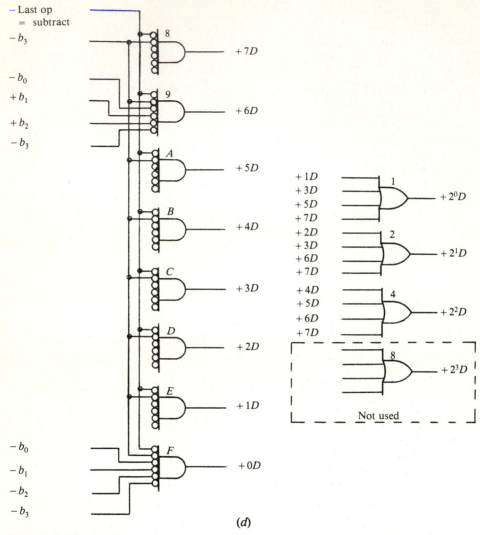

Figure 3.58 (Continued)

crease in speed can be realized by replacing the multiplicand table RAM by nine discrete registers.

Multiplicand × 0 register ⇒ force 0s to the adder

Multiplicand × 1 register ⇒ load register with multiplicand

Multiplicand × 2 register ⇒ load register with multiplicand shifted left one bit position

Multiplicand × 4 register ⇒ load register with multiplicand shifted left two bit positions

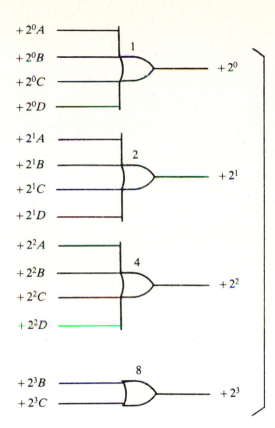

To multiplicand table RAM

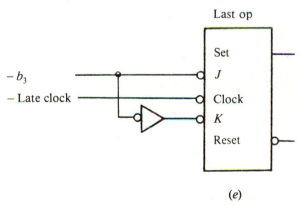

(e)

Figure 3.58 (Continued)

The previous operations can be done in the same cycle. The remaining registers are loaded in the manner already prescribed.

PROBLEMS

3.1 Use the paper-and-pencil method to perform the operation $A \times B$ on the following five-bit 2s-complemented operands.

    (a) A (multiplicand) = 0 1 1 1 0
         B (multiplier)   = 0 0 1 1 1
    (b) A (multiplicand) = 1 1 1 1 1
         B (multiplier)   = 0 1 0 1 1

3.2 Multiply the following 2s-complemented operands using the sequential add-shift method shown in Fig. 3.2.

    (a) A (multiplicand) = 1 1 1 1
         B (multiplier)   = 0 1 0 1
    (b) A (multiplicand) = 0 1 0 1
         B (multiplier)   = 0 1 1 1

3.3 Use the Booth algorithm to multiply the following 2s-complemented operands.

    (a) A (multiplicand) = 0 0 1 1 1
         B (multiplier)   = 0 1 1 0 1
    (b) A (multiplicand) = 0 1 0 1 1 1
         B (multiplier)   = 0 0 1 1 0 1
    (c) A (multiplicand) = 0 1 0 1 1 0
         B (multiplier)   = 1 1 0 1 1 0

3.4 Use bit-pair recoding to multiply the following 2s-complemented operands.

    (a) A (multiplicand) = 0 1 1 1 1
         B (multiplier)   = 0 1 1 0 1
    (b) A (multiplicand) = 0 0 0 1 1
         B (multiplier)   = 1 1 1 0 1

3.5 Use the Booth algorithm to multiply the following operands.

                    A (multiplicand) = 0 1 0 1 1
                    B (multiplier)   = 1 1 0 1 0

3.6 Use bit-pair recoding to multiply the following operands.

                    A (multiplicand) = 0 0 0 0 1 1
                    B (multiplier)   = 0 1 0 1 0 1

3.7 Multiply the following two unsigned operands using the array shown below.

                    A (multiplicand) = 1 0 1
                    B (multiplier)   = 1 1 1

Show all partial products and carries.

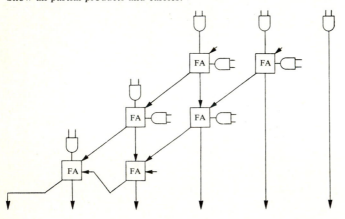

3.8 Use the table lookup method of four-bit-pair recoding to determine the multiplicand versions to be added or subtracted for each multiplier segment shown below.

(a) | 0 0 0 0 | 1 0 0 1 | 1 1 0 0 | 0 x x x |

(b) | 1 0 0 0 | 1 1 1 1 | 1 0 1 1 | 0 0 1 1 | 1 x x x |

3.9 Draw a block diagram using carry-save full adders and a carry lookahead adder to add the following three unsigned binary operands.

$$A = 1 1 0$$
$$B = 1 1 1$$
$$C = 1 0 1$$

3.10 Use carry-save full adders to design a nine-bit-slice Wallace tree.

3.11 Use the table lookup method for four-bit-pair recoding to determine the multiplicand versions to be added or subtracted for each multiplier segment shown below. Indicate the rule that is used for each segment.

(a) | 1 0 1 1 | 0 0 1 1 | 1 1 1 1 | 0 1 1 1 | 0 x x x |

(b) | 1 1 1 0 | 0 1 1 0 | 0 1 0 1 | 1 1 0 1 | 1 x x x |

3.12 Multiply the two 16-bit operands below using the table lookup method for four-bit-pair recoding.

$$A \text{ (multiplicand)} = 0 0 0 0 0 0 0 0 0 0 0 0 0 0 1 0$$
$$B \text{ (multiplier)} = 0 0 0 1 1 0 1 0 0 0 1 0 1 1 0 0$$

3.13 Design a 2×2 fixed-point binary array multiplier for unsigned operands using only the cell shown below.

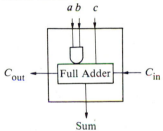

3.14 Use bit-pair recoding to multiply the following operands.

$$A \text{ (multiplicand)} = 0 0 1 1 0$$
$$B \text{ (multiplier)} = 1 1 0 1 0$$

3.15 What are the advantages and disadvantages of implementing a fixed-point binary multiplication algorithm with:

(a) Hardware only?

(b) Hardware and firmware?

(c) Software only?

3.16 Why must the multiplier be positive in the sequential add-shift multiplication technique?

3.17 Show that the fixed-point multiplication of two n-digit operands with radix r produces a product $\leqslant 2n$ digits in length. Show that no overflow can occur.

3.18 Design a 2×2 fixed-point binary array multiplier using AND gates and half adders.

3.19 Design a 3×3 fixed-point binary array multiplier using AND gates, half adders, and full adders.

3.20 Illustrate the carry-save addition principle by performing the addition operation on three n-bit operands A, B, and C such that

$$\text{Sum} = A + B + C$$

Use carry-save adders and a ripple-carry adder.

FOUR

FIXED-POINT DIVISION

4.1 INTRODUCTION

In most computers, division is a considerably slower operation than multiplication. The nature of division is such that it does not easily lend itself to speedup techniques, as does multiplication. Division also occurs less frequently than multiplication and its slower speed can thus be better tolerated. Division is derived from multiplication and is defined as the determination of the quotient, which, when multiplied by the divisor, produces the dividend; that is,

$$\text{Dividend} = \text{divisor} \times \text{quotient}$$

or
$$\frac{\text{Dividend}}{\text{Divisor}} = \text{quotient}$$

or
$$\text{Divisor} \overline{\smash{\big)}\text{dividend}}^{\text{quotient}}$$

In contrast to multiplication, the division operation is not commutative; that is, $A/B \neq B/A$, except when $A = B$. It is not always possible to obtain an integer quotient for an integer dividend and divisor, and this leads to the concept of a remainder. The remainder has a smaller magnitude than the divisor and the same sign as the dividend. Division is basically the inverse of multiplication, with the dividend, divisor, and quotient corresponding to the product, multiplicand, and multiplier, respectively. Because division is the inverse of multiplication, a 16-bit dividend divided by an eight-bit divisor will yield an eight-bit quotient. The remainder is also an eight-bit number.

Division differs from multiplication in many aspects. Division is a shift-subtract divisor operation, whereas multiplication is a shift-add multiplicand operation. The results of one subtraction (which requires a comparison check) determine the next operation in a division sequence. Therefore, division has an inherent dependency on the previous subtraction and this occurs serially for all subsequent cycles. This problem does not occur in multiplication and, as a result, all summands can be generated simultaneously, if required. Division is usually not a deterministic process; that is, the procedure is not fixed. Instead, it is a trial-and-error process in which successive quotient digits are selected from a digit set. In binary arithmetic, the process is easier, because the number of digits in the set of radix 2 consists of 0 and 1 only.

In decimal division, the divisor is compared to the dividend (or current partial remainder) to determine how many multiples it is of the divisor. The estimate thus obtained is checked by multiplying the divisor by the quotient digit and subtracting the resultant product from the partial remainder. If the subtraction yields a negative result, then the quotient digit q_i was too large and a smaller value is tried. If subtraction yields a positive result, but one that is larger than or equal to the divisor, then q_i was too small and a larger value is necessary. The correct digit q_i is such that

$$0 \leqslant \text{dividend} - \text{divisor} \times q_i < \text{divisor}$$

Binary division is considerably simpler, because there are only two possible guesses, either 0 or 1. If the divisor is smaller than the partial remainder, the quotient bit is 1 and a subtraction is performed; if it is larger, the quotient bit is 0 and no subtraction takes place. The quotient digits are selected sequentially from the most-significant digit to the least-significant digits. The remainder is usually obtained automatically once the quotient has been determined.

This chapter will present the sequential add/subtract method for restoring and nonrestoring division, a technique for generating strings of 0s and 1s by which division is speeded up in much the same way as multiplication, a convergence technique using high-speed multipliers, and methods of high-speed hardware division using two-dimensional iterative cellular arrays.

4.2 SEQUENTIAL SHIFT-SUBTRACT/ADD RESTORING DIVISION

Division of two fixed-point binary numbers is done with paper and pencil by a process of successive subtraction, shift, and comparison operations. Binary division is simpler than decimal division, because the quotient digits are either 0 or 1 and there is no need to estimate the number of times the divisor will fit into the dividend or partial remainder. Let A and B be the dividend and divisior, respectively, where

$$A = a_{2n-1} \, a_{2n-2} \cdots a_n \, a_{n-1} \cdots a_1 a_0$$

and

$$B = b_{n-1} \, b_{n-2} \cdots b_1 b_0$$

The dividend is a $2n$-bit signed integer and the divisor is an n-bit signed integer. The quotient Q and remainder R are also n-bit signed integers, where

$$Q = q_{n-1} q_{n-2} \cdots q_1 q_0$$

and

$$R = r_{n-1} r_{n-2} \cdots r_1 r_0$$

In machine operation, the dividend is divided by the divisor and is usually replaced by the quotient and remainder. The sign of the quotient is determined by the rules of algebra. The sign of the dividend is a_{2n-1}, and the sign of the divisor is b_{n-1}. Therefore, the sign of the quotient is

$$q_{n-1} = a_{2n-1} \veebar b_{n-1}$$

Thus, $q_{n-1} = 1$ (negative quotient) if

$$a_{2n-1} = 0 \quad \text{and} \quad b_{n-1} = 1$$

or

$$a_{2n-1} = 1 \quad \text{and} \quad b_{n-1} = 0$$

Otherwise, $q_{n-1} = 0$ (positive quotient). The remainder has the same sign as the dividend.

The division process is illustrated by a binary numerical example in Fig. 4.1. Divisor B consists of five bits and dividend A has 10 bits. The divisor is subtracted from the five most-significant bits of the dividend. The result of this subtraction is negative, indicating that the value of the divisor is greater than the five dividend bits. Because the result is a negative value, a 0 is placed in the quotient high-order bit. The divisor is then shifted right one bit position and is again subtracted from the corresponding bits of the dividend (not the partial remainder). The result is again negative, which places a 0 in the next lower-order bit of the quotient. The divisor is shifted right one bit position and subtracted from the dividend. This sequence continues for five shift-subtract cycles. Note that the fourth shift-subtract operation results in a positive difference, which indicates that the value of the divisor was smaller than the value of the corresponding dividend bits. In this case, a 1 is placed in the next lower-order bit position of the quotient. Since the result was positive, the dividend (or previous partial remainder) is not restored and this result (0 0 0 0 1) becomes the new partial remainder together with the next lower-order bit of the dividend, which is right-concatenated.

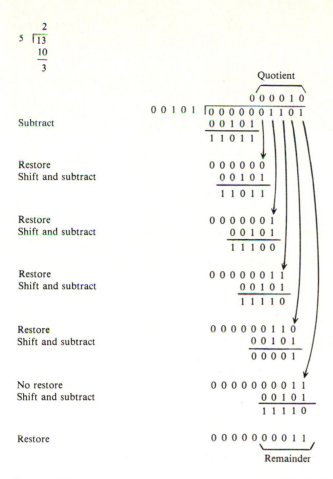

Figure 4.1 Binary division example using paper-and-pencil method.

The difference is called a *partial remainder*, because the division could have stopped at this cycle to obtain a quotient of 1 and a remainder equal to the partial remainder. The logic that implements binary division must methodically position the divisor with respect to the appropriate bits in the dividend (or partial remainder) and perform a subtraction. If the partial remainder is 0 or positive, a 1 is placed in the quotient and the remainder is right-concatenated with another bit of the dividend. The divisor is then repositioned and another subtraction is performed. If the partial remainder is negative, a 0 is placed in the quotient and the dividend (or previous partial remainder) is restored by adding back the divisor. The divisor is then repositioned for another subtraction. This is called the *restoring division technique*.

When division is implemented in a digital computer, the process is changed slightly. Instead of shifting the divisor to the right, the dividend or partial remainder is shifted to the left, thus leaving the two numbers in the required relative position. Subtraction can be achieved by adding the 2s complement of the divisor. The information about the relative magnitude is then available from the carry-out of the high-order bit position.

Binary restoring division requires a maximum of one subtraction and one addition for each quotient digit, that is, for each cycle. The following recursive formula is used repeatedly during a division operation.

$$R_j = R_{j-1} - q_j \times B \tag{4.1}$$

where

$$
\begin{aligned}
R_j &= \text{current partial remainder} \\
R_{j-1} &= \text{previous partial remainder} \\
q_j &= \text{current quotient bit} \\
B &= \text{divisor}
\end{aligned}
$$

and each quotient digit $q_j \in \{0, 1\}$. Each quotient digit is selected based upon the following selection criteria:

$$
q_j = \begin{cases} 0 & \text{if } R_{j-1} < B \\ 1 & \text{if } R_{j-1} \geq B \end{cases} \tag{4.2}
$$

That is, if the value of the previous partial remainder is less than the divisor (R_j will be negative), then quotient bit q_j is set to 0; if the value of the previous partial remainder is greater than or equal to the divisor (R_j will be positive), then quotient bit q_j is set to 1.

Each subtraction produces a tentative current partial remainder

$$R_{j(t)} = R_{j-1} - B \tag{4.3}$$

If the sign of $R_{j(t)}$ is positive, then $q_j = 1$ and $R_j = R_{j(t)}$. Otherwise, quotient bit $q_j = 0$ and one addition is required to restore the previous partial remainder

$$R_{j-1} = R_{j(t)} + B \tag{4.4}$$

If it is assumed that an equal probability exists for generating quotient digits of 0 or 1, n subtractions and $n/2$ additions are required for an n-bit divisor. To produce successive partial remainders, n one-bit left shifts are also required.

A hardware algorithm example for a positive dividend and positive divisor is shown in Figs. 4.2 and 4.3. The algorithm is implemented with a subtractor, and a $2n$-bit shift register in a manner similar to the multiplication algorithm of Sec.

3.2. Referring to Fig. 4.2, the dividend is shifted left one bit position and the divisor is subtracted. The subtraction is accomplished by 2s complement addition. The initial left shift negates the high-order quotient bit q_n that would otherwise occur (see Fig. 4.1). The quotient is contained in $q_{n-1} q_{n-2} \cdots q_1 q_0$. Since the result of the subtraction was negative (the divisor was larger than the high-order half of the dividend), the dividend is restored by adding back the divisor, and the low-order quotient bit q_0 is set to 0. This shift-subtract sequence repeats for each cycle. However, when the result of the subtraction is positive, the result (partial remainder) is placed in the high-order half of register A, and q_0 is set to 1.

In Fig. 4.2, the low-order quotient bit q_0 is left blank after each left-shift operation. It does not matter what state q_0 is in after the shift, because it will be set again before the next shift. Thus, the logic associated with q_0 can either maintain the present state of q_0 or reset q_0 to 0.

The division of two binary numbers when negative numbers are in 2s complement form is more complicated than multiplication. There are no simple algorithms for performing negative 2s complement division that are comparable to multiplication. This is because the quotient bits must be in the correct positive or negative representation. For example, if dividend A is negative and divisor B is positive, then quotient Q must be negative and in 2s complement representation. But the division algorithm assumes a positive binary number representation so that, if A or B is negative (2s complement), then subtraction may be attempted on a bit (1 for example) that is not a 1 in $|A|$ or $|B|$. In division, preprocessing of the operands and/or postprocessing of the results are usually required. The negative numbers are converted to positive numbers by 2s complementation and the division is performed. The resulting quotient is complemented, if required.

4.2.1 Overflow

Another problem encountered with division is when the dividend is so large relative to the divisor that the value of the quotient exceeds the range of the set of numbers used by the machine. The quotient will have 1s in positions of higher order than those represented by the hardware. When this occurs, the division operation results in an overflow. This is not a problem when working with pencil and paper, but it is critical when division is implemented with hardware, because the length of the registers is fixed and they cannot contain a number exceeding that length. Provisions to detect this condition must be included in the system hardware or software, or both.

In most computers, the dividend is two times the length of the divisor, and the condition for overflow can be stated as follows:

A divide overflow condition occurs if the value of the high-order half of the dividend is greater than or equal to the divisor.

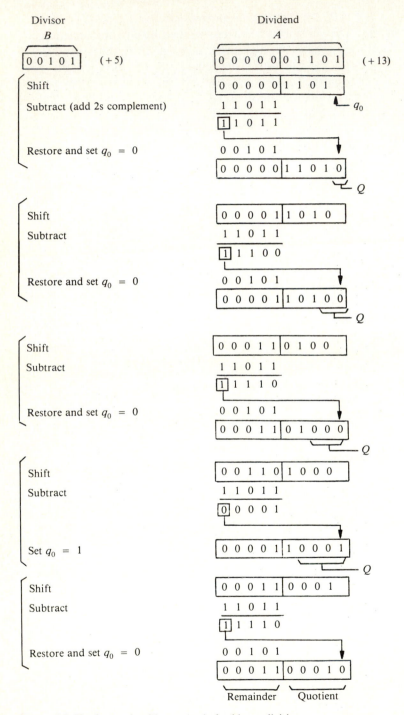

Figure 4.2 Hardware algorithm example for binary division.

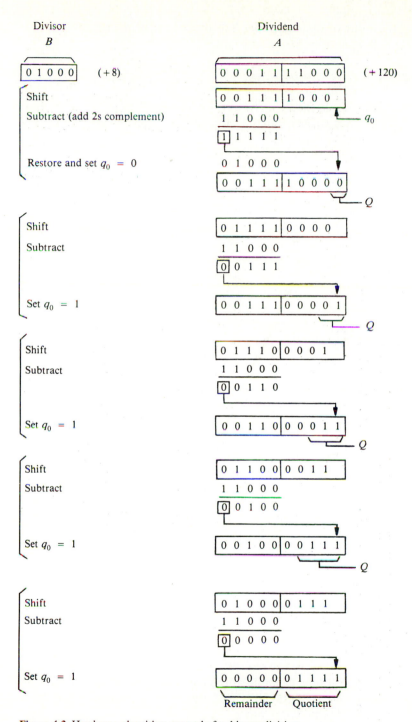

Figure 4.3 Hardware algorithm example for binary division.

For example, if the value of the high-order half of the dividend was equal to the divisor, that is,

$$b_{n-1} \cdots b_1 b_0 = a_{2n-1} \cdots a_{n+1} a_n$$

then the quotient result would exceed n bits as shown in the example below. If the value of the dividend bits is greater than the value of the divisor, then the value of the quotient will be even greater.

$$A = \frac{256}{8} = 32 = Q$$
$$B = $$

$$\overbrace{}^{n}$$
$$B = \boxed{0\ 1\ 0\ 0\ 0}$$

$$\overbrace{}^{2n}$$
$$A = \boxed{0\ 1\ 0\ 0\ 0\ |\ 0\ 0\ 0\ 0\ 0}$$

$$\overbrace{}^{n}$$
$$\Rightarrow \boxed{\qquad\qquad 1\ |\ 0\ 0\ 0\ 0\ 0}$$
$$\underbrace{}_{\text{Quotient}}$$

A common method for detecting overflow is to subtract the divisor from the high-order bits of the dividend. This occurs before the first shift-subtract cycle. If the difference is positive, then an overflow has been detected. If the difference is negative, then the dividend and divisor have correct relative magnitudes and the division operation can continue.

Another problem associated with division is that division by 0 must be avoided. The preceding method of detecting overflow will also detect a 0 divisor, because any high-order dividend bits will be greater than or equal to a divisor of 0. The occurrence of a divide overflow can be handled in a number of different ways. The action that is taken depends on the application of the system. The programmer may check a divide overflow flip-flop and, if the flip-flop is set, branch to a subroutine that takes corrective action, such as scaling the data to avoid overflow. Another approach is to provide an interrupt that causes the computer to suspend the current program and branch to a service routine that removes the program from the system and presents an error message to the user. It is then the user's responsibility to correct the problem. The problem of divide overflow does not occur in floating-point number representation, and this will be further discussed in Chap. 6.

4.2.2 Hardware Organization

Before presenting the hardware for the sequential shift-subtract restoring division technique, consider an additional example of the hardware algorithm. Figure 4.4 illustrates the sequence for a 10-bit dividend and a 5-bit divisor. A carry flip-flop is used to indicate the value that is set into q_0. If carry-out $c_{n-1} = 0$ after subtraction, then $q_0 = 0$; if carry-out $= 1$ after a subtraction then $q_0 = 1$. The setting of q_0 is identical to that described previously in which sign bit a_{n-1} of the high-order bits of the dividend was used to determine the state of q_0. In that case, however, $q_0 = \bar{a}_{n-1}$. Figure 4.4 also shows a separate restore cycle in which the divisor is added to the subtraction result to restore the partial remainder to its previous value. There are a total of eight cycles for this five-bit divisor: five shift-subtract cycles and three restore cycles. If each cycle is sufficiently long, then only five cycles are needed; the second half of each cycle is reserved for the restore operation.

Whenever the carry flip-flop is equal to 1 (On), the next cycle will be a subtract cycle; when it is equal to 0 (Off), the next cycle will be an add (restore) cycle. Near the end of each add cycle, the carry flip-flop is set to 1 so that the next cycle will be a shift-subtract cycle. Figure 4.4(b) shows the sequence during a divide operation.

Figure 4.5 shows the organization of the hardware required for a fixed-point divide operation. Notice the similarity between this and the hardware required for the fixed-point add-shift multiply operation of Fig. 3.3. A $2n$-bit dividend is loaded into the concatenated registers A and Q, with register A containing the high-order n bits and register Q containing the low-order n bits. An n-bit positive divisor is loaded into register B, and the carry flip-flop is set to 1. The dividend is shifted to the left one bit position, and the divisor is subtracted by adding its negated value. The information about the relative magnitudes is available in the carry flip-flop C. If $C = 1$, this signifies that $A \geqslant B$, and a quotient bit of 1 is inserted into q_0. The partial remainder is then shifted to the left and the process is repeated. If $C = 0$, this signifies that $A < B$, and a quotient bit of 0 is inserted into q_0 (the value set into q_0 could also be loaded during the shift). The value of B is then added to restore the partial remainder in A to its previous value, and the carry flip-flop is set to 1. The partial remainder is shifted to the left and the process repeats until all n bits of the quotient have been formed. There will never be a valid situation where sign bit $a_{n-1} = c_{n-1}$. This will occur only in an overflow condition or when negative operands are used.

The partial remainder R_j for the jth cycle is obtained by shifting the concatenated registers $A \cdot Q$ one bit to the left, with the new quotient bit entering the right end of register Q after the subtraction. The comparison operation specified in Eq. 4.2 is implemented with 2s complement subtraction. The input-output relationship of the n-bit adder is described by the following arithmetic equation:

$$c_{n-1} \cdot s_{n-1} \cdots s_0 = (a_{n-1} \cdots a_0) - (b_{n-1} \cdots b_0)$$

$$= (a_{n-1} \cdots a_0) + [(\bar{b}_{n-1} \cdots \bar{b}_0) + 1] \quad (4.5)$$

where c_{n-1} is the carry-out of the n-bit adder and $s_{n-1} \cdots s_0$ is the sum outputs of the adder right-concatenated with c_{n-1}.

The hardware divide unit tends to decrease the initial partial remainder from $2n$ bits to n bits and, at the same time, increase the quotient to n bits. At the in-

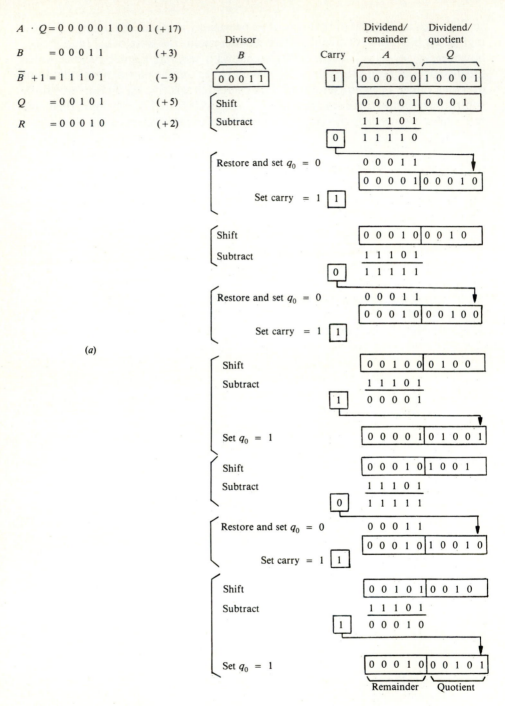

$A \cdot Q = 0\ 0\ 0\ 0\ 0\ 1\ 0\ 0\ 0\ 1\ (+17)$

$B = 0\ 0\ 0\ 1\ 1 \qquad (+3)$

$\bar{B} + 1 = 1\ 1\ 1\ 0\ 1 \qquad (-3)$

$Q = 0\ 0\ 1\ 0\ 1 \qquad (+5)$

$R = 0\ 0\ 0\ 1\ 0 \qquad (+2)$

(a)

	Divisor	Carry	Dividend/remainder	Dividend/quotient
	B		A	Q
	0 0 0 1 1	1	0 0 0 0 0	1 0 0 0 1
Shift			0 0 0 0 1	0 0 0 1
Subtract			1 1 1 0 1	
		0	1 1 1 1 0	
Restore and set $q_0 = 0$			0 0 0 1 1	
			0 0 0 0 1	0 0 0 1 0
Set carry $= 1$		1		
Shift			0 0 0 1 0	0 0 1 0
Subtract			1 1 1 0 1	
		0	1 1 1 1 1	
Restore and set $q_0 = 0$			0 0 0 1 1	
			0 0 0 1 0	0 0 1 0 0
Set carry $= 1$		1		
Shift			0 0 1 0 0	0 1 0 0
Subtract			1 1 1 0 1	
		1	0 0 0 0 1	
Set $q_0 = 1$			0 0 0 0 1	0 1 0 0 1
Shift			0 0 0 1 0	1 0 0 1
Subtract			1 1 1 0 1	
		0	1 1 1 1 1	
Restore and set $q_0 = 0$			0 0 0 1 1	
			0 0 0 1 0	1 0 0 1 0
Set carry $= 1$		1		
Shift			0 0 1 0 1	0 0 1 0
Subtract			1 1 1 0 1	
		1	0 0 0 1 0	
Set $q_0 = 1$			0 0 0 1 0	0 0 1 0 1
			Remainder	Quotient

Figure 4.4 (*a*) Hardware algorithm example with carry FF and separate restore cycle; (*b*) timing diagram.

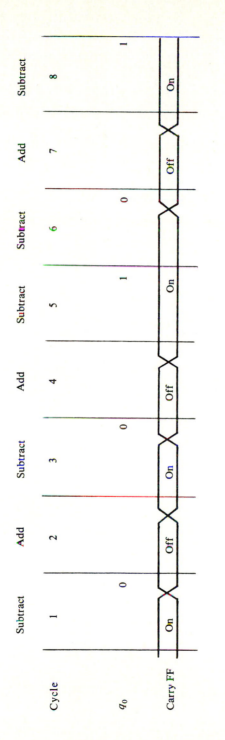

Figure 4.4 (Continued)

247

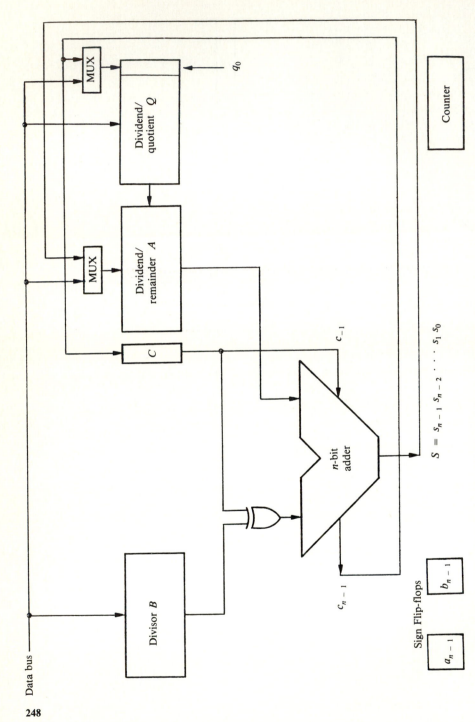

Figure 4.5 Hardware organization for fixed-point shift-subtract restoring division.

248

termediate shift cycle j, the effective partial remainder occupies the leftmost $2n - j$ bits of the cascaded register $A \cdot Q$, whereas the quotient occupies the rightmost j bits. The sum of the two number lengths is always $2n$ bits. The n-bit quotient enters the cascaded registers from the right end and pushes the upper part of the partial remainder (initially, the dividend) off the left end. The implementation of the restoring binary division requires $n + 2$ cycles: two cycles for loading the dividend and divisor and n cycles for shift-subtract operations. This assumes that shift-subtract-restore can be accomplished in one cycle; otherwise, one cycle must be added for each restore operation. Also, if the data bus is sufficiently wide, then both operands can be loaded in one cycle. In any case, when the divide operation has been completed, the quotient resides in the n-bit register Q and the remainder resides in the n-bit register A.

The divisor register B is required to only load information (from the data bus); it is not required to have shift properties. The design of a register of this type has been discussed previously, as has the design for the carry JK flip-flop, the carry lookahead adder, the cycle counter, and the sign flip-flops. The only new design is for the A and Q registers, which are shown in Figs. 4.6 and 4.7, respectively. These registers must be able to store the $2n$-bit dividend from the data bus and shift left one bit position. Register A must also store the n-bit sum from the adder. During a left shift operation, q_0 is set to 0.

4.2.3 Restoring Division Using a Multiplexer

A faster method of restoring division than that illustrated in Fig. 4.5 can be realized at the expense of additional hardware. The technique, shown in Fig. 4.8, entails bypassing the restoration addition and loading the previous partial remainder, which was kept unchanged, into register A. The additional hardware includes an n-bit multiplexer with inputs from register A and the adder, the selection of which is controlled by the state of c_{n-1}.

A numerical example will best illustrate the operation of this technique. Figure 4.9 repeats a previous example that is modified for this procedure. The adder is always used as a subtractor. Whenever $c_{n-1} = 0$, the previous partial remainder (register A) is selected by the multiplexer and is loaded into register A, while c_{n-1} is loaded into q_0. Whenever $c_{n-1} = 1$, the adder sum output is selected by the multiplexer and loaded into register A at the same time that c_{n-1} is loaded into q_0. The above functions are illustrated by the following operations. If $c_{n-1} = 0$, then

$$a_{n-1} \cdots a_1 a_0 \leftarrow a_{n-1} \cdots a_1 a_0$$

If $c_{n-1} = 1$, then

$$a_{n-1} \cdots a_1 a_0 \leftarrow s_{n-1} \cdots s_1 s_0$$

As before, when the divide operation is finished, the quotient resides in the n-bit register Q and the remainder resides in the n-bit register A.

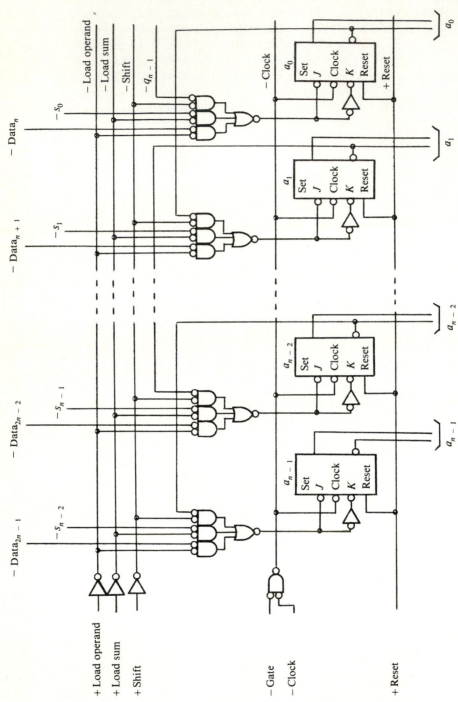

Figure 4.6 Logic diagram for dividend/remainder register A.

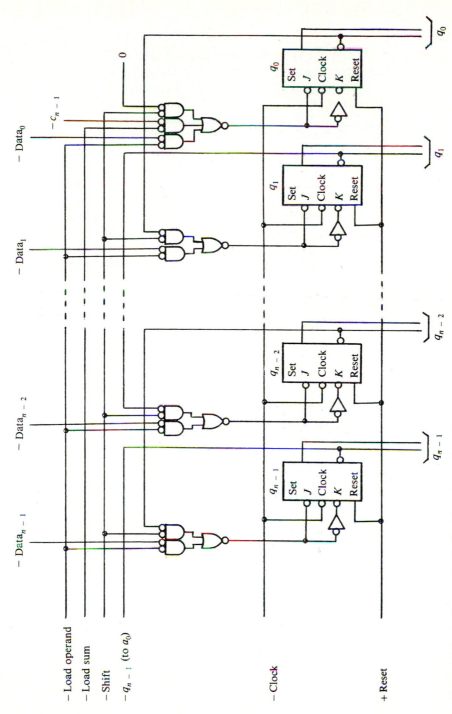

Figure 4.7 Logic diagram for dividend/quotient register Q.

251

4.3 SEQUENTIAL SHIFT-SUBTRACT/ADD NONRESTORING DIVISION

It is possible to improve the speed of the sequential shift-subtract division by redefining the algorithm to avoid the need for restoring the partial remainder after an unsuccessful subtraction. The subtraction is considered unsuccessful if the result is negative. The restoring addition step slows the division process considerably. Even the multiplexed method of restoration slows the operation slightly due to the delay through the multiplexer and the associated controls. This section will present an improved method that will completely eliminate the need to restore the partial remainder. The technique does not consume additional time due to extra add, subtract, or shift operations. The shortcoming of restoring division can be overcome by allowing a negative as well as a positive partial remainder and by restoring only the final partial remainder to a positive value. In nonrestoring division, a negative partial remainder is not restored to a positive value, but is used as it is in the following cycle. The absolute value of the partial remainder is thus reduced in every cycle by either adding the divisor to it or subtracting the divisor from it.

If partial remainder A is positive after the subtract operation, then A is shifted left and B is subtracted; that is, the operation $2A - B$ is performed. If A is negative, the partial remainder is restored by performing $A + B$, and then it is shifted left and B is subtracted. This is equivalent to performing $2A + B$; that is,

$$2(A + B) - B = 2A + B$$

Thus, in nonrestoring division, we have only the operations $2A - B$ or $2A + B$ for each cycle. If $q_0 = 1$ (A is positive), then shift $A \cdot Q$ left one bit position and add B with no restoring of the partial remainder being required. The quotient bit q_0 is set as it was in the restoring division method; that is, if the sign of A (partial remainder) is positive, then set $q_0 = 1$. If the sign of A is negative, then set $q_0 = 0$. The same selection for q_0 can be determined by the carry-out bit c_{n-1} according to the following criteria:

$$q_0 = \begin{cases} 0 & \text{if } c_{n-1} = 0 \\ 1 & \text{if } c_{n-1} = 1 \end{cases}$$

The first time the dividend is shifted, B must be subtracted. Also, if the last bit of the quotient is 0, then the previous partial remainder must be restored in order to obtain the correct final remainder. Therefore, in nonrestoring division, either n or $n + 1$ shift-subtract/add cycles are required. Two previous examples from restoring division will now be presented to illustrate the technique of nonrestoring division. These are shown in Figs. 4.10 and 4.11. The carry-out bit c_{n-1} is initialized to 1 so that a subtraction will occur during the first cycle. Note

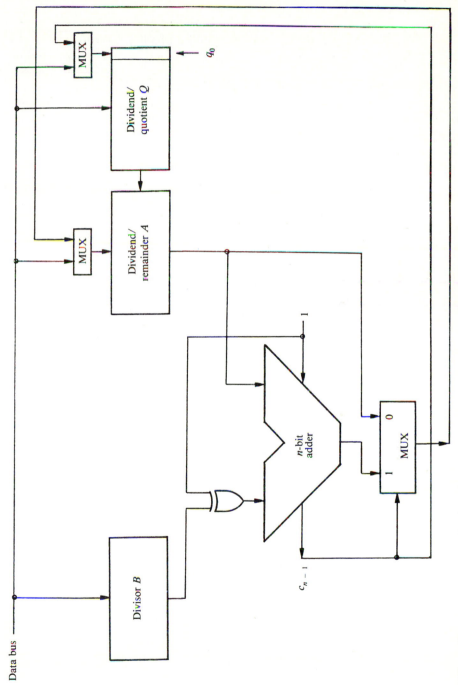

Figure 4.8 Hardware organization for a faster version of fixed-point shift-subtract restoring division.

253

$A \cdot Q = 0\ 0\ 0\ 0\ 0\ 1\ 0\ 0\ 0\ 1$ (+17)

$B \quad\quad = 0\ 0\ 0\ 1\ 1$ (+3)

$\bar{B} + 1 = 1\ 1\ 1\ 0\ 1$ (−3)

$Q \quad\quad = 0\ 0\ 1\ 0\ 1$ (+5)

$R \quad\quad = 0\ 0\ 0\ 1\ 0$ (+2)

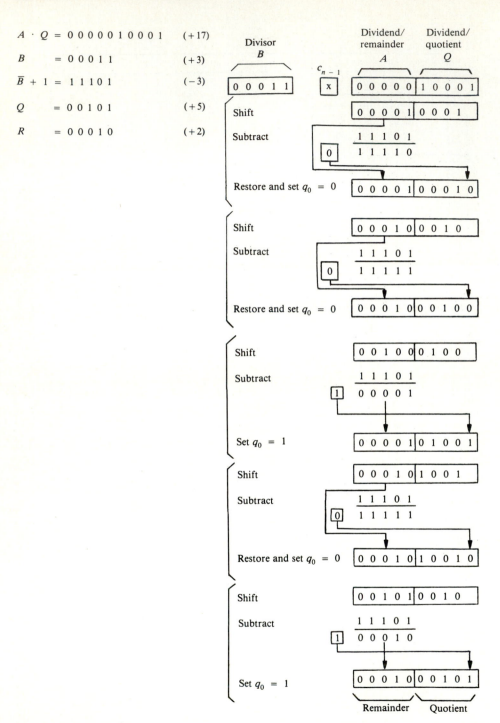

Figure 4.9 Example of restore division without the restoration addition cycle.

that in both examples only the operations $2A - B$ and $2A + B$ are performed. In Fig. 4.10, an additional cycle is required to restore the partial remainder in order to obtain the correct final remainder. This was necessary because the low-order bit of the quotient was a 0.

4.3.1 Hardware Organization

The hardware for the shift-subtract nonrestoring division is identical to that shown in Fig. 4.5 for restoring division. The difference in operation is in the microcode. In the restoring method, the restoration addition is accomplished in a separate cycle without shifting. In nonrestoring division, a shift occurs every cycle and a subtraction or an addition is executed. The carry flip-flop, which is set from c_{n-1}, has the same function in both techniques. When $c_{n-1} = 1$, a subtraction is performed during the next cycle; when $c_{n-1} = 0$, an add operation is performed.

4.4 SRT DIVISION

Faster direct division schemes can be implemented on normalized numbers by observing sequences of more than one bit of the dividend or partial remainder. For example, sequences of 0s or 1s can be skipped. Shifting over 0s or 1s in multiplication suggested that perhaps a similar method for acceleration could be applied to division. The widely used SRT method accomplishes this. The SRT method, discovered independently by Sweeney, Robertson, and Tocher, is a powerful shortcut for division and provides a speedup over the methods previously described, including the nonrestoring method. The version of SRT division that is presented in this section produces quotient bits q_i, where $q_i \in \{0, 1\}$.

It shifts over strings of 0s when 0s occur and shifts over strings of 1s when 1s appear. A string can be one or more bits. There are situations in which addition and subtraction must still be performed, but these are done in a nonrestoring fashion and the result thus obtained is examined for strings of 0s and 1s. Two approaches will be presented: one using positive operands, the other using a negative dividend with a positive divisor in 2s complement notation. Because this method of division is more complex than any previously given, numerous examples will be given to clarify the procedure.

The time required to perform division is proportional to the number of additions required to complete the operation. The SRT method reduces the required number of additions. SRT division was proposed to improve binary floating-point arithmetic, which uses fractional notation for the operands. Thus, the dividend and divisor are binary fractions, with the binary point to the immediate left of the high-order bit. Also, the divisor is to be normalized before starting the actual division by shifting it left until there is a 1 in the high-order bit position. Thus, for a divisor of

$$B = b_{n-1} b_{n-2} \cdots b_1 b_0$$

$A \cdot Q = 0\ 0\ 0\ 0\ 0\ 0\ 1\ 1\ 0\ 1 \quad (+13)$

$B \qquad = 0\ 0\ 1\ 0\ 1 \qquad (+5)$

$\overline{B} + 1 = 1\ 1\ 0\ 1\ 1 \qquad (-5)$

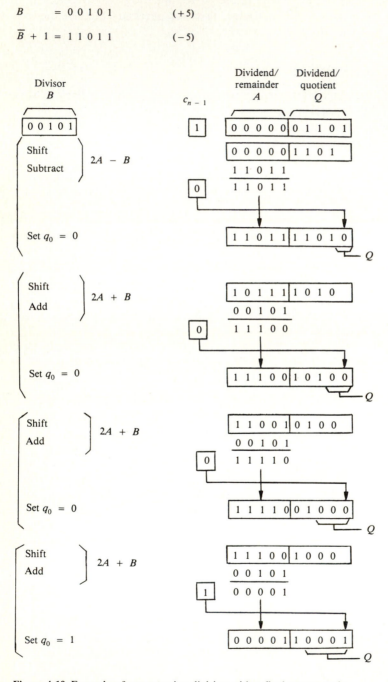

Figure 4.10 Example of nonrestoring division with a final restore cycle.

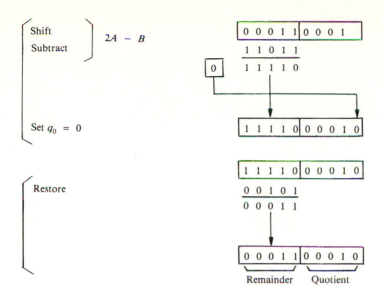

Figure 4.10 (Continued)

the binary (or radix) point is located such that

$$B = 0 \cdot b_{n-1} \, b_{n-2} \, \cdots \, b_1 b_0$$
$$= 0 \cdot \quad 1 \quad b_{n-2} \, \cdots \, b_1 b_0$$

is the normalized divisor, where $b_{n-2} \cdots b_1 b_0$ may be 0s or 1s. Since only positive operands are being considered initially, the sign bit and the high-order value bit must be 0 and 1, respectively. The dividend is normalized in a similar manner, but this is done during the division operation. With the radix point positioned as shown, the divisor becomes a binary fraction with a value greater than or equal to 0.5 and less than 1, such that

$$0.5 \leqslant B < 1$$

These assumptions do not negate the principles of the division operation, and they simplify the hardware design and description.

The reason for normalizing the divisor is to permit a fixed reference point for comparing the divisor and partial remainder. It is possible to develop a method that uses a variable reference point, but this would needlessly complicate the operation. With a normalized divisor, the reference point always corresponds to the radix point, and thus it becomes a fixed point of reference for both operands.

A division process can be categorized by listing the permissible values of each quotient bit that occurs during the operation. For radix r, each quotient digit has one of the values 0, 1, $\cdots$, $r-1$, which, for the binary number system, where

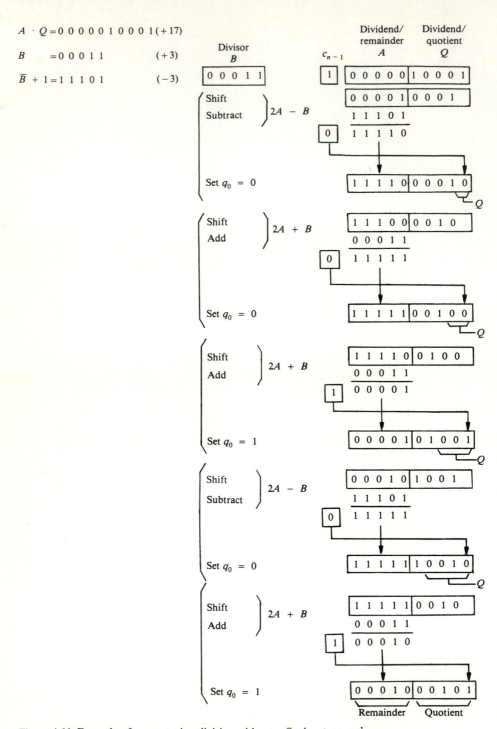

Figure 4.11 Example of nonrestoring division without a final restore cycle.

$r = 2$, is simply 0 or 1. Division is performed by executing a recursive operation, as shown below.

$$R_{j + 1} = rR_j - q_{j + 1}B \tag{4.6}$$

where $\quad R_{j + 1}$ = next partial remainder

$\qquad\quad r$ = radix

$\qquad\quad rR_j$ = left-shifted current partial remainder, which, for $r = 2$, is $2R_j$ (R_j shifted left one bit position; that is, R_j is doubled)

$\qquad\quad q_{j + 1}$ = next quotient bit (0 or 1)

$\qquad\quad B$ = divisor

For $j = 0 \qquad R_1 = rR_0 - q_1B$

For $j = 1 \qquad R_2 = rR_1 - q_2B$

$\qquad\qquad\qquad = r(rR_0 - q_1B) - q_2B$

$\qquad\qquad\qquad = r^2R_0 - (rq_1 + q_2)B$

For $j = 3 \qquad R_4 = rR_3 - q_4B$

$\qquad\qquad\qquad = r[r^3R_0 - (r^2q_1 + rq_2 + q_3)B] - q_4B$

$\qquad\qquad\qquad = r^4R_0 - (r^3q_1 + r^2q_2 + rq_3 + q_4)B$

For $j = n \qquad R_{n + 1} = r^{n + 1}R_0 - (r^nq_1 + r^{n - 1}q_2 +$

$$\qquad\qquad\qquad \cdots + rq_n + q_{n + 1})B \tag{4.7}$$

The shifted remainder $r^{-(n + 1)}R_{n + 1}$ then becomes

$$r^{-(n + 1)}R_{n + 1} = R_0 - B\sum_{i = 1}^{n + 1} r^{-i}q_i \tag{4.8}$$

where

$$\sum_{i = 1}^{n + 1} r^{-i}q_i$$

is quotient Q. Substituting

$$Q = \sum_{i = 1}^{n + 1} r^{-i}q_i$$

in Eq. 4.8 and rearranging results in

$$R_0 = QB + r^{-(n + 1)}R_{n + 1} \tag{4.9}$$

which states that the dividend is equal to the sum of the quotient multiplied by the divisor and the shifted remainder. The result of any division operation should agree with Eq. 4.9. If the remainder is 0, then the result is simply

$$\text{Dividend} = \text{quotient} \times \text{divisor}$$

as illustrated earlier.

The rationale for shifting over 0s in the dividend is explained below. Whenever there is a 0 to the immediate right of the radix point in the dividend, this means that the value is less than 0.5. Also, since the divisor is normalized, it contains a value greater than or equal to 0.5. Therefore, the divisor, is obviously larger than the dividend and will result in a 0 bit being entered in the quotient. This is because the division process attempts to reduce the dividend by an amount equal to the divisor. If this cannot be done, then the two operands are shifted with respect to each other and a 0 is placed in the quotient. If an attempt is made to subtract the divisor from the dividend before the dividend has been normalized, the subtraction would result in a negative number, which may be considered as an unsuccessful subtraction. Therefore, since the divisor is normalized and the dividend remains unnormalized, subtraction will be unsuccessful and a 0 will be placed in the quotient. If there are n leading 0s in the dividend, then n positions may be shifted across in one operation, with a 0 being inserted in the quotient for each position shifted.

With dividend A and divisor B being defined as

$$A = a_{2n-1}a_{2n-2} \cdot \cdot \cdot a_1 a_0$$

and

$$B = b_{n-1}b_{n-2} \cdot \cdot \cdot b_1 b_0$$

then the normalized A and B will be

$$A = 0.1a_i a_{i-1} \cdot \cdot \cdot a_1 a_0$$

and

$$B = 0.1b_j b_{j-1} \cdot \cdot \cdot b_1 b_0$$

where $a_i a_{i-1} \cdot \cdot \cdot a_1 a_0$ and $b_j b_{j-1} \cdot \cdot \cdot b_1 b_0$ may be 0s or 1s. Since the operands are now both normalized, a subtraction must be performed to determine whether or not the dividend is larger than the divisor.

Consider now the reasons for shifting over 1s in order to normalize a negative partial remainder. After an unsuccessful subtraction, partial remainder A and divisor B will be

$$A = 1.1 \, a_i a_{i-1} \cdot \cdot \cdot a_1 a_0$$

and

$$B = 0.1 \, b_j b_{j-1} \cdot \cdot \cdot b_1 b_0$$

The value of A is greater than -0.5; that is,

$$-0.5 < A < 0$$

This is because A is a negative number and the leading 1s in a negative number correspond to leading 0s in a positive number. Thus, the 1s are considered to be 0s when calculating the value of A. Since the divisor is

$$0.5 \leqslant B < 1$$

when A is added to B, the sum will be a number greater than 0.

Now consider what happens when the partial remainder is doubled, that is, shifted left one bit position. Shifting an unnormalized number to the left does not destroy any information. It is true that 1s are being discarded from the left, but these 1s represent only positional information. This is because the number is in 2s complement notation and the 1s represent 0s that have been complemented. Therefore, shifting an unnormalized number one bit position to the left doubles it, but preserves all significant bits. Since the high-order bit of the divisor always contains a 1, and if the high-order bit of the dividend contains a 1, then a positive result will always be obtained when adding A and B. This justifies shifting across a string of high-order 1s in the partial remainder and entering a 1 in the quotient for each position shifted.

Another way to look at the above reasoning is described below. Shifting the partial remainder left one bit position is equivalent to dividing the divisor by 2 with respect to the original partial remainder. After the subtraction, which resulted in a negative partial remainder A, A is shifted left and B is added, then $B/2$, then $B/4$, and so forth. This can continue as long as the result is positive, and the result will be positive as long as the negative partial remainder is unnormalized. When both the dividend and divisor are normalized, a subtraction or addition must take place.

During the division operation when both the dividend and divisor are normalized, an addition or subtraction must occur in order to diminish the partial remainder and determine the quotient bit. In diminishing the partial remainder, its magnitude is reduced toward 0. This is accomplished by adding a number of opposite sign to it. The next partial remainder R_{j+1} is characterized by

$$R_{j+1} = \begin{cases} 2R_j - B & \text{if } 2R_j \text{ is positive} \\ 2R_j & \text{if } R_j \text{ is unnormalized} \\ 2R_j + B & \text{if } 2R_j \text{ is negative} \end{cases}$$

Next, some general comments will be presented that describe the SRT method for determining the quotient of two positive operands. This will be followed by examples illustrating the SRT technique. First, the divisor is normalized and the dividend is adjusted by shifting it left the same number of positions that the divisor was shifted during normalization. The operands are now properly positioned in their respective registers (dividend in $A \cdot Q$ and divisor in B), and shifting over 0s, if possible, can commence. It is assumed that overflow checking has already been performed. At the end of the positioning process, the operands will be

$$A \cdot Q = 0.\overset{n}{\overline{0 \cdots 0}} 1 \cdots a_1 a_0 q_{n-1} \cdots q_1 q_0$$
$$B = 0.1 \cdots b_1 b_0$$

where n is the number of 0s between the radix point and the first high-order 1 in the $A \cdot Q$ concatenated register pair. The number n is a positive integer such that

$$0 \leqslant n \leqslant 2n - 1$$

assuming a $2n$-bit dividend contained in register pair $A \cdot Q$.

Next, registers $A \cdot Q$ are shifted left until the high-order 1 is positioned immediately to the right of the radix point. The number of shifts required to normalize $A \cdot Q$ is equal to n. For each shift of registers $A \cdot Q$, a 0 is entered into the right end of quotient register Q. The contents of the registers are now

$$A \cdot Q = 0.1 \cdots a_1 a_0 q_{n-1} \cdots 0.\overset{n}{\overline{0 \cdots 0}}$$
$$B = 0.1 \cdots b_1 b_0$$

Next, the aligned operands are compared by subtracting the divisor from the dividend. If the result is positive, a 1 is entered in the quotient followed by a left shift of one bit position. Then shifting over 0s is performed until a 1 appears in the $A \cdot Q$ register pair to the immediate right of the radix point. The operation then continues as before.

If the result is negative, then the shifted registers contain

$$A \cdot Q = 1.1 \cdots a_1 a_0 q_{n-1} \cdots 0.\overset{n+1}{\overline{0 \cdots 0}}$$
$$B = 0.1 \cdots b_1 b_0$$

The added 0 in register Q was entered because the result was negative. Next, a shift over 1s is performed on registers $A \cdot Q$. The shifting over 1s continues until register A is normalized, that is, until a 0 is positioned to the immediate right of the radix point. For each 1 that is shifted over in register A, a 1 is entered in register Q. At the end of the shifting, register A contains a normalized negative number and the register contents are

$$A \cdot Q = 1.0 \cdots a_1 a_0 q_{n-1} \cdots 0.\overset{n+1}{\overline{0 \cdots 0}} \overset{m}{\overline{1 \cdots 1}}$$
$$B = 0.1 \cdots b_1 b_0$$

where m is the number of 1s between the radix point and the first high-order 0 in register A before normalization.

Next, the divisor is added to the partial remainder. Addition is performed instead of subtraction, because the partial remainder is to be diminished toward 0. This is always the case after shifting over 1s. The result of this addition will yield either a positive or negative number, which is shifted and loaded into A. Thus,

$$A \leftarrow 2(A + B)$$

To summarize, when the result is positive, a 1 is entered into the right side of register Q followed by a shift; when the result is negative, a 0 is entered into the right side of register Q followed by a shift. When a positive number is in register A, shifting over 0s is performed and 0s are entered into register Q. This is followed by subtraction. When a negative number is in register A, shifting over 1s is performed and 1s are entered into register Q. This is followed by addition.

An example of SRT division is shown in Fig. 4.12. Only shifting over 0s is presented in this example; examples of shifting over 0s and 1s will be illustrated in later examples. Step 1 shows the normalized divisor and the dividend before adjustment. Step 2 adjusts the dividend by shifting it left two bit positions. The asterisked (*) entries in register Q are simply delimiters between the quotient and the diminishing partial remainder. The bit to the immediate left of the leftmost asterisk is the low-order bit of the partial remainder. This bit eventually becomes the low-order bit of the final remainder. Since there is a positive number in register A, step 3 shifts over 0s. There are three 0s, which results in a left shift over three bit positions. The dividend is now normalized and three 0s are entered into register Q.

Now both the dividend and divisor are normalized, and the next quotient bit cannot be determined without performing a subtraction or addition. Since the operands have the same sign, a subtraction is performed. This is done by adding the 2s complement of the normalized divisor, as in step 4. Since the subtraction has produced a positive result, a 1 is entered into the low-order bit position q_0 of register Q. At the same time, register pair $A \cdot Q$ is shifted left one bit position, as demonstrated in step 5. Since the result was positive, step 6 shifts over 0s; in this example, two 0s are shifted over and two 0s are entered into register Q. Six shifts ($n + 1$, where $n = 5$) have occurred, the quotient 4_{10} resides in register Q, and the remainder 3_{10} is in register A.

As mentioned previously, the low-order bit of the remainder is to the immediate left of the leftmost asterisk. If desired, only register A can be shifted right to align the remainder such that

$$\begin{aligned} A &= a_4 \; a_3 \; a_2 \; a_1 \; a_0 \\ &= 0 \;\; 0 \;\; 0 \;\; 1 \;\; 1 \end{aligned}$$

As the contents of register A are shifted right, the sign bit is propagated. The contents of register Q are not shifted.

$A \cdot Q$ $= 0 . 0 0 0 0 0 1 0 1 1 1$ $(+23 \times 2^{-10})$

B $= 0 . 0 0 1 0 1$ $(+5 \times 2^{-5})$

Normalized B $= 0 . 1 0 1 0 0$

$\neg$ (Normalized B) $+ 1$ $= 1 . 0 1 1 0 0$

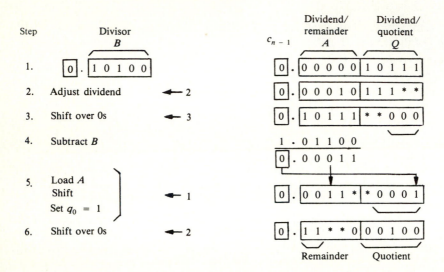

$$\frac{23}{5} = Q4, \ R3$$

$$\frac{23 \times 2^{-10}}{5 \times 2^{-5}} = \frac{20 \times 2^{-10}}{5 \times 2^{-5}} + \frac{3 \times 2^{-10}}{5 \times 2^{-5}}$$

$$= \underbrace{4 \times 2^{-5}}_{\text{Quotient}} + \underbrace{3 \times 2^{-5}}_{\text{Remainder}}$$

Figure 4.12 Example of SRT division with positive operands; shifting over 0s.

The fractional notation in Fig. 4.12 may require an explanation. Divisor B is shown as

$$B = 0 . 0 0 1 0 1 \ \ (+5 \times 2^{-5})$$

where

$$5 \times 2^{-5} = 5 \times \frac{1}{2^5} = \frac{5}{32}$$

The binary weighted value of B is

$$B = 0 \times 2^{-1} + 0 \times 2^{-2} + 1 \times 2^{-3} + 0 \times 2^{-4} + 1 \times 2^{-5}$$

$$= \frac{1}{8} + \frac{1}{32}$$

$$= \frac{4 + 1}{32}$$

$$= \frac{5}{32}$$

The number 5×2^{-5} is another way of representing the fractional value of the divisor. In the above example, a variable-shift register is required, one that can shift over n positions at one time. Alternatively, a high-speed single-bit shift register can be utilized in which n separate shifts can occur in one machine cycle.

Figure 4.13 illustrates another example. Although the operation is similar to the previous example, additional steps are required because the dividend required less adjustment and fewer 0s are shifted over. Figure 4.14 presents an example in which no acceleration is achieved over the standard nonrestoring technique due to a poor bit configuration in all partial remainders.

Figure 4.15 shows an example in which shifting over both 0s and 1s occurs. Step 3 shifts over a 0, which is followed by a subtraction in step 4 (because register A contains a positive number). The result of the subtraction is loaded into register A and shifted left one bit position. Since the result was negative, we would want to normalize the negative number in register A by shifting over 1s until a 0 was positioned in the bit position immediately to the right of the radix point. But this position already contains a 0, so an addition is performed instead because the number is already normalized. The same occurs in step 7, except that now the positive number is already normalized.

4.4.1 Remainder Correction

After the termination cycle, this method of division will produce a remainder with a sign that is the same as the dividend or opposite it. To be correct, the remainder must have the same sign as the original dividend. In Fig. 4.15, the remainder is negative and should be corrected so that it agrees with the sign of the positive dividend. To correct the remainder, shift register A one bit position to the right (register Q is not shifted). This restores the result of the previous operation, which in this case was an addition (step 11). The normalized divisor is then added to the contents of register A, producing a correct positive remainder.

4.4.2 Termination

There are two ways to terminate an SRT division operation. One way is to perform an addition or subtraction followed by a left shift of one bit position; the

$$
\begin{aligned}
A \cdot Q && = 0.0000110111 && (+55 \times 2^{-10}) \\
B && = 0.01010 && (+10 \times 2^{-5}) \\
\text{Normalized } B && = 0.10100 \\
\lnot \text{ (Normalized } B) + 1 && = 1.01100
\end{aligned}
$$

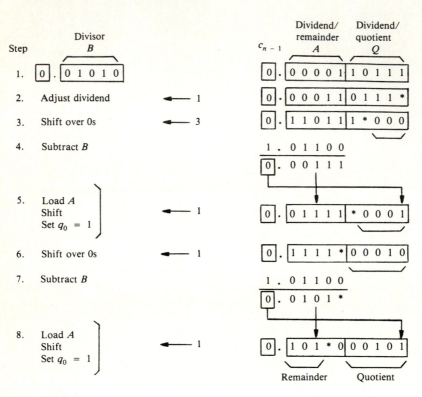

$$
\frac{55}{10} = Q5, \; R5
$$

$$
\frac{55 \times 2^{-10}}{10 \times 2^{-5}} = \frac{50 \times 2^{-10}}{10 \times 2^{-5}} + \frac{5 \times 2^{-10}}{10 \times 2^{-5}}
$$

$$
= \underbrace{5 \times 2^{-5}}_{\text{Quotient}} + \underbrace{5 \times 2^{-5}}_{\text{Remainder}}
$$

Figure 4.13 Example of SRT division with positive operands; shifting over 0s.

$A \cdot Q$ $\qquad = 0.0001111100 \quad (+124 \times 2^{-10})$
B $\qquad\qquad = 0.01000 \quad\quad (+8 \times 2^{-5})$
Normalized B $\quad = 0.10000$
$\neg$ (Normalized B) + 1 $= 1.10000$

		Divisor			c_{n-1}	Dividend/ remainder A	Dividend/ quotient Q
Step		B					
1.		$\boxed{0}$. $\boxed{1\ 0\ 0\ 0\ 0}$			$\boxed{0}$.	$\boxed{0\ 0\ 0\ 1\ 1}$	$\boxed{1\ 1\ 1\ 0\ 0}$
2.	Adjust dividend		⟵ 1		$\boxed{0}$.	$\boxed{0\ 0\ 1\ 1\ 1}$	$\boxed{1\ 1\ 0\ 0}$ *
3.	Shift over 0s		⟵ 2		$\boxed{0}$.	$\boxed{1\ 1\ 1\ 1\ 1}$	$\boxed{0\ 0}$ * $0\ 0$
4.	Subtract B				$1\ .\ 1\ 0\ 0\ 0\ 0$		
					$\boxed{0}$. $0\ 1\ 1\ 1\ 1$		
5.	Load A Shift Set $q_0 = 1$		⟵ 1		$\boxed{0}$.	$\boxed{1\ 1\ 1\ 1\ 0}$	$\boxed{0}$ * $0\ 0\ 1$
6.	Subtract B				$1\ .\ 1\ 0\ 0\ 0\ 0$		
					$\boxed{0}$. $0\ 1\ 1\ 1\ 0$		
7.	Load A Shift Set $q_0 = 1$		⟵ 1		$\boxed{0}$.	$\boxed{1\ 1\ 1\ 0\ 0}$	* $0\ 0\ 1\ 1$
8.	Subtract B				$1\ .\ 1\ 0\ 0\ 0\ 0$		
					$\boxed{0}$. $0\ 1\ 1\ 0\ 0$		
9.	Load A Shift Set $q_0 = 1$		⟵ 1		$\boxed{0}$.	$\boxed{1\ 1\ 0\ 0}$ *	$0\ 0\ 1\ 1\ 1$
10.	Subtract B				$1\ .\ 1\ 0\ 0\ 0\ 0$		
					$\boxed{0}$. $0\ 1\ 0\ 0$ *		
11.	Load A Shift Set $q_0 = 1$		⟵ 1		$\boxed{0}$.	$\boxed{1\ 0\ 0}$ * 0	$0\ 1\ 1\ 1\ 1$
						Remainder	Quotient

$\dfrac{124}{8} = Q15, R4$

$\dfrac{124 \times 2^{-10}}{8 \times 2^{-5}} = \dfrac{120 \times 2^{-10}}{8 \times 2^{-5}} + \dfrac{4 \times 2^{-10}}{8 \times 2^{-5}}$

$\qquad\qquad = \underbrace{15 \times 2^{-5}}_{\text{Quotient}} + \underbrace{4 \times 2^{-5}}_{\text{Remainder}}$

Figure 4.14 Example of SRT division, shifting over 0s, and poor bit configuration resulting in many cycles.

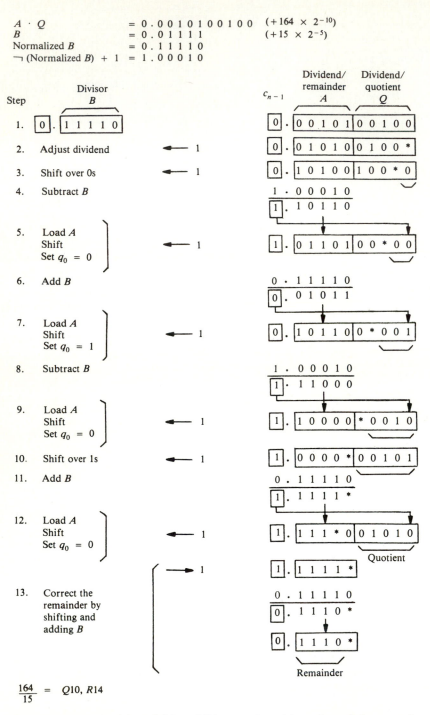

$$A \cdot Q \quad\quad = 0 . 0\,0\,1\,0\,1\,0\,0\,1\,0\,0 \quad (+164 \times 2^{-10})$$
$$B \quad\quad\quad\; = 0 . 0\,1\,1\,1\,1 \quad\quad\quad\;\; (+15 \times 2^{-5})$$
$$\text{Normalized } B \quad = 0 . 1\,1\,1\,1\,0$$
$$\neg \text{(Normalized } B) + 1 \; = 1 . 0\,0\,0\,1\,0$$

$$\frac{164}{15} = Q10, R14$$

Figure 4.15 Example of SRT division, shifting over 0s and 1s, and remainder correction.

shift counter then becomes 0. At this point, all quotient bits have been determined. Only corrections may be required. The second way to terminate an SRT division is to shift into termination. Termination will occur when a string of 0s or 1s is encountered that is greater than or equal to the number of quotient bits that have yet to be formed; that is, the number of shifts required for the string is greater than or equal to the number of shifts remaining in the shift counter before it counts down to 0. In this case, the shift counter is the determining factor. When the counter reaches 0, the operation is terminated regardless of the number of 0s or 1s that remain unshifted in the string. When this occurs, all quotient bits have been determined and only corrections may be required. An example of this type of termination is shown in Fig. 4.16.

4.4.3 Negative Operands

The principles developed for SRT division can also be applied to negative operands. The same procedure is followed. The first step is to normalize the divisor and adjust the dividend. Next, the adjusted dividend is normalized. This means shifting over 0s for positive dividends and shifting over 1s for negative dividends. Regardless of whether 0s or 1s are shifted over, the result is the same; that is, the dividend is normalized with either a 1 or a 0 in the high-order bit position immediately to the right of the radix point. The shifted 0s or 1s carry only positional information and, therefore, no numerical information is lost.

For negative operands, the bits that are inserted into the quotient depend upon the sign of the quotient being developed. If one operand is negative, 1s are entered in the quotient when normalizing a partial remainder by shifting over 0s; 0s are entered in the quotient when shifting over 1s. When both operands have been normalized, an addition or a subtraction must take place. Either the normalized divisor or the 2s complement of the normalized divisor is added to the partial remainder. The version of the divisor that is added is the one with the sign that is opposite the sign of the partial remainder.

If the sign of the resulting partial remainder is positive after the arithmetic has been performed, then a 0 is entered into register Q; if the sign is negative, then a 1 is entered into register Q. This contrasts to division with positive operands. When dividing using one negative operand, the roles of addition and subtraction are interchanged. If both are negative, then the roles are the same as when both are positive.

Figure 4.17 shows an example of SRT division using a negative dividend and a positive divisor. The operation follows the method outlined above. Since the dividend is negative and the divisor is positive, the quotient must be negative. The terminal quotient is 0.0 0 1 0 1, which is positive. Therefore, it must be converted into negative 2s complement notation, which results in the correct quotient of -5. The remainder must agree with the sign of the dividend, and it does. Therefore, the remainder is in correct notation—also -5.

If the terminal quotient is negative, it is in 1s complement notation, because the rules for entering 0s and 1s in the quotient are the reverse of those used when

$A \cdot Q$ $= 0 . 0 0 1 0 1 1 0 1 0 1$ $(+181 \times 2^{-10})$
B $= 0 . 0 1 1 0 1$ $(+13 \times 2^{-5})$
Normalized B $= 0 . 1 1 0 1 0$
$\neg$ (Normalized B) $+ 1 = 1 . 0 0 1 1 0$

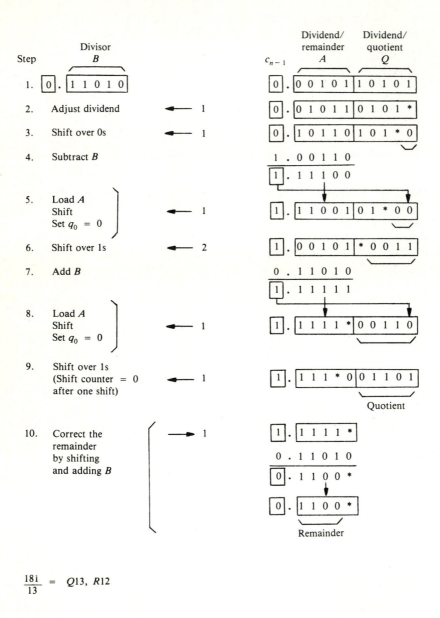

$$\frac{181}{13} = Q13, \ R12$$

Figure 4.16 Example of SRT division, shifting over 0s and 1s, and remainder correction.

both operands are positive. In order to correct the quotient, a 1 must be added in the low-order bit position. This converts the quotient to correct 2s complement number representation.

The algorithm for a positive dividend and a negative divisor is similar to that described previously for a negative dividend. SRT division using negative operands requires minor variations to the algorithm that is used when both operands are positive. In order to be consistent and use the same hardware algorithm for all SRT divisions, it may be worthwhile to 2s complement all negative operands before division.

4.4.4 Hardware Organization

The architecture for SRT division is shown in Fig. 4.18. The dividend and sign are loaded into register pair $A \cdot Q$ from the data bus and the divisor and sign are loaded into register B, all under microprogram control. The microprogram then issues a command to normalize the divisor in register B. The normalization can be accomplished with one shift pulse such that all bits that must be shifted over to acquire normalization can be shifted in one step. This may require too much hardware, so an alternative approach would be to shift groups of bits in one step or even to shift one bit at a time. The number of bit shifts that are required to normalize B are also sent to the $A \cdot Q$ shift control to adjust the dividend.

Next, the dividend is normalized under the control of the microprogram. This is followed by a subtraction operation in which the normalized divisor is subtracted from the normalized dividend. It might be stated here that microprogram control is not essential; the same sequence could be controlled by a finite-state machine, but this would require more hardware and would not be as flexible as microprogram control. The results of the first subtraction are loaded into register A, and the complement of the carry-out c_{n-1} is loaded into q_0 at the same time as registers $A \cdot Q$ are shifted left one bit position. Depending upon the sign of the result, the new partial remainder in A is normalized by shifting over 0s or 1s, if possible. The sequence then repeats, with the following operations occurring at the end of each subtraction or addition:

$$q_0 \leftarrow \bar{c}_{n-1}$$
$$q_{i+1} \leftarrow q_i$$
$$a_0 \leftarrow q_{n-1}$$
$$a_1 \leftarrow s_0$$
$$a_{i+1} \leftarrow s_i$$
$$S \leftarrow a_{n-1}$$

The operation of subtracting or adding the normalized divisor from or to the partial remainder is controlled by the sign bit of the partial remainder. If the sign is 0 (positive), then the divisor is subtracted because this would tend to diminish

$$A \cdot Q \qquad\qquad = 1 \,.\, 1\,1\,1\,1\,0\,0\,1\,0\,0\,1 \;(-55 \times 2^{-10})$$
$$B \qquad\qquad\qquad = 0 \,.\, 0\,1\,0\,1\,0 \qquad\qquad (+10 \times 2^{-5})$$
$$\text{Normalized } B \qquad = 0 \,.\, 1\,0\,1\,0\,0$$
$$\neg(\text{Normalized } B) + 1 \;= 1 \,.\, 0\,1\,1\,0\,0$$

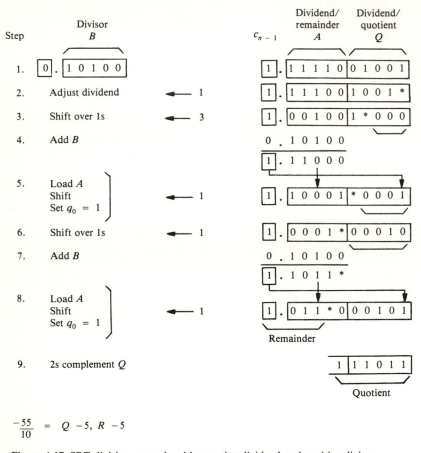

$$\frac{-55}{10} \;=\; Q \;-5, \; R \;-5$$

Figure 4.17 SRT division example with negative dividend and positive divisor.

the remainder. If the sign is 1 (negative), then the divisor is added for the same reason. It is for this reason that an inverter is placed on the output of the partial remainder sign flip-flop S in Fig. 4.18. The remainder pointer indicates the low-order bit of the final remainder in register A. The position of the low-order bit is dependent upon the number of bits that were shifted over when the divisor was normalized. If normalization is not required, the low-order remainder bit is in position a_1; if one bit is shifted over during normalization, the low-order remainder bit is in position a_2.

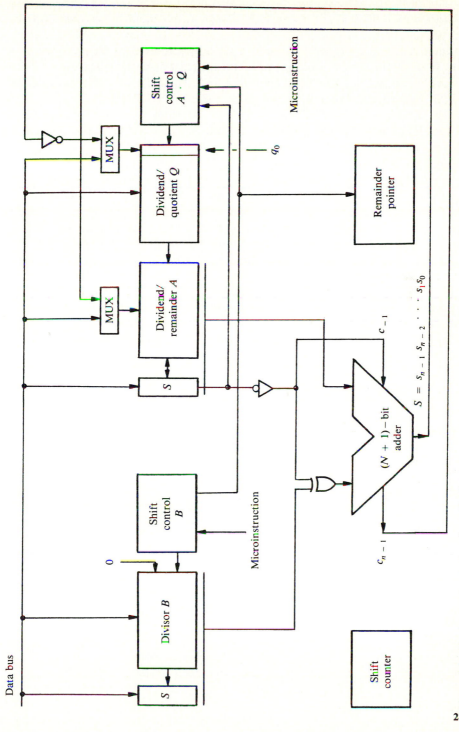

Data bus

Shift control
A · Q

Microinstruction

Dividend/
quotient Q

q_0

Remainder
pointer

MUX

MUX

Dividend/
remainder A

S

$(N + 1)$-bit
adder

$S = s_{n-1} \, s_{n-2} \cdots s_1 s_0$

c_{-1}

c_{n-1}

Shift control
B

Microinstruction

Divisor B

0

S

Shift
counter

Figure 4.18 Hardware organization for SRT division.

273

The shift control equations for normalizing register B and a positive partial remainder are tabulated in Table 4.1. For large n, the circuitry becomes impractical because of the large number of gates as well as the large number of inputs per gate. A better approach may be to shift only one to eight bit positions at a time. If more than eight positions must be shifted during normalization of the divisor, then additional shift cycles are required. The shift control equations for normalizing a negative partial remainder are shown in Table 4.2.

The designs for most components of Fig. 4.18 have been presented in earlier sections. The main difference in this organization is the multiple shifts required to normalize the divisor and to adjust and normalize the dividend. A typical stage (bit position) of register B is shown in Fig. 4.19. The shift equation inputs on the left, for example, "logic equation for four shifts," come from the logic in the B shift control, which is designed from the equations in Table 4.1. It is assumed that no more than eight positions will be shifted over at one time. The logic diagram for bit position b_5 is shown in Fig. 4.20. Notice here that as the positive divisor is normalized logic 0s are shifted into the low-order positions of register B, that is, into those positions for which no low-order position exists for the number of shifts required.

The shift control logic and the register design for registers A and Q are similar to those for register B. Register A must be capable of shifting both right (to correct the termination remainder) and left for adjustment, normalization, and the one bit position shift after a subtraction or addition. The one-bit left shift

Table 4.1 Shift control equations for divisor and positive partial remainder normalization

Number of shifts	Logic equations
0	b_{n-1}
1	$\bar{b}_{n-1} \wedge b_{n-2}$
2	$\bar{b}_{n-1} \wedge \bar{b}_{n-2} \wedge b_{n-3}$
3	$\bar{b}_{n-1} \wedge \bar{b}_{n-2} \wedge \bar{b}_{n-3} \wedge b_{n-4}$
4	$\bar{b}_{n-1} \wedge \bar{b}_{n-2} \wedge \bar{b}_{n-3} \wedge \bar{b}_{n-4} \wedge b_{n-5}$
.	.
.	.
.	.
$n-2$	$\bar{b}_{n-1} \wedge \bar{b}_{n-2} \wedge \cdots \wedge \bar{b}_3 \wedge \bar{b}_2 \wedge b_1$
$n-1$	$\bar{b}_{n-1} \wedge \bar{b}_{n-2} \wedge \cdots \wedge \bar{b}_2 \wedge \bar{b}_1 \wedge b_0$
n	$\bar{b}_{n-1} \wedge \bar{b}_{n-2} \wedge \cdots \wedge \bar{b}_2 \wedge \bar{b}_1 \wedge \bar{b}_0$
	$=$ divide check

Table 4.2 Shift control equations for negative partial remainder normalization

Number of shifts	Logic equations
0	$\bar{a}_{n-1}$
1	$a_{n-1} \wedge \bar{a}_{n-2}$
2	$a_{n-1} \wedge a_{n-2} \wedge \bar{a}_{n-3}$
3	$a_{n-1} \wedge a_{n-2} \wedge a_{n-3} \, \bar{a}_{n-4}$
4	$a_{n-1} \wedge a_{n-2} \wedge a_{n-3} \wedge a_{n-4} \wedge \bar{a}_{n-5}$
.	.
.	.
.	.
$2n-2$	$a_{n-1} \wedge \cdots \wedge a_0 \wedge q_{n-1} \wedge \cdots \wedge q_2 \wedge \bar{q}_1$
$2n-1$	$a_{n-1} \wedge \cdots \wedge a_0 \wedge q_{n-1} \wedge \cdots \wedge q_1 \wedge \bar{q}_0$
$2n$	$a_{n-1} \wedge \cdots \wedge a_0 \wedge q_{n-1} \wedge \cdots \wedge q_1 \wedge q_0$

can be accomplished by simply ORing a signal with the equation in Table 4.1 that represents a left shift of one bit position; that is,

$$(\bar{b}_{n-1} \wedge b_{n-2}) \vee \text{ (left shift after arithmetic)}$$

The remainder pointer can be a shift register that shifts a single logic 1 through the register, with all other positions containing a logic 0. When no shifts are required to adjust the dividend, the remainder pointer will indicate that a_1 is the low-order bit position of the remainder. The contents of the remainder pointer register will then be

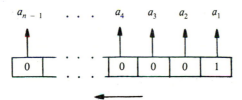

For each left shift that adjusts the dividend, the remainder pointer is also shifted left. Thus, if two shifts are required to adjust the dividend, then the contents of the remainder pointer register will be

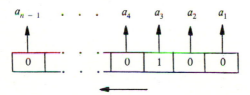

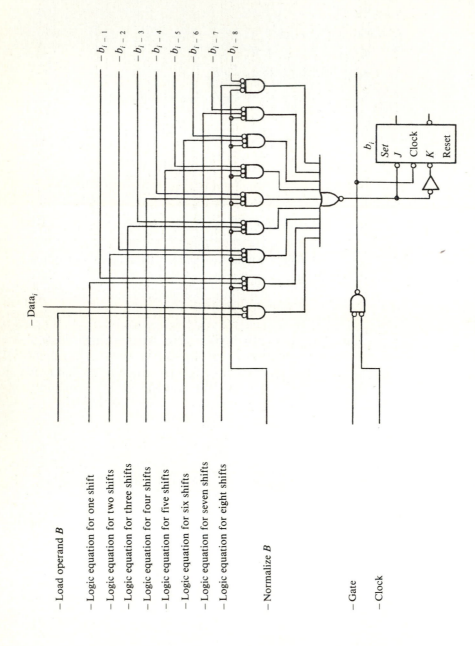

Figure 4.19 Typical stage b_i of register B for shifts of one to eight bit positions, where $i \geqslant 8$.

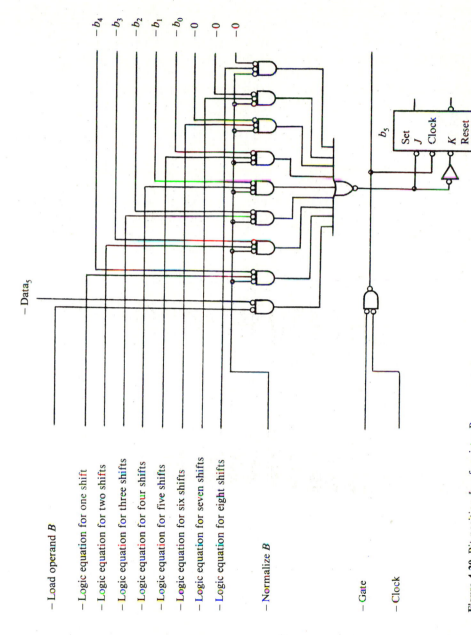

— Data₅

— Load operand B

— Logic equation for one shift
— Logic equation for two shifts
— Logic equation for three shifts
— Logic equation for four shifts
— Logic equation for five shifts
— Logic equation for six shifts
— Logic equation for seven shifts
— Logic equation for eight shifts

— Normalize B

— Gate

— Clock

Figure 4.20 Bit position b_5 of register B.

277

When register A is large, a large shift register, implying much hardware, is necessary. A counter could be used instead of a shift register; its contents are read by the microprogram and used for positioning the final remainder.

The procedure described in this section will result in the minimum number of addition/subtraction operations for most bit combinations that might be encountered in a division operation. Worst-case bit combinations will result in a division operation in which the total time required is no more than that of nonrestoring division. *Worst case* is defined as a bit configuration in which no 0s or 1s can be skipped over. Therefore, it can be concluded that the efficiency of the SRT division method, like the Booth algorithm for multiplication, is data-dependent.

4.5 CONVERGENCE DIVISION

Division methods different from those previously presented employ iterative processes that require only addition, subtraction, and multiplication. Two methods will be described in this section. The first method involves the reciprocal of the divisor, and the second uses a constant factor to multiply both the dividend and the divisor without changing the value of the ratio. Both methods employ the multiplication hardware to execute the division operation through a convergence approach.

4.5.1 Divisor Reciprocation

This convergence method for binary division generates the reciprocal of the divisor by an iterative process, and then obtains the quotient by multiplying the dividend by the divisor reciprocal. A convergence algorithm that performs the required reciprocation is presented. The method is ideally suited to binary reciprocation, because of its ease of implementation with combinational logic circuits.

Thus, to evaluate A/B, it is necessary to compute $A(1/B)$. An iterative procedure can be used to evaluate the term $1/B$. A simple, but effective iterative technique is the *Newton-Raphson iteration*. This method is very useful for improving a first approximation to a root of an equation of the form $f(x) = 0$. A brief description and development of the Newton-Raphson iteration equation follows.

Consider the graph in Fig. 4.21, and assume that x_i is a first approximation of a root. If a tangent is drawn to the curve at $x = x_i$, then the tangent will intersect the x axis at x_{i+1}. This is an improved approximation for the root of $f(x) = 0$. Since the slope of a curve is defined as the first derivative of the function, then the slope of the tangent is

$$f'(x_i) = \frac{f(x_i)}{x_i - x_{i+1}} \tag{4.10}$$

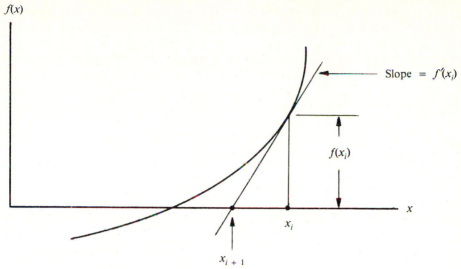

$f(x)$

Slope $= f'(x_i)$

$f(x_i)$

x

x_i

x_{i+1}

Figure 4.21 Newton-Raphson method.

or

$$x_{i+1} = x_i - \frac{f(x_i)}{f'(x_i)} \qquad (4.11)$$

The value of the function and the value of the derivative of the function are determined at $x = x_i$. The new approximation of the root is obtained by substituting these values in Eq. 4.11 to obtain x_{i+1}.

This procedure is repeated, using the approximation, to obtain a more precise approximation of the root. This continues until successive values of the approximate root differ by less than a prescribed small ε, which controls the allowable error in the root. Thus, for function f and initial value x_0, the Newton-Raphson method can be used to evaluate a root of $f(x) = 0$.

Let us now define a function $f(x)$ that will be useful in determining a quotient for this method of division. Let the function be

$$f(x) = \frac{1}{x} - B \qquad (4.12)$$

where B is the divisor. The root for this equation, when $f(x) = 0$, corresponds to

$$x = \frac{1}{B} \qquad (4.13)$$

which is the desired reciprocal. Equation 4.12 gives the function and, in order to use the Newton-Raphson method, the first derivative must also be available. The first derivative of Eq. 4.12 is

$$
\begin{aligned}
f'(x) &= f'(x^{-1}) - f'(B) \\
&= (-1)(x^{-2}) - 0 \\
&= -\frac{1}{x_2}
\end{aligned}
$$

(4.14)

Substituting Eqs. 4.12 and 4.14 in Eq. 4.11 yields

$$
\begin{aligned}
x_{i+1} &= x_i - \left[\frac{(1/x_i) - B}{-(1/x_i^2)}\right] \\
&= x_i - \left[\left(\frac{1}{x_i} - B\right)(-x_i^2)\right] \\
&= x_i - (-x_i + Bx_i^2) \\
&= 2x_i - Bx_i^2 \\
&= x_i(2 - Bx_i)
\end{aligned}
$$

(4.15)

where B is the divisor and the x_i are successively closer approximations to the reciprocal $1/B$. When x_i comes very close to $1/B$, then x_{i+1} approaches $1/B$ as a limit. This divisor reciprocal is the goal of this method, because once the value $1/B$ is obtained, then the quotient can be calculated by multiplying the dividend by the divisor reciprocal.

In order to use the Newton-Raphson method to obtain the quotient, the function must converge. When the function converges, the divisor reciprocal $1/B$ is obtained. By applying the function to a Taylor series with remainder, it can be seen that this method does converge; in fact, it converges quadratically, as will be shown later.

The Taylor series is one of the most useful methods to easily generate a polynomial approximation of a function, which results from truncation of the power series expansion after the nth-degree term. In order to establish a bound for the error introduced by the truncation process, the Taylor series with remainder is used. If a continuous function $f(x)$ possesses a continuous $(n + 1)$th derivative everywhere on the interval (x_{i+1}, x_i), then it can be represented by the Taylor finite power series

$$
f(x_i) = f(x_{i+1}) + (x_i - x_{i+1})f'(x_{i+1}) + (x_i - x_{i+1})^2\frac{f''(x_{i+1})}{2!}
$$

$$
+ (x_i - x_{i+1})^3\frac{f^3(x_{i+1})}{3!} + \cdots + (x_i - x_{i+1})^k\frac{f^k(x_{i+1})}{k!}
$$

$$+ \cdots + (x_i - x_{i+1})^n \frac{f^n (x_{i+1})}{n!} + R(x_i) \qquad (4.16)$$

where $R(x_i)$ is the remainder and is given by

$$R(x_i) = (x_i - x_{i+1})^{n+1} \frac{f^{n+1} \xi}{(n+1)!} \qquad (4.17)$$

where ξ is an unknown function of x_i and $x_{i+1} < \xi < x_i$. Therefore, it is difficult to evaluate $R(x_i)$ exactly. It is for this reason that division methods using convergence techniques do not commonly provide a remainder. The quotient is accurate, but the remainder may not be accurate.

The first approximation is crucial to the success of this method. For the process to converge, the first approximation x_0 of the divisor reciprocal must fall in the range $0 < x_0 < 2/B$. Let Q as defined by Eq. 4.18 be the quotient to be evaluated.

$$Q = \frac{A \text{ (dividend)}}{B \text{ (divisor)}} \qquad (4.18)$$

The divisor B is assumed to be a positive, normalized fraction within the range

$$\frac{1}{2} \leqslant B < 1$$

Therefore, the reciprocal of B, denoted by $1/B$, is bounded in the range

$$1 < \frac{1}{B} \leqslant 2$$

The initial x_0 should be reasonably accurate so that the number of required iterations is not excessive. An initial approximation for x_0 (to obtain $1/B$) can be found by designing a combinational logic circuit or by using a ROM. The circuit should transform the divisor bits into a string of bits that is the initial approximation. Only the k high-order bits need be used, that is, the first k bits to the right of the radix point in the normalized divisor fraction. The value for k is determined by the hardware and the precision demanded by the processor. The circuit should perform the transformation

$$B = 0.1 \ b_2 b_3 \ \cdots \ b_k \rightarrow x_0 = 1/B = 1 \cdot d_i d_2 \ \cdots \ d_t$$

where the value for t is again determined by the precision required by the processor. The value for k will usually be such that no more than the eight high-order bits of the divisor will be used.

A partial table that specifies the translation logic for the initial approximation of x_0 is given in Table 4.3 for $k = t = 4$. The objective of this scheme is to develop a quotient as quickly as possible, that is, with as few iterations as possible and with the least number of steps per iteration. While the number of operations per iteration is fundamentally intrinsic to the iteration process, a table of initial values for x_0 (similar to Table 4.3) can greatly minimize the initial error. If a ROM is used to contain the table of initial values, then the high-order bits of the divisor would form the address to the ROM.

Table 4.3 Partial table for initial approximation of the divisor reciprocal

B inputs	Approximate $1/B$ outputs
0 . 1 0 0 0	1 . 1 1 1 1
0 . 1 0 0 1	1 . 1 1 0 0
0 . 1 0 1 0	1 . 1 0 0 1
0 . 1 0 1 1	1 . 0 1 1 1
0 . 1 1 0 0	1 . 0 1 0 1
0 . 1 1 0 1	1 . 0 0 1 1
0 . 1 1 1 0	1 . 0 0 1 0
0 . 1 1 1 1	1 . 0 0 0 1

The iterative process will now be described. Equation 4.15, which was derived from the Newton-Raphson method, is restated below.

$$x_{i+1} = x_i (2 - Bx_i) \tag{4.19}$$

Let $a_i = Bx_i$. Then, Eq. 4.19 becomes

$$x_{i+1} = x_i (2 - a_i) \tag{4.20}$$

Multiplying both sides of Eq. 4.20 by B, gives

$$Bx_{i+1} = Bx_i (2 - a_i)$$

which becomes

$$a_{i+1} = a_i (2 - a_i) \tag{4.21}$$

The above sequence states that given a positive, normalized divisor B and some initial approximation x_0 to $1/B$, set $a_0 = Bx_0$ and iterate using Eqs. 4.20 and 4.21:

$$x_{i+1} = x_i (2 - a_i)$$

and

$$a_{i+1} = a_i (2 - a_i)$$

The reason for using two equations in the iteration process is to eliminate the divisor from the operation and thus speed up the process. Looking at the iteration equation of Eq. 4.19, it can be seen that the divisor for which the reciprocal is sought is required as a factor during each cycle of iteration, whereas, using Eqs. 4.20 and 4.21, the divisor enters into the computations only as an initial step. Although two equations are now used, both have the same multiplier $(2 - a_i)$, thereby reducing the amount of hardware required and also speeding up the iteration process.

The successive approximations x_i for all i approach the final reciprocal quadratically as the number of iterations increases; that is,

$$\lim_{i \to \infty} x_i = \frac{1}{B} \tag{4.22}$$

and

$$\lim_{i \to \infty} a_i = 1 \tag{4.23}$$

The initial approximation x_0 is obtained from the table. This value is multiplied by the divisor B to obtain a_0. The iteration cycles can now begin as outlined by the following sequence.

$$a_0 = Bx_0$$

$$\text{Cycle 1} \quad \begin{cases} x_1 = x_0 (2 - a_0) \\ a_1 = a_0 (2 - a_0) \end{cases}$$

$$\text{Cycle 2} \quad \begin{cases} x_2 = x_1 (2 - a_1) \\ a_2 = a_1 (2 - a_1) \end{cases}$$

$$\cdot$$
$$\cdot$$
$$\cdot$$

$$\text{Cycle } n \quad \begin{cases} x_n = x_{n-1} (2 - a_{n-1}) \\ a_n = a_{n-1} (2 - a_{n-1}) \end{cases}$$

A method of termination must be established to determine when the iteration process should end. One way to determine the number of iterations necessary to attain the required accuracy for $1/B$ is to subtract each x_{i+1} from its corresponding x_i. If the magnitude of the difference is equal to or less than some predetermined roundoff error, then the process is terminated. The actual number of iterations is determined by the precision of the processor. Let ε be a very small number reflecting this roundoff error, which could be the magnitude of the least-significant bit in the normalized divisor. Then, the required n iterations will satisfy

$$|1 - Bx_n| \leqslant \varepsilon \tag{4.24}$$

where x_n is the final approximation of the calculated divisor reciprocal.

As can be seen from Eqs. 4.20 and 4.21, the hardware involves a multiplier and an adder. Any of the multipliers or adders previously described can be used in the design of this iterative division technique. For higher-speed division, it is recommended that a variation of the nonadditive multiply modules be used with a Wallace tree network (see Sec. 3.5). The bit-pair recoding scheme can also be incorporated in the hardware multiplier to further increase the speed of the divide operation.

4.5.2 Multiplicative Division

In systems containing a high-speed multiplier, division can be performed efficiently and at very high speeds by using a process of repeated multiplication. Again, letting

$$Q = \frac{A}{B} \tag{4.25}$$

the operation of division can be replaced by that of finding a factor F such that $B \times F = 1$ and $A \times F = Q$. On each iteration a constant factor F_i is used to multiply both dividend A and divisor B so that the value of the ratio of Eq. 4.25 is not changed. The sequence of multiplying factors F_i for $i = 0, 1, \ldots, n$ is chosen such that the resulting sequence of denominators converges rapidly (quadratically) toward 1, and the resulting sequence of numerators converges toward the desired quotient Q.

The concept can be stated mathematically as

$$Q = \frac{A \times F_0 \times F_1 \times \cdots \times F_n}{B \times F_0 \times F_1 \times \cdots \times F_n}$$

which, for sufficiently large n,

$$B \times F_0 \times F_1 \times \cdots \times F_n \to 1$$

and

$$A \times F_0 \times F_1 \times \cdots \times F_n \to Q$$

which states that if the denominator converges toward 1, then the numerator must converge toward Q.

The numerator (dividend) and the denominator (divisor) are both positive fractions, for which the divisor is normalized and the dividend is shifted accordingly. The convergence of this method depends on the selection of F_i. This is facilitated by the fact that B is a normalized positive fraction, which can be expressed as

$$B = 1 - \delta \qquad (4.26)$$

where

$$0 < \delta \leqslant \frac{1}{2} \qquad (4.27)$$

The successive multipliers F_i for $i = 0, 1, \ldots, n$ are chosen such that

$$B_{i-1} < B_i \qquad (4.28)$$

for $i = 0, 1, 2, \ldots, n$. The sequence of denominators can be written as

$$B_0 = B \times F_0$$
$$B_1 = B \times F_0 \times F_1$$
$$B_2 = B \times F_0 \times F_1 \times F_2$$

$$B_{i-1} = B \times F_0 \times F_1 \times F_2 \times \cdots \times F_{i-1}$$
$$B_i = B \times F_0 \times F_1 \times F_2 \times \cdots \times F_{i-1} \times F_i$$
$$= B_{i-1} \times F_i$$

$$B_n = B_{n-1} \times F_n \qquad (4.29)$$

The process continues, with each B_i being multiplied by F_{i+1} until, for some n,

$$B_n \rightarrow 1$$

Since $B = 1 - \delta$, F_0 can be chosen such that

$$F_0 = 1 + \delta$$

We can then write

$$
\begin{aligned}
B_0 &= B \times F_0 \\
&= (1 - \delta)(1 + \delta) \\
&= 1 - \delta^2
\end{aligned}
\tag{4.30}
$$

Clearly, B_0 is closer to 1 than B. For the next iteration, select

$$F_1 = 1 + \delta^2$$

Then

$$
\begin{aligned}
B_1 &= B \times F_0 \times F_1 \\
&= B_0 \times F_1 \\
&= (1 - \delta^2)(1 + \delta^2) \\
&= 1 - \delta^4
\end{aligned}
\tag{4.31}
$$

For the next iteration, select

$$F_2 = 1 + \delta^4$$

Therefore, it can be seen that at the ith iteration

$$F_i = 1 + \delta^{2^i} \tag{4.32}$$

and

$$
\begin{aligned}
B_i &= B_{i-1} \times F_i \\
&= (1 - \delta^{2^i})(1 + \delta^{2^i}) \\
&= 1 - \delta^{2^i} \times \delta^{2^i} \\
&= 1 - \delta^{2^i + 2^i} \\
&= 1 - \delta^{2^1 \times 2^i} \\
&= 1 - \delta^{2^{i+1}}
\end{aligned}
\tag{4.33}
$$

The $1 - \delta^{2^i}$ term in Eq. 4.33 can be realized by examining Eq. 4.31 for $i = 2$; that is,

$$B_1 = 1 - \delta^4$$
$$= 1 - \delta^{2^i}$$

It was stated in Eq. 4.28 that B_{i-1} must be less than B_i. This is true because the δ's used in determining B_i are fractions, and

$$\delta^{2^i} > \delta^{2^{i+1}}$$

which makes each succeeding B_i greater than the previous B_i, thus bringing the sequence of denominators closer to 1. Thus, Eq. 4.28 can be restated as

$$B_{i-1} = 1 - \delta^{2^i} < 1 - \delta^{2^{i+1}} = B_i$$

Recall that δ was less than or equal to ½ (Eq. 4.27) and that $B_0 = 1 - \delta^2$ (Eq. 4.30). This indicates that

$$0 < \delta^2 \leqslant \frac{1}{4}$$

which means that B_0 is of the form

$$B_0 \geqslant \frac{3}{4}$$

or

$$B_0 = 0.1 \ 1 \ x \ x \ x \ \cdot \cdot \cdot$$

Using the same approach, where $B_1 = 1 - \delta^4$, B_1 is then of the form

$$B_1 \geqslant \frac{15}{16}$$

or

$$B_1 = 0.1 \ 1 \ 1 \ 1 \ x \ x \ x \ \cdot \cdot \cdot$$

Thus, as i increases, B_i converges rapidly toward 1, and the process terminates when $B_i = 0.1 \ 1 \ 1 \ 1 \ \cdot \cdot \cdot \ 1 \ 1$, which is the number closest to 1 for the word size of the machine. For a 64-bit operand, only six δ's are required, providing a very fast division technique.

Because this division method uses binary fractions, the 2s complement of B_{i-1} can be written as $2 - B_{i-1}$ (a few examples will verify this). Also,

$$
\begin{aligned}
F_i &= 1 + \delta^{2^i} \\
&= 2 - (1 - \delta^{2^i}) \\
&= 2 - B_{i-1}
\end{aligned}
\tag{4.34}
$$

The fact that $B_{i-1} = 1 - \delta^{2^i}$ above can be better understood by examining Eq. 4.33. Thus, factor F_i can be obtained directly by taking the 2s complement of the B_{i-1} term. It is this simplicity of obtaining F_i from B_{i-1} that makes this method of division so attractive.

To summarize, two multiplications are required for each iteration: one that produces the next denominator in a sequence of denominators, and from which the next multiplying factor is obtained; and one that produces the next numerator in a sequence of numerators that converge toward the quotient. The quotient can be expressed as

$$
Q = \frac{A}{B} = A \times F_0 \times F_1 \times \cdots \times F_n
$$

$$
= A \times (1 + \delta) \times (1 + \delta^2) \times (1 + \delta^4) \times \cdots \times (1 + \delta^{2^n})
$$

The smaller the initial value of δ, the faster the process will converge.

The initial multiplying factor $F_0 = 1 + \delta$ can be obtained by a table lookup procedure in a manner similar to that of divisor reciprocal division. The high-order bits of the divisor are used to address the ROM table. The output of the ROM (F_0) is multiplied by divisor B to yield B_0. Dividend A is also multiplied by F_0 to yield A_0. The operation continues as shown in the following sequence.

$$
\begin{aligned}
B_0 &= B \times F_0 \\
A_0 &= A \times F_0
\end{aligned}
$$
2s complement B_0 to yield F_1

$$
\begin{aligned}
B_1 &= B_0 \times F_1 \\
A_1 &= A_0 \times F_1
\end{aligned}
$$
If $B_1 = 1$, then $A_1 = Q$; terminate

If $B_1 \neq 1$, then 2s complement B_1 to yield F_2

$$B_2 = B_1 \times F_2$$
$$A_2 = A_1 \times F_2$$

If $B_2 = 1$, then $A_2 = Q$; terminate

If $B_2 \neq 1$, then 2s complement B_2 to yield F_3

.

.

.

The hardware for this method of multiplicative division should include one of the high-speed multipliers presented in a previous section. The 2s complementation of the B_i terms can be accomplished with a carry lookahead adder. Two multipliers would normally be required: one for numerator multiplication and one for denominator multiplication. However, if overlapping is designed into the architecture, then only one multiply unit is required and the two multiply operations can be sequenced through the single multiply unit. A detection circuit is also required to detect the presence of 0.1 1 1 1 $\cdots$ 1 1 for the value of B_i, at which point A_i contains the desired quotient.

4.6 ARRAY DIVISION

Combinational arrays can be used for division as well as for multiplication. Unlike multiplication, however, the rows of summands developed in the array are not independent of each other. The version to be used in each row depends upon the sign of the partial remainder developed in the previous row. This section presents two methods of array division. The first method is a nonrestoring technique using ripple carry. The implementation of this method requires the carry-out of each stage in a row to be rippled to the following stage. The ripple carry adds more delay to the division operation, but it is still much faster than the shift-subtract/add techniques described earlier. The second method, which is also nonrestoring, uses an approach that is similar to the speedup technique found in the carry lookahead adder.

4.6.1 Nonrestoring Array Divider

The algorithm for nonrestoring division is particularly well suited for iterative arrays. The division is performed by a series of shifts, additions, and subtractions. The iterative array is an important design consideration when VLSI technology is used. Array implementation also simplifies diagnostic procedures, because fewer machine cycles are required to obtain the result. The nonrestoring divider array is presented here as a beginning method from which modifications will lead to a much faster iterative array divider.

Recall that in shift-subtract/add nonrestoring division only two operations are required for each cycle:

$$2A - B$$

or

$$2A + B$$

where A is a $2n$-bit dividend and B is an n-bit divisor defined as

$$A = a_{2n-1} \, a_{2n-2} \cdots a_1 \, a_0$$

and

$$B = b_{n-1} \, b_{n-2} \cdots b_1 \, b_0$$

In binary nonrestoring division, successively right-shifted versions of the divisor are subtracted from or added to the dividend or resulting partial remainder. The carry-out c_{n-1} of the partial remainder determines the quotient bit q_0 according to the following criteria

$$q_0 = \begin{cases} 0 & \text{if } c_{n-1} = 0 \\ 1 & \text{if } c_{n-1} = 1 \end{cases}$$

Also, in nonrestoring division the sign determines whether to subtract or add the shifted divisor on the next cycle. If the sign is 1, then the next cycle will be a shift-subtract $(2A - B)$; if the sign is 0, then the next cycle will be a shift-add $(2A + B)$.

A two-dimensional iterative array can be used to implement the nonrestoring algorithm directly. The array consists of rows of add/subtract cells incorporating a full adder in each cell, as shown in Fig. 4.22. The mode line selects the operation of addition or subtraction. The full adder is of the type described in Sec. 2.2.2. Table 4.4 is the truth table representing the sum and carry-out for cell ij, based upon the dividend, divisor, and carry-in, under control of the mode line. The equation for the sum s_{ij} is

$$
\begin{aligned}
s_{ij} = & \left(\bar{A}_j \, \bar{B}_j \, c_{i(j-1)} \, \overline{M} \right) \vee \left(\bar{A}_j \, B_j \, \bar{c}_{i(j-1)} \, \overline{M} \right) \\
& \vee \left(A_j \, \bar{B}_j \, \bar{c}_{i(j-1)} \, \overline{M} \right) \vee \left(A_j \, B_j \, c_{i(j-1)} \, \overline{M} \right) \\
& \vee \left(\bar{A}_j \, \bar{B}_j \, \bar{c}_{i(j-1)} \, M \right) \vee \left(\bar{A}_j \, B_j \, c_{i(j-1)} \, M \right) \\
& \vee \left(A_j \, \bar{B}_j \, c_{i(j-1)} \, M \right) \vee \left(A_j \, B_j \, \bar{c}_{i(j-1)} \, M \right)
\end{aligned}
$$

$$= \left[\bar{c}_{i(j-1)} \, \bar{M} \, (A_j \veebar B_j)\right] \vee \left[c_{i(j-1)} \, M \, (A_j \veebar B_j)\right]$$

$$\vee \left[c_{i(j-1)} \, \bar{M} \, \overline{(A_j \veebar B_j)}\right] \vee \left[\bar{c}_{i(j-1)} \, M \, \overline{(A_j \veebar B_j)}\right]$$

$$= \left[(A_j \veebar B_j) \, \overline{(c_{i(j-1)} \veebar M)}\right] \vee \left[\overline{(A_j \veebar B_j)} \, (c_{i(j-1)} \veebar M)\right]$$

$$= \left[(A_j \veebar B_j) \veebar (c_{i(j-1)} \veebar M)\right] \tag{4.35}$$

The equation for carry-out c_{ij} is

$$c_{ij} = (\bar{A}_j \, B_j \, c_{i(j-1)} \, \bar{M}) \vee (A_j \, \bar{B}_j \, c_{i(j-1)} \, \bar{M})$$

$$\vee (A_j \, B_j \, \bar{c}_{i(j-1)} \, \bar{M}) \vee (A_j \, B_j \, c_{i(j-1)} \, \bar{M})$$

$$\vee (\bar{A}_j \, \bar{B}_j \, c_{i(j-1)} \, M) \vee (A_j \, \bar{B}_j \, \bar{c}_{i(j-1)} \, M)$$

$$\vee (A_j \, \bar{B}_j \, c_{i(j-1)} \, M) \vee (A_j \, B_j \, c_{i(j-1)} \, M)$$

which can be simplified by means of a Karnaugh map to

$$c_{ij} = (A_j \, c_{i(j-1)}) \vee (B_j \, c_{i(j-1)} \, \bar{M})$$

$$\vee (\bar{B}_j \, c_{i(j-1)} \, M) \vee (A_j \, \bar{B}_j \, M) \vee (A_j \, B_j \, \bar{M})$$

$$= (A_j \, c_{i(j-1)}) \vee \left[c_{i(j-1)} \, (B_j \veebar M)\right] \vee \left[A_j \, (B_j \veebar M)\right]$$

$$= (A_j \, c_{i(j-1)}) \vee \left[(B_j \veebar M)(A_j \vee c_{i(j-1)})\right] \tag{4.36}$$

The cell is implemented in the 4×4 array shown in Fig. 4.23 for a seven-bit dividend and a four-bit divisor. This yields a four-bit quotient and a four-bit remainder. Each cell contains a full adder and an EXCLUSIVE-OR gate. The mode line controls the divisor input to the adder through the EXCLUSIVE-OR gate. When the mode line is 0, an add operation is performed; when it is 1, a subtraction is performed. Subtraction is executed in 2s complement notation by forming the 1s complement of the divisor and forcing a carry-in to the low-order bit position.

The upper left cell $i = j = 1$ has mode $= 1$, thus forcing a subtraction for the first row; that is, the divisor is subtracted from the four high-order bits of the dividend

$$
\begin{array}{r}
a_6 \quad a_5 \quad a_4 \quad a_3 \\
-) \; b_3 \quad b_2 \quad b_1 \quad b_0 \\
\hline
pr_6 \quad pr_5 \quad pr_4 \quad pr_3 \\
\end{array}
$$

to yield the first partial remainder. Note that the mode line is propagated through each cell in a row, and is connected to the carry-in line of the low-order cell in each row. The first row, which performs a subtraction, thus has carry-in = 1 for the low-order bit position, which is necessary for 2s complement subtraction.

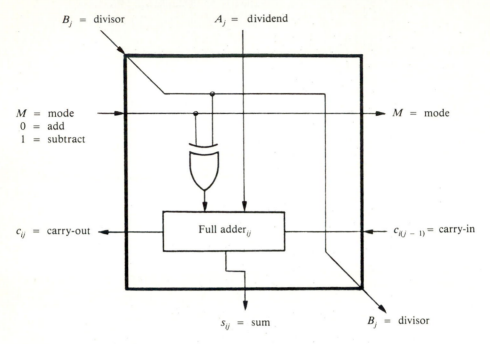

Figure 4.22 Typical cell for nonrestoring division array.

The carry-out of the high-order cell in each row represents the quotient bit. This carry-out is connected to the mode line of the row beneath it. If the high-order carry-out = 0, indicating an unsuccessful subtraction, then the next operation at the next lower level will be an addition (mode = 0). If the high-order carry-out = 1, indicating a successful subtraction, then the next operation at the next lower level will be a subtraction (mode = 1). This conforms to the nonrestoring division algorithm. The shift that takes place before each addition or subtraction is accomplished by moving the divisor to the right along the diagonal. This is equivalent to the operation $2A - B$ or $2A + B$.

The nonrestoring division algorithm can be summarized as follows:

1. Subtract the divisor from the dividend. This is accomplished by 2s complement subtraction, that is, $A + \bar{B} + 1$. This yields the first partial remainder.
2. If the high-order carry-out = 0, the partial remainder was negative. Therefore, the quotient bit at this level is 0, the divisor is shifted to the right, and an add operation is performed at the next lower level. This is equivalent

Table 4.4 Truth table for add/subtract cell in nonrestoring division array

	a_j	b_j	$c_{i(j-1)}$	M	s_{ij}	c_{ij}
	0	0	0	0	0	0
	0	0	1	0	1	0
	0	1	0	0	1	0
	0	1	1	0	0	1
Add	1	0	0	0	1	0
	1	0	1	0	0	1
	1	1	0	0	0	1
	1	1	1	0	1	1
	0	0	0	1	1	0
	0	0	1	1	0	1
	0	1	0	1	0	0
Subtract*	0	1	1	1	1	0
	1	0	0	1	0	1
	1	0	1	1	1	1
	1	1	0	1	1	0
	1	1	1	1	0	1

*B_j is inverted to determine s_{ij} and c_{ij}.

    to adding one-half the divisor to the partial remainder.
3. If the high-order carry-out $= 1$, the partial remainder was positive. Therefore, the quotient bit at this level is 1, the divisor is shifted to the right, and a subtract operation is performed at the next lower level. This is equivalent to subtracting one-half the divisor from the partial remainder.

    An example will now be given using the array illustrated in Fig. 4.23. First, the example will be presented in the manner that was used in previous sections of this chapter. This will allow the computation to be followed and compared at each level of the operation. Figure 4.24 shows a nonrestoring division example using a seven-bit dividend and a four-bit divisor, both of which are positive operands. The sign of the dividend is extended one bit position to accommodate register A. The same example is presented in Fig. 4.25, using the array implementation.

    The nonrestoring division array technique works equally well for normalized fractional operands. Also, as in the sequential shift-subtract/add method, the algorithm is simpler if both operands are positive. Restoring a negative remainder is much easier and faster in the array implementation than in the sequential method. In the sequential technique, recall that a negative remainder ($q_0 = 0$) was restored by adding back the divisor to obtain the previous partial remainder. This resulted in an extra cycle. However, in the combinational iterative array, the previous partial remainder is still available, and can be found at the sum outputs of

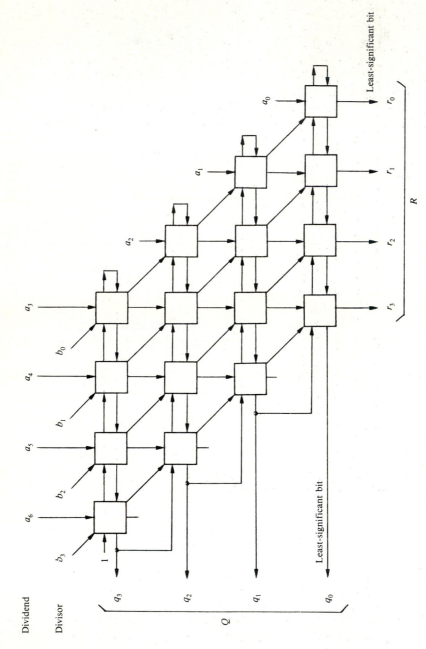

Figure 4.23 Nonrestoring division array for a seven-bit dividend and a four-bit divisor.

$A \cdot Q = 0\ 0\ 0\ 0\ 1\ 1\ 1 \quad (+7)$

$B \quad\quad = 0\ 0\ 1\ 0 \quad\quad (+2)$

$\overline{B} + 1 = 1\ 1\ 1\ 0$

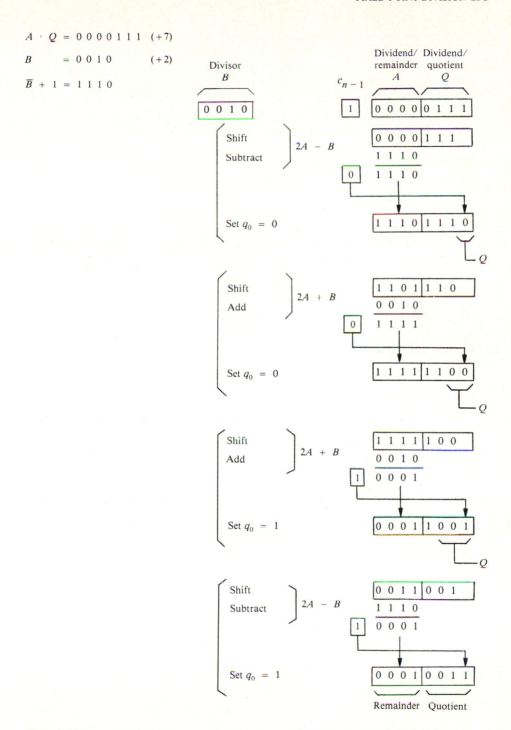

Figure 4.24 Nonrestoring division example using a seven-bit dividend and a four-bit divisor.

each cell at the previous higher level. A multiplexer can be used to select the correct final remainder, as a function of the quotient bit q_0. If $q_0 = 1$, the remainder is correct; if $q_0 = 0$, the remainder must be restored to the previous partial remainder. An example is shown in Fig. 4.26.

The number of cells required for a four-bit divisor, quotient, and remainder is 16. For an m-bit divisor, quotient, and remainder, the number of cells is m^2. The carry-in to the low-order cell of the ith row occurs only after the quotient bit q_{i-1} is available for the $(i-1)$th row. This is because q_{i-1} is connected to the mode line for row i, and the mode line feeds through each cell and is connected to the carry-in of the low-order cell. If the propagation delay for both the sum and carry outputs is 2 $\triangle$, then the delay for the 4 $\times$ 4 array of Fig. 4.26 is 32 $\triangle$, that is, 2 $\triangle$ to propagate the carry through each cell and 2 $\triangle$ to form the sum. Thus, the delay for a divide operation for an m-bit divisor, quotient, and remainder is $2m^2$ $\triangle$, where $\triangle$ is the gate propagation delay of the technology being used.

4.6.2 Carry Lookahead (CLA) Array Divider

A method will now be presented to increase the speed of the array divider mentioned previously. The basic idea of the modification is to eliminate the carry ripple time, which is proportional to the length of the divisor along each row of the array. The array presented here will perform high-speed nonrestoring division. The high speed is obtained by replacing the ripple carry in each cell in a row with carry lookahead logic.

The cell used for this array is the one shown in Fig. 4.22, with the exception that no carry-out is required. This improved technique can be implemented with an augmented cellular array, which is entirely combinational and very applicable to LSI and VLSI technology. A minimum of external timing and control is required. This method results in a division time that increases linearly with blocks of cells in a row; in other words, it increases linearly with the quotient length. This is in contrast to the quadratic increase in time of the ripple carry array divider.

The array organization utilizing the CLA principle is illustrated in Fig. 4.27 for a seven-bit positive dividend and a four-bit positive divisor. The divisor bits are connected to the upper left corner of the cells in the first row and propagate down the diagonals to the appropriate cells in the next row. The dividend bits enter the top of each cell in the first row and also the cells along the right diagonal. For all subsequent rows, the partial remainder enters the top of the cells.

The carry-out c_{out} of each CLA circuit becomes the appropriate quotient bit in the same manner as the ripple carry array. Bit c_{out} is the final carry-out for each row, that is, the carry-out of the leftmost cell in each row. Bit $c_{i\ out}$ also connects to the add/subtract mode control line for each cell in the $i + 1$ row directly below. This bit also becomes the carry-in bit c_{in} to the CLA logic in the $i + 1$ row. Bit c_{in} is then used in the generate and propagate functions for that row.

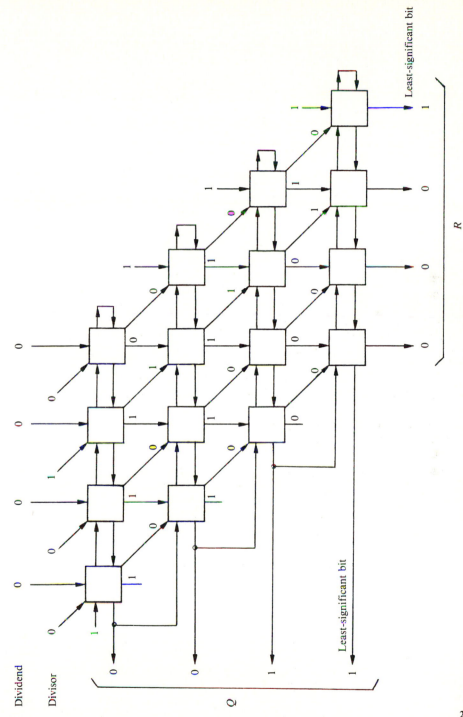

Figure 4.25 Nonrestoring division example for a seven-bit dividend and a four-bit divisor.

297

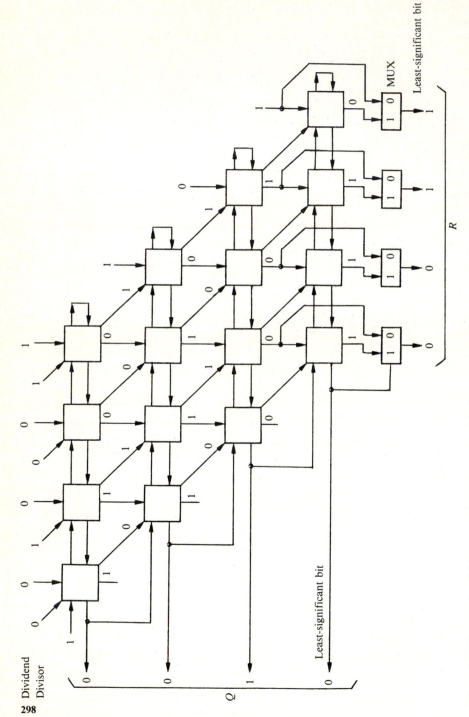

Figure 4.26 Nonrestoring division example for a seven-bit dividend and a four-bit divisor, with remainder correction capability.

Note also that the mode control line feeds back to connect to the carry-in line of the low-order cell in each row. Bit c_{out}, used in this manner, accomplishes 2s complement arithmetic. When $q_i = 1$, the divisor in the $i + 1$ row is subtracted from the previous partial remainder. This is accomplished because $M = q_i = 1$, which 1s-complements the divisor and forces a 1 into the low-order carry-in as well as into the CLA logic. The CLA logic then uses $c_{in} = 1$ to produce the carries into each cell in the $i + 1$ row.

The equations for the carry outs of each cell into the next higher-order cell in the row (produced by the CLA logic) are shown in Eq. 4.37. The carry-out for cell$_i$ (c_i), which is formed by CLA logic, becomes the carry-in to cell$_{i + 1}$. Thus,

$$\text{Carry-in}_{i + 1} \leftarrow \text{carry-out}_i \ (c_i)$$

and the carry-out equations are

$$
\begin{aligned}
c_0 \quad &= \ G_0 \vee P_0 \, c_{in} \\
c_1 \quad &= \ G_1 \vee P_1 \, G_0 \vee P_1 \, P_0 \, c_{in} \\
c_2 \quad &= \ G_2 \vee P_2 \, G_1 \vee P_2 \, P_1 \, G_0 \vee P_2 \, P_1 \, P_0 \, c_{in} \\
c_3 = c_{out} \ &= \ G_3 \vee P_3 \, G_2 \vee P_3 \, P_2 \, G_1 \vee P_3 \, P_2 \, P_1 \, G_0 \\
&\quad \vee P_3 \, P_2 \, P_1 \, P_0 \, c_{in}
\end{aligned}
\tag{4.37}
$$

where

$$
\begin{aligned}
G_i \ &= \ a_i \wedge b_i \\
P_i \ &= \ a_i \vee b_i
\end{aligned}
$$

In general,

$$
\begin{aligned}
c_i = \ &G_i \vee P_i \, G_{i-1} \vee \cdots \vee P_i \, P_{i-1} \cdots P_1 \, G_0 \\
&\vee P_i \, P_{i-1} \cdots P_1 \, P_0 \, c_{in}
\end{aligned}
\tag{4.38}
$$

and $c_{n-1} = c_{out} = G_{n-1} \vee P_{n-1} \, G_{n-2} \vee P_{n-1} \, P_{n-2} \, G_{n-3}$

$$
\begin{aligned}
&\vee \cdots \vee P_{n-1} \cdots P_{i+1} \, G_i \\
&\vee P_{n-1} \cdots P_{i+1} \, P_i \, G_{i-1} \\
&\vee \cdots \vee P_{n-1} \cdots P_1 \, G_0 \vee P_{n-1} \cdots P_1 \, P_0 \, c_{in}
\end{aligned}
\tag{4.39}
$$

The example of Fig. 4.24 will be executed in the CLA array. This is shown in Figure 4.28 for the seven-bit dividend and four-bit divisor. To facilitate the operation of this example, the generate and propagate terms have been determined for each cell in each row, as shown in Table 4.5. These generate and propagate functions are to be used in Eq. 4.37 to form c_0, c_1, c_2, and c_3.

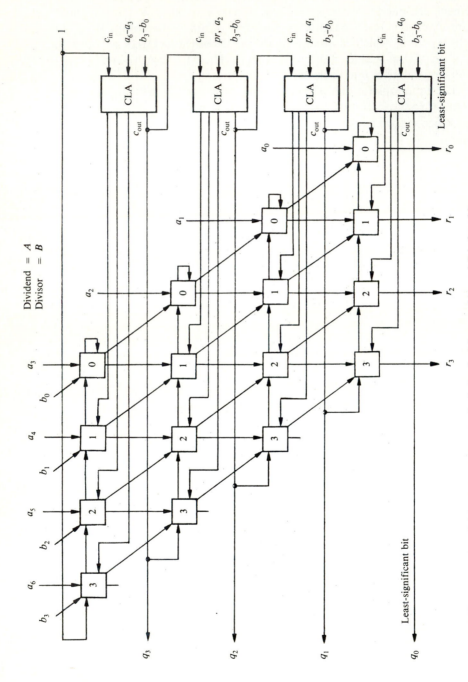

Figure 4.27 Nonrestoring division array using carry lookahead. A is seven bits and B is four bits.

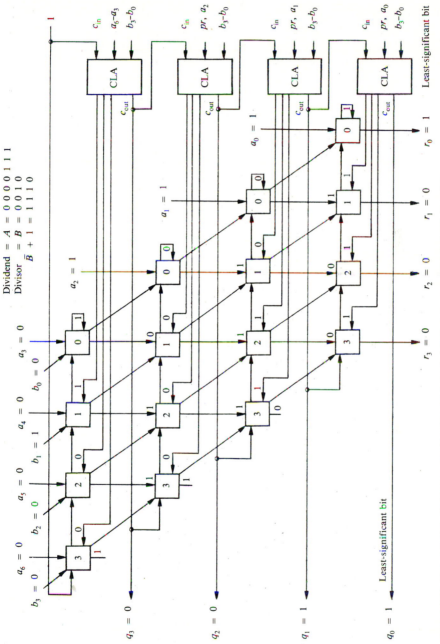

Figure 4.28 Nonrestoring division example using carry lookahead: A is seven bits and B is four bits.

301

Table 4.5 Generate and propagate functions for the example of Fig. 4.28

Row number	G_3 P_3	G_2 P_2	G_1 P_1	G_0 P_0	c_{in}
1	0 1	0 1	0 0	0 1	1
2	0 1	0 1	0 1	0 1	0
3	0 1	0 1	1 1	0 1	0
4	0 1	0 1	0 1	1 1	1

The generate and propagate functions and the formation of the carry-outs are used with the divisor and previous partial remainder, under control of the mode line, to produce the next partial remainder. It is recommended that this example be examined in detail to aid in understanding the operation of the nonrestoring division array technique using the CLA principle.

Correction for the final remainder can be realized in the same manner as previously described, that is, multiplexing as shown in Fig. 4.26. The 4×4 CLA array presented in this section can be extended to include divisors and quotients of up to 16 bits without any loss in carry generation time, using current LSI technology. Also, current LSI technology permits operands for large n ($n \gg 16$) to be used in the CLA array. This results from having equivalent gates with many inputs. Each additional input is wired-ORed to the previous inputs to add more inputs to the equivalent gate. Logic diagrams for the AND and OR functions are shown in Fig. 4.29. However, it should be noted that each wire-ORed input adds a proportional delay to the propagation delay of the function.

The divide time for 4×4 CLA array is 20 Δ, as compared with 32 Δ for a 4×4 ripple carry array. The 20 Δ was calculated from 3 Δ for CLA logic and 2 Δ for sum generation of each cell. A much greater increase in speed is realized for larger operands. For example, an 8×8 ripple carry array has a divide time of 128 Δ, whereas an 8×8 CLA array has a divide time of only 40 Δ.

PROBLEMS

4.1 Use the paper-and-pencil method for fixed-point binary restoring division to perform the following divide operations using eight-bit dividends and four-bit divisors:

(a) $\dfrac{41}{3}$ (b) $\dfrac{73}{5}$

4.2 How can quotient overflow be detected for fixed-point binary division?

4.3 After the completion of a division operation, what should be the sign of the remainder? Why?

4.4 Use the sequential restoring method to perform the following divide operation:

$$A \cdot Q \text{ (dividend)} = 0\ 0\ 0\ 0\ 1\ 1\ 0\ 0\ 0\ 0$$

$$B \text{ (divisor)} \qquad = 0\ 0\ 1\ 1\ 1$$

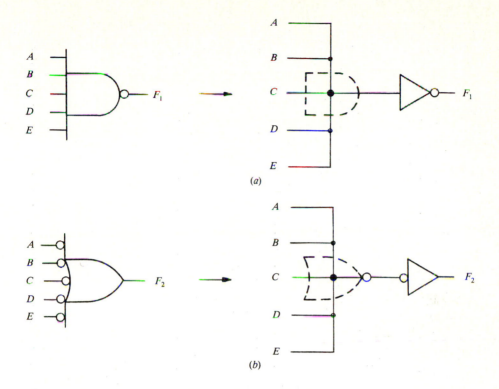

Figure 4.29 Logic diagrams for AND and OR functions using an inverter.
(a) $F_1 = \overline{A \wedge B \wedge C \wedge D \wedge E}$; (b) $F_2 = \overline{A} \vee \overline{B} \vee \overline{C} \vee \overline{D} \vee \overline{E}$.

4.5 Use the sequential nonrestoring method to perform the following divide operation:
$$A \cdot Q \text{ (dividend)} = 0\ 0\ 0\ 0\ 0\ 1\ 1\ 1$$
$$B \text{ (divisor)} = 0\ 0\ 1\ 0$$

4.6 Use the sequential nonrestoring method to perform the following divide operation:
$$A \cdot Q \text{ (dividend)} = 0\ 0\ 0\ 1\ 1\ 0\ 0\ 0\ 1\ 1$$
$$B \text{ (divisor)} = 0\ 1\ 0\ 0\ 0$$

4.7 Compare the processing speed and hardware requirements of fixed-point binary restoring and nonrestoring division.

4.8 What are the advantages of SRT division over the standard shift-add/subtract methods?

4.9 Name two ways to terminate an SRT division.

4.10 Use SRT division to perform the following divide operation:
$$A \cdot Q \text{ (dividend)} = 0\ .\ 0\ 0\ 1\ 0\ 0\ 0\ 0\ 0$$
$$B \text{ (divisor)} = 0\ .\ 0\ 1\ 1\ 0$$

4.11 Use SRT division to perform the following divide operation:
$$A \cdot Q \text{ (dividend)} = 0\ .\ 0\ 0\ 0\ 1\ 0\ 1\ 1\ 1$$
$$B \text{ (divisor)} = 0\ .\ 0\ 1\ 0\ 0$$

4.12 Determine whether the following operands produce an overflow condition for a fixed-point binary divide operation:

(a)
$$\text{Dividend} = 0\ 0\ 0\ 1\ 1\ 1\ 1\ 1$$
$$\text{Divisor}\ \ = 0\ 0\ 0\ 1$$

(b)
$$\text{Dividend} = 0\ 0\ 0\ 0\ 1\ 1\ 1\ 1$$
$$\text{Divisor}\ \ = 0\ 0\ 0\ 1$$

(c)
$$\text{Dividend} = 0\ 1\ 0\ 0\ 0\ 0\ 0\ 1$$
$$\text{Divisor}\ \ \ = 0\ 0\ 1\ 1$$

4.13 Design a 5×5 nonrestoring array divider using the cell shown in Fig. 4.22. Test the design with the following operands:

$$A\ \text{(dividend)} = 0\ 0\ 1\ 0\ 0\ 1\ 0\ 0\ 1\ 1$$
$$B\ \text{(divisor)}\ \ \ = 0\ 1\ 1\ 0\ 0$$

Show all partial remainders.

4.14 Design a 4×4 nonrestoring array divider for positive operands with remainder correction. The design should allow for the situation where:

(a) The final remainder is negative.

(b) The remainder directly before the final remainder is also negative.

4.15 What are the main differences between fixed-point binary multiplication and division?

4.16 Explain in general the convergence division method of obtaining the quotient using multiplicative division. Write the generalized equation for finding the quotient.

4.17 For $i = 0, 1, 2, 3$, write the equations for the constant factor in terms of d and the corresponding equations for the divisor in terms of d using the multiplicative division technique for convergence division. Comment on the convergence of the divisor.

4.18 Write the ith equation of constant factor F_i in terms of the denominator for multiplicative division using convergence. Why is this method of division so attractive?

4.19 For a 16-bit processor, what is the bit configuration of the final value of the denominator after convergence, using multiplicative division?

DECIMAL ARITHMETIC

5.1 INTRODUCTION

Computer users generally prepare input data and receive the computed results in decimal form. A binary processor can perform arithmetic operations on decimal data if it first converts the input decimal numbers into binary form, executes the operations, and then converts the results into decimal form. This is satisfactory for small input-output requirements and a large number of calculations. However, if the opposite is true—that is, large amounts of input-output data and a relatively small number of computations—then it is more efficient to perform the calculations using decimal arithmetic.

The radix complement is the primary representation used for subtraction. In binary fixed-point arithmetic, with radix equal to 2, this becomes the 2s complement. In decimal fixed-point arithmetic, the 10s complement is used in the subtraction operation. A single element in a decimal arithmetic processor has nine inputs and five outputs, as shown below. Each of the two operands is represented by a four-bit BCD-encoded digit. A carry-in bit is also provided from the next lowest element. The outputs are a four-bit BCD-encoded digit and a carry-out bit. The carry bit is never greater than 1, regardless of the radix that is used, and thus only one line is needed.

The most commonly used code in decimal arithmetic is the 8, 4, 2, 1 code, because simple binary addition methods may be used. However, other codes, such as the 5, 4, 2, 1 code, are also readily adaptable to decimal arithmetic. The 4, 2, and 1 bits are used in the standard binary fashion, but the code generation for decimal 5, 6, and 7 is different.

The algorithms used for decimal arithmetic are similar to those used for fixed-point arithmetic. The main difference is that fixed-point arithmetic treats each bit as a digit, whereas decimal arithmetic treats four bits as a digit. Shifting

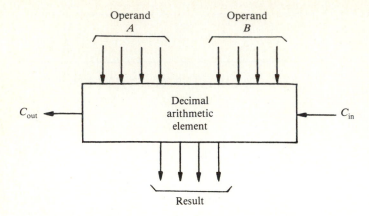

operations are also different in decimal arithmetic, because a shift of one digit position necessitates a shift over four bits. All shifting is performed in 4-bit increments. Thus, to shift

$$1\ 0\ 0\ 1 \qquad 0\ 1\ 1\ 1 \qquad 0\ 1\ 1\ 0 \qquad 0\ 0\ 1\ 1 \qquad 0\ 1\ 0\ 0$$

two digit positions to the right, with 0 0 0 0 filling the vacated positions, results in

$$0\ 0\ 0\ 0 \qquad 0\ 0\ 0\ 0 \qquad 1\ 0\ 0\ 1 \qquad 0\ 1\ 1\ 1 \qquad 0\ 1\ 1\ 0$$

The 2s complement is used in fixed-point binary arithmetic. Recall that a subtraction was written as

$$A \leftarrow A + (\bar{B} + 1)$$

where $\bar{B}$ is the 1s complement and 1 is added to the low-order bit position to form the 2s complement. The same notation is also used in decimal arithmetic. However, in this case, $\bar{B}$ indicates the 9s complement and 1 is added to the low-order digit position to form the 10s complement.

5.2 ADDITION AND SUBTRACTION

There are basically three approaches available to add and subtract decimal numbers. The first is the parallel approach, in which all bits of all digits of both operands are added in parallel. The second is the digit-serial, bit-parallel approach, in which all four bits of both operand digits are added in parallel, but the digits enter the adder serially. The third is the digit-serial, bit-serial approach, in which the four bits of both operands enter a single full adder serially and the digits also enter serially. Only the first approach will be considered here, and several different methods with examples will be presented.

There are 16 possible bit combinations using four binary bits, as shown in Table 5.1. Of these, only 10 are valid BCD digits. Thus, when two BCD digits are added, the result has a value range from 0 to 18, as shown below. When a carry-in is asserted, then the range is from 0 to 19.

$$
\begin{array}{llll}
0\ 0\ 0\ 0 & \text{to} & 1\ 0\ 0\ 1 \\
0\ 0\ 0\ 0 & & 1\ 0\ 0\ 1 \\
\hline
0\ 0\ 0\ 0 & & 1\leftarrow0\ 0\ 1\ 0
\end{array}
$$

Table 5.1 Possible bit combinations of four binary bits

Decimal	Binary			
	8	4	2	1
0	0	0	0	0
1	0	0	0	1
2	0	0	1	0
3	0	0	1	1
4	0	1	0	0
5	0	1	0	1
6	0	1	1	0
7	0	1	1	1
8	1	0	0	0
9	1	0	0	1
10	1	0	1	0
11	1	0	1	1
12	1	1	0	0
13	1	1	0	1
14	1	1	1	0
15	1	1	1	1

Valid BCD digits (0–9)

Invalid BCD digits (10–15)

When a BCD sum digit exceeds 9, it must be adjusted to a valid digit by adding $0\ 1\ 1\ 0_2$ (6_{10}). The excess-6 technique generates both a valid sum and a carry-in to the next higher-order digit.

Table 5.2 shows the 20 possible result digits when adding two BCD digits and a carry-in. The first 10 digits (0 through 9) require no adjustment. The last 10 digits (10 through 19) require an adjustment—the addition of $0\ 1\ 1\ 0$—to produce a valid BCD digit. The logic that detects whether a 6 should be added is determined from the table entries. Whenever the unadjusted BCD sum produces a carry-out, the sum must be corrected by adding 6. Also, whenever bit positions 8 and 4 are both 1s or bit positions 8 and 2 are both 1s, then the sum must be corrected. The condition for a correction that also produces a carry-out can be expressed by the following boolean function:

$$\text{Carry} = c_8 \lor b_8 b_4 \lor b_8 b_2 \qquad (5.1)$$

Table 5.2 Binary-coded decimal sum digits

Decimal	Unadjusted BCD sum						Adjusted BCD sum				
	C	8	4	2	1		C	8	4	2	1
0	0	0	0	0	0						
1	0	0	0	0	1						
2	0	0	0	1	0	No					
3	0	0	0	1	1						
4	0	0	1	0	0	adjustment					
5	0	0	1	0	1						
6	0	0	1	1	0	required					
7	0	0	1	1	1						
8	0	1	0	0	0						
9	0	1	0	0	1						
10	0	1	0	1	0		1	0	0	0	0
11	0	1	0	1	1		1	0	0	0	1
12	0	1	1	0	0		1	0	0	1	0
13	0	1	1	0	1	Adjustment	1	0	0	1	1
14	0	1	1	1	0		1	0	1	0	0
15	0	1	1	1	1	required	1	0	1	0	1
16	1	0	0	0	0		1	0	1	1	0
17	1	0	0	0	1		1	0	1	1	1
18	1	0	0	1	0		1	1	0	0	0
19	1	0	0	1	1		1	1	0	0	1

where c_8 is the carry-out of the high-order bit position and the b_i's are the bits of the unadjusted BCD sum digit.

5.2.1 Addition with Sum Correction

A decimal adder is a device that adds two decimal (BCD) digits in parallel and produces a decimal sum. The adder must also include correction logic for intermediate sum digits equal to or greater than 1 0 1 0. Two adders are involved, as shown in Fig. 5.1. These are standard four-bit binary adders of the type described in Chap. 2 for fixed-point addition. The decimal digits are the low-order digits of two n-bit operands: operand A (augend) and operand B

(addend) as defined below.

$$A = a(n-1)_8\ a(n-1)_4\ a(n-1)_2\ a(n-1)_1$$
$$a(n-2)_8\ a(n-2)_4\ a(n-2)_2\ a(n-2)_1$$

$$\cdot$$
$$\cdot$$
$$\cdot$$

$$a(1)_8\ a(1)_4\ a(1)_2\ a(1)_1 \qquad\qquad (5.2)$$
$$a(0)_8\ a(0)_4\ a(0)_2\ a(0)_1$$

$$B = b(n-1)_8\ b(n-1)_4\ b(n-1)_2\ b(n-1)_1$$
$$b(n-2)_8\ b(n-2)_4\ b(n-2)_2\ b(n-2)_1$$

$$\cdot$$
$$\cdot$$
$$\cdot$$

$$b(1)_8\ b(1)_4\ b(1)_2\ b(1)_1$$
$$b(0)_8\ b(0)_4\ b(0)_2\ b(0)_1$$

The carry-out bit from the decimal adder agrees with Eq. 5.1. The carry-out signal is applied to the b_4 and b_2 inputs of the lower adder (with $b_8 = b_1 = 0$), which corrects the invalid decimal digit. All sum digits that require correction also produce a carry. The carry-out of the lower adder may be ignored since it supplies no new information to the carry-out function for this element of a decimal adder. This decimal adder element may be used with other identical elements to perform parallel addition of decimal operands. A decimal parallel adder that adds n decimal digits requires n decimal adder stages, with the carry-out of stage$_i$ connected to the carry-in of stage$_{i+1}$. The propagation of the ripple carry in this manner may be too slow for some machines. A later section will describe a decimal adder that uses the carry lookahead technique presented in Chap. 2. Also, the lower adder of Fig. 5.1 does not need four full adders, and this can permit a reduction in logic.

5.2.2 Addition/Subtraction Element

The same adder that was described in the previous section can also be utilized to subtract two decimal digits. A small amount of additional circuitry is required in the form of a 9s complementer. The BCD code is not a self-complementing code, and thus the 9s complement cannot be obtained by simply inverting each of the four bits in the decimal digit. It can be obtained at the expense of an extra adder, but a more economical and faster method is to use a combinational circuit that is defined by the following boolean equations:

$$f_1 = b_1\overline{M} \vee \overline{b}_1 M$$
$$= b_1 \veebar M$$
$$f_2 = b_2$$
$$f_4 = b_4\overline{M} \vee (\overline{b}_4 b_2 \vee b_4\overline{b}_2) M$$
$$= b_4\overline{M} \vee (b_4 \veebar b_2) M$$
$$f_8 = b_8\overline{M} \vee \overline{b}_8\overline{b}_4\overline{b}_2 M \qquad (5.3)$$

where the f_i's are the outputs of the 9s complementer, and are under control of the mode bit M such that

$$\text{Add} \qquad M = 0$$
$$\text{Subtract} \quad M = 1$$

Equation 5.3 shows that $f_i = b_i$ when $M = 0$. When $M = 1$, the f_i's produce the 9s complement of the b_i's. The 9s complement of a number is obtained by subtracting the number from 9. The logic diagram for a 9s complementer is shown in Fig. 5.2.

A single element of a decimal addition/subtraction unit is shown in Fig. 5.3. It consists of the decimal adder stage of Fig. 5.1 and a 9s complementer on the inputs of the addend/subtrahend. The mode line controls the operation of the element. When $M = 0$, the outputs form the sum of $A(i) + B(i)$. When $M = 1$, the outputs form the sum of A plus the 9s complement of B. If $i = 0$, then the mode line is connected to C_{i-1}, so that $C_{i-1} = M$. The outputs then form the sum of A plus the 10s complement of B. The carry-out of the last stage is discarded. Figure 5.4 shows the organization for an n-digit adder/subtractor unit that can perform the operations $A + B$, $A - B$, and $B - A$. Twelve examples are given in Fig. 5.5 that illustrate the principles of decimal addition and subtraction. Negative results can either remain in 10s complement form or be recomplemented into sign-magnitude notation. Both operands are assumed to have 9s complementers on their inputs. Although the operation in the examples is addition, both true addition and true subtraction are performed.

5.2.3 Addition Using Multiplexer

In Figure 5.1, the carry associated with the sum from the upper adder determined whether 6 was to be added to the intermediate sum by means of the lower adder. An alternative approach is described here. The two operands are added in the upper adder as before. The intermediate sum thus generated is always added to +6, as shown in Fig. 5.6. The two different sums—the sum from the upper adder and the sum from the lower adder—are then sent to a multiplexer. Selection of the up-

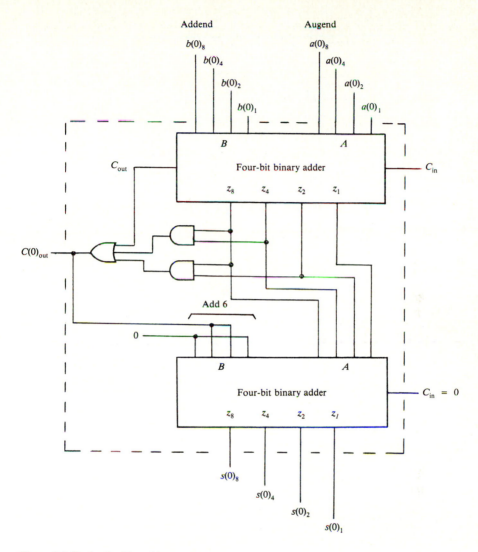

Figure 5.1 Decimal adder with sum correction.

per or lower sum is determined by the OR of the upper and lower carries. The carry-out of the upper adder is ORed with the carry-out of the lower adder to generate C_{out}.

$$C_{out} = C_{out} \text{ (upper)} \vee C_{out} \text{ (lower)} \tag{5.4}$$

$$\text{Multiplexer select} = \begin{cases} \text{upper sum} & \text{if } C_{out} = 0 \\ \text{lower sum} & \text{if } C_{out} = 1 \end{cases} \tag{5.5}$$

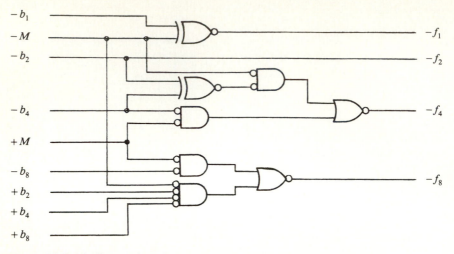

Figure 5.2 Logic diagram for a 9s complementer.

The time required for carry propagation can be decreased if CLA logic is used. Two separate lookahead circuits are needed—one for the upper adder and one for the lower adder. The carry-out in Eq. 5.4 can also be described in terms of the upper and lower group generate GG and group propagate GP:

$$
\begin{aligned}
C_{out} &= C_{out} \text{ (upper)} \lor C_{out} \text{ (lower)} \\
&= [GG \lor (GP \land C_{in})]_{upper} \\
&\quad \lor [GG \lor (GP \land C_{in})]_{lower}
\end{aligned}
$$

By incorporating a 9s complementer into the design, the unit becomes an adder/subtractor, as shown in Fig. 5.7 for two elements. Six examples are shown in Fig. 5.8 to illustrate the selection determination of the upper and lower sums.

5.2.4 Addition with Correction ROM

The operation that adds 6 in order to correct an invalid decimal digit can be implemented with a ROM. High-speed ROMs using current technology can correct a decimal digit in less than 10 ns. This approach may require less hardware and less cost than having a second level of addition. In any event, it is certainly simpler. The technique is shown in Fig. 5.9. The ROM is addressed by the decimal sum outputs concatenated on the left with the carry-out of the stage. The carry is provided by the following expression:

$$
Carry = c_8 \lor b_8 b_4 \lor b_8 b_2
$$

Table 5.3 lists the ROM outputs that are associated with each address. Figure 5.10 gives some examples using this method of decimal addition.

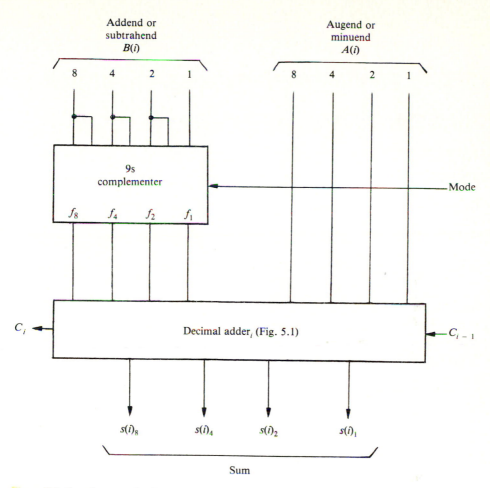

Figure 5.3 One element of a decimal addition/subtraction unit.

5.2.5 Addition with Bias

As demonstrated, there are a variety of schemes for performing decimal addition. The method presented in this section preprocesses and postprocesses the decimal digits. This allows a standard binary adder to be used. Carry propagation occurs when any sum digit exceeds 9, even though a four-bit binary adder can represent digits up to 15. Thus, a decimal number (for example, the augend) can be preconditioned (or biased) by adding 6 to each decimal digit without generating a carry-out of the high-order bit position. Each augend digit can be independently biased this way in one parallel operation.

Next, the addend digits are added to the biased augend digits, and carries are allowed to propagate in the standard way for binary addition. Since any biased 9 in the augend has been translated to a 15, any nonzero digit that is added to a 9

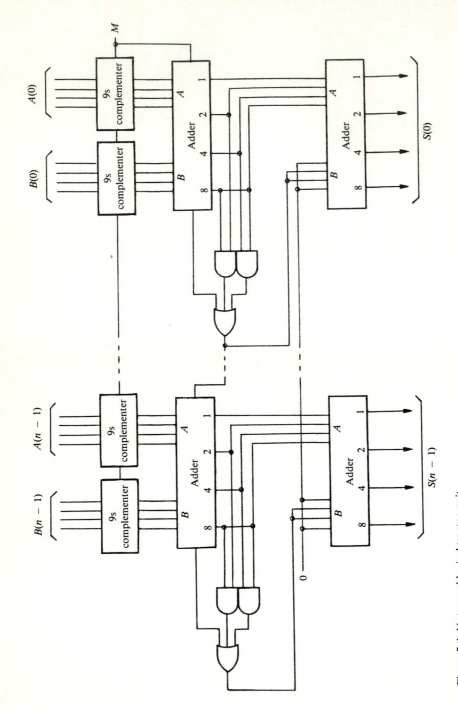

Figure 5.4 *N*-stage adder/subtractor unit.

314

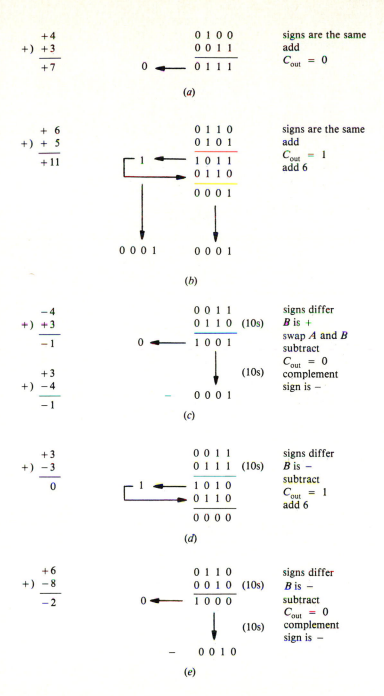

Figure 5.5 Examples of decimal addition and subtraction.

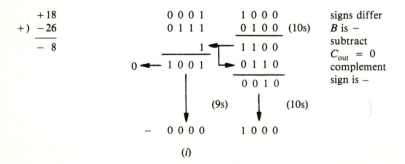

Figure 5.5 (Continued)

```
     + 26        0 0 1 0      0 1 1 0     signs are the same
+)   + 18        0 0 0 1      1 0 0 0     add
   ───────                                Cₒᵤₜ = 1
     + 44                1 ◄──── 1 1 1 0  add 6
                 0 1 0 0 └──► 0 1 1 0
                              ─────────
                              0 1 0 0
```

$C_{out} = 1$
add 6

(j)

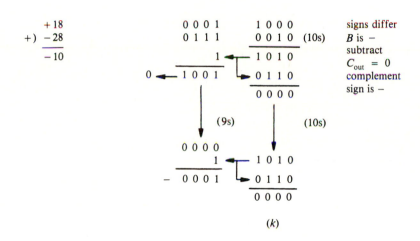

```
     + 18        0 0 0 1      1 0 0 0     signs differ
+)   − 28        0 1 1 1      0 0 1 0 (10s) B is −
   ───────                              subtract
     − 10                1 ◄──── 1 0 1 0   Cₒᵤₜ = 0
              0 ◄─── 1 0 0 1 └──► 0 1 1 0  complement
                              ─────────   sign is −
                              0 0 0 0

                 (9s)            (10s)

              0 0 0 0        1 0 1 0
                      1 ◄──── 1 0 1 0
            −  0 0 0 1 └──► 0 1 1 0
                              ─────────
                              0 0 0 0
```

(k)

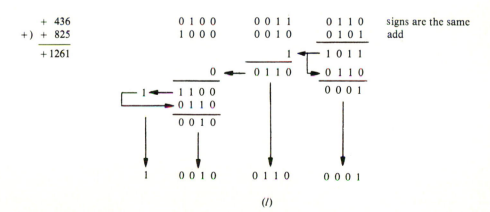

```
     +  436      0 1 0 0    0 0 1 1     0 1 1 0   signs are the same
+)   +  825      1 0 0 0    0 0 1 0     0 1 0 1   add
   ────────                          1 ◄──── 1 0 1 1
     + 1261            0 ◄─── 0 1 1 0 └──► 0 1 1 0
                                           0 0 0 1
           ┌─1 ◄──── 1 1 0 0
           └──► 0 1 1 0
                 0 0 1 0

       1       0 0 1 0       0 1 1 0     0 0 0 1
```

(l)

Figure 5.5 (Continued)

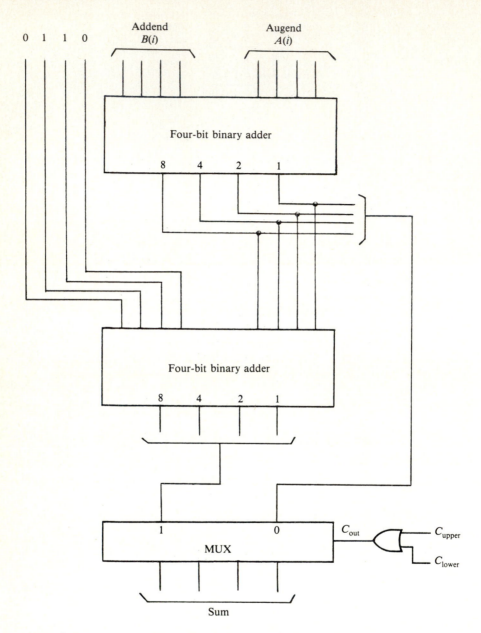

Figure 5.6 Decimal adder with multiplexer.

will cause a carry-out of the high-order bit position. Any decimal digit that generates a carry in this way contains a valid decimal sum digit.

Finally, any decimal sum digit that did not generate a carry must be corrected by subtracting the bias of 6. This can also be accomplished by adding 10_{10}

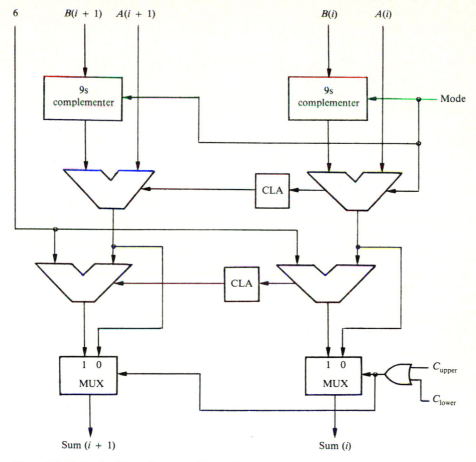

Figure 5.7 Decimal adder/subtractor with multiplexer.

(1 0 1 0), and can be performed on all sum digits of this type simultaneously. The example in Fig. 5.11 illustrates this technique.

5.2.6 Three-Operand Adder

The final method for decimal addition and subtraction involves a technique in which 6 is always added in the addition operation. The two operands (augend and addend) are added in the usual manner, and 6 is added to the sum whether correction is required or not. The sum that is generated in this way is then interrogated to determine if, indeed, 6 should have been added.

Correction is accomplished by subtracting 6 (adding 1 0 1 0). There is no carry propagation to consider in the correction circuitry, except within each four-bit digit segment. There is no carry between digits. Therefore, the time required to correct a digit is faster than the addition performed on the augend and addend.

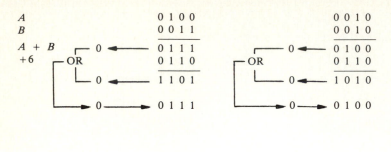

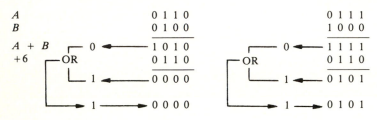

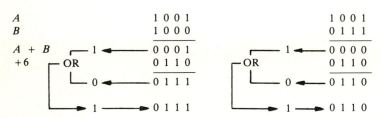

Figure 5.8 Examples using decimal adder with multiplexer.

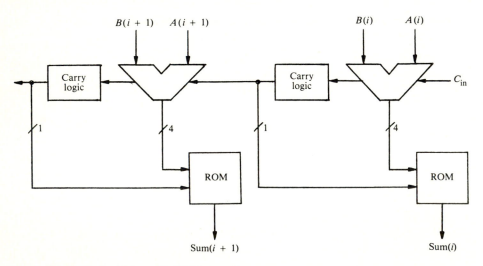

Figure 5.9 Decimal addition with ROM correction.

Table 5.3 ROM correction codes for decimal addition

	ROM addresses					ROM outputs			
	C	8	4	2	1	8	4	2	1
	0	0	0	0	0	0	0	0	0
	0	0	0	0	1	0	0	0	1
	0	0	0	1	0	0	0	1	0
	0	0	0	1	1	0	0	1	1
	0	0	1	0	0	0	1	0	0
	0	0	1	0	1	0	1	0	1
	0	0	1	1	0	0	1	1	0
	0	0	1	1	1	0	1	1	1
	0	1	0	0	0	1	0	0	0
	0	1	0	0	1	1	0	0	1
$C_{8 \wedge 2}$	1	1	0	1	0	0	0	0	0
	1	1	0	1	1	0	0	0	1
	1	1	1	0	0	0	0	1	0
$C_{8 \wedge 4}$	1	1	1	0	1	0	0	1	1
	1	1	1	1	0	0	1	0	0
	1	1	1	1	1	0	1	0	1
	1	0	0	0	0	0	1	1	0
C_8	1	0	0	0	1	0	1	1	1
	1	0	0	1	0	1	0	0	0
	1	0	0	1	1	1	0	0	1

The organization for one digit is shown in Fig. 5.12. The carry lookahead logic is the same as that used in fixed-point addition.

Figure 5.12 shows a three-operand adder using two cascaded adders. The same result can be achieved, and at a much higher speed, if a single adder were used in which the three operands A, B, and 6 were added simultaneously. Figure 5.13 shows such a method. The CLA logic may appear deceptively simple, whereas it is, in fact, extremely complex. The problem occurs because the three-operand adder must add more than the three basic operands. It is a five-operand adder when the carries from the lower-order stages are considered. For example, when adding one bit from each of three operands, the maximum sum is 11_2,

Operand number	$i + 1$	i
1	x	1
2	x	1
3	x	1
	1	1

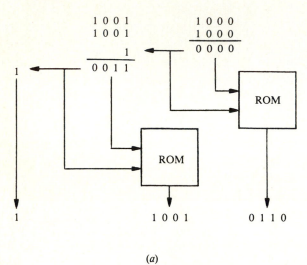

(a)

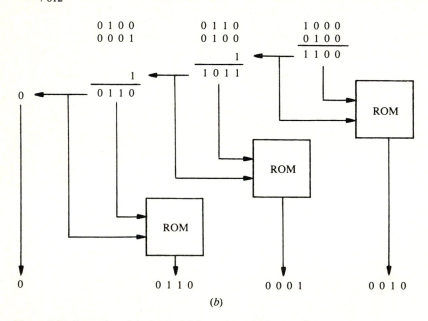

(b)

Figure 5.10 Examples of decimal addition using ROM correction.

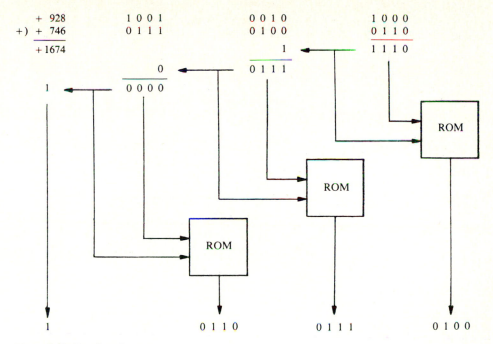

Figure 5.10 (Continued)

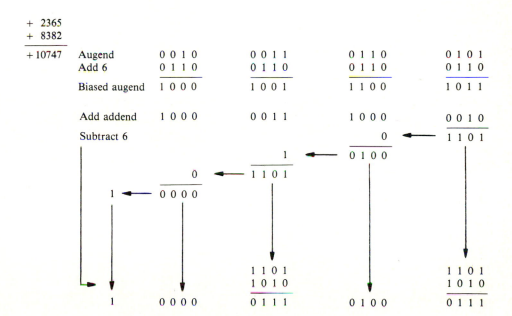

Figure 5.11 Decimal addition with biased augend.

which generates a carry-in to the $i + 1$ position. However, when a carry-in is also considered in the sum, a carry-in to the $i + 2$ position can occur:

Operand number	$i + 2$	$i + 1$	i	
1	x	x	1	
2	x	x	1	
3	x	x	1	
			1	$\leftarrow C_{in}$
	1	0	0	

Thus, in general, position i can receive a carry-in from position $i - 1$ as well as from position $i - 2$.

The sum bit formation is not difficult. It is simply the output of a combinational circuit that generates a 1 corresponding to $S_i = 1$ in Table 5.4. This requires 16 five-input AND gates connected to a 16-input OR gate. Slightly fewer gates are needed if the sum is generated using a five-input EXCLUSIVE-OR circuit. In VLSI logic design, a five-input EXCLUSIVE-OR circuit requires 12 gates. The EXCLUSIVE-OR technique produces six levels of gate delay, compared with two levels of delay when designing directly from the truth table.

The generate and propagate equations require much more logic. If the generate function is restricted to the use of the three main operands only, then the generate function can generate a carry-in to the $i + 1$ position only and is defined as

$$G_{i + 1} = AB \lor AC \lor BC \tag{5.6}$$

The propagate function will produce a carry-in to the $i + 1$ position whenever two or three of the five operands A_i, B_i, C_i, $Cy_{i - 1}$, and $Cy_{i - 2}$ are equal to 1, and will produce a carry-in to the $i + 2$ position whenever four or five of the operands are equal to 1. The generate and propagate equations for the individual bit positions within each four-bit digit are not lengthy, except when these equations are expanded to include carry generation between digits and between groups of digits. Figure 5.14 shows a generalized block diagram of four stages of a three-operand adder.

5.3 MULTIPLICATION

The multiplication algorithms for fixed-point decimal numbers are similar to those for fixed-point binary numbers except in the way that partial products are formed. Although the algorithms have an overall structure that is similar, they are more complex than the same operation in fixed-point binary arithmetic. A decimal multiplier has digits that range in value from 0 to 9, whereas a binary

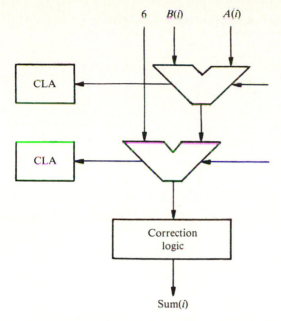

Figure 5.12 Three-operand decimal adder using cascaded adders.

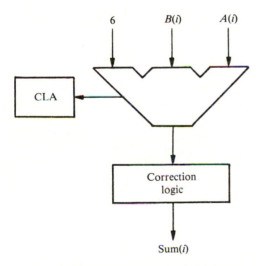

Figure 5.13 Three-operand decimal adder using a single adder.

multiplier has digits that have the value 0 or 1. In binary multiplication, the multiplicand is added to the previous partial product if the low-order multiplier bit is 1. However, in decimal multiplication, the multiplicand must first be

Table 5.4 Sum, carry, generate, and propagate truth table for three-input adder

A_i	B_i	C_i	Cy_{i-1}	Cy_{i-2}	S_i	Cy_{i+1}	Cy_{i+2}	G_{i+1}	P_{i+1}	P_{i+2}
0	0	0	0	0	0	0	0	0	0	0
0	0	0	0	1	1	0	0	0	0	0
0	0	0	1	0	1	0	0	0	0	0
0	0	0	1	1	0	1	0	0	1	0
0	0	1	0	0	1	0	0	0	0	0
0	0	1	0	1	0	1	0	0	1	0
0	0	1	1	0	0	1	0	0	1	0
0	0	1	1	1	1	1	0	0	1	0
0	1	0	0	0	1	0	0	0	0	0
0	1	0	0	1	0	1	0	0	1	0
0	1	0	1	0	0	1	0	0	1	0
0	1	0	1	1	1	1	0	0	1	0
0	1	1	0	0	0	1	0	1	1	0
0	1	1	0	1	1	1	0	1	1	0
0	1	1	1	0	1	1	0	1	1	0
0	1	1	1	1	0	0	1	1	0	1
1	0	0	0	0	1	0	0	0	0	0
1	0	0	0	1	0	1	0	0	1	0
1	0	0	1	0	0	1	0	0	1	0
1	0	0	1	1	1	1	0	0	1	0
1	0	1	0	0	0	1	0	1	1	0
1	0	1	0	1	1	1	0	1	1	0
1	0	1	1	0	1	1	0	1	1	0
1	0	1	1	1	0	0	1	1	0	1
1	1	0	0	0	0	1	0	1	1	0
1	1	0	0	1	1	1	0	1	1	0
1	1	0	1	0	1	1	0	1	1	0
1	1	0	1	1	0	0	1	1	0	1
1	1	1	0	0	1	1	0	1	1	0
1	1	1	0	1	0	0	1	1	0	1
1	1	1	1	0	0	0	1	1	0	1
1	1	1	1	1	1	0	1	1	0	1

multiplied by the low-order multiplier digit and then this result is added to the previous partial product. This section will describe three methods of decimal multiplication:

Multiplication by repeated addition
Multiplication using combinational logic or ROM
Multiplication by table lookup

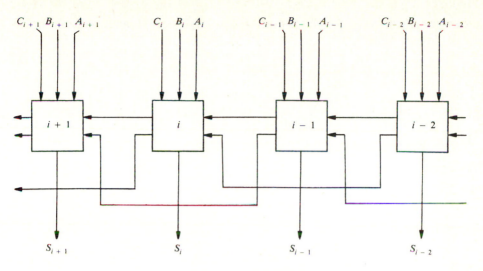

C_{i+1} B_{i+1} A_{i+1} C_i B_i A_i C_{i-1} B_{i-1} A_{i-1} C_{i-2} B_{i-2} A_{i-2}

$i+1$ i $i-1$ $i-2$

S_{i+1} S_i S_{i-1} S_{i-2}

Figure 5.14 Three-operand adder showing carry arrangement.

5.3.1 Multiplication by Repeated Addition

It is possible to perform decimal multiplication by a series of repeated additions, but this process is relatively slow and is not deemed satisfactory for high-speed arithmetic processors. The operation can be accomplished by adding the multiplicand to the partial product the number of times that is equal to the multiplier digit.

The organization for a decimal multiplier unit using repeated addition is shown in Fig. 5.15. As can be seen, it is almost identical to that used for fixed-point multiplication. Registers A, B, and D each have a sign flip-flop A_s, B_s, and D_s, respectively. Registers A and D have an additional digit (four bits) to provide an extension for those registers. The extension bits are labeled A_x and D_x. The unit adds decimal digits in parallel and places the sum in register D. The purpose of D_x is to accommodate an overflow digit that may occur when adding the multiplicand to the previous partial product.

The low-order multiplier digit is loaded into a count-down counter. (Or the low-order digit of register B could be a count-down counter.) The counter is used to determine the number of times that the multiplicand is added to the previous partial product.

The decimal multiplication algorithm using repeated addition is shown in Fig. 5.16. The multiplicand and multiplier are loaded into registers A and B, respectively. Register D is reset to 0. The sequence counter is set to n, which is the number of four-bit decimal digits in the multiplier, and the low-order multiplier digit is loaded into a count-down counter (digit counter). If digit counter $DC \neq 0$, then the multiplicand in A is added to the partial product in D, and DC

is decremented by 1. The decimal adder produces valid decimal digits only; no correction is needed. The multiplicand is added repeatedly until the $DC = 0$. Then, the partial product and the multiplier are shifted one digit (four bits) to the right, as follows:

$$D_x \cdot D_{n-1} \cdots D_0 \cdot B_{n-1} \cdots B_0 \leftarrow 0 \cdot D_x \cdot D_{n-1} \cdots D_0 \cdot B_{n-1} \cdots B_1$$

The process is then repeated until the sequence counter equals 0. The $2n$-digit product is then in concatenated registers $D \cdot B$.

The technique can be improved to obtain higher speeds if subtraction can also be executed. In this case, if the low-order multiplier digit has a value 6–9, then the multiplicand is subtracted the number of times equal to the 10s complement of the digit value, and 1 is added to the next-highest multiplier digit. Adding 1 to the next-highest multiplier digit has the effect of adding the multiplicand 10 times. The following example will illustrate this.

$43 \times 26 = 1118$
10s complement of $6 = 4$
Subtracting 43 four times $= -172$
Add 1 to multiplier digit $2 = 3$
$3 \times 43 = 129$; shift left one digit and add to previous partial product -172:

$$
\begin{array}{r}
-172 \\
+) \quad 129 \\
\hline
\end{array}
\quad \rightarrow \quad
\begin{array}{r}
1290 \\
+) - \quad 172 \\
\hline
1118
\end{array}
$$

5.3.2 Multiplication Using ROM

High-speed ROMs can greatly facilitate decimal multiplication when multiplying the multiplicand by the low-order multiplier digit. Each digit of the multiplicand is multiplied by the low-order multiplier digit. The two-digit product obtained when multiplying one multiplicand digit by one multiplier digit is saved as a subpartial product. All subpartial products are then aligned and added in a decimal adder to produce a partial product.

A ROM is used to obtain a subpartial product directly. The four bits each of the multiplicand digit and the multiplier digit form the address lines to a ROM, as shown in Fig. 5.17. The outputs are valid decimal digits that form a subpartial product. As each subpartial product is generated, it is added to the previous shifted subpartial product. This continues until a complete partial product is obtained. The partial product thus obtained is added to the previous shifted partial product. The sequence continues until all partial products have been added, yielding the final product.

Table 5.5 lists the ROM entries required to generate the subpartial products as determined by the address formed by the multiplicand and multiplier digits. All correction is accomplished in the ROM programming so that only valid decimal digits are produced.

Four ROMs are required when multiplying a four-digit multiplicand by one multiplier digit, as shown in Fig. 5.18. The different levels of the hardware-aligned subpartial products are added using decimal adders. The resulting partial product is shifted and stored. Then the next higher-order multiplier digit is applied to the ROMs, and the new partial product is added to the previous partial product. The rectangular blocks in the middle of Fig. 5.18 are not registers; these blocks simply show the alignment of the subpartial products before the addition operation. Carry lookahead may be used to increase the speed of the decimal multiplication operation. A self-explanatory example using this technique is shown in Fig. 5.19.

5.3.3 Multiplication Using Table Lookup

In fixed-point binary arithmetic, it was shown that multiplication could be speeded up by using a table lookup method. The same is true for decimal multiplication. The organization of the unit is shown in Fig. 5.20. The multiplicand table resides in RAM and contains the multiplicand times 0, 1, 2, 4, and 8. Register D is n digits wide and is concatenated on the left with a one-digit extension register D_x. The n-digit multiplier is stored in register B. The bits of the low-order multiplier digit $B(0)$ generate an address function for the multiplicand table, as follows:

$$\text{If } B(0)_1 = \begin{cases} 0 & \text{address multiplicand} \times 0 \text{ location} \\ 1 & \text{address multiplicand} \times 1 \text{ location} \end{cases}$$

$$\text{If } B(0)_2 = \begin{cases} 0 & \text{address multiplicand} \times 0 \text{ location} \\ 1 & \text{address multiplicand} \times 2 \text{ location} \end{cases}$$

$$\text{If } B(0)_4 = \begin{cases} 0 & \text{address multiplicand} \times 0 \text{ location} \\ 1 & \text{address multiplicand} \times 4 \text{ location} \end{cases}$$

$$\text{If } B(0)_8 = \begin{cases} 0 & \text{address multiplicand} \times 0 \text{ location} \\ 1 & \text{address multiplicand} \times 8 \text{ location} \end{cases}$$

A four-state count-down counter assists the RAM address generation by sequencing through the bits of $B(0)$ from right to left. A sequence counter is again employed to determine the end of the multiply operation.

The multiply operation commences with the loading of the multiplicand table. Multiplicand $\times$ 1 is loaded into the RAM multiplicand table and register D. The multiplicand $\times$ 1 entry and register D are added in the decimal adder, and the sum (multiplicand $\times$ 2) is loaded into RAM location multiplicand $\times$ 2

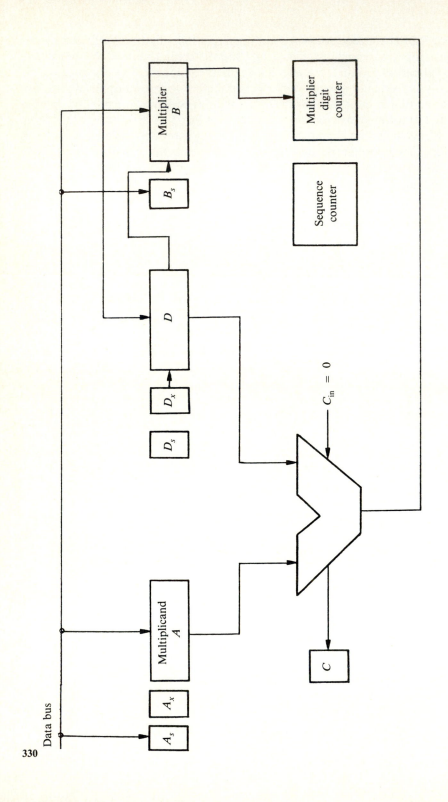

Figure 5.15 Decimal multiplier unit for repeated addition.

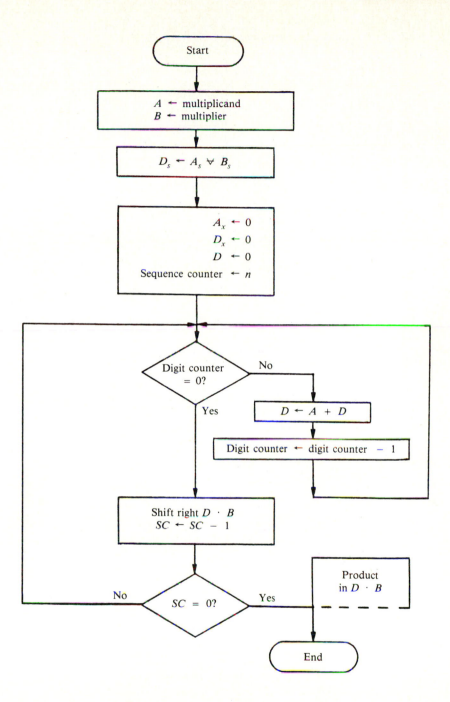

Figure 5.16 Decimal multiplication algorithm using repeated addition.

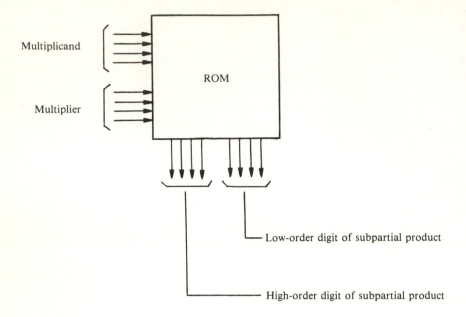

Figure 5.17 Generation of subpartial products using a ROM.

and also into register D. The multiplicand $\times$ 2 entry and register D are added, and the sum (multiplicand $\times$ 4) is loaded into RAM location multiplicand $\times$ 4 and register D. The same procedure is used to load the multiplicand $\times$ 8 location in RAM.

Next, registers D_x and D are reset to 0 and the add-shift sequence begins. An example will best illustrate the sequence. Assume that $B(0) = 0\ 1\ 1\ 0$; that is, the multiplicand is to be multiplied by the low-order multiplier digit $B(0)$, where

$$
\begin{array}{c|cccc}
 & 2^3 & 2^2 & 2^1 & 2^0 \\
\hline
B_0 = & 0 & 1 & 1 & 0 \\
\end{array}
$$

Since bit $2^0 = 0$, RAM location multiplicand $\times$ 0 is added to the partial product (initially all 0s), and the sum is loaded into register D. Since bit $2^1 = 1$, location multiplicand $\times$ 2 is added to the partial product, and the sum is loaded into register D. Since bit $2^2 = 1$, multiplicand $\times$ 4 is added to the partial product in D, and the sum is returned to D. Bit 2^3 does not change the partial product, because it causes an access to location multiplicand $\times$ 0. The result of the above sequence is that the multiplicand was multiplied by 6. The partial product is then shifted to the right four bit positions (one digit) as defined below.

$$
D_x \cdot D_{n-1} \cdots D_0\, B_{n-1} \cdots B_0 \leftarrow 0 \cdot D_x \cdot D_{n-1} \cdots D_0 \cdot B_{n-1} \cdots B_1
$$

The sequence counter is decremented by 1, and the above procedure repeats until the sequence counter equals 0.

In the preceding description of this method, it was apparent that four cycles were required for each multiplier digit, even when one or more of the bits were 0. There is really no need to add multiplicand × 0 to the partial product in these instances. The 0 bit can be simply shifted over and the next higher-order bit ex-

Table 5.5 ROM entries for generating subpartial products

								Subpartial product							
Multiplicand				Multiplier				Tens				Units			
8	4	2	1	8	4	2	1	8	4	2	1	8	4	2	1
0	0	0	0	0	0	0	0	0	0	0	0	0	0	0	0
					⋮				⋮				⋮		
0	0	0	0	1	0	0	1	0	0	0	0	0	0	0	0
0	0	0	1	0	0	0	0	0	0	0	0	0	0	0	0
0	0	0	1	0	0	0	1	0	0	0	0	0	0	0	1
0	0	0	1	0	0	1	0	0	0	0	0	0	0	1	0
					⋮				⋮				⋮		
0	0	0	1	1	0	0	1	0	0	0	0	1	0	0	1
0	0	1	0	0	0	0	0	0	0	0	0	0	0	0	0
0	0	1	0	0	0	0	1	0	0	0	0	0	0	1	0
0	0	1	0	0	0	1	0	0	0	0	0	0	1	0	0
0	0	1	0	0	0	1	1	0	0	0	0	0	1	1	0
0	0	1	0	0	1	0	0	0	0	0	0	1	0	0	0
0	0	1	0	0	1	0	1	0	0	0	1	0	0	0	0
0	0	1	0	0	1	1	0	0	0	0	1	0	0	1	0
0	0	1	0	0	1	1	1	0	0	0	1	0	1	0	0
0	0	1	0	1	0	0	0	0	0	0	1	0	1	1	0
0	0	1	0	1	0	0	1	0	0	0	1	1	0	0	0
0	0	1	1	0	0	0	0	0	0	0	0	0	0	0	0
0	0	1	1	0	0	0	1	0	0	0	0	0	0	1	1
0	0	1	1	0	0	1	0	0	0	0	0	0	1	1	0
					⋮				⋮				⋮		
0	0	1	1	1	0	0	0	0	0	1	0	0	1	0	0
0	0	1	1	1	0	0	1	0	0	1	0	0	1	1	1

Table 5.5 (Continued)

Multiplicand				Multiplier				Subpartial product							
								Tens				Units			
8	4	2	1	8	4	2	1	8	4	2	1	8	4	2	1
0	1	0	0	0	0	0	0	0	0	0	0	0	0	0	0
0	1	0	0	0	0	0	1	0	0	0	0	0	1	0	0
		·				·				·				·	
		·				·				·				·	
		·				·				·				·	
0	1	0	0	1	0	0	0	0	0	1	1	0	0	1	0
0	1	0	0	1	0	0	1	0	0	1	1	0	1	0	0
0	1	0	1	0	0	0	0	0	0	0	0	0	0	0	0
0	1	0	1	0	0	0	1	0	0	0	0	0	1	0	1
		·				·				·				·	
		·				·				·				·	
		·				·				·				·	
0	1	0	1	1	0	0	0	0	1	0	0	0	0	0	0
0	1	0	1	1	0	0	1	0	1	0	0	0	1	0	1
		·				·				·				·	
		·				·				·				·	
		·				·				·				·	
1	0	0	0	0	0	0	0	0	0	0	0	0	0	0	0
1	0	0	0	0	0	0	1	0	0	0	0	1	0	0	0
		·				·				·				·	
		·				·				·				·	
		·				·				·				·	
1	0	0	0	1	0	0	0	0	1	1	0	0	1	0	0
1	0	0	0	1	0	0	1	0	1	1	1	0	0	1	0
1	0	0	1	0	0	0	0	0	0	0	0	0	0	0	0
1	0	0	1	0	0	0	1	0	0	0	0	1	0	0	1
		·				·				·				·	
		·				·				·				·	
		·				·				·				·	
1	0	0	1	1	0	0	0	0	1	1	1	0	0	1	0
1	0	0	1	1	0	0	1	1	0	0	0	0	0	0	1

amined. The number of cycles that are needed for each multiplier decimal digit is data-dependent and is shown in Table 5.6.

Figure 5.21 presents two examples of this method of decimal multiplication. The multiplicand and multiplier are both two-digit positive operands. Note that correction can take place during any decimal addition operation in which the sub-partial products are formed.

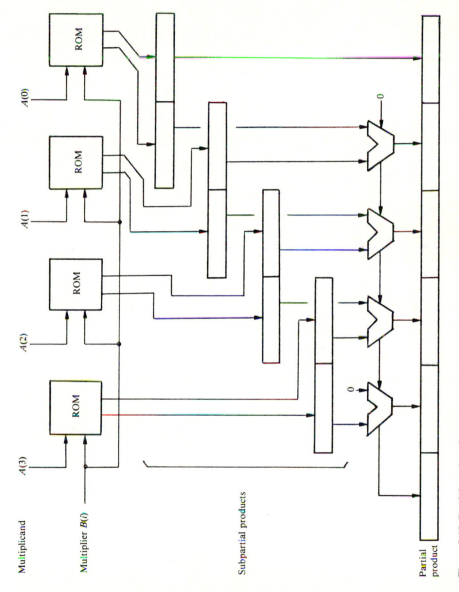

Figure 5.18 Partial product formation using ROMs. The unlabeled rectangular blocks below each arrow do not represent hardware, but indicate the alignment of subpartial products.

335

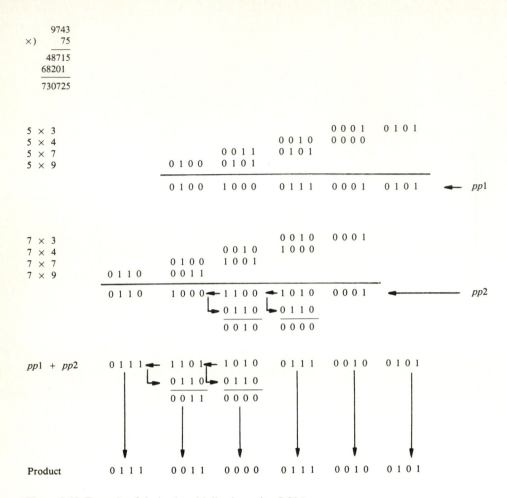

Figure 5.19 Example of decimal multiplication using ROM.

5.4 DIVISION

In many respects, decimal division can be considered to be the inverse of decimal multiplication. Decimal division is similar to fixed-point division, except that in fixed-point representation the quotient digits are either 0 or 1, and in decimal representation the quotient digits can range in value from 0 to 9. The dividend, divisor, and quotient in division correspond to the product, multiplicand, and multiplier, respectively, in multiplication.

Even with the many similarities between multiplication and division, some difficulties are encountered in the division operation that do not occur in multiplication. For example, correct alignment of the dividend and divisor must

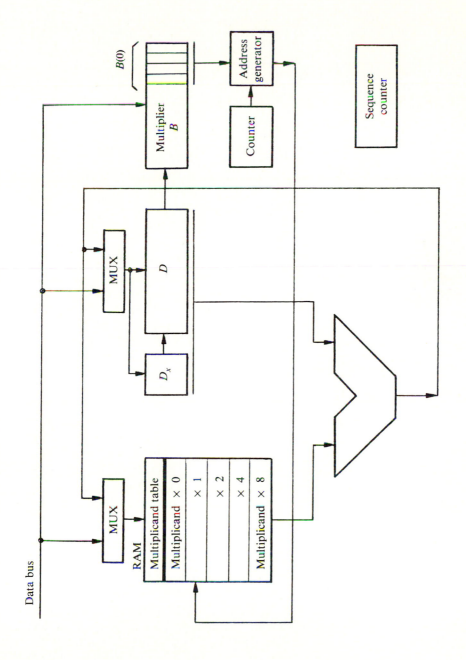

Figure 5.20 Decimal multiplication using table lookup.

Table 5.6 Number of cycles needed for different multiplier decimal digits

	Multiplier digit			
	2^3	2^2	2^1	2^0
One cycle	0	0	0	0
	0	0	0	1
	0	0	1	0
	0	1	0	0
	1	0	0	0
Two cycles	0	0	1	1
	0	1	0	1
	0	1	1	0
	1	0	0	1
Three cycles	0	1	1	1

be established when the divisor is initially subtracted from the dividend. This is easy when using paper and pencil; the proper alignment can be accomplished by inspection. However, "inspection" is not easily designed into a processor. One method utilized to circumvent this problem is to align the highest-order nonzero digit in the divisor with the highest-order nonzero digit in the dividend. This is applicable to all combinations of numbers. However, in some cases, this will result in a 0 quotient digit. This presents no problem, because a leading 0 digit in the quotient does not affect the correctness of the quotient.

Another difficulty is in deciding whether to subtract the divisor from the dividend or previous partial remainder so that a valid subtraction will result. The simplest procedure is to actually perform the subtraction and then to add back the divisor if the subtraction was unsucessful, that is, if it produced a negative partial remainder.

Two types of decimal division will be presented in this section. The first type is division by repeated subtraction; the second type describes an algorithm that adds or subtracts a multiple of the divisor depending on the results of the previous addition or subtraction.

5.4.1 Division by Repeated Subtraction

Repeated subtraction is the most straightforward method of decimal division. In the restoring division method, the divisor is subtracted from the dividend or previous partial remainder until a 0 or negative partial remainder results. If a negative partial remainder is produced, this indicates that the quotient has become too large. The previous partial remainder and quotient must then be restored. Restoration is accomplished by adding the divisor to the negative partial remainder and decrementing the quotient digit by 1, if necessary.

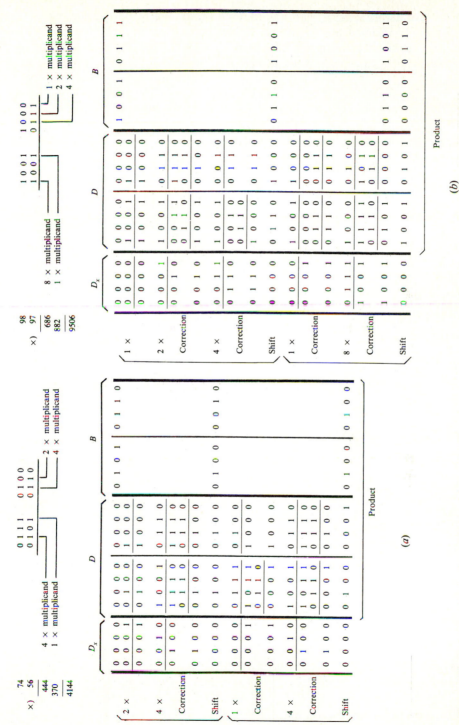

Figure 5.21 Decimal multiplication examples using table lookup.

An alternative scheme, and one that was described in fixed-point restoring division, is to incorporate a multiplexer in the design such that the multiplexer can select either the output of the decimal adder or the previous partial remainder. This negates the extra add operation resulting from a negative partial remainder.

The organization for decimal division using repeated subtraction is shown in Fig. 5.22. The dividend is loaded into concatenated register-pair $A_x \cdot A \cdot Q$ with the sign bit in A_s, and the divisor is loaded into $B_s \cdot B_x \cdot B$. The sequence counter contains the number of decimal digits that is desired in the quotient. The quotient counter is a four-bit decimal counter that is utilized in the determination of each quotient digit.

The algorithm for decimal division is summarized in Fig. 5.23. In many ways, it is similar to the binary algorithm, except for the way in which the quotient digits are formed. The dividend and the divisor are loaded into registers $A \cdot Q$ and B, respectively. Other initialization steps include checking for overflow, determining the quotient sign, initializing the sequence counter SC to the number of digits in the quotient, setting the quotient counter QC to 0, and setting the register B extension digit B_x to 0. The quotient counter establishes the quotient digit by incrementing by 1 for each successful subtraction, that is, for each subtraction that yields a positive partial remainder.

The dividend (or partial remainder) is shifted left one digit position so that the high-order digit is in the extension digit register A_x. The divisor is then subtracted from the dividend (or partial remainder) by adding its 10s complement. The resulting sum determines the relative magnitude of A and B. If the sum is less than 0, indicating $A < B$, then the divisor is added to the sum in order to restore the partial remainder. The quotient counter is not incremented.

If the sum is greater than or equal to 0, indicating $A \geqslant B$, then the quotient counter is incremented by 1 and the divisor is subtracted again. If this subtraction results in a sum that is greater than or equal to 0, then the quotient counter is again incremented and another subtraction takes place. This process loop continues until the sum is less than 0 (negative). When this occurs, the quotient counter is not incremented, the divisor is added to the partial remainder to restore the previous partial remainder, and the sequence counter is decremented. In this way, the quotient counter is made equal to the number of times that the partial remainder can be divided by the divisor.

The partial remainder and the quotient bits (right-concatenated with QC) are shifted to the left one digit position and the process repeats until the sequence counter equals 0, that is, until n quotient digits have been formed. The quotient then resides in register Q and the remainder is in register A.

5.4.2 Division Using Table Lookup

Decimal division using table lookup is similar in function to the binary search technique utilized in programming. A binary search is a systematic way of

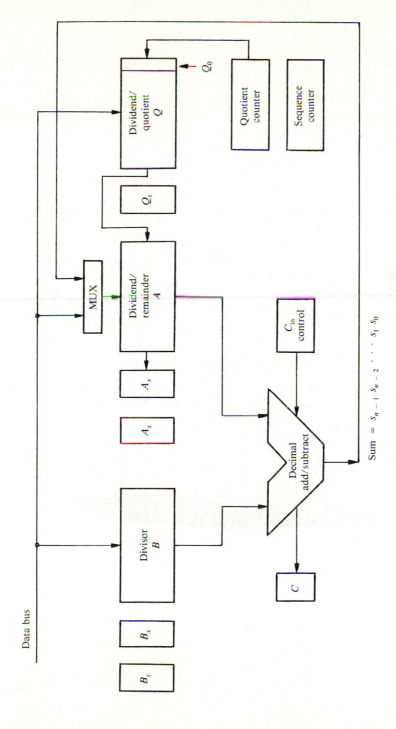

Figure 5.22 Organization for decimal divide unit using repeated subtraction.

Sum $= s_{n-1} \, s_{n-2} \cdots s_1 \, s_0$

Data bus

B_s

B_x

Divisor
B

MUX

Dividend/
remainder
A

A_s

A_x

Dividend/
quotient
Q

Q_0

Q_s

Quotient
counter

Sequence
counter

C_{in}
control

Decimal
add/subtract

C

341

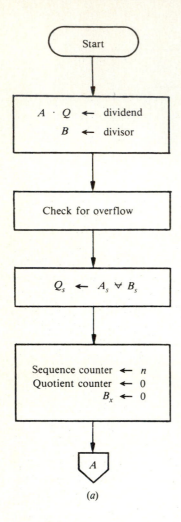

(a)

Figure 5.23 Algorithm for decimal division: (a) initialization; and (b) quotient determination.

searching an ordered table. The method begins by examining the entry at the middle of the table (or the middle ±1 for tables with an even number of entries) and comparing a keyword with the middle entry. The keyword may be less than, equal to, or greater than the item checked. The next step for each of the above results is as follows:

1. If less than, use the bottom half of the table as a new table to search.
2. If equal to, the entry is found.
3. If greater than, use the top half of the table as a new table to search.

This method effectively divides the table in half for each comparison, systematically bracketing the item that is being sought. The search is terminated

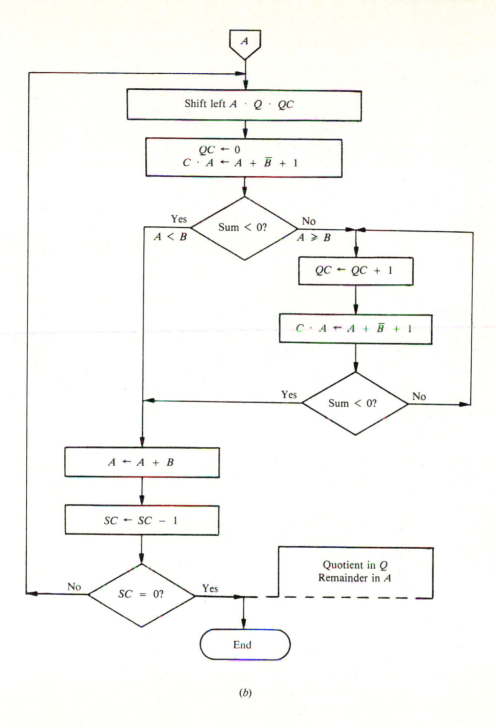

Figure 5.23 (Continued)

when the item is found or when the length of the last subtable is 1 and the item is not found.

The table lookup method adds or subtracts multiples of the divisor from the dividend or partial remainder in the following order:

$$\pm \quad \text{Divisor} \quad \times \quad 8$$
$$\pm \quad \text{Divisor} \quad \times \quad 4$$
$$\pm \quad \text{Divisor} \quad \times \quad 2$$
$$\pm \quad \text{Divisor} \quad \times \quad 1$$

The sequence is always the same: add or subtract eight times the divisor; then add or subtract four times the divisor; then add or subtract two times the divisor; and, finally, add or subtract one times the divisor. This is done for each quotient digit. However, to establish the initial digit, the first step is always a subtraction of eight times the divisor.

The number of cycles required for each quotient digit when performing decimal division by repeated subtraction is clearly data-dependent. However, the table lookup method guarantees only four cycles for each quotient digit, regardless of the data configuration.

The organization of a decimal division unit using table lookup is shown in Fig. 5.24, and the algorithm is presented in Fig. 5.25. It is evident from the flowchart that the tree structure is similar to the binary search technique.

The operands are loaded and any other initialization is performed. Next, the divisor table is constructed. The divisor is loaded into RAM location divisor $\times$ 1 and also into register A. The contents of A and the contents of RAM location divisor $\times$ 1 are added, and the result (divisor $\times$ 2) is loaded into RAM location divisor $\times$ 2 and register A. The contents of A and the contents of RAM location divisor $\times$ 2 are then added to yield a sum of divisor $\times$ 4, which is loaded into the RAM and register A. In this way, the table is built to contain the entries shown in Fig. 5.24.

Next, the actual division sequence begins. Eight times the divisor is subtracted from the dividend. If the result is less than 0 (negative), four times the divisor is added to this result. If the result is greater than or equal to 0 (positive), then 8 is added to the quotient counter and four times the divisor is subtracted from the result.

If the result of the previous addition or subtraction is less than 0, then two times the divisor is added to the dividend. If the result is greater than or equal to 0, then 4 is added to the quotient counter and two times the divisor is subtracted from the result. This sequence of "bracketing" continues until one times the divisor is added to or subtracted from the previous result. The quotient digit then resides in the quotient counter. Registers A and Q and the quotient counter are shifted left in concatenation such that the digit in the quotient counter is shifted into the low-order digit position of register Q. The above procedure then repeats

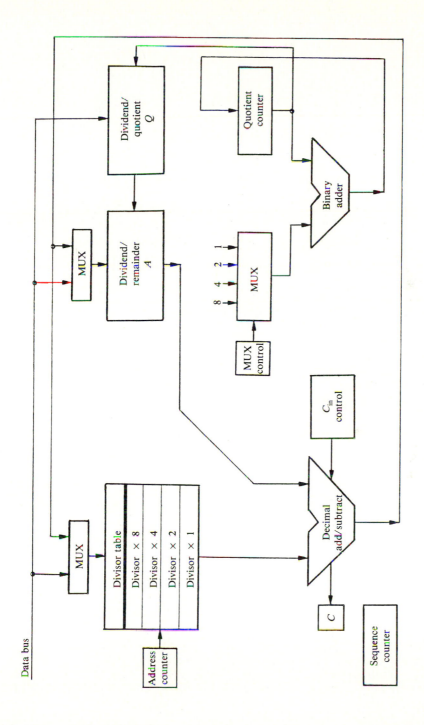

Figure 5.24 Decimal division unit using table lookup.

345

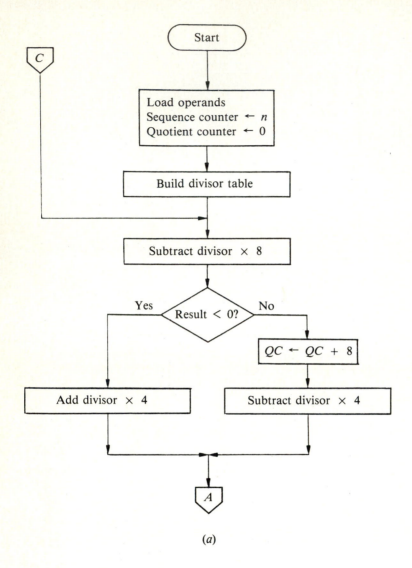

(a)

Figure 5.25 Algorithm for decimal division using table lookup: (a) initialization and first subtraction, (b) successive addition/subtraction, and (c) ending sequence.

for the next quotient digit. When the required number of quotient digits have been obtained ($SC = 0$), the decimal division operation is complete, with the quotient in register Q and the remainder in register A. As always, the algorithm is better understood with the aid of examples, several of which are shown in Fig. 5.26.

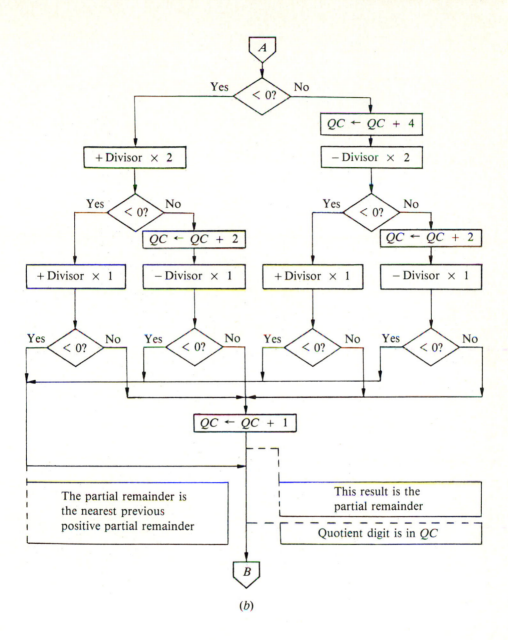

(b)

Figure 5.25 (Continued)

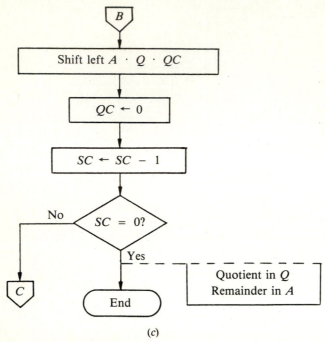

(c)

Figure 5.25 (Continued)

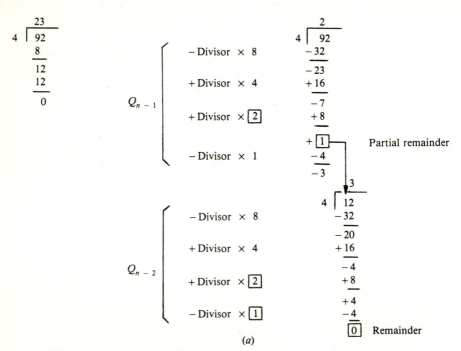

(a)

Figure 5.26 Examples of decimal division using table lookup.

$$
\begin{array}{r}
37 \\
2\,\overline{\smash{\big)}\,75} \\
6 \\
\hline
15 \\
14 \\
\hline
1
\end{array}
$$

Q_{n-1}
- Divisor × 8
+ Divisor × 4
+ Divisor × $\boxed{2}$
- Divisor × $\boxed{1}$

Q_{n-2}
- Divisor × 8
+ Divisor × $\boxed{4}$
- Divisor × $\boxed{2}$
- Divisor × $\boxed{1}$

$$
\begin{array}{r}
3 \\
2\,\overline{\smash{\big)}\,75} \\
-16 \\
\hline
-9 \\
+8 \\
\hline
-1 \\
+4 \\
\hline
+3 \\
-2 \\
\hline
+\boxed{1}
\end{array}
$$
Partial remainder

$$
\begin{array}{r}
7 \\
2\,\overline{\smash{\big)}\,15} \\
-16 \\
\hline
-1 \\
+8 \\
\hline
+7 \\
-4 \\
\hline
+3 \\
-2 \\
\hline
+\boxed{1}
\end{array}
$$
Remainder

(b)

$$
\begin{array}{r}
5 \\
3\,\overline{\smash{\big)}\,16} \\
15 \\
\hline
1
\end{array}
$$

Q_{n-1}
- Divisor × 8
+ Divisor × $\boxed{4}$
- Divisor × 2
+ Divisor × $\boxed{1}$

$$
\begin{array}{r}
5 \\
3\,\overline{\smash{\big)}\,16} \\
-24 \\
\hline
-8 \\
+12 \\
\hline
+4 \\
-6 \\
\hline
-2 \\
+3 \\
\hline
+\boxed{1}
\end{array}
$$
Remainder

(c)

$$
\begin{array}{r}
7 \\
11\,\overline{\smash{\big)}\,79} \\
77 \\
\hline
2
\end{array}
$$

Q_{n-1}
- Divisor × 8
+ Divisor × $\boxed{4}$
- Divisor × $\boxed{2}$
- Divisor × $\boxed{1}$

$$
\begin{array}{r}
7 \\
11\,\overline{\smash{\big)}\,79} \\
-88 \\
\hline
-9 \\
+44 \\
\hline
+35 \\
-22 \\
\hline
+13 \\
-11 \\
\hline
+\boxed{2}
\end{array}
$$
Remainder

(d)

Figure 5.26 (Continued)

```
        85                                                    8
   3 |  255                                              3 |  255
        24                                                  − 24
      ─────                                                ─────
        15                                                  +  1  ──── Partial remainder
        15                                                  − 12
      ─────                                                  − 11
         0                                                  +  6
                                                             − 5
                                                            +  3
                                                             − 2
```

Q_{n-1}
- − Divisor × 8
- − Divisor × 4
- + Divisor × 2
- + Divisor × 1

```
                                                               5
                                                        3 |  15
                                                            − 24
                                                            −  9
                                                            + 12
                                                            +  3
                                                            −  6
                                                            −  3
                                                            +  3
                                                          ─────
                                                             0   Remainder
```

Q_{n-2}
- − Divisor × 8
- + Divisor × 4
- − Divisor × 2
- + Divisor × 1

(e)

```
        22                                                    2
  17 |  378                                             17 |  378
        34                                                 − 136
      ─────                                                 − 99
        38                                                 + 68
        34                                                 − 31
      ─────                                                + 34
         4                                                ─────
                                                           +  3  ──── Partial remainder
                                                            − 17
                                                            − 14
```

Q_{n-1}
- − Divisor × 8
- + Divisor × 4
- + Divisor × 2
- − Divisor × 1

```
                                                               2
                                                       17 |  38
                                                           − 136
                                                           − 98
                                                           + 68
                                                           − 30
                                                           + 34
                                                          ─────
                                                           +  4   Remainder
                                                            − 17
                                                            − 13
```

Q_{n-2}
- − Divisor × 8
- + Divisor × 4
- + Divisor × 2
- − Divisor × 1

(f)

Figure 5.26 (Continued)

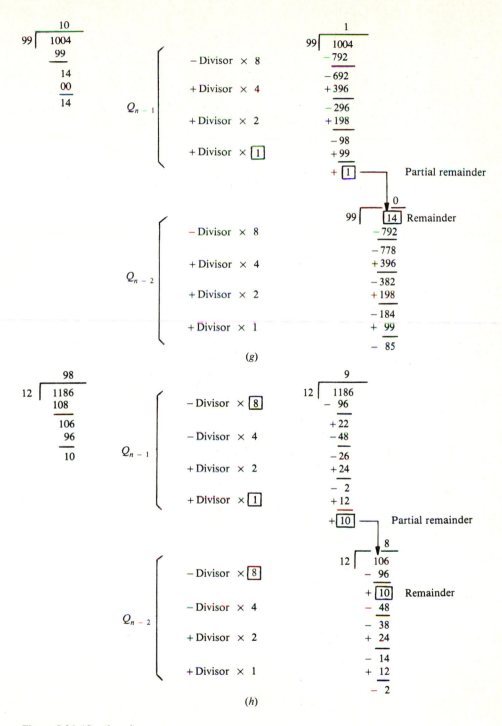

Figure 5.26 (Continued)

```
       64                                                              6
35 | 2267                                                    35 | 2267
     210              ⎧   − Divisor × 8                         − 280
     ───              ⎪                                         ─────
     167              ⎪   + Divisor × ④                         −  54
     140              ⎨                                         + 140
     ───         Qₙ₋₁ ⎪   − Divisor × ②                         ─────
      27              ⎪                                         +  86
                      ⎩   − Divisor × 1                         −  70
                                                               ─────
                                                               + ⑯ ──┐   Partial remainder
                                                               −  35 │
                                                               ─────  │
                                                               −  19  │
                                                                      │ 4
                                                              ┌───────▼──
                                                           35 │   167
                      ⎧   − Divisor × 8                         − 280
                      ⎪                                         ─────
                      ⎪   + Divisor × ④                         − 113
                      ⎨                                         + 140
                 Qₙ₋₂ ⎪                                         ─────
                      ⎪   − Divisor × 2                         + ㉗   Remainder
                      ⎪                                         −  70
                      ⎩   + Divisor × 1                         ─────
                                                               −  43
                                                               +  35
                                                               ─────
                                                               −   8
```

(i)

Figure 5.26 (Continued)

PROBLEMS

5.1 For a decimal adder, what is the carry equation that determines whether or not the intermediate sum requires correction?

5.2 Draw a flowchart algorithm for decimal addition.

5.3 Show that the lower four-bit fixed-point binary adder in Fig. 5.1 can be replaced by one full adder and two half adders.

5.4 Develop an algorithm to convert from binary to decimal form using a shift register and adder.

5.5 Develop an algorithm to convert from decimal to binary form using a shift register and adder.

5.6 Perform the indicated decimal arithmetic operations on the following decimal operands:

```
    (a)      − 4      (b)      + 20      (c)      + 725
        +)  + 8           +)  − 32           +)  + 536
```

5.7 Perform decimal multiplication using ROM on the following operands:

```
        736
     ×)   48
```

5.8 Multiply the following two decimal numbers using the decimal multiplication table lookup method.

```
        63
     ×) 56
```

5.9 Divide the following decimal numbers using the decimal division table lookup method.

```
    (a) 86       (b) 786
         5            8
```

FLOATING-POINT ARITHMETIC

6.1 INTRODUCTION

Fixed-point number notation is convenient for representing small-valued integers and scaled fractional numbers. The same algorithms could be applied to real (floating-point) numbers with a provision for scaling, that is, keeping track of the implied radix point. In fixed-point processors, the programmer must maintain the correct position of the radix point at all times, and this can be very complicated. While it is possible to handle scaling problems with programming, the resulting programs tend to be inefficient due to the additional steps required to maintain the scaling factors. This also imposes an unnecessary burden on the programmer and results in a process that is prone to errors.

Floating-point processors handle the scaling factor automatically. The additional hardware is relatively complex and adds to the cost of the computer, but the operation of the machine is more efficient. Consider the range of values represented by a 16-bit fixed-point number. When interpreted as an integer, the value range is

$$+2^{15} - 1 = +32,767$$

with the high-order bit representing the sign

$$2^{15} = 32,768 \qquad\qquad 2^0$$
$$\downarrow \qquad\qquad\qquad\qquad\qquad\qquad \downarrow$$
$$| \ 0 \ 1 \ 1 \ 1 \ | \ 1 \ 1 \ 1 \ 1 \ | \ 1 \ 1 \ 1 \ 1 \ | \ 1 \ 1 \ 1 \ 1 \ |$$

The maximum negative value is

$$-2^{15} = 32,768$$

with the high-order bit representing the sign

$$2^{15} = 32,768$$
$$\downarrow$$
$$|\,1\;0\;0\;0\,|\,0\;0\;0\;0\,|\,0\;0\;0\;0\,|\,0\;0\;0\;0\,|$$

Neither of these limits is sufficient for scientific calculations, which might involve such numbers as

$$34,200,000,000 \times 0.0000000762$$

The above multiplication is much easier to read and understand if it is written in scientific notation, such as

$$(342 \times 10^8) \times (7.62 \times 10^{-8})$$

Floating-point notation is nothing more than scientific notation. Even 32-bit machines have values restricted to $+2^{31} - 1$ and -2^{31}, which approximates $\pm 10^{11}$.

6.1.1 Floating-Point Format

Floating-point arithmetic offers the advantage of eliminating the scaling factor problem and also expanding the range of values over that of fixed-point arithmetic. A floating-point number consists of two parts: a fraction f and an exponent e. The two parts represent a number that is obtained by multiplying f times a radix that is raised to the power e; that is, the floating-point number A can be expressed as

$$A = f \times r^e \tag{6.1}$$

where f and e are both signed, fixed-point numbers and r is the radix (base). The fractional and exponent parts of a floating-point number have been called by a variety of names, none of which are standardized. For example, the fraction is often referred to as the *mantissa*, and the exponent is sometimes called the *characteristic*.

The fraction can be represented in any one of the three fixed-point number systems described in Chap. 1—that is, sign-magnitude, diminished-radix complement (1s complement in binary), and radix complement (2s complement in binary). Most machines use the sign-magnitude number representation for the floating-point processor. By adjusting the magnitude of exponent e, the radix point can be made to float around the fraction. For this reason, the notation $f \times r^e$ is called the *floating-point representation* of the number A (Eq. 6.1). Consider a numerical example in a decimal ($r = 10$) floating-point system.

$$A = 0.0000068421 \times 10^{+3}$$

This can be represented in either of the following two formats:

$$A = 0.0000068421, +3$$

or

$$A = 0.6842100000, -2$$

where the $+3$ and -2 entries are the magnitudes of the exponents, with an implied base of 10. The fraction can be shifted k positions to the left, and simultaneously the value of the exponent can be decremented by k without changing the real value of the number. The fraction can also be shifted to the right with a corresponding increment in the exponent. In the preceding example, the fraction was shifted to the left five digit positions and the exponent was decremented accordingly. This shifting of the fraction and scaling of the exponent occurs frequently in floating-point operations.

A 32-bit binary format for a floating-point number is shown in Fig. 6.1. This includes a 24-bit fractional part, a 7-bit signed (positive or negative) exponent, and a sign bit that indicates the sign for the number. The high-order bit of the exponent (bit 30) indicates the sign of the 2s complement exponent; that is,

$$e = \begin{cases} \text{positive} & \text{if bit } 30 = 0 \\ \text{negative} & \text{if bit } 30 = 1 \end{cases}$$

Since precision is important, there should be as many significant bits as possible in the fraction. This is accomplished by normalizing the real number. Normalization for radix 2 is achieved by shifting the fraction left until the bit to the immediate right of the radix point is a 1, decreasing the exponent accordingly. An example of this is shown in Fig. 6.2. A seven-bit 2s complement exponent has a range of -64 to $+63$, which means that the scale factor for radix 2 has a range of 2^{-64} to 2^{63}. If this range is still not large enough, it can be increased further by changing the radix. This will be discussed later in this chapter. The magnitude of the normalized fraction has an absolute value within the range

$$\frac{1}{r} \leqslant |f| < 1$$

where r is the radix. For binary numbers ($r = 2$), this range becomes

$$\frac{1}{2} \leqslant |f| < 1 \tag{6.2}$$

which states that all normalized binary numbers must have a fraction $\geqslant \frac{1}{2}$. The

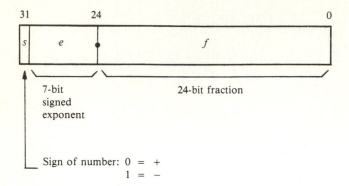

Figure 6.1 A 32-bit binary floating-point format.

only exception is a floating-point number equal to 0. A 0 cannot be normalized because it does not have a nonzero digit. It is represented in floating-point by an all-zero fraction and an all-zero exponent.

All floating-point operations can produce an overflow or underflow condition if the result is too large or too small to be represented by the machine. Overflow or underflow resulting from a fraction operation can usually be corrected by shifting the fraction of the result and adjusting the exponent. However, exponent overflow or underflow should generate an error indication. Overflow and underflow will be discussed in more detail later.

Arithmetic operations with floating-point numbers are more complicated than the same operations using fixed-point numbers. The execution of the operations takes longer and requires more complex hardware. Computers that do not have hardware for floating-point computations usually perform the same operations by means of software subroutines.

6.1.2 Biased Exponents

The exponent e can be either a positive or negative integer. When adding or subtracting two floating-point numbers, the exponents must be compared and made equal, resulting in a shift operation on one of the fractions. The comparison operation can be accomplished without involving the signs of the exponents. This occurs by converting all exponents to positive numbers by adding a positive constant to each exponent as the floating-point number is being formed. Internally, this makes all exponents positive. This bias constant has a magnitude equal to that of the most negative exponent. If the exponent field is m bits long, then the bias constant is $+2^{m-1}$ and all exponents e are biased by 2^{m-1}; that is, they are represented by

$$e_{\text{biased}} = e + 2^{m-1} \tag{6.3}$$

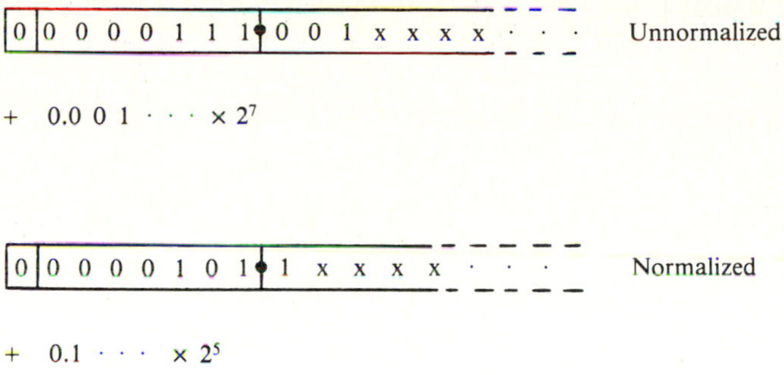

```
0 0 0 0 0 1 1 1 0 0 1 x x x x · · ·        Unnormalized
```

$+ \quad 0.0 \ 0 \ 1 \cdots \times 2^7$

```
0 0 0 0 0 1 0 1 1 x x x x · · ·            Normalized
```

$+ \quad 0.1 \cdots \times 2^5$

Figure 6.2 Binary normalization example.

An unbiased exponent in 2s complement notation has the following range of values:

$$-2^{m-1} \leqslant e_{\text{unbiased}} \leqslant 2^{m-1} - 1 \qquad (6.4)$$

After adding the bias constant, the exponents then become positive integers in the following range:

$$0 \leqslant e_{\text{biased}} \leqslant 2^m - 1 \qquad (6.5)$$

The 2^m term is obtained as follows:

$$2^{m-1} + 2^{m-1} = 2^1 \times 2^{m-1}$$
$$= 2^{1 + (m-1)}$$
$$= 2^m$$

There are two major reasons for using biased exponents. The first is that all-positive exponents may provide some simplification to the exponent hardware. The second reason relates to the way that 0 is represented in floating-point notation. Mathematically, 0 multiplied by any value is equal to 0. Theoretically, there can be many ways to represent 0 in floating-point notation, provided that the fraction equals 0 regardless of the value of the exponent. In some machines, when a computation results in a 0 fraction, the exponent is left at whatever value it was at the end of the operation. This result is a 0 that is not unique. A unique 0 is desired in any processor design. In fixed-point arithmetic, a unique 0 is represented by a number containing all 0s. In floating-point arithmetic, a unique 0 can be defined as a 0 fraction with a biased exponent that is in its most negative form, that is, an exponent of all zeros (Eq. 6.5). With unbiased exponents, the smallest possible exponent is the most negative exponent; with a biased exponent, the smallest possible exponent is 0. Using biased exponents, comparison of the exponents is relatively straightforward, because the exponents are positive. A simple comparator will suffice.

Another way of comparing two operands is to subtract one from the other and check the sign of the result. If the two exponents are e_1 and e_2, then the absolute value is $|\ e_1 - e_2\ |$, which is the shift count required to shift the fraction. Also, if the exponents are biased,

$$e_{1_{biased}} = e_1 + 2^{m-1}$$

and

$$e_{2_{biased}} = e_2 + 2^{m-1}$$

then the subtraction can be performed by adding the 1s complement of $e_{2_{biased}}$ to $e_{1_{biased}}$ following the rules for 1s complement addition. If the subtraction produces a carry-out of the high-order position, then $e_1 > e_2$, and the fraction f_2 that is associated with e_2 is gated to the shifting logic. The result of the subtraction yields the shift count when the end-around carry is added to the result. However, if $e_1 \leq e_2$, then there will be no carry-out of the high-order position; that is, there will be no end-around carry. In this case, the fraction f_1 that is associated with e_1 is gated to the shifting logic. The shift count is the 1s complement of the result. This is illustrated in the two examples below.

$$
\begin{array}{ll}
e_{1_{biased}} = 1\ 0\ 0\ 1 & \qquad 1\ 0\ 0\ 1 \\[2em]
e_{2_{biased}} = 0\ 1\ 0\ 0 & \qquad +)\ 1\ 0\ 1\ 1 \\
& \qquad\ \ \ \ \ 0\ 1\ 0\ 0 \\
& \qquad\qquad\qquad 1 \\
& \qquad\ \ \ \ \ 0\ 1\ 0\ 1
\end{array}
\qquad \Big\}\ e_1 > e_2
$$

$$
\begin{array}{ll}
e_{1_{biased}} = 0\ 1\ 0\ 0 & \qquad 0\ 1\ 0\ 0 \\[2em]
e_{2_{biased}} = 1\ 0\ 0\ 1 & \qquad\ \ 0\ 1\ 1\ 0 \\
& \qquad 0 \longleftarrow 1\ 0\ 1\ 0 \\[1em]
\text{(1s complement)}\ \ 0\ 1\ 0\ 1
\end{array}
\qquad \Big\}\ e_1 \leq e_2
$$

Consider now a numerical example of fraction alignment using biased exponents and normalized operands. Let A_1 and A_2 be normalized operands such that

$$A_1 = 0 . 1\ 0\ 1\ 1\ 0\ 0 \times 2^{101}$$
$$A_2 = 0 . 1\ 1\ 1\ 0\ 0\ 0 \times 2^{010}$$

and let the operation on A_1 and A_2 be addition. The addition process requires equal exponents, in which case the fractions must be aligned by shifting to the right the fraction with the smaller exponent, and adjusting the smaller exponent. After alignment and exponent adjustment, A_1 and A_2 become

$$A_1 = 0 . 1\ 0\ 1\ 1\ 0\ 0 \times 2^{101}$$
$$A_2 = 0 . 0\ 0\ 0\ 1\ 1\ 1 \times 2^{101}$$

Thus, $A_1 + A_2$ becomes

$$A_1 + A_2 = 0 . 1\ 1\ 0\ 0\ 1\ 1 \times 2^{101}$$

The sum may overflow to the left by one bit position. If this occurs, then renormalization is required to position the high-order 1 in the result to the immediate right of the radix point. This may cause a bit to drop off the right end due to the right shift. If there is a choice between discarding a bit from the right end or from the left end of the word, then the choice is obviously the right end, which is the low-order end. Various methods for disposal of low-order bits that minimize the errors incurred will be discussed in Chap. 7.

In summarizing the principles of biased exponents, the sign bit is removed from being a separate entity. The bias is a positive number that is added to the exponent as the floating-point number is being formed, which results in all exponents being positive internally. The following decimal example will clarify this type of exponent representation. Consider an exponent that ranges from -32 to $+31$. Internally, it is represented by two digits with no sign attached. This is done by adding a bias of $+32$ to each exponent such that the new (biased) exponent $= e + 32$, where e is the original exponent. The exponents are now represented as positive operands in the range 00-63.

The advantage of biased exponents is that they are always positive numbers. It is then easier to compare their relative magnitude without concern for their signs. Thus, a simple magnitude comparator can be used to compare their relative magnitude during the alignment of the fractions. This is the primary reason for biasing—to determine the number of bit positions to shift a fraction so that both fractions may be properly aligned by their radix points during addition or subtraction. Another advantage is that the smallest-valued biased exponent contains all 0s. The floating-point representation of 0 is then a 0 fraction and a 0 exponent.

6.1.3 Normalized Floating-Point Arithmetic Definitions

This section defines floating-point arithmetic operations: addition, subtraction, multiplication, and division. These operations can be performed by a floating-point processor, which gives them a wider operating range and greater precision than their fixed-point counterparts. These operations are defined using normalized floating-point operands A_1 and A_2 such that

$$A_1 = f_1 \times r^{e_1}$$

and

$$A_2 = f_2 \times r^{e_2}$$

where f is the normalized fraction, e the exponent, and r the radix. The fraction f, which is a signed operand with n significant digits (excluding the sign), has the following range:

$$\frac{1}{r} \leqslant |f| \leqslant 1 - r^{-n} < 1 \tag{6.6}$$

The $1 - r^{-n}$ term gives the maximum value of the fraction, which, for $n = 3$, becomes

$$1 - r^{-3} = 1 - 2^{-3}$$
$$= 1 - \frac{1}{8}$$
$$= \frac{7}{8}$$

where the bit configuration of the fraction is

$$\overbrace{}^{n = 3}$$

$$0.1 \quad 1 \quad 1$$
$$\downarrow \quad \downarrow \quad \downarrow$$
$$\frac{1}{2} + \frac{1}{4} + \frac{1}{8} = \frac{7}{8}$$

Also, the biased exponent e is a positive integer with m significants digits that has the following range:

$$0 \leqslant |e| \leqslant r^m - 1 \tag{6.7}$$

For a four-bit exponent, where $m = 4$, the maximum value of e will be

$$e_3 \; e_2 \; e_1 \; e_0$$
$$1 \quad 1 \quad 1 \quad 1$$
$$r^m - 1 = 2^4 - 1 = 15$$

Floating-point addition is defined as

$$
\begin{aligned}
A_1 + A_2 &= (f_1 \times r^{e_1}) + (f_2 \times r^{e_2}) \\
&= [f_1 + (f_2 \times r^{-(e_1-e_2)})] \times r^{e_1} \qquad \text{for } e_1 > e_2 \\
&= [(f_1 \times r^{-(e_2-e_1)}) + f_2] \times r^{e_2} \qquad \text{for } e_1 \leqslant e_2 \qquad (6.8)
\end{aligned}
$$

where $r^{-(e_1-e_2)}$ is a shifting factor that is multiplied by the fraction with the smaller exponent. Equation 6.8 states that, for $e_1 > e_2$, f_1 is added to the aligned (right-shifted) f_2 fraction, and the resulting fraction is characterized with the larger exponent. An example using the shifting factor is shown below for

$$
\begin{aligned}
A_1 &= f_1 \times r^5 \\
&= 0.1\,0\,1\,1\,0\,0 \times r^5
\end{aligned}
$$

and

$$
\begin{aligned}
A_2 &= f_2 \times r^2 \\
&= 0.1\,1\,1\,0\,0\,0 \times r^2
\end{aligned}
$$

The fraction f_2 has the smaller exponent and $e_1 - e_2 = 3$. Therefore,

$$
\begin{aligned}
f_{2_{\text{aligned}}} &= 0.1\,1\,1\,0\,0\,0 \times r^{-(3)} \\
&= 0.1\,1\,1\,0\,0\,0 \times \frac{1}{8} \qquad \text{for } r = 2
\end{aligned}
$$

This indicates that $f_{2_{\text{aligned}}} = f_2/8$. Division by 8 is accomplished by a right shift of three bit positions, which properly aligns f_2 with f_1.

Equation 6.8 shows that the radix point of the two operands A_1 and A_2 must be aligned before addition can be performed. This is accomplished by comparing the relative magnitudes of the two exponents and shifting the fraction with the smaller exponent $|e_1 - e_2|$ bit positions to the right. The addition of the fractions then proceeds with the larger exponent used as the exponent for the resulting fractional sum. Since a carry-out of the high-order bit position may occur, the resulting fraction has a value of

$$
0 \leqslant |f| < 2
$$

The compare-shift-add process is sequential, which results in a longer execution time than a fixed-point addition.

Floating-point subtraction is defined as

$$A_1 - A_2 = (f_1 \times r^{e_1}) - (f_2 \times r^{e_2})$$
$$= [f_1 - (f_2 \times r^{-(e_1 - e_2)})] \times r^{e_1} \qquad \text{for } e_1 > e_2$$
$$= [(f_1 \times r^{-(e_2 - e_1)}) - f_2] \times r^{e_2} \qquad \text{for } e_1 \leqslant e_2$$

(6.9)

The comments mentioned for addition also apply to subtraction. The same comparison and alignment procedure is used; however, the subtraction is performed in 2s complement addition.

Floating-point multiplication is defined as

$$A_1 \times A_2 = (f_1 \times r^{e_1}) \times (f_2 \times r^{e_2})$$
$$= f_1 \times f_2 \times r^{e_1 + e_2}$$

(6.10)

This is obviously a simpler procedure than addition or subtraction. The fractions and exponents can be processed independently. Floating-point multiplication requires a fixed-point multiplication of the fractions and a fixed-point addition of the exponents. No alignment is necessary. Since the fractions and exponents can be processed independently, they can be operated on simultaneously. Therefore, for the same length of normalized operands, a floating-point multiplication takes the same amount of execution time as a corresponding fixed-point multiplication. Floating-point operations do not require any scaling instructions, but the time thus saved is offset by the requirement to bias the exponents and postnormalize the result, if required.

When a multiply operation takes place according to Eq. 6.10, the value of the resulting fraction is in the range

$$\frac{1}{r^2} \leqslant |f_1 \times f_2| < 1$$

for $f_1 \neq 0 \neq f_2$. For $r = 2$, the lower limit becomes ¼, which is shown below for a multiplication of the two smallest normalized numbers.

$$\frac{1}{2^2} \leqslant \begin{cases} \qquad\quad 0.1\,0\,0\,0 \quad \times\ 2^4 \\ \qquad \times\ 0.1\,0\,0\,0 \quad \times\ 2^4 \\ \hline \qquad\qquad 0\,0\,0\,0 \\ \qquad\quad\ 0\,0\,0\,0 \\ \qquad 0\,0\,0\,0 \\ \quad 1\,0\,0\,0 \\ \hline 0.0\,1\,0\,0\,0\,0\,0\,0 \end{cases}$$

$$\frac{1}{2} \quad \frac{1}{4} \quad \frac{1}{8}$$

The product in the preceding example falls within the range

$$\frac{1}{r^2} \leqslant |f_1 \times f_2| < \frac{1}{r}$$

and normalization is required. A left shift of one bit position is sufficient to normalize the result. The binary configuration for this range, for $r = 2$, is

$$0.010 \cdots 0 \leqslant |f_1 \times f_2| < 0.011 \cdots 1$$

In this case, Eq. 6.10 is replaced by

$$A_1 \times A_2 = [(f_1 \times f_2) \times r] \times r^{(e_1 + e_2) - 1}$$

That is, the result is multiplied by 2 ($r = 2$), which is equivalent to a left shift of one bit position, and the resulting exponent is decremented by 1. However, when the result falls within the range

$$\frac{1}{r} \leqslant |f_1 \times f_2| < 1$$

postnormalization is not required, because the resulting product is already in normalized form.

Floating-point division is defined as

$$\frac{A_1}{A_2} = \frac{f_1 \times r^{e_1}}{f_2 \times r^{e_2}}$$

$$= \frac{f_1}{f_2} \times r^{e_1 - e_2} \tag{6.11}$$

When a divide operation takes place according to Eq. 6.11, the value of the resulting fraction is in the range

$$\frac{1}{r} \leqslant \left| \frac{f_1}{f_2} \right| < r$$

for $f_1 \neq 0 \neq f_2$ and the dividend less than the divisor. This indicates that postnormalization is not needed. However, when the dividend is greater than or equal to the divisor, then a fraction overflow occurs because

$$1 \leqslant \left| \frac{f_1}{f_2} \right| < r$$

and Eq. 6.11 becomes

$$\frac{A_1}{A_2} = \frac{f_1}{f_2} \times r^{-1} \times r^{(e_1 - e_2) + 1}$$

The r^{-1} term shifts the quotient right one bit position, and the resulting exponent is incremented by 1.

Most of the statements made for floating-point multiplication also apply to floating-point division, with the exception that floating-point division requires fixed-point division of the fractions and fixed-point subtraction of the exponents. An additional step may be required for each of the four floating-point operations in order to normalize the result.

6.1.4 Overflow and Underflow

Some complications may occur as a result of floating-point arithmetic operations. An addition may generate a carry-out of the high-order bit position, resulting in a fraction overflow. That is, when adding two numbers of the same sign or subtracting two numbers of the opposite sign, a situation may occur where $1 \leqslant |f| < 2$. This states that the result may be in the range $1.00 \cdots 0$ to $1.11 \cdots 1$. The problem can be corrected by simply shifting the fraction and the carry-out one bit position to the right and incrementing the exponent by 1, as shown in the following equation for a floating-point add operation.

$$A_1 + A_2 = \left\{[f_1 + (f_2 \times r^{-(e_1 - e_2)})] \times r^{-1}\right\} \times r^{e_1 + 1} \qquad \text{for } e_1 > e_2$$

$$= \left\{[(f_1 \times r^{-(e_2 - e_1)}) + f_2] \times r^{-1}\right\} \times r^{e_2 + 1} \qquad \text{for } e_1 \leqslant e_2$$

$$(6.12)$$

The r^{-1} term in Eq. 6.12 is the shifting factor that moves the result one bit position to the right. The shifting factor for $r = 2$ is $\frac{1}{2}$, which divides the result by 2 and is accomplished by a right shift of one bit position. Also, the exponent is incremented by 1. Notice the similarity between Eqs. 6.12 and 6.8; the latter represents a sum that does not require any shifting. The equation for a floating-point subtract operation, which corrects for a fraction overflow, is given below.

$$A_1 - A_2 = \left\{[f_1 - (f_2 \times r^{-(e_1 - e_2)})] \times r^{-1}\right\} \times r^{e_1 + 1} \qquad \text{for } e_1 > e_2$$

$$= \left\{[(f_1 \times r^{-(e_2 - e_1)}) - f_2] \times r^{-1}\right\} \times r^{e_2 + 1} \qquad \text{for } e_1 \leqslant e_2$$

$$(6.13)$$

Two examples are given in Fig. 6.3 to further illustrate the alignment procedure as well as postnormalization for fraction overflow.

When aligning the operands and adjusting the exponent in addition or subtraction, low-order bits may be lost from the right end of the fraction, which is shifted to the right. This is referred to as *fraction underflow*. Another complication arises when the fraction that results from an arithmetic opertion is 0. In this case, the exponent is reset to 0. Also, the fraction cannot be normalized, which may require that a status bit be sent to the user. A number with a 0 fraction and a 0 exponent is called a *true* 0. A true 0 may result from an arithmetic operation due to the particular magnitude of the operands. A true 0 may be forced when:

1. The result fraction of an add or subtract operation is 0.
2. One or both fractions in a multiply operation are 0s.
3. The dividend fraction is 0 during a divide operation.
4. An exponent underflow occurs.

During multiplication or division, the exponents are added or subtracted, respectively. When the exponents are added, the resulting number may be too large, thereby exceeding the upper limit allowed in the exponent field. This is called *exponent overflow*. When the exponents are subtracted, the resulting number may be too small to be represented. This is called *exponent underflow*, and indicates that the number exceeds the minimum allowable value.

If, during addition or subtraction, the difference in exponents corresponds to a number of shifts that is greater than the length of the fraction, then the result is set equal to the larger operand (or its negative). This happens because $| e_1 - e_2 |$ is very large, indicating that one of the operands is insignificant when compared with the other operand. It would be more efficient to terminate the shifting after n shifts (length of fraction $= n$ bits) instead of $| e_1 - e_2 |$. Alternatively, logic could be designed to detect if $| e_1 - e_2 | > n$. In this event, shifting would not occur and the result is set equal to the larger operand. Whenever an exponent overflow or underflow occurs, a signal should be generated by the floating-point hardware.

6.1.5 Precision

If the fraction has a length of n bits, then the number may be represented with n bits of precision. In other words, the precision of a floating-point number system is the number of digits representable in the fraction. This is normally measured in digits of radix r. Single precision refers to those operations defined with standard operands, for example, a floating-point format of 32 bits. Double precision is simply double the format length, that is, 64 bits. The standard proposed by the Institute of Electrical and Electronics Engineers (IEEE) for single-precision and double-precision floating-point formats is shown as follows:

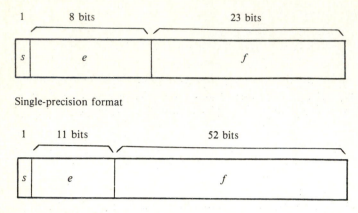

Single-precision format

Double-precision format

There are numerous floating-point formats; most manufacturers have different designs. Some designs also include hardware for extended single precision and extended double precision. In multiplication, the precision of the result is the sum of the precisions of the operands. Multiple-precision formats are needed to increase the number of significant bits in the fractions, thereby permitting greater accuracy or a wider range of values. It should be noted that when numbers are entered into a computer, regardless of their original accuracy, they become limited to the precision of the machine. Thus, some accuracy may be lost after data has been entered. Most machines provide hardware for double-precision operation, but perform it much slower than single-precision calculations.

After adding or subtracting two n-bit single-precision numbers, the sum will be single precision, but there may also be a carry-out of the high-order bit position. This could be considered as a multiple-precision format. When multiplying two n-bit single-precision numbers, the product will be a $2n$-bit (or $2n - 1$ bit) number, which is also multiple precision. If only single precision is allowed for the product, then the lower half must be truncated or rounded, which may produce an error. Also, when dividing a $2n$-bit dividend by an n-bit divisor, an n-bit quotient and n-bit remainder are produced. A double-precision word is needed to store the quotient and remainder.

Whether single or multiple precision is required for a particular operation, the floating-point processor must be conditioned to operate in a particular mode. This can be accomplished by a length field in the instruction or by the operation code of the instruction. Other methods of controlling the precision of binary numbers will be discussed in a later section.

6.1.6 General Implementation

Floating-point arithmetic is inherently more complex than fixed-point arithmetic. However, the same hardware organization that was used for fixed-point

A_1 = 0 0 1 0 1 0 1 1 (+43)

A_2 = 0 0 0 0 0 1 1 0 (+6)

Normalize operands

A_1 = 0 . 1 0 1 0 1 1 0 0 × 2^{110}

A_2 = 0 . 1 1 0 0 0 0 0 0 × 2^{011}

Align fractions and adjust exponents

A_1 = 0 . 1 0 1 0 1 1 0 0 × 2^{110}

A_2 = 0 . 0 0 0 1 1 0 0 0 × 2^{110}

$A_1 + A_2$ = 0 . 1 1 0 0 0 1 0 0 × 2^{110}

No postnormalization required

$A_1 + A_2$ = 0 0 1 1 0 0 0 1 (+49)

(*a*)

A_1 = 0 0 0 0 1 1 1 0 (+14)

A_2 = 0 0 0 0 0 1 0 0 (+4)

Normalize operands

A_1 = 0 . 1 1 1 0 0 0 0 0 × 2^{100}

A_2 = 0 . 1 0 0 0 0 0 0 0 × 2^{011}

Align fractions and adjust exponents

A_1 = 0 . 1 1 1 0 0 0 0 0 × 2^{100}

A_2 = 0 . 0 1 0 0 0 0 0 0 × 2^{100}

$A_1 + A_2$ = 1 . 0 0 1 0 0 0 0 0 × 2^{100}

Postnormalize (fraction overflow) and adjust exponent

$A_1 + A_2$ = 0 . 1 0 0 1 0 0 0 0 × 2^{101}

= 0 0 0 1 0 0 1 0 (+18)

(*b*)

Figure 6.3 (*a*) Example of alignment procedure for a floating-point add operation; (*b*) example of floating-point add operation showing fraction overflow.

arithmetic can be used for processing fractions. Any of the implementations that were used for fixed-point addition, subtraction, multiplication, and division can be used in an identical configuration for the corresponding floating-point fraction operations. However, additional circuitry is needed for fraction alignment, exponent comparison, shift control, rounding, and other features that are unique to floating-point processors.

Floating-point arithmetic may be implemented by two fixed-point arithmetic units, one for fraction computation and one for exponent computation, as shown by the generalized block diagram in Fig. 6.4. The fraction unit must be capable of performing all of the four operations on the fraction; thus, a general-purpose fixed-point arithmetic unit is needed. However, the exponent unit needs a simpler circuit with the sole requirement to add, subtract, and compare. Exponent comparison may be performed by either subtraction of the exponents or by a comparator. The registers labeled F contain the multiplicand, multiplier, and product, or the dividend, divisor, quotient, and remainder, depending on whether the operation is a multiplication or division.

The exponents of the operands are placed in registers E_1 and E_2, which are connected to a carry lookahead adder that calculates $E_1 \pm E_2$. The exponents are also connected to a comparator. The shifting of one fraction with respect to the other is controlled by the shift count resulting from $| e_1 - e_2 |$. The magnitude of the shift count register is decremented toward 0. With each decrement, the appropriate fraction is shifted right one bit position. When the fractions have been aligned, they are processed as fixed-point numbers according to the operation being performed. The exponent of the result is also calculated and placed in the shift counter or E_1 register for transfer with the resulting fraction.

It is sometimes desirable to design an arithmetic unit that has facilities for both fixed-point and floating-point operations. Although this does not present great conceptual problems, the control of such a unit is more complex than either a stand-alone fixed-point or floating-point unit. Essentially, it has the form of a fixed-point unit in which the registers and adder can be partitioned into fraction and exponent sections when floating-point operations are being performed.

The block diagram of Fig. 6.4 and the preceding description were intended to provide a general overview of floating-point hardware, leading to a more detailed implementation and description in the following sections. As stated previously, any of the implementation techniques described in Chaps. 2, 3, and 4 can be used for floating-point fraction computation. However, for the purpose of clarity, only sequential shift techniques will be used in the description of floating-point multiplication and division. There is no advantage in presenting higher-speed methods, such as skipping over 0s and 1s and array operations, since each of these methods still requires the additional features that are needed by a floating-point processor; the operation is merely faster.

6.2 ADDITION AND SUBTRACTION

Addition and subtraction will be described together since the same hardware is used for both operations. Subtraction is performed by addition using a 2s-complemented subtrahend. All floating-point operands will be assumed to

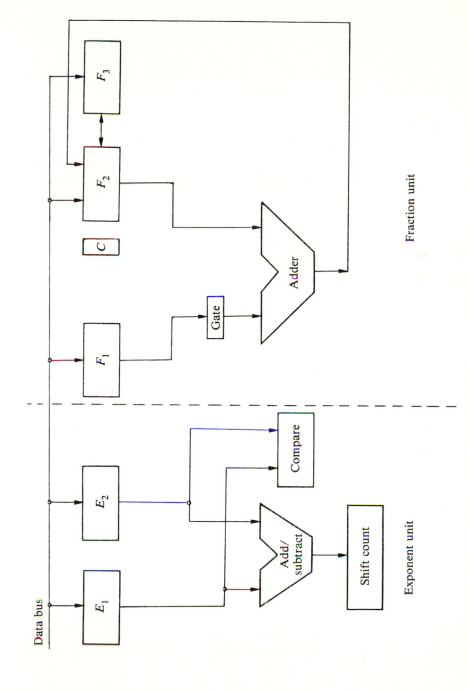

Figure 6.4 Generalized block diagram for a floating-point arithmetic unit.

consist of normalized fractions and biased exponents. The addition process requires equal exponents, so the fractions must first be aligned by shifting to the right the one with the smaller exponent and then adjusting the smaller exponent by incrementing it by the shift amount. Fraction underflow will be discussed separately in a later section. It is important now to understand the general principles of floating-point addition and subtraction without giving too much consideration to the many details that are uniquely applicable to floating-point operations.

The addition/subtraction algorithm can be divided into six consecutive steps.

1. Check for 0 operands.
2. Align the fractions by selecting the fraction with the smaller exponent. Then shift that fraction to the right and increment the smaller exponent until both exponents are equal.
3. Add or subtract the fractions.
4. Set the exponent of the result equal to the larger exponent.
5. Normalize the result, if necessary.
6. Check for overflow or underflow.

Considerable saving in execution time can be realized by not performing the alignment-shift operation if $| e_1 - e_2 |$ is greater than the number of bits in the fraction. In this case, the result is set equal to the larger fraction or its negative. The results of a floating-point operation may require rounding. Rounding deletes one or more of the low-order digits of an operand and adjusts the retained part in accordance with a specified rule. Rounding is discussed in greater detail in Sec. 7.2.

The registers reuired for an addition/subtraction operation are shown in Fig. 6.5. There are two registers AR and BR, each subdivided into three parts to form concatenated registers as follows:

$$AR = a \cdot A_s \cdot A$$
$$BR = b \cdot B_s \cdot B \qquad (6.14)$$

where a is the exponent register, A_s the sign flip-flop, and A the fraction register for operand A. Operand B is similarly defined. Thus, register AR has a fraction with a sign in A_s and a magnitude in A. For the registers to be normalized, bits A_{n-1} and B_{n-1} must be equal to 1; that is, $A_{n-1} = B_{n-1} = 1$.

The operands used in the design of this addition/subtraction unit will be 32-bit floating-point operands using the format of Fig. 6.1, which has a 24-bit fraction, a 7-bit exponent, and a sign bit. A carry lookahead (CLA) adder adds the two fractions and transfers the sum into register A. A separate CLA adder is used for the exponents. The exponents are positive-biased numbers that are connected to a magnitude comparator with outputs $a < b$, $a = b$, and $a > b$.

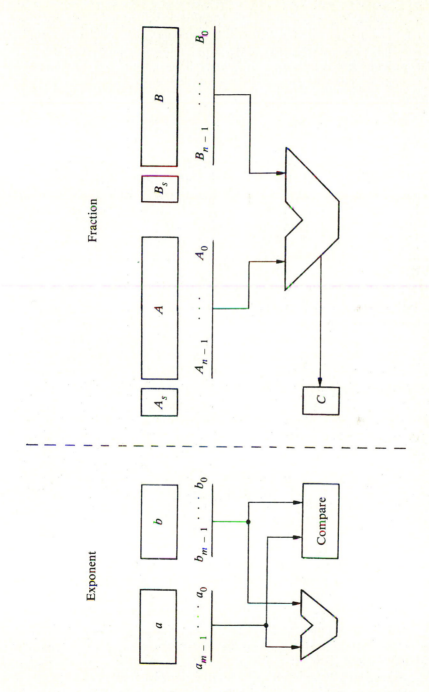

Figure 6.5 Register organization for floating-point addition/subtraction.

371

6.2.1 Addition/Subtraction Algorithm

A flowchart depicting the algorithm for the addition/subtraction of two floating-point numbers is shown in Fig. 6.6. Before the actual addition/subtraction operation, the two operands—augend and addend or minuend and subtrahend—are loaded into registers AR and BR. The operands are in normalized form and the resulting sum/difference will be normalized and loaded into register AR. The operation that takes place is

$$AR \leftarrow AR \pm BR$$

A floating-point number that is 0 cannot be normalized. Time can be saved in the operation if 0 operands are detected early, and thus terminate the operation after only a few steps. Figure 6.6(a) shows the sequence of checking for zero-valued operands. If the contents of BR equal 0, then the operation is terminated with the value in AR being the result. If the contents of AR equal 0, then the contents of BR are transferred to AR (B_s is complemented if the operation is subtraction). Thus, when the second operand (addend/subtrahend) in register BR is 0, no execution is required. When the first operand (augend/minuend) in register AR is 0, the result is equal to the addend if the operation is addition and equal to the negative subtrahend if the operation is subtraction. If both operands are nonzero, then the operation proceeds.

The exponents a and b are compared for relative magnitude. If the two exponents are equal, this indicates that the fractions are already aligned and the arithmetic operation can be executed; see Fig. 6.6(b). If the exponents are not equal, then the fraction with the smaller exponent is shifted right and its exponent is incremented by 1. This process continues until the exponents are of equal magnitude. Register concatenation is indicated by the center dot ($\cdot$), and the replacement operator is indicated by $\leftarrow$. Thus, for $a < b$, A is shifted right one bit position, where

$$A \leftarrow 0 \cdot A_{n-1} \cdots A_1$$

means that

$$A_{n-1} \leftarrow 0$$
$$A_{n-2} \leftarrow A_{n-1}$$
$$\cdot$$
$$\cdot$$
$$\cdot$$
$$A_1 \leftarrow A_2$$

Once the fractions have been aligned, the sequence can proceed to the arithmetic operation of addition or subtraction; see Fig. 6.6(b). The addition and

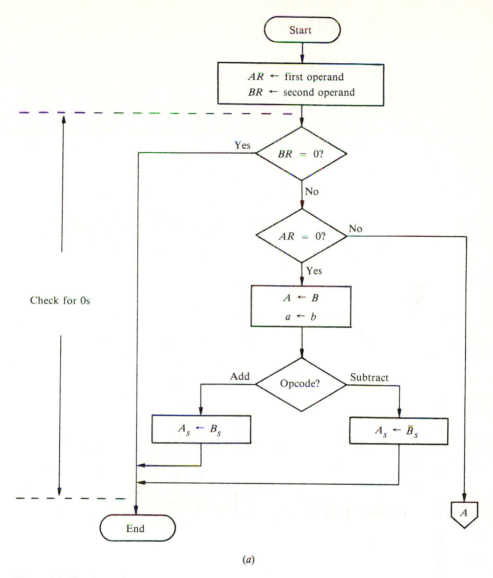

Check for 0s

(a)

Figure 6.6 Floating-point addition/subtraction algorithm: (*a*) check for 0s; (*b*) align fractions and add/subtract fractions; and (*c*) and (*d*) postnormalization.

subtraction of the two fractions is identical to the addition and subtraction algorithm presented under fixed-point addition/subtraction. The magnitude parts of the operands are added or subtracted, depending on the operation being performed and on the signs of the operands. If the operation is addition and the signs of the operands are the same ($A_s \lor B_s = 0$), then the fractions are added and any carry that is generated is stored in flip-flop C. If the signs are not the

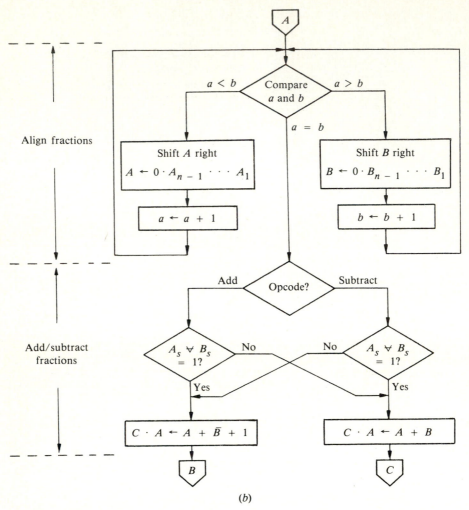

(b)

Figure 6.6 (Continued)

same, then the operation is equivalent to subtraction and the addend is 2s complemented and added to the augend. A similar process occurs if the operation is a subtraction. In this case, if the signs are different ($A_s \;\forall\; B_s = 1$), then the fractions are simply added, with any carry that is generated being stored in C. This is equivalent to the arithmetic rule, "Change the bottom sign and add." If the signs of the operands are the same during a subtraction, then the subtrahend is 2s complemented and added to the minuend.

Postnormalization is shown in Fig. 6.6(c) and (d). When the result of a subtraction does not produce a carry-out of the fraction high-order bit position, then the result must be 2s complemented when stored in register A and the sign of A is complemented. That is, when true subtraction is performed through 2s comple-

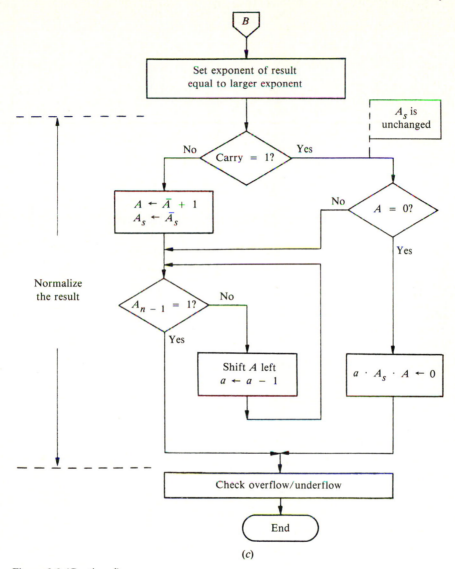

(c)

Figure 6.6 (Continued)

ment addition, the resulting difference may be positive, negative, or 0. When the result is negative ($|A| < |B|$), it is in 2s complement form and should be recomplemented to its sign-magnitude form. Examples of this will be given later.

Recall that this point in the algorithm was reached because the signs of the operands were different and the operation was addition, or the signs were the same and the operation was subtraction. In either case, the resulting arithmetic operation is a true subtraction. This true subtraction may result in a carry-out of the fraction high-order bit position. In this situation, the result does not require

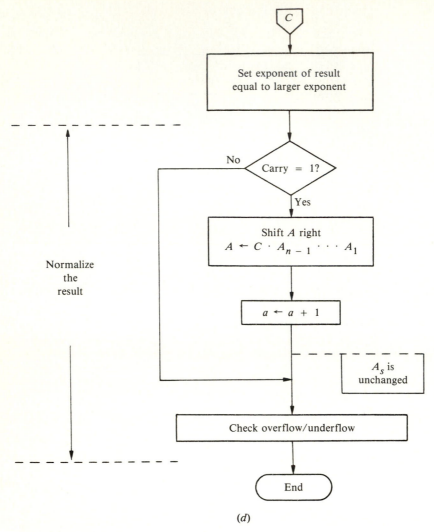

(d)

Figure 6.6 (Continued)

complementation and normalization proceeds. Examples of this will be given later.

If the high-order bit position of the resulting difference is not a 1 (that is, if $A_{n-1} = 0$), then the result is shifted left one bit position and the exponent is decremented. This repeats until $A_{n-1} = 1$. A rounding bit may be needed after the left-shift operation. Rounding is discussed in detail in Sec. 7.2.

When the sum of a true addition is equal to or greater than unity, the resulting fraction is shifted to the right one bit position and the exponent is incremented by 1. The carry bit is shifted right into the high-order A_{n-1} bit of the fraction and the sign of A (A_s) remains unchanged. Since the carry bit was a 1 and was shifted into A_{n-1}, no further normalization is required. It is possible that the incrementation of the exponent may cause an exponent overflow. When this happens, there is no need to enter the normalization sequence and the overflow should be indicated in a status bit.

The preceding discussion on true addition and true subtraction indicates that a carry-out of the high-order bit position of the result does not necessarily mean that an overflow has occurred, as it does in fixed-point arithmetic. Instead, the exponent is incremented by 1, which positions the radix point one bit to the left so that the fraction can be properly contained in register A. This is accomplished by shifting the fraction one position to the right. The low-order bit may be lost during the shift, so rounding may be required. Exponent overflow can occur only during a true addition when the exponent value exceeds the limit of the exponent field.

6.2.2 Addition/Subtraction Examples

Figure 6.7 gives several examples of floating-point addition and subtraction that follow the algorithm presented in Fig. 6.6. The two operands used in these examples are

$$0 0 0 0 1 0 1 1 \quad (+11)$$
$$0 0 1 0 0 0 1 0 \quad (+34)$$

which, when normalized, become

$$0 . 1 0 1 1 0 0 0 0 \times 2^4$$
$$0 . 1 0 0 0 1 0 0 0 \times 2^6$$

After alignment, the fractions become

$$0 . 0 0 1 0 1 1 0 0 \times 2^6$$
$$0 . 1 0 0 0 1 0 0 0 \times 2^6$$

It is strongly suggested that these many examples be followed through to completion using the flowcharts of Fig. 6.6 in a step-by-step procedure. Figure 6.7 presents examples in which no postnormalization is required ($A_{n-1} = 1$), and examples in which postnormalization is required; that is, the result is such that $A_{n-1} = 0$. Additional examples are presented in Fig. 6.8 in which postnormalization is accomplished by shifting the result one bit position to the right. A right shift is required because of fraction overflow from a carry-out of the high-order bit position. These examples take a different path through the flowchart.

The lower section of the flowchart in Fig. 6.6 (*b*) illustrates the fraction addition or subtraction operations. Subtraction of operands A and B is accomplished with 2s complement arithmetic; that is,

$$A - B = A + \bar{B} + 1$$

where $\bar{B}$ is the 1s complement (bit complement) with a 1 added to form the 2s complement notation. The block that exits to $\boxed{C}$ and contains $C \cdot A \leftarrow A + B$ represents true addition corresponding to one of the following four situations:

$$
\begin{aligned}
(+A) &+ (+B) \\
(-A) &+ (-B) \\
(+A) &- (-B) \\
(-A) &- (+B)
\end{aligned}
\tag{6.15}
$$

where $A \leqslant B$ or $A > B$. The block that exits to $\boxed{B}$ and contains $C \cdot A \leftarrow A + \bar{B} + 1$ represents true subtraction corresponding to one of the following four situations:

$$
\begin{aligned}
(+A) &- (+B) \\
(-A) &- (-B) \\
(+A) &+ (-B) \\
(-A) &+ (+B)
\end{aligned}
\tag{6.16}
$$

where $A \leqslant B$ or $A > B$. The sign of the result depends upon the operation being performed, the comparison of the signs, and whether $A \leqslant B$ or $A > B$.

6.2.3 Hardware Organization

Figure 6.9 shows the hardware organization for a floating-point addition/subtraction unit. The structure is divided into two sections: one for the fraction and one for the exponent. The two operands, the augend/minuend and the addend/subtrahend, are loaded into registers A and B, respectively, in normalized form. The biased exponents for the respective operands are loaded into registers a and b.

The resulting sum/difference will be normalized and loaded into register A, and the exponent of the result will be placed in register a. The register concatenation of $a \cdot A_s \cdot A$ will then be available on an output data bus. Control of the unit is assumed to be under microprogram control. Not shown on the logic diagram, but essential to the operation, are exponent overflow/underflow detection and the microprogram control register.

The first step is to check for 0 operands. If register B contains 0, then the operation is complete and the final result is in register A. If register A contains 0 and B is not 0, then A is added to B and the result is placed in A. A similar operation is performed on the exponents. The sign of B becomes the sign of A according to the following rule:

$$
\begin{aligned}
\text{Operation is add} \quad & A_s \leftarrow B_s \\
\text{Operation is subtract} \quad & A_s \leftarrow \bar{B}_s
\end{aligned}
$$

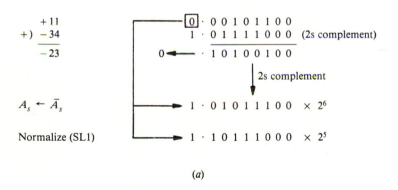

$$
\begin{array}{r}
+11 \\
+) \ +34 \\
\hline
+45
\end{array}
$$

$A_s \leftarrow A_s$

No normalization required

$$
\begin{array}{r}
-11 \\
+) \ -34 \\
\hline
-45
\end{array}
$$

$A_s \leftarrow A_s$

No normalization required

$$
\begin{array}{r}
+11 \\
+) \ -34 \\
\hline
-23
\end{array}
$$

$A_s \leftarrow \bar{A}_s$

Normalize (SL1)

(a)

Figure 6.7 (a) Floating-point addition with and without postnormalization; (b) floating-point addition with a shift-left postnormalization; (c) floating-point subtraction with a shift-left postnormalization; and (d) floating-point subtraction with and without postnormalization.

The next step is executed if and only if both operands are nonzero. The exponents are compared to determine the number of bit positions to shift the fraction with the smaller exponent. The shift count value p is

$$
p = |a - b|
$$

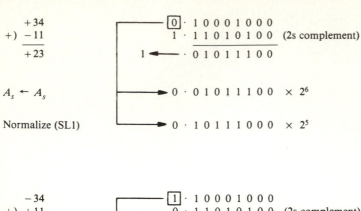

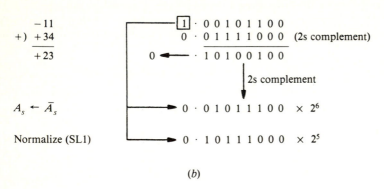

(b)

Figure 6.7 (Continued)

which is determined by first comparing the relative magnitude of a and b. The output of the comparator selects a and b through multiplexers such that the larger value is the minuend for the seven-bit subtractor. Thus, $a - b$ or $b - a$ results in a positive difference. The count value could also be obtained by a subtractor without using a comparator. However, this may require an extra cycle to 2s-complement the result if the carry-out of the high-order bit position is 0. This occurs when the subtrahend is greater than the minuend. The comparator approach requires additional hardware, but is faster.

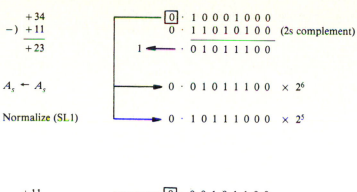

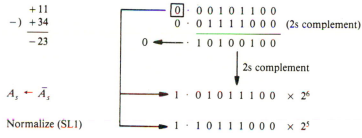

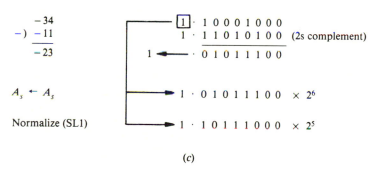

(c)

Figure 6.7 (Continued)

The shift count is loaded into a count-down counter called the *shift counter*. There are cases in which the shift count may exceed the number of bits in the fraction. When this occurs, the operand with the smaller exponent becomes 0; that is, the fraction and exponent are both reset to 0. The addition of this 0 fraction with the other fraction can now take place with the assumption that the two operands have equal exponents. The result is equal to either the positive or negative version of the larger operand.

The next step is to align the two fractions by shifting to the right the fraction with the smaller exponent. The number of bit positions that the fraction is shifted

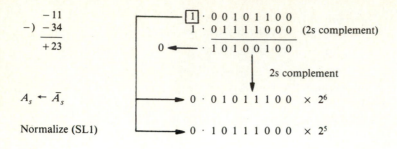

$$
\begin{array}{r}
-11 \\
-) \ -34 \\
\hline
+23
\end{array}
$$

$$\boxed{1} \cdot 0\ 0\ 1\ 0\ 1\ 1\ 0\ 0$$
$$1 \cdot 0\ 1\ 1\ 1\ 1\ 0\ 0\ 0 \quad \text{(2s complement)}$$
$$0 \longleftarrow \cdot \ 1\ 0\ 1\ 0\ 0\ 1\ 0\ 0$$

2s complement

$A_s \leftarrow \bar{A}_s$

$$0 \cdot 0\ 1\ 0\ 1\ 1\ 1\ 0\ 0 \quad \times \ 2^6$$

Normalize (SL1)

$$0 \cdot 1\ 0\ 1\ 1\ 1\ 0\ 0\ 0 \quad \times \ 2^5$$

$$
\begin{array}{r}
+34 \\
-) \ -11 \\
\hline
+45
\end{array}
$$

$$\boxed{0} \cdot 1\ 0\ 0\ 0\ 1\ 0\ 0\ 0$$
$$1 \cdot 0\ 0\ 1\ 0\ 1\ 1\ 0\ 0$$
$$0 \longleftarrow \cdot \ 1\ 0\ 1\ 1\ 0\ 1\ 0\ 0 \quad \times \ 2^6$$

$A_s \leftarrow A_s$

$$0 \cdot 1\ 0\ 1\ 1\ 0\ 1\ 0\ 0 \quad \times \ 2^6$$

No normalization required

$$
\begin{array}{r}
-34 \\
-) \ +11 \\
\hline
-45
\end{array}
$$

$$\boxed{1} \cdot 1\ 0\ 0\ 0\ 1\ 0\ 0\ 0$$
$$0 \cdot 0\ 0\ 1\ 0\ 1\ 1\ 0\ 0$$
$$0 \longleftarrow \cdot \ 1\ 0\ 1\ 1\ 0\ 1\ 0\ 0 \quad \times \ 2^6$$

$A_s \leftarrow A_s$

$$1 \cdot 1\ 0\ 1\ 1\ 0\ 1\ 0\ 0 \quad \times \ 2^6$$

No normalization required

(*d*)

Figure 6.7 (Continued)

is equal to the shift count. If the comparator indicates that $a < b$, then register A will be shifted to the right; $a > b$ will cause a right-shift operation on register B. When the output of the comparator is $a = b$, then no shifting is required because the fractions are already aligned. The shift operation terminates when the shift counter has decremented to 0, as indicated by the zero detect logic. Normally, the smaller exponent is incremented by 1 for each bit position the corresponding fraction is shifted. However, in this design, incrementing the exponent is not necessary because the alignment is controlled by the shift counter and the larger exponent is automatically selected to become the exponent of the result before the postnormalization step.

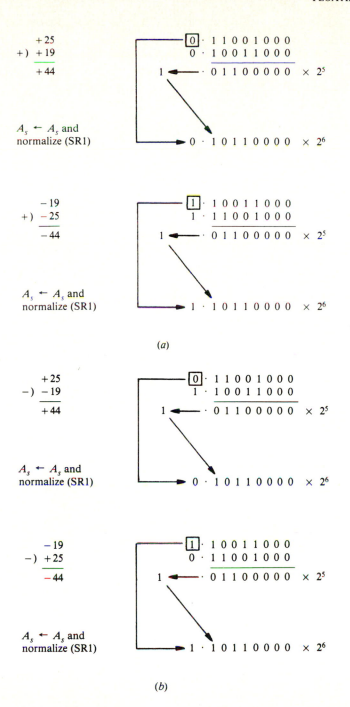

Figure 6.8 (*a*) Floating-point addition with shift-right postnormalization; (*b*) floating-point subtraction with shift-right postnormalization.

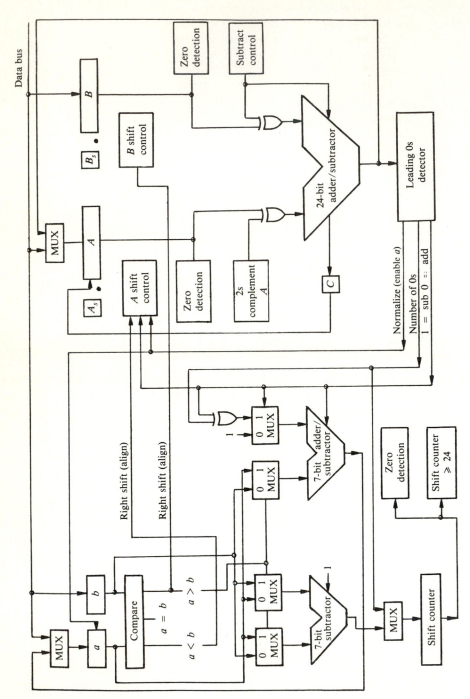

Figure 6.9 Floating-point addition/subtraction unit.

The aligned fractions are now ready for the arithmetic operation. The operation and the signs of the operands determine whether the arithmetic is true addition or true subtraction, as determined by Eqs. 6.15 and 6.16, respectively. These equations are also used in the determination of the sign of the result. For example, if A is negative ($A_s = 1$), B is positive ($B_s = 0$), and the operation is subtraction ($A - B$), then the fractions are added and the sign of the result is negative. However, if A and B are both positive ($A_s = B_s = 0$) and the operation is subtraction, then the fractions are subtracted. The resulting difference may be positive, negative, or 0, and the sign of the result depends on the subtraction operation. If $A > B$, the result will be positive. If $A < B$, the result will be negative and in 2s-complement form, which must then be recomplemented to sign-magnitude form.

The next operation following the fraction addition/subtraction is normalization. Register A will be shifted left one bit position at a time until the high-order bit is a 1; that is, $A_{n-1} = 1$. The number of bits that A is shifted is determined by the number of leading (high-order) 0s in the result. The number of 0s detected is determined by the block labeled *leading 0s detector*. The number of leading 0s is loaded into the shift counter, which controls the number of left shifts required to normalize the result that is now contained in register A. When the shift counter decrements to 0, the normalization of the resulting fraction is complete. If the value of the contents of the shift counter is greater than or equal to 24, then the final result should be considered to be 0.

The number of 0s is also entered into a seven-bit adder/subtractor in which it is subtracted from the larger of the two exponents. Thus, the number of leading 0s causes the result to be shifted left n bit positions and the corresponding exponent to be decreased by n.

Normalization may require a right shift if there is a carry-out of the high-order bit position during a true addition. This will occur when two fractions of the form 0.1 x x $\cdots$ x are added. The sum will then have the form 1.x x $\cdots$ x. The carry-out bit is shifted into A_{n-1} of register A and a 1 is added to the result exponent in register a. During normalization, the resulting exponent may overflow or underflow. When underflow occurs, the final result can be assigned a value of 0.

6.2.4 Hardware Implementation

The logic design for most blocks in Fig. 6.9 has already been presented. However, some functions are shown here for the first time and will be described in greater detail.

The *magnitude comparator* that compares the two exponents is shown in Fig. 6.10. A magnitude comparator is a combinational circuit that compares two numbers A and B and determines their relative magnitude. The outputs of the circuit are $A < B$, $A = B$, and $A > B$. Consider 2 seven-bit exponents as follows:

$$e_a = a_6a_5a_4a_3a_2a_1a_0$$
$$e_b = b_6b_5b_4b_3b_2b_1b_0$$

where each subscripted letter represents one of the digits in the exponent. The two numbers are equal if and only if all pairs of bits are equal; that is, if

$$a_6 = b_6, \; a_5 = b_5, \; \ldots \; , \; a_0 = b_0$$

The equality relation of the individual bits can be expressed by the following boolean equation:

$$\text{Equality}_i = a_i b_i \vee \bar{a}_i \bar{b}_i$$

where $i = 0, 1, \ldots, 6$. This states that the bits in position i must be equal; that is, both are 1s or both are 0s.

In Fig. 6.10, the output of the EXCLUSIVE-OR circuit is positive if $a_i \neq b_i$ and negative if $a_i = b_i$. Let the outputs of the seven EXCLUSIVE-OR circuits be $x_6, x_5, x_4, \ldots, x_0$. Then $a = b$ if $x_i = 0$ (negative); that is,

$$(a = b) = \bar{x}_6 \wedge \bar{x}_5 \wedge \bar{x}_4 \wedge \bar{x}_3 \wedge \bar{x}_2 \wedge \bar{x}_1 \wedge \bar{x}_0$$

To determine if a is greater than or less than b, the relative magnitude of pairs of bits must be inspected starting from most-significant position a_6. If two bits are equal ($x_i = -$), then the next-lowest significant pair are compared. This comparison continues until a pair of unequal digits is found. If digit a_i is greater than the corresponding digit b_i (that is, $a_i = 1$ and $b_i = 0$), then $a > b$. If $a_i = 0$ and $b_i = 1$, then $a < b$. This sequential comparison of bits can be expressed by the following two equations:

$$\begin{aligned}
a < b = \quad & \bar{a}_6 b_6 \vee \bar{x}_6 \bar{a}_5 b_5 \vee \bar{x}_6 \bar{x}_5 \bar{a}_4 b_4 \\
& \vee \bar{x}_6 \bar{x}_5 \bar{x}_4 \bar{a}_3 b_3 \vee \bar{x}_6 \bar{x}_5 \bar{x}_4 \bar{x}_3 \bar{a}_2 b_2 \\
& \vee \bar{x}_6 \bar{x}_5 \bar{x}_4 \bar{x}_3 \bar{x}_2 \bar{a}_1 b_1 \\
& \vee \bar{x}_6 \bar{x}_5 \bar{x}_4 \bar{x}_3 \bar{x}_2 \bar{x}_1 \bar{a}_0 b_0
\end{aligned}$$

$$\begin{aligned}
a > b = \quad & a_6 \bar{b}_6 \vee \bar{x}_6 a_5 \bar{b}_5 \vee \bar{x}_6 \bar{x}_5 a_4 \bar{b}_4 \\
& \vee \bar{x}_6 \bar{x}_5 \bar{x}_4 a_3 \bar{b}_3 \vee \bar{x}_6 \bar{x}_5 \bar{x}_4 \bar{x}_3 a_2 \bar{b}_2 \\
& \vee \bar{x}_6 \bar{x}_5 \bar{x}_4 \bar{x}_3 \bar{x}_2 a_1 \bar{b}_1 \\
& \vee \bar{x}_6 \bar{x}_5 \bar{x}_4 \bar{x}_3 \bar{x}_2 \bar{x}_1 a_0 \bar{b}_0
\end{aligned}$$

The outputs $a < b$, $a > b$, and $a = b$ are equal to 1 when the respective functions are true. The magnitude comparator presented here can be easily expanded to accommodate numbers with a larger number of bits.

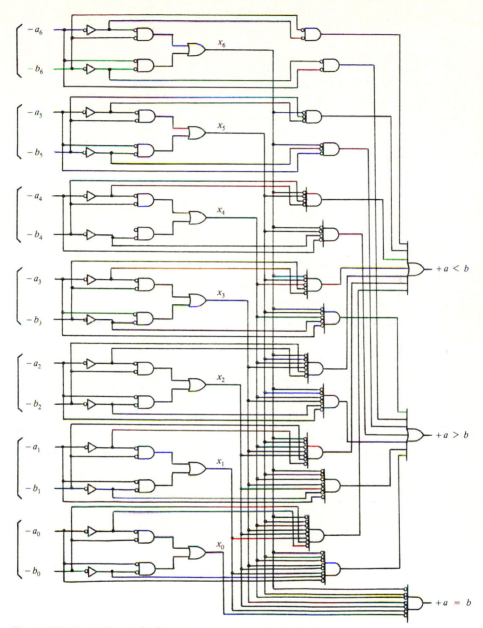

Figure 6.10 Seven-bit magnitude comparator.

The logic diagrams for *detecting all 0s* and *detecting a shift count greater than or equal to 24* are straightforward and are shown in Fig. 6.11.

The *leading 0s detector* is based on the following design, which detects up to seven 0s and encodes that number in binary. The bits to be detected for 0s are

7	6	5	4	3	2	1	0

The number of 0s detected is determined by the following equations.

Number of 0s detected	Bits
$0 = 7$	
$1 = \overline{7} \wedge 6$	
$2 = \overline{7} \wedge \overline{6} \wedge 5$	
$3 = \overline{7} \wedge \overline{6} \wedge \overline{5} \wedge 4$	
$4 = \overline{7} \wedge \overline{6} \wedge \overline{5} \wedge \overline{4} \wedge 3$	
$5 = \overline{7} \wedge \overline{6} \wedge \overline{5} \wedge \overline{4} \wedge \overline{3} \wedge 2$	
$6 = \overline{7} \wedge \overline{6} \wedge \overline{5} \wedge \overline{4} \wedge \overline{3} \wedge \overline{2} \wedge 1$	
$7 = \overline{7} \wedge \overline{6} \wedge \overline{5} \wedge \overline{4} \wedge \overline{3} \wedge \overline{2} \wedge \overline{1} \wedge 0$	

The logic and the encoding for the preceding equations are shown in Fig. 6.12. This can be easily expanded to detect 23 leading 0s, although this expansion may require two or more levels of decoding. The design of the subtraction control for the 24-bit adder/subtractor is based on Eqs. 6.15 and 6.16.

6.3 MULTIPLICATION

The multiplication of two floating-point numbers requires that the fractions are multiplied and the exponents are added. The fractions are multiplied by any of the techniques described for fixed-point arithmetic; however, the add-shift architecture will be used here as the vehicle to present floating-point multiplication. In many respects, floating-point multiplication is simpler than addition or subtraction, because no comparison of exponents or alignment of fractions is required and there are fewer special conditions to handle.

Multiplication is executed on two normalized floating-point operands A_1 and A_2, using biased exponents such that

$$A_1 = f_1 \times r^{e_1}$$

and

$$A_2 = f_2 \times r^{e_2}$$

(6.17)

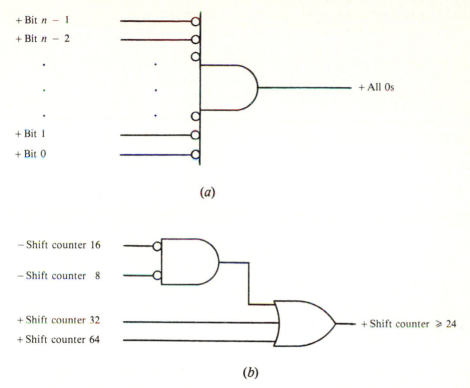

Figure 6.11 (*a*) Detecting all zeros; (*b*) detecting a count $\geqslant 24$.

where f is the normalized fraction, e the exponent, and r the radix. The operands are in sign-magnitude representation such that the fraction f is a signed number with n significant digits (excluding the sign). Floating-point multiplication is defined as

$$A_1 \times A_2 = (f_1 \times r^{e_1}) \times (f_2 \times r^{e_2})$$
$$= (f_1 \times f_2) \times r^{e_1 + e_2} \tag{6.18}$$

The arithmetic operations on the fractions and exponents are two independent operations. Thus, fraction multiplication and exponent addition can be done at the same time.

The sign of the product is determined by the signs of the fractions. If the signs are the same, then the sign of the result is positive. If the signs are not the same, then the result is negative. However, if all digits of the product fraction are 0, then the sign of the result is made positive, regardless of the signs of the individual operands. If both exponents are positive (before biasing), exponent overflow may occur, indicating that the magnitude of the product exceeds the representation capacity of the machine. Likewise, when both exponents are negative, exponent underflow may occur, indicating that the magnitude of the product is too small to be represented, even though the magnitude is greater than 0 and the digits are significant. In some situations, exponent overflow/underflow may be brought within range when the product contains a string of 0s in the high-order or low-order portions. In this case, shifting the product fraction in the appropriate direction together with a corresponding change in the value of the exponent may clear the overflow/underflow condition.

Multiplication of the fractions provides a double-precision product. In fixed-point arithmetic, the double-precision result is used to increase the accuracy of the product. However, in floating-point arithmetic, the range of a single-precision fraction combined with the exponent is usually sufficiently accurate so that only single-precision results are required. Thus, the low-order half of the product can be truncated, with a possible rounding bit added to the high-order half of the product. The adding of the rounding bit may cause a fraction overflow so that renormalization may be required.

6.3.1 Multiplication Algorithm

The multiplication algorithm is divided into five parts:

1. Check for 0 operands.
2. Determine product sign.
3. Add exponents.
4. Multiply fractions.
5. Normalize the product.

Steps 3 and 4 can be done in parallel, but must be properly synchronized before the normalization step is initiated. Also, separate adders are required to obtain this parallelism.

The registers required for a multiplication operation are shown in Fig. 6.13. There are three registers, two of which are subdivided into three parts to form concatenated registers as follows:

$$AR = a \cdot A_s \cdot A$$
$$BR = b \cdot B_s \cdot B$$

where a is the exponent register, A_s the sign flip-flop, and A the fraction register. Register BR is similarly defined. Register AR contains the multiplicand, register BR contains the multiplier, and register D contains the high-order n bits of the partial product. Registers AR and BR contain normalized floating-point operands such that $A_{n-1} = B_{n-1} = 1$. The operands conform to the format of Fig. 6.1 which has a 24-bit fraction, a seven-bit exponent, and a sign bit. A 24-bit carry lookahead adder is used for the addition operations involving the multiplicand and partial products. The product resides in register D, since the low-order half of the $2n$-bit product in register B was truncated. The floating-

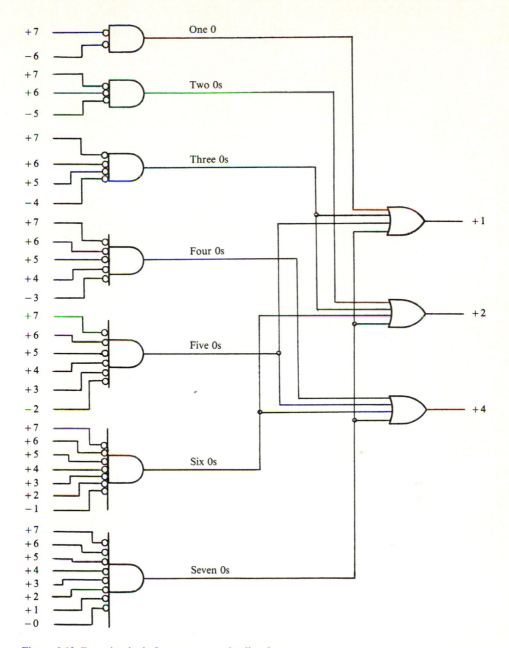

Figure 6.12 Detection logic for up to seven leading 0s.

point multiplication unit is normally integrated with the addition hardware in which register A is connected to the output bus. Therefore, the product in register D should be transferred to register A, where postnormalization will take place.

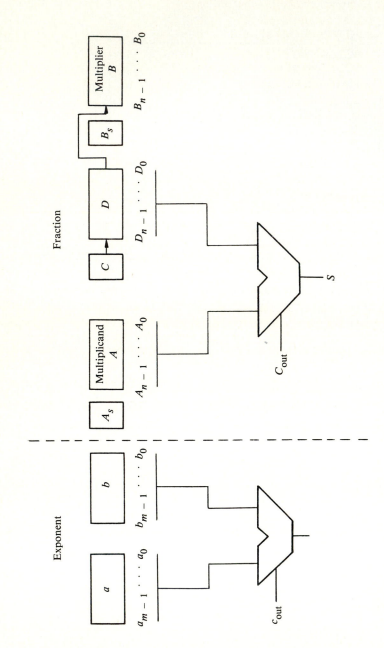

Figure 6.13 Register organization for floating-point multiplication.

The flowchart for the floating-point multiplication algorithm is shown in Fig. 6.14. Initially, the multiplicand is loaded into register AR, the multiplier into register BR, and register D is reset to 0. The two operands are checked to determine if either one contains a 0 value. If either operand is equal to 0, the product in AR is set to 0 and the operation is terminated. If neither of the operands is equal to 0, then the process continues with setting the product sign. The product is positive when the two operands have the same sign; otherwise, it is negative.

The sequence continues by executing in parallel the next two operations, that is, exponent addition and fraction multiplication. The flowchart of Fig. 6.14(a) indicates this parallelism by exiting at $\boxed{A}$ and proceeding to the next two sequences, both of which have entering points at $\boxed{A}$. The exponents are added and the sum is transferred into register a. The exponent adder produces the sum of the two biased exponents; therefore, the resulting sum has a double bias. The correct biased exponent for the product is obtained by subtracting the bias number from the exponent sum. For an m-bit exponent, where $m = 7$, this means that $2^{m-1} = 2^6 = 64$ must be subtracted to restore the exponent to a single bias. The subtraction of the bias value is implemented with 2s complement addition. Thus, subtracting $64 = 1\ 0\ 0\ 0\ 0\ 0\ 0$ is the same as adding $1\ 0\ 0\ 0\ 0\ 0\ 0$, since the 2s complement of $1\ 0\ 0\ 0\ 0\ 0\ 0$ is $1\ 0\ 0\ 0\ 0\ 0\ 0$. When the carry-out of the exponent adder equals 1 ($c_{out} = 1$), an exponent overflow has occurred.

Multiplication of fractions can be implemented by any of the fixed-point multiplication techniques described in Chap. 3. The add-shift method is used in this section to describe the floating-point multiplication procedure. Sequence counter SC is loaded with value n, which represents the number of bits in the multiplier. Register D contains the initial partial product, which is 0. The value of least-significant bit B_0 of register B is checked. If $B_0 = 1$, addition of the multiplicand and the partial product is performed through the n-bit CLA adder. If $B_0 = 0$, then 0s are added to the partial product in D. In both cases, the sum output of the adder

$$S = S_{n-1}\ S_{n-2} \cdot \cdot \cdot S_1\ S_0$$

is loaded into register D and bit C_{out} is loaded into flip-flop C. It is not necessary to add 0s to the partial product when $B_0 = 0$, since this requires only a shift with no addition, but it may mean simpler control logic if the same sequence occurs during each cycle; that is, always do an add-shift operation.

The contents of the concatenated registers $C \cdot D \cdot B$ are then shifted right one bit position as follows:

$$C \cdot D_{n-1} \cdot \cdot \cdot D_0 \cdot B_{n-1} \cdot \cdot \cdot B_0 \leftarrow 0 \cdot C \cdot D_{n-1} \cdot \cdot \cdot D_0 \cdot B_{n-1} \cdot \cdot \cdot B_1 \quad (6.19)$$

The sequence counter is then decremented by 1. The process repeats with the inspection of the next higher-order bit of the multiplier and concludes when $SC = 0$. At that time, all multiplier bits will have been examined.

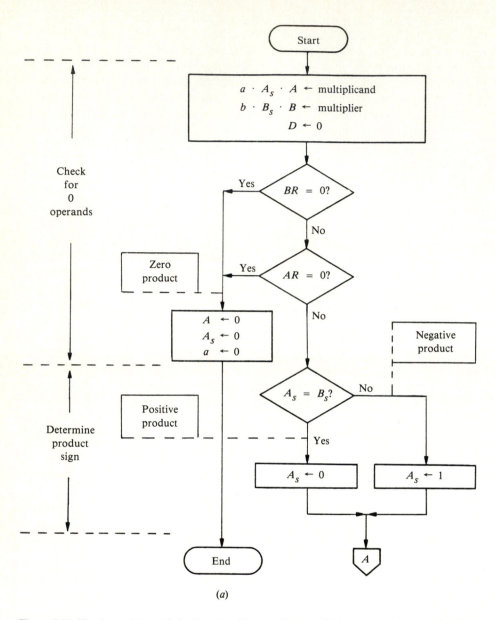

(a)

Figure 6.14 Floating-point multiplication algorithm; (a) 0 operand detection and product sign determination; (b) exponent addition; (c) fraction multiplication; and (d) postnormalization.

The value of the resulting fraction is within the range

$$\frac{1}{r^2} \leqslant |f_1 \times f_2| < 1 \tag{6.20}$$

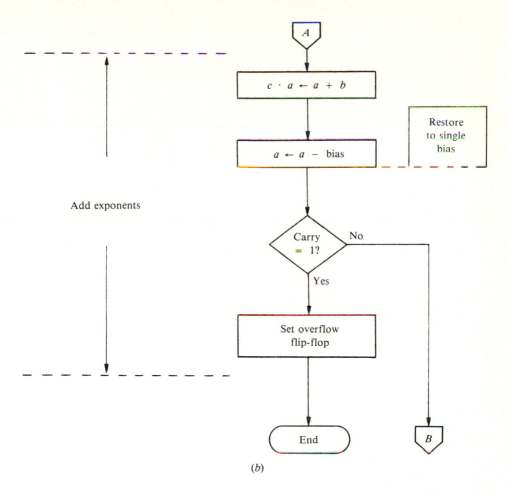

(b)

Figure 6.14 (Continued)

and at most one leading 0 may exist in the final product, in which case only one left shift is required to normalize the result. The multiplicand and multiplier were originally normalized fractions of the form $0 \cdot 1 \text{ x x} \cdots \text{x}$, so that the smallest possible product is $0 \cdot 0 1 0 0 \cdots 0$. When the product fraction is shifted left, the result exponent is decremented by 1. The multiply operation results in a double-length $(2n)$ product residing in register pair $D \cdot B$. The lower half of the product in register B can be rounded off. If $B_{n-1} = 1$ and $D_0 = 0$, then D_0 can be set to 1 during the rounding operation.

The operations during normalization implement the fraction shifting and exponent decrementing as specified by

$$AR \times BR = [(A \times B) \times r] \times r^{(e_1 + e_2) - 1} \tag{6.21}$$

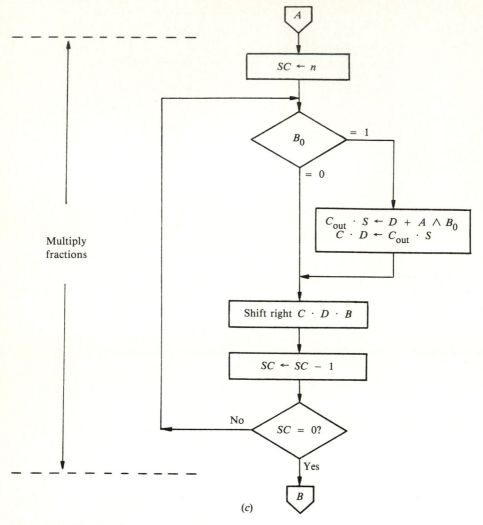

(c)

Figure 6.14 (Continued)

The final normalized product with correctly biased exponent resides in concatenated registers $a \cdot A_s \cdot A$.

Figure 6.15 gives an example of floating-point multiplication in which no postnormalization is required. However, Fig. 6.16 requires normalization with an accompanying decrement of the exponent.

6.3.2 Hardware Organization

Figure 6.17 shows the hardware organization for a floating-point multiplication unit. The structure is divided into two sections: one for the fraction and one for

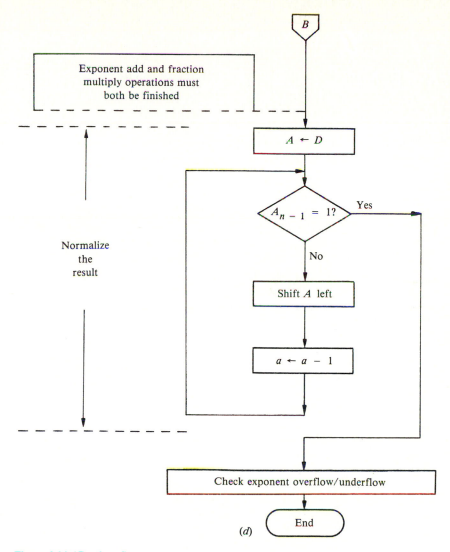

Figure 6.14 (Continued)

the exponent. The two operands, the multiplicand and multiplier, are loaded into registers A and B, respectively, in normalized form. Register D, which will contain the partial product, is reset to 0. The biased exponents for the respective operands are loaded into registers a and b. The resulting product will be normalized and loaded into register A, and the exponent of the result will be in register a. The concatenated registers $a \cdot A_s \cdot A$ will then be available on the output bus. The unit is controlled by a microprogram.

The first step is to check for 0 operands. If either zero detection circuit finds a value of 0 in register A or B, then register AR is set to 0; that is,

$$A \leftarrow 0$$
$$A_s \leftarrow 0$$
$$a \leftarrow 0$$

and the operation is terminated, with the result in register AR. The sign bits are compared by means of an EXCLUSIVE-OR circuit, and the sign of the result is determined by the rules of algebra:

$$\text{Sign of result } A_s = \begin{cases} 0 \text{ (positive)} & \text{if } A_s \veebar B_s = 0 \\ 1 \text{ (negative)} & \text{if } A_s \veebar B_s = 1 \end{cases}$$

The next two steps are executed in parallel, and are performed if and only if both operands are nonzero. The exponents are added and the bias is subtracted using an m-bit CLA adder/subtractor. If the exponents are to be added, then the subtract bias signal is 0, which selects register b through the multiplexer and forces c_{in} to be a logical 0. When the bias is to be subtracted, the subtract bias signal is 1, which selects the 1s complement of the bias and forces $c_{in} = 1$ to permit the 2s complement of the bias number to be added to the exponent in register a.

The low-order bit B_0 of register B is used to generate a vector V that is added to the previous partial product in D. This auxiliary vector V is defined as

$$V = \begin{cases} A & \text{if } B_0 = 1 \\ \Phi & \text{if } B_0 = 0 \end{cases}$$

where Φ refers to a 0 vector of n bits. The adder performs the following addition during each cycle, with $C_{in} = 0$.

$$C_{out} \cdot S \leftarrow D + A \wedge B_0$$

where the center dot ($\cdot$) is concatenation, the plus sign ($+$) is addition, and $\wedge$ is the AND function. The addition may yield $C_{out} = 1$. The sum and carry-out are loaded into registers D and C, respectively; that is,

$$C \cdot D \leftarrow C_{out} \cdot S$$

The concatenated registers C, D, and B are then shifted right one bit position, as defined by Eq. 6.19. The process repeats until the sequence counter has decremented to 0. When exponent addition and fraction multiplication have both been completed, then the result can be normalized and exponent overflow/underflow can be checked. There is no new hardware design to be described.

Multiplicand $= 0 . 1 1 1 1 0 0 0 0 \times 2^4$ $(+15)$
Multiplier $= 0 . 1 0 1 0 0 0 0 0 \times 2^3$ $(+5)$

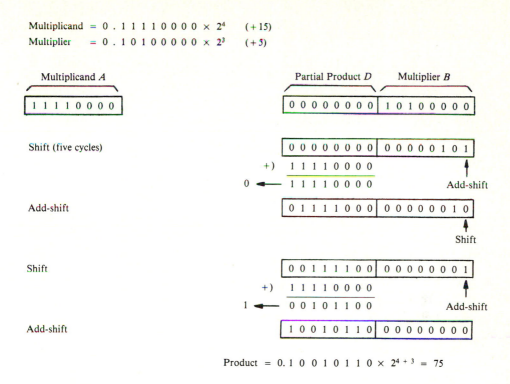

Product $= 0. 1 0 0 1 0 1 1 0 \times 2^{4+3} = 75$

Figure 6.15 Floating-point multiplication example without postnormalization.

6.4 DIVISION

The division of two floating-point numbers requires that the fractions be divided and the exponents subtracted. The fractions are divided by any of the techniques described for fixed-point arithmetic; however, the restoring architecture with a multiplexer will be used here as the vehicle to describe floating-point division. The dividend can have a single-precision fraction. In processor operation, the dividend is divided by the divisor and replaced by the normalized quotient. The remainder may or may not be retained. Both operands have prenormalized fractions and biased exponents.

Divide overflow is checked in the same manner as in fixed-point division. Recall that divide overflow occurs when the quotient overflows, that is, when the number of bits in the quotient exceeds the word length of the machine. If a double-precision dividend is adopted, then a divide-overflow condition occurs if the value of the high-order half of the dividend is greater than or equal to the value of the divisor. For single-precision floating-point division, a divide overflow occurs if the dividend is greater than or equal to the divisor. This presents no problem when dealing with floating-point numbers. The dividend

Multiplicand $= 0 . 1 1 0 0 1 0 0 0 \times 2^5$ $(+25)$

Multiplier $= 0 . 1 0 0 1 0 0 0 0 \times 2^4$ $(+9)$

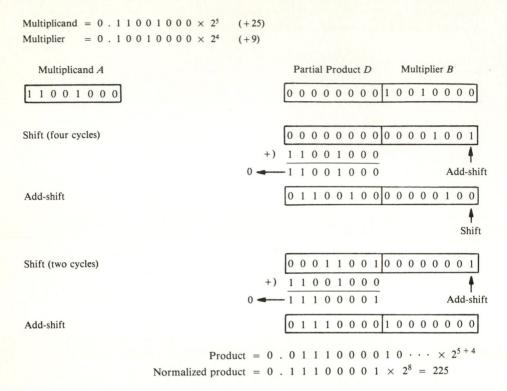

Product $= 0 . 0 1 1 1 0 0 0 0 1 0 \cdots \times 2^{5 + 4}$

Normalized product $= 0 . 1 1 1 0 0 0 0 1 \times 2^8 = 225$

Figure 6.16 Floating-point multiplication example with postnormalization.

fraction is shifted right one bit position and the exponent is incremented by 1. This ensures that the dividend is smaller than the divisor. Both operands were normalized and of the form $0.1 \; x \; x \cdots x$. If the dividend is shifted right one bit position (divided by 2), then the forms of the two operands are

$$\text{Dividend} = 0 . 0 1 \; x \; x \cdots x$$
$$\text{Divisor} \; = 0 . 1 \; x \; x \cdots x$$

where the ranges are

$$\frac{1}{4} \leqslant \text{dividend} < \frac{1}{2}$$

$$\frac{1}{2} \leqslant \text{divisor} < 1$$

thus forcing the dividend to be less than the divisor. This is referred to as *dividend alignment*.

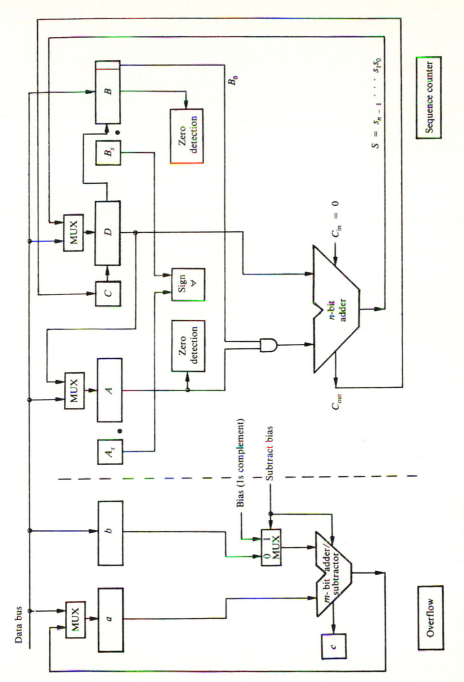

Figure 6.17 Floating-point multiplication unit.

401

Fraction alignment is essentially an overflow prevention operation, ensuring that the dividend fraction is smaller than the divisor fraction. This permits meaningful fraction division. The division of two normalized floating-point operands always results in a normalized quotient if the dividend alignment is performed before the division operation. Therefore, no postnormalization is required on the quotient.

A 0 dividend or divisor must also be detected. If the dividend is 0, then the quotient, remainder, and exponent of the result are made 0 and the operation is terminated. If the divisor is 0, this indicates an attempt to divide by 0, which is an illegal operation. An error is generated and the operation is terminated.

During the execution of the divide operation, a 0 remainder may be produced. This effect is caused by "even" division; that is, the result is an integer. When this situation occurs, time may be saved by terminating the shift-subtract cycles and adjusting the quotient fraction and exponent so that they are in proper form.

Consider two normalized floating-point operands A_1 and A_2 with biased exponents

$$A_1 = f_1 \times r^{e_1} \quad \text{and} \quad A_2 = f_2 \times r^{e_2} \qquad (6.22)$$

where f is the normalized fraction, e the exponent, and r the radix. The fractions are in sign-magnitude representation, with n significant bits (excluding the sign). Floating-point division is defined as

$$\frac{A_1}{A_2} = \frac{f_1 \times r^{e_1}}{f_2 \times r^{e_2}}$$

$$= \frac{f_1}{f_2} \times r^{e_1 - e_2} \qquad (6.23)$$

The value of the resulting quotient fraction is in the range

$$\frac{1}{r} \leqslant \left| \frac{f_1}{f_2} \right| < r$$

for $f_1 \neq 0 \neq f_2$ and the dividend less than the divisor. Fraction overflow occurs when the dividend is greater than or equal to the divisor because the range of the result is

$$1 \leqslant \left| \frac{f_1}{f_2} \right| < r$$

As in floating-point multiplication, the operations on the fractions and exponents can be done in parallel. Thus, fraction division and exponent subtraction can be done at the same time. Exponent overflow/underflow may occur when the subtraction of exponents involves true addition on two exponents of opposite sign; that is,

$$(+e_1) - (-e_2)$$
$$(-e_1) - (+e_2)$$

Correct synchronization must be maintained between these two processes so that the next process can be entered with the correctly calculated fraction and exponent.

The sign of the quotient is determined by the rules of algebra, with a positive sign being given to a quotient value of 0. The quotient sign is also positive when the dividend and divisor have identical signs; otherwise, the quotient sign is negative. If the remainder is preserved, then the sign of the dividend becomes the sign of the remainder.

6.4.1 Division Algorithm

The division algorithm is divided into five parts:

1. Check for 0 operands.
2. Determine the sign of the quotient.
3. Align the dividend.
4. Subtract exponents.
5. Divide fractions.

Steps 4 and 5 can be done in parallel, but must be properly synchronized before terminating the operation.

The three registers required for a floating-point division operation are shown in Fig. 6.18. Two registers are subdivided into three parts to form concatenated registers as follows:

$$AR = a \cdot A_s \cdot A$$
$$BR = b \cdot B_s \cdot B$$

where a is the exponent register, A_s the sign flip-flop, and A the fraction register for operand A, which is the high-order half of the dividend. Register BR is similarly defined for the divisor. The low-order half of the dividend resides in register Q, which ultimately contains the quotient. Registers AR and BR are loaded with normalized operands such that $A_{n-1} = B_{n-1} = 1$. The divisor conforms to the format of Fig. 6.1, which has a 24-bit fraction, a 7-bit exponent, and a sign bit. However, the dividend consists of a double-precision fraction in register pair $A \cdot Q$. A 24-bit carry lookahead adder is used for the subtraction operations involving the divisor and the partial remainders. The initial and final

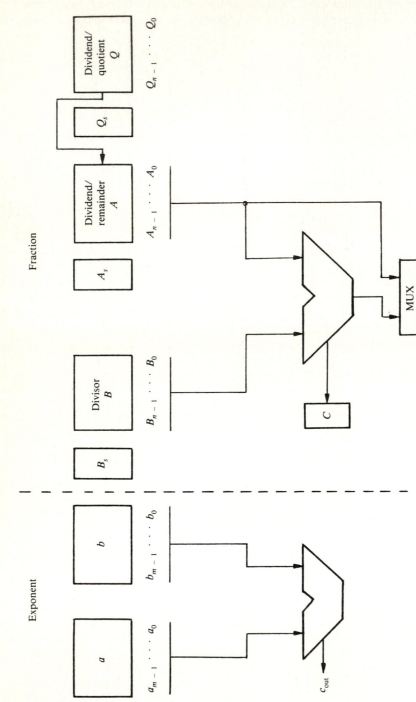

Figure 6.18 Register organization for floating-point division.

register assignments before and after the execution of a floating-point division operation are shown in Fig. 6.19.

The flowchart for the floating-point division algorithm is shown in Fig. 6.20. The dividend is loaded into $AR \cdot Q$ and the divisor is loaded into BR. Both operands are in normalized form with biased exponents, where

$$\text{Dividend} = a_{m-1} \cdots a_0 \cdot A_s \cdot A_{n-1} \cdots A_0 \cdot Q_{n-1} \cdots Q_0$$
$$\text{Divisor} = b_{m-1} \cdots b_0 \cdot B_s \cdot B_{n-1} \cdots B_0$$

and $A_{n-1} = B_{n-1} = 1$. The fractions are checked for a 0 value. If the divisor equals 0, then a flag is set and the operation is terminated. If the dividend equals 0, then $a \cdot Q_s \cdot Q$ and $A_s \cdot A$ are set to 0 and the operation is terminated.

The sign of dividend A_s is left unchanged to become the sign of the remainder. Quotient sign Q_s is positive if the dividend and divisor have the same signs; otherwise, it is negative, as defined below:

$$Q_s \leftarrow A_s \not\forall B_s$$

that is,

$$Q_s = \begin{cases} 0 & \text{if } A_s \not\forall B_s = 0 \\ 1 & \text{if } A_s \not\forall B_s = 1 \end{cases}$$

Next, the dividend is aligned, if necessary. If the high-order half of the dividend (contents of A) is greater than or equal to the value of the divisor, then the dividend must be aligned. The relative magnitude of the two fractions can be determined by a combinational magnitude comparator similar to Fig. 6.10. An alternative approach, which is used in this design, employs the fraction adder, in which the divisor is subtracted from the dividend. The carry-out bit is then used to determine whether alignment is required.

The block immediately after entry symbol $\boxed{A}$ in Fig. 6.20(b) indicates that operation $A - B$ is performed but only the carry-out bit is retained. The operation could have been $C \cdot A \leftarrow A + \bar{B} + 1$, but then the dividend would have to be restored. The microcode prevents register A from being loaded. If there is no carry-out, then the dividend is less than the divisor ($A < B$) and alignment is not required.

However, if carry-out equals 1, then the dividend is greater than or equal to the divisor ($A \geqslant B$) and alignment is required. The alignment always results in a normalized quotient, and thus no postnormalization is necessary. The concatenated register pair $A \cdot Q$ is shifted right one bit position as defined below.

$$A_{n-1} \cdots A_0 \cdot Q_{n-1} \cdots Q_0 \leftarrow 0 \cdot A_{n-1} \cdots A_0 \cdot Q_{n-1} \cdots Q_1$$

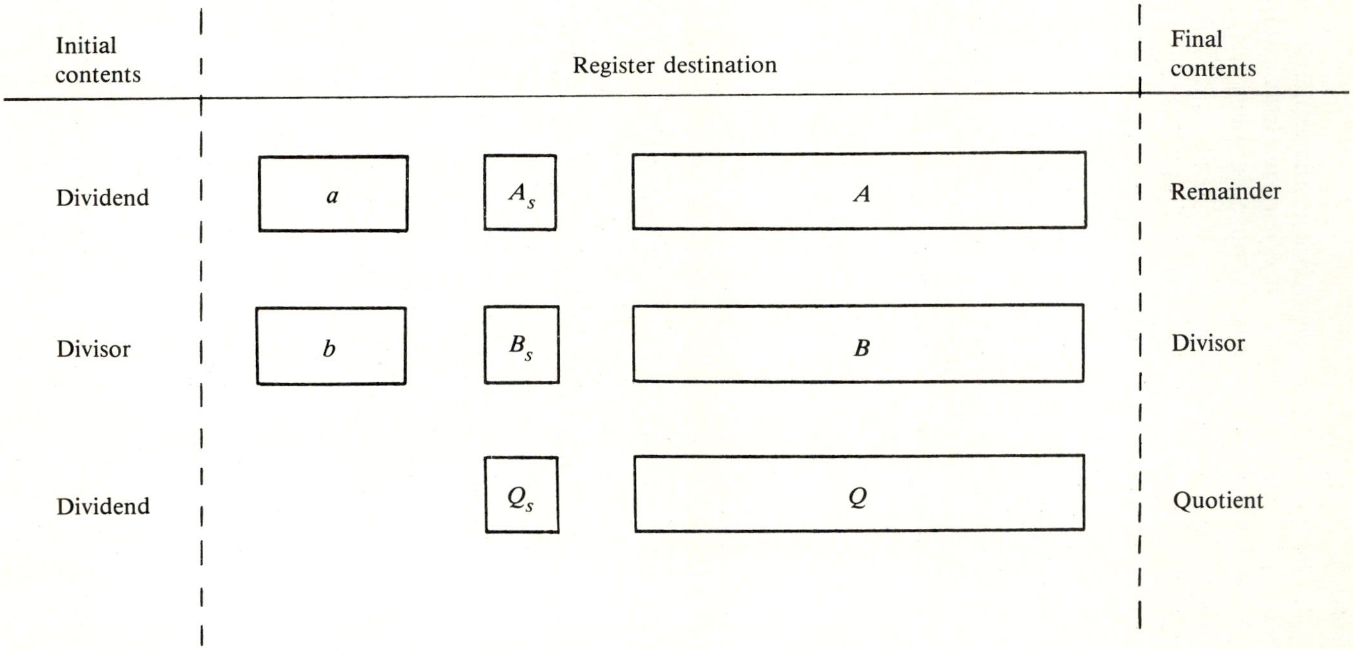

Figure 6.19 Register assignments for floating-point division.

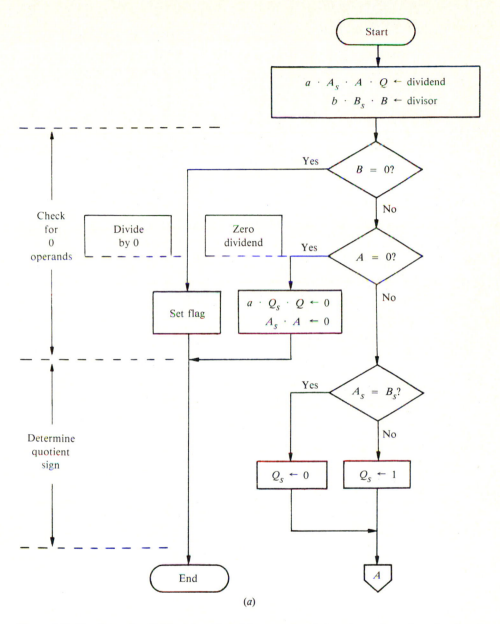

Figure 6.20 Floating-point division algorithm: (*a*) zero operand detection and quotient sign deter-mination; (*b*) dividend alignment; (*c*) exponent subtraction; and (*d*) fraction division.

The dividend exponent is then incremented by 1. This incrementation may result in an exponent overflow, in which case a flag is set and the operation is ter-minated; otherwise, the process continues with the parallel operations of expo-nent subtraction and fraction division.

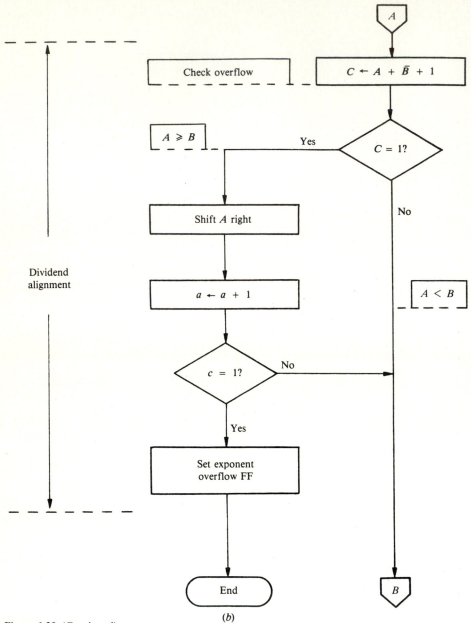

Figure 6.20 (Continued)

(b)

The divisor exponent is subtracted from the dividend exponent, and carry-out bit c_{out} is examined. If $c_{out} = 1$, then the dividend exponent was greater than or equal to the divisor exponent ($a \geqslant b$). If $c_{out} = 0$, then the dividend exponent was less than the divisor exponent ($a < b$). In either case, since both exponents

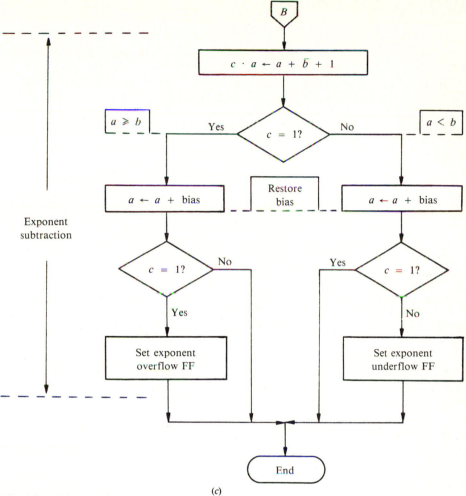

Figure 6.20 (Continued)

(c)

were originally biased, the subtraction operation yields a difference without the bias, as shown below.

$$a - b = (e_a + \text{bias}) - (e_b + \text{bias})$$
$$= e_a + \text{bias} - e_b - \text{bias}$$
$$= e_a - e_b$$

The bias is then added back. For seven-bit exponents, the bias is $1\ 0\ 0\ 0\ 0\ 0\ 0$ ($+64_{10}$). Thus,

$$a_{m-1} \cdots a_0 \leftarrow (a_{m-1} \cdots a_0) + 1\ 0\ 0\ 0\ 0\ 0\ 0$$

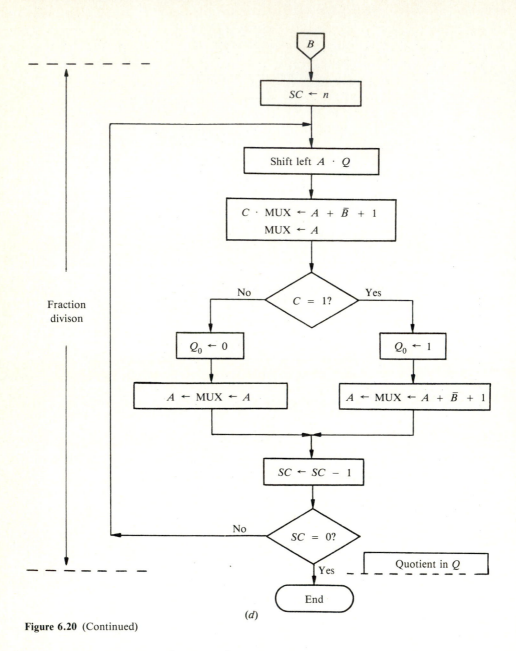

Figure 6.20 (Continued)

The preceding operation could be replaced by

$$q_{m-1} \cdots q_0 \leftarrow (a_{m-1} \cdots a_0) + 1\ 0\ 0\ 0\ 0\ 0\ 0$$

but this would require another register to contain the quotient exponent. Less hardware is required to simply load the restored-bias result exponent back into register a through a multiplexer. The resulting quotient is then in the concatenated registers $a \cdot Q_s \cdot Q$. Restoring the bias may result in an exponent overflow or underflow. If either occurs, a corresponding flag is set and the operation is terminated. If no exponent overflow or underflow condition occurs, then the exponent subtraction process is completed.

It is appropriate at this time to discuss exponent overflow/underflow with some examples. For seven-bit exponents, the largest unbiased exponent is 0 1 1 1 1 1 1 (+63) and the smallest unbiased exponent is 1 0 0 0 0 0 0 (−64). The largest biased exponent is 1 1 1 1 1 1 1 and the smallest biased exponent is 0 0 0 0 0 0 0, obtained from adding the bias 1 0 0 0 0 0 0 to the largest and smallest unbiased exponents, respectively.

Let

$$e_{a_{\text{unbiased}}} = 0\ 1\ 1\ 1\ 1\ 1\ 1 \quad (+63)$$

Then,

$$
\begin{aligned}
a_{\text{biased}} &= 0\ 1\ 1\ 1\ 1\ 1\ 1\ +\ 1\ 0\ 0\ 0\ 0\ 0\ 0 \\
&= 1\ 1\ 1\ 1\ 1\ 1\ 1
\end{aligned}
$$

Also, let

$$e_{b_{\text{unbiased}}} = 0\ 1\ 1\ 1\ 1\ 1\ 0 \quad (+62)$$

Then,

$$b_{\text{biased}} = 1\ 1\ 1\ 1\ 1\ 1\ 0$$

Thus, for $a > b$, in binary,

$$
\begin{array}{r}
a - b = \quad 1\ 1\ 1\ 1\ 1\ 1\ 1 \\
-)\ 1\ 1\ 1\ 1\ 1\ 1\ 0 \\
\hline
\end{array}
$$

$$
\begin{array}{r}
= \quad 1\ 1\ 1\ 1\ 1\ 1\ 1 \\
+)\ 0\ 0\ 0\ 0\ 0\ 1\ 0 \quad \text{(2s complement)} \\
\hline
1 \leftarrow \quad 0\ 0\ 0\ 0\ 0\ 0\ 1
\end{array}
$$

$$
\begin{array}{r}
\text{Add bias} \quad +)\ 1\ 0\ 0\ 0\ 0\ 0\ 0 \\
\hline
\boxed{0} \leftarrow \quad 1\ 0\ 0\ 0\ 0\ 0\ 1 \quad (+65)
\end{array}
$$

$\longrightarrow$ No overflow

In decimal,

$$a - b = (63 + \text{bias}) - (62 + \text{bias})$$
$$= 63 - 62 = 1$$

Add bias $\quad 1 + 64 = +65$

which is within the range of 0–127 for biased exponents.

If $e_a = e_b = 0\ 0\ 1\ 0\ 1\ 1\ 0\ (+22)$, then for $a = b$, in binary,

$$a - b = \quad\quad 1\ 0\ 1\ 0\ 1\ 1\ 0$$
$$-)\ 1\ 0\ 1\ 0\ 1\ 1\ 0$$

$$= \quad\quad 1\ 0\ 1\ 0\ 1\ 1\ 0$$
$$+)\ 0\ 1\ 0\ 1\ 0\ 1\ 0 \quad \text{(2s complement)}$$

$$1 \quad \leftarrow \quad 0\ 0\ 0\ 0\ 0\ 0\ 0$$

Add bias $\quad\quad 1\ 0\ 0\ 0\ 0\ 0\ 0$

$$\boxed{0} \quad \leftarrow \quad 1\ 0\ 0\ 0\ 0\ 0\ 0$$
$$\quad\quad\quad \longrightarrow \quad \text{No overflow}$$

In decimal,

$$a - b = (22 + \text{bias}) - (22 + \text{bias})$$
$$= 22 - 22 = 0$$

Add bias $\quad 0 + 64 = 64$

which is within the range of 0–127 for biased exponents.

If $e_a = 0\ 1\ 0\ 0\ 0\ 0\ 0\ (+32)$ and $e_b = 1\ 1\ 0\ 0\ 0\ 0\ 0\ (-32)$, then for $a > b$, in binary,

$$a - b = \quad\quad 1\ 1\ 0\ 0\ 0\ 0\ 0$$
$$-)\ 0\ 1\ 0\ 0\ 0\ 0\ 0$$

$$= \quad\quad 1\ 1\ 0\ 0\ 0\ 0\ 0$$
$$+)\ 1\ 1\ 0\ 0\ 0\ 0\ 0$$

$$1 \quad \leftarrow \quad 1\ 0\ 0\ 0\ 0\ 0\ 0$$

Add bias $\quad\quad 1\ 0\ 0\ 0\ 0\ 0\ 0$

$$\boxed{1} \quad \leftarrow \quad 0\ 0\ 0\ 0\ 0\ 0\ 0$$
$$\quad\quad\quad \longrightarrow \quad \text{Overflow}$$

In decimal,

$$(32 + \text{bias}) - [(-32) + \text{bias}] = 32 + 32 = 64$$

Add bias $64 + 64 = 128$

which is not within the range of 0–127 for biased exponents, and an overflow results.

If $e_a = 1\ 0\ 0\ 0\ 0\ 0\ 0\ (-64)$ and $e_b = 1\ 1\ 1\ 1\ 1\ 1\ 1\ (-1)$, then for $a < b$, in binary,

$$
\begin{array}{rl}
a - b = & 1\ 0\ 0\ 0\ 0\ 0\ 0 \\
-) & 1\ 1\ 1\ 1\ 1\ 1\ 1 \\
\hline
\end{array}
$$

$$
\begin{array}{rl}
= & 1\ 0\ 0\ 0\ 0\ 0\ 0 \\
+) & 0\ 0\ 0\ 0\ 0\ 0\ 1 \\
\hline
0 \quad \leftarrow & 1\ 0\ 0\ 0\ 0\ 0\ 1 \\
\end{array}
$$

Add bias $1\ 0\ 0\ 0\ 0\ 0\ 0$

$$
\boxed{1} \quad \leftarrow \quad 0\ 0\ 0\ 0\ 0\ 0\ 1
$$

⎿ ⟶ No underflow

In decimal,

$$[(-64) + \text{bias}] - [(-1) + \text{bias}] = -64 + 1 = -63$$

Add bias $-63 + 64 = 1$

which is within the range of 0–127 for biased exponents, and no underflow results.

If $e_a = 1\ 0\ 0\ 0\ 0\ 0\ 0\ (-64)$ and $e_b = 0\ 0\ 0\ 0\ 0\ 1\ 0\ (+2)$, then for $a < b$, in binary,

$$
\begin{array}{rl}
a - b = & 0\ 0\ 0\ 0\ 0\ 0\ 0 \\
-) & 1\ 0\ 0\ 0\ 0\ 1\ 0 \\
\hline
\end{array}
$$

$$
\begin{array}{rl}
= & 0\ 0\ 0\ 0\ 0\ 0\ 0 \\
+) & 0\ 1\ 1\ 1\ 1\ 1\ 0 \\
\hline
0 \quad \leftarrow & 0\ 1\ 1\ 1\ 1\ 1\ 0 \\
\end{array}
$$

Add bias $1\ 0\ 0\ 0\ 0\ 0\ 0$

$$
\boxed{0} \quad \leftarrow \quad 1\ 1\ 1\ 1\ 1\ 1\ 0
$$

⎿ ⟶ Underflow

In decimal,

$$[(-64) + \text{bias}] - [2 + \text{bias}] = -64 - 2 = -66$$

Add bias $\quad -66 + 64 = -2$

which is not within the range of 0–127 for biased exponents, and an underflow results.

Figure 6.20(d) contains the flowchart for fraction division. Sequence counter SC is set to value n, the length of the quotient. The shift-subtract restoring division is implemented using a multiplexer to restore the previous partial remainder. The concatenated registers $A \cdot Q$ are shifted left one bit position according to the following expression.

$$A_{n-1} \cdots A_0 \cdot Q_{n-1} \cdots Q_0 \leftarrow A_{n-2} \cdots A_0 \cdot Q_{n-1} \cdots Q_0 \cdot 0$$

Divisor B is then subtracted from dividend A and the sum is sent to the multiplexer, with C_{n-1} sent to the carry flip-flop. The previous partial remainder in A is also applied to the inputs of the multiplexer.

The subtraction follows the expression below.

$$C \cdot s_{n-1} \cdots s_0 \leftarrow A_{n-1} \cdots A_0 + \bar{B}_{n-1} \cdots \bar{B}_0 + 1$$

If $C_{n-1} = 0$ (that is, if the carry-out is 0, indicating an unsuccessful subtraction), then the previous partial remainder (in register A) is selected by the multiplexer and loaded into register A, thus restoring the previous partial remainder. Flip-flop C, which equals 0, is loaded into Q_0. If $C_{n-1} = 1$, then the sum output from the adder is selected by the multiplexer and loaded into register A, while flip-flop C, which equals 1, is loaded into Q_0. The above sequences are illustrated by the following operations. If $C_{n-1} = 0$, then

$$A_{n-1} \cdots A_1 A_0 \leftarrow A_{n-1} \cdots A_1 A_0$$
$$Q_0 \leftarrow C = 0$$

If $C_{n-1} = 1$, then

$$A_{n-1} \cdots A_1 A_0 \leftarrow s_{n-1} \cdots s_1 s_0$$
$$Q_0 \leftarrow C = 1$$

The sequence counter is then decremented by 1 and checked for a 0 value. If $SC \neq 0$, then the fraction division operation continues with the preceding procedure. If $SC = 0$, then the floating-point division operation is finished and the quotient fraction is in register $Q_s \cdot Q$ and the quotient exponent is in register a. Figure 6.21 presents an example of floating-point division.

Dividend $= 0 . 1 1 1 1 0 0 0 0 \times 2^4$ $(+15)$
Divisor $= 0 . 1 0 1 0 \qquad \times 2^3$ $(+5)$

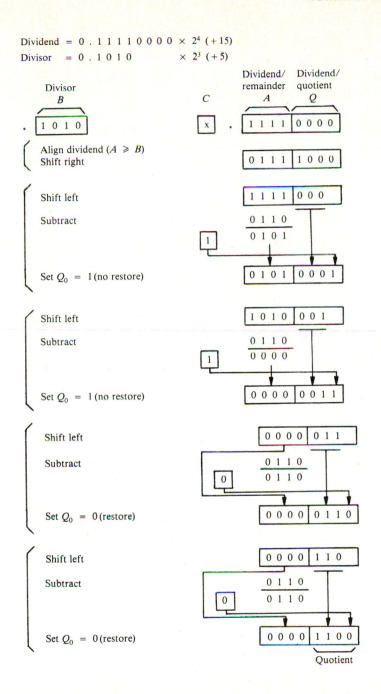

Figure 6.21 Floating-point division example. The sign of the quotient is $A_s \veebar B_s = 0 \veebar 0 = 0$ (positive). The quotient exponent is $2^{4 + 1 - 3} = 2^2$. Therefore, the quotient is $0 . 1 1 0 0 \times 2^2$ $(+3)$. The dividend exponent is incremented by 1, because of a right shift of the dividend during alignment.

6.4.2 Hardware Organization

Figure 6.22 shows the hardware organization for a floating-point division unit. The unit is divided into two sections: one for the fraction and one for the exponent. The two operands, the dividend and divisor, are loaded into registers $A \cdot Q$ and B, respectively, in normalized form. The biased exponents for the respective operands are loaded into registers a and b. The resulting normalized quotient will be in register Q, and the exponent of the quotient will be in register a. The concatenated registers $a \cdot Q_s \cdot Q$ will then be available on the output bus. The division unit is controlled by a microprogram.

The operands are checked for a 0 value and an appropriate action is taken. The sign of the quotient is determined by the block *sign* $\forall$. The fractions are checked for magnitude comparison. If $A \geqslant B$, flip-flop C will be set to 1. This will cause register A to be shifted one bit position to the right and a 1 to be added to register a, with the result placed back into register a. The effect of this procedure is to align the dividend so that $A < B$. If the result of the comparison does not produce a carry-out of the adder, then $A < B$ and the operation continues.

The exponents are now subtracted. As mentioned previously, this subtraction produces an exponent without a bias. The bias is applied to the exponent adder through a multiplexer, where it is added to the unbiased exponent in register a, and the result is returned to register a. The fraction division process is straightforward and was described previously in this section. The function of the n-bit fraction adder is to perform subtraction only. Thus, if the floating-point division unit is a stand-alone unit (that is, if its function is only fixed-point or floating-point division), then the hardware could be reduced by eliminating the EXCLUSIVE-OR circuits on the input to the fraction adder by loading the 1s complement of the divisor into register B and maintaining $C_{in} = 1$.

PROBLEMS

6.1 What is the minimum and maximum value of a seven-bit biased floating-point exponent?

6.2 Perform the following floating-point addition operation:

$$A_1 + A_2$$

where

$$A_1 = 0 . 1 0 1 1 0 0 \times r^5$$
$$A_2 = 0 . 1 1 1 0 0 0 \times r^2$$

for $r = 2$.

6.3 What is the lower limit of the product when multiplying the two smallest normalized fractions for $r = 2$?

6.4 What operations does the following equation represent for $r = 2$?

$$A_1 \times A_2 = [(f_1 \times f_2) \times r] \times r^{(e_1 + e_2) - 1}$$

6.5 What operations does the following equation represent for $r = 2$?

$$\frac{A_1}{A_2} = \left(\frac{f_1}{f_2} \times r^{-1} \right) \times r^{(e_1 - e_2) + 1}$$

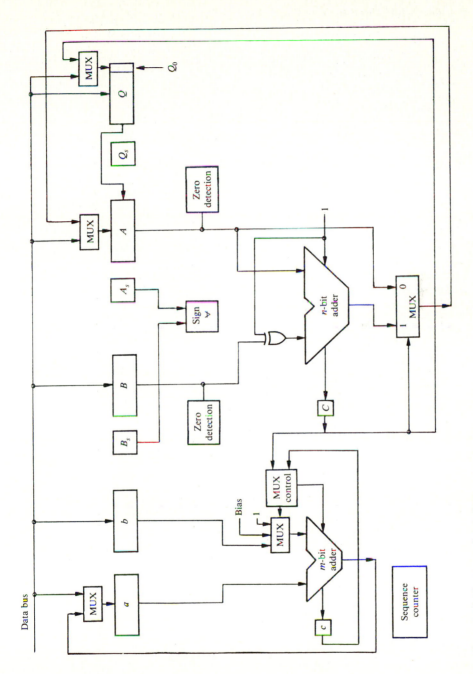

Figure 6.22 Floating-point division unit.

6.6 Perform the following floating-point addition operation:

$$A_1 + A_2$$

where

$$A_1 = 0\ 0\ 0\ 0\ 1\ 1\ 1\ 1$$
$$A_2 = 0\ 0\ 0\ 0\ 0\ 1\ 0\ 1$$

for $r = 2$. The operands should be in fractional normalized notation and the sum should be normalized.

6.7 Perform the following floating-point addition operation:

$$A_1 + A_2$$

where

$$A_1 = 0\ 0\ 1\ 1\ 1\ 0\ 1\ 1$$
$$A_2 = 0\ 0\ 0\ 0\ 0\ 1\ 1\ 0$$

for $r = 2$. The operands should be in fractional normalized notation and the sum should be normalized.

6.8 Under what conditions can there be an exponent overflow during floating-point arithmetic?

6.9 Compare fixed-point arithmetic and floating-point arithmetic with respect to:

(a) Operand range
(b) Speed of execution
(c) Precision
(d) Hardware design
(e) Software requirements

6.10 What are the advantages of floating-point arithmetic over fixed-point arithmetic?

6.11 What are the advantages of biased exponents in floating-point arithmetic?

6.12 Add the two floating-point numbers below.

31		24		0

$A = $ | 0 | 0 0 0 0 1 0 1 | 1 0 1 1 0 0 · · · 0 |

31		24		0

$B = $ | 0 | 0 0 0 0 0 1 0 | 1 1 1 0 0 0 · · · 0 |

6.13 Under what conditions do the following overflow/underflow situations occur?

(a) Fraction overflow
(b) Fraction underflow
(c) Exponent overflow
(d) Exponent underflow

6.14 Find the normalized machine representation for the following floating-point numbers using a 24-bit fraction, a seven-bit biased exponent, and a sign bit:

(a) $+9.75_{10}$ (b) -0.125_{10}

6.15 For a 24-bit fraction with a seven-bit exponent and a sign bit, determine:

(a) The largest positive number with an unbiased exponent
(b) The largest positive number with a biased exponent
(c) The most negative number with the most negative unbiased exponent
(d) The most negative number with the smallest biased exponent

Write your answers using the following format:

31	24	0

6.16 Perform the operations indicated for the following floating-point numbers using eight-bit fractions. Normalize the results, if necessary.

(a) -10
   $+)\ -35$

(b) -10
   $+)\ +33$

(c) $+24$
   $+)\ +20$

6.17 Perform the operations indicated for the following floating-point numbers using eight-bit fractions. Normalize the results, if necessary.

(a) $+35$
   $-)\ +12$

(b) -33
   $-)\ -10$

(c) $+36$
   $-)\ -\ 9$

6.18 Perform the operations indicated for the following floating-point numbers using eight-bit fractions. Normalize the results, if necessary.

(a) $+21$
   $+)\ -36$

(b) $+27$
   $+)\ +13$

(c) -18
   $-)\ +26$

6.19 Perform the operation indicated below for the floating-point operands using eight-bit fractions. Normalize the operands and write the result as a normalized floating-point fraction.

$$0\ .\ 0\ 0\ 1\ 0\ 1\ 1\ 0\ 0 \times 2^7$$
$$+)\ 0\ .\ 0\ 0\ 1\ 1\ 1\ 0\ 0\ 0 \times 2^4$$

6.20 Develop an algorithm in flowchart form to compare two biased floating-point exponents:

(a) By a subtraction operation
(b) By scanning and comparing bits of each exponent

6.21 During a floating-point addition operation on two n-bit operands, a shift count that is greater than or equal to n is produced during fraction alignment. What happens to the operands as a result of this shift-count value?

6.22 Design a logic circuit to detect leading 0s for the floating-point addition/subtraction unit of Fig. 6.9.

6.23 Design a magnitude comparator for two 16-bit operands. The logic family is ECL and the available logic gates are:

2 input
3 input
5 input
8 input
10 input

Use two 8-bit comparison circuits with provision for expanding the high-order 8 bits to accommodate 16-bit operands.

6.24 Multiply the following floating-point fractions using the sequential add-shift method. Normalize the results, is necessary.

(a)
A (multiplicand) $=\ 0\ .\ 1\ 1\ 0\ 0\ 1\ 0\ 0\ 0 \times 2^5$
$D \cdot B$ (multiplier) $=\ 0\ .\ 1\ 0\ 0\ 1\ 0\ 0\ 0\ 0 \times 2^4$

(b)
A (multiplicand) $=\ 0\ .\ 1\ 1\ 1\ 0\ 0\ 0\ 0\ 0 \times 2^4$
$D \cdot B$ (multiplier) $=\ 0\ .\ 1\ 0\ 1\ 0\ 0\ 0\ 0\ 0 \times 2^3$

6.25 How is quotient overflow determined in floating-point division? How is the problem resolved? After the problem is resolved, what is the range of the two operands for radix 2?

6.26 Comment on the biasing problem when the exponents are operated on during:

(a) Floating-point multiplication
(b) Floating-point division

In each case, how is the problem resolved?

6.27 Show that there can be no fraction overflow after a floating-point multiplication operation.

6.28 Show that the division of two normalized floating-point operands will result in a normalized quotient if the dividend is aligned before the division operation.

6.29 Show how an exponent overflow and underflow can be detected using biased exponents.

6.30 Explain the differences between:

(*a*) Fixed-point addition and floating-point addition

(*b*) Fixed-point subtraction and floating-point subtraction

(*c*) Fixed-point multiplication and floating-point multiplication

(*d*) Fixed-point division and floating-point division

SEVEN

ADDITIONAL FLOATING-POINT TOPICS

Previously, only normalized floating-point arithmetic was presented. This section will discuss unnormalized arithmetic operations and the advantages and disadvantages of such an approach. The design of a floating-point unit should be considered in terms of machine speed, machine cost, and numerical considerations. The processor should have the highest speed for the lowest cost; this is always true. Numerical considerations entails that the arithmetic processor should produce results that are as near as possible to the exact results. Errors resulting from a floating-point computation result primarily from normalization, truncation, or other roundoff procedures. Different roundoff techniques—and their accuracy—will be presented.

Guard digits are also discussed for the different floating-point operations. Exponent overflow and underflow are examined in greater detail. Multiple precision, as a means of obtaining high-precision results using existing small word lengths, is also included in this section. Finally, a change to the value of the implied base to increase the range of the scale factor is presented, and the IEEE proposal for floating-point arithmetic is outlined.

7.1 UNNORMALIZED FLOATING-POINT ARITHMETIC

The use of normalized floating-point notation may cause difficulty in determining the number of significant bits in the result. In many applications, the sequence of arithmetic operations may be sufficiently long so that the number of significant bits in the result may be much less than the word length. An indication of the number of significant bits in the intermediate and final results can be obtained more readily by adopting an unnormalized floating-point notation.

An unnormalized floating-point number A

$$A = f \times r^e \tag{7.1}$$

has a fraction with a value that is less than unity; that is,

$$|f| < 1$$

In fact, the unnormalized fraction may have a value less than r^{-1}, because the high-order fraction bit is not required to be a 1. For a radix of 2, this gives the fraction a form of 0.0 1 x x $\cdots$ x through 0.0 0 $\cdots$ 1 for nonzero fractions, which permits the unnormalized floating-point number to have many internal representations.

Let fraction f be a signed fraction in sign-magnitude form with n magnitude bits to the right of the radix point, and let the exponent e be a sign-magnitude integer with m bits plus sign and satisfying

$$0 \leqslant |e| \leqslant r^m - 1 \tag{7.2}$$

All previous floating-point operations have assumed normalized operands. However, the processor could receive unnormalized operands and prenormalize them before being processed by the floating-point hardware. This normalization process would decrease operational speed and require more hardware.

Unnormalized floating-point addition and subtraction are essentially the same as the normalized operations. However, a carry-out of the highest-order 1 does not cause a shift operation, unless the carry was from the high-order bit of the fraction. After the addition operation has been completed, the sum is truncated to the proper fraction length without performing normalization. Leading 0s are not eliminated in the result fraction.

Assume two unnormalized operands A_1 and A_2 such that

$$A_1 = f_1 \times r^{e_1}$$

and

$$A_2 = f_2 \times r^{e_2}$$

where f is the unnormalized fraction, e is the exponent, and r is the radix. Since addition is commutative, the assumption can be made that $e_1 \geqslant e_2$, without loss of generality. Also, addition and subtraction can be treated as same operation. The addition of two unnormalized floating-point operands is then defined as

$$A_1 + A_2$$
$$= (f_1 \times r^{e_1}) + (f_2 \times r^{e_2})$$
$$= [f_1 + (f_2 \times r^{e_2 - e_1})] \times r^{e_1} \qquad \text{for } | f_1 + (f_2 \times r^{e_2 - e_1}) | < 1$$
$$= \{[f_1 + (f_2 \times r^{e_2 - e_1})] \times r^{-1}\} r^{e_1 + 1} \quad \text{for } | f_1 + (f_2 \times r^{e_2 - e_1}) | \geqslant 1$$

$$(7.3)$$

The notation

$$| f_1 + (f_2 \times r^{e_2 - e_1}) | \geqslant 1$$

means that the resulting sum has a fraction that exceeds the upper limit. Thus, a right shift of one bit position is required. The definition of Eq. 7.3 is similar to the definition of normalized operand addition; however, no postnormalization is needed. Exponent underflow cannot occur.

Two examples are presented in Fig. 7.1, which demonstrate both situations of Eq. 7.3. The radix in these examples is 2. In Fig. 7.1(a), the result fraction 0.0 1 0 0 0 0 is less than unity, thereby requiring no adjustment. However, Fig. 7.1(b) produces a sum 1.0 0 1 0 1 0, which is in the range greater than or equal to unity. In this case, the result is multiplied by r^{-1} (2^{-1} for radix 2), which shifts the result one bit position to the right (equivalent to dividing by 2). The e_1 exponent is then taken as the result exponent and incremented by 1 to accommodate the right shift.

For unnormalized floating-point multiplication, additional nomenclature will be employed. Let z be defined as the number of leading 0s in the unnormalized fraction, for example,

$$f_1 = 0 . \overbrace{\underbrace{0\ 0\ 0\ 0\ 1}_{z_1}\ \text{x x x}}^{n}$$

Note that the value of $f_1 = 0$ when $z_1 = n$. Let e' be the adjusted exponent if normalization were to occur. Then, an unnormalized operand A_1 can be written as

$$A_1 = f_1' \times r^{e_1'} \qquad (7.4)$$

where

$$f_1' = f_1 \times r^{z_1} \qquad \text{and} \qquad e_1' = e_1 - z_1 \qquad (7.5)$$

For $\left| f_1 + (f_2 \times r^{e_2 - e_1}) \right| < 1$

$f_1 \times r^{e_1} = 0 . 0 0 1 1 0 0 \times 2^4 \qquad (+3)$

$f_2 \times r^{e_2} = 0 . 0 1 0 0 0 0 \times 2^2 \qquad (+1)$

$\downarrow$

$\qquad 0 . 0 0 1 1 0 0 \times 2^4$

$\qquad 0 . 0 1 0 0 0 0 \times 2^{2 - 4}$

$\downarrow$

$\qquad 0 . 0 0 1 1 0 0 \times 2^4$

$+)\ 0 . 0 0 0 1 0 0 \times 2^4$

Result $= \underbrace{0 . 0 1 0 0 0 0}_{< 1} \times 2^4 \qquad (+4)$

(*a*)

For $\left| f_1 + (f_2 \times r^{e_2 - e_1}) \right| \geqslant 1$

$f_1 \times r^{e_1} = 0 . 0 1 1 0 1 0 \times 2^5 \qquad (+13)$

$f_2 \times r^{e_2} = 0 . 1 1 0 0 0 0 \times 2^5 \qquad (+24)$

$\downarrow$

$\qquad 0 . 0 1 1 0 1 0 \times 2^5$

$\qquad 0 . 1 1 0 0 0 0 \times 2^{5 - 5} \qquad \text{(No shift required)}$

$\downarrow$

$\qquad 0 . 0 1 1 0 1 0 \times 2^5$

$+)\ 0 . 1 1 0 0 0 0 \times 2^5$

Result $= \underbrace{1 . 0 0 1 0 1 0}_{\geqslant 1} \times 2^5$

$\downarrow$

$\qquad 0 . 1 0 0 1 0 1 \times 2^6 \qquad (+37)$

(*b*)

Figure 7.1 Examples of unnormalized floating-point addition: (*a*) sum less than 1; (*b*) sum greater than or equal to 1.

Equation 7.5 represents the operand as the equivalent normalized number. Using the previous example, where $f_1 = 0.00001$ x x x and $r = 2$,

$$f_1' = f_1 \times 2^4$$

which multiplies the unnormalized fraction by 16, thereby normalizing the fraction. The equation $e_1' = e_1 - z_1$ simply adjusts the exponent due to the left shift.

This method now permits an unnormalized operand to be written as a normalized operand, thereby permitting use of Eq. 6.10, which is rewritten here.

$$
\begin{aligned}
A_1 \times A_2 &= (f_1 \times r^{e_1}) \times (f_2 \times r^{e_2}) \\
&= (f_1 \times f_2) \times r^{e_1 + e_2}
\end{aligned}
\tag{7.6}
$$

Assume $|f_1| \leqslant |f_2|$, which ensures that $z_1 \geqslant z_2$, as shown below.

$$
\overbrace{}^{z_1}
$$
$$A_1 = 0.00001 \text{ x x x}$$

$$
\overbrace{}^{z_2}
$$
$$A_2 = 0.0001 \text{ x x x x}$$

Then, the multiplication of two unnormalized operands A_1 and A_2 is as follows:

$$
\begin{aligned}
A_1 \times A_2 &= (f_1' \times r^{e_1'}) \times (f_2' \times r^{e_2'}) \\
&= (f_1' \times f_2') \times r^{e_1' + e_2'} \\
&= [(f_1 \times r^{z_1}) \times (f_2 \times r^{z_2})] \times r^{(e_1 - z_1) + (e_2 - z_2)} \\
&= [(f_1 \times f_2) \times r^{z_1 + z_2}] \times r^{e_1 + e_2 - z_1 - z_2} \\
&= (f_1 \times f_2) \times r^{e_1 + e_2}
\end{aligned}
\tag{7.7}
$$

which is identical to Eq. 7.6, indicating a similar procedure for multiplication of unnormalized numbers. However, the processor must be equipped with the ability to detect leading 0s, and thus determine which of the two numbers has the greater number of 0s to the left of the highest-order 1. This would be the number with the fewer significant bits. The product fraction should be shifted, if necessary, so that it contains the same number of leading 0s. The product exponent is adjusted accordingly.

Floating-point division of unnormalized operands can be similarly defined as

$$\frac{A_1}{A_2} = \frac{f_1' \times r^{e_1'}}{f_2' \times r^{e_2'}}$$

$$= \frac{f_1'}{f_2'} \times r^{e_1' - e_2'} \tag{7.8}$$

The processor must be similarly equipped for detecting leading 0s in the dividend and divisor and must have the ability to shift the quotient digits to obtain the same number of leading 0s to the left of the highest-order 1.

Normalized floating-point arithmetic may be less subject to roundoff errors, because rounding occurs over the full length of n of the fraction (the high-order bit always being equal to 1).

7.2 ROUNDING METHODS

Rounding a number deletes one or more of the least-significant digits in a positional number representation and adjusts the retained part in accordance with some specified rule. The purpose of rounding is to reduce the number of digits in the operand so that it can be contained within the word size of the machine. Rounding usually limits the precision of the number.

In many situations, the results of a floating-point operation may exceed the n digits allowed for a fraction. For example, the addition of two n-bit normalized numbers may result in a sum of $n + 1$ bits. In this case, the fraction sum overflow is handled by shifting the result one bit position to the right. This results in the loss of the least-significant bit. This section will discuss different methods for disposing of the additional low-order digits while preserving accurate results of high quality.

Rounding can be accomplished by rounding down, rounding up, or rounding off. Rounding down requires deleting the necessary low-order digits and making no adjustment to the retained part of the number. If a number is rounded down, its absolute value is not increased. This is a form of truncation. Rounding up requires deleting the necessary low-order digits and adjusting the retained part of the number by adding 1 to the low-order digit and executing any necessary carries. A 1 is added if and only if one or more nonzero digits have been deleted. If a number is rounded up, its absolute value is not decreased. Rounding off adjusts the retained part of the number by adding a 1 to the low-order digit and executing any necessary carries. A 1 is added if and only if the most significant digit deleted was equal to or greater than one-half the radix of its digit position. Whenever a number is rounded, a rounding error may result.

7.2.1 Truncation

Truncation is sometimes called *chopping*. It involves removing the additional bits and making no change to the remaining bits. While aligning fractions during a floating-point addition or subtraction, truncation could result in loss of several bits. There is obviously an error associated with truncation. For example, assume that it is necessary to truncate an eight-bit fraction

$$0 \cdot d_{-1} d_{-2} \cdots d_{-7} d_{-8}$$

to a four-bit fraction. All fractions in the range

$$0 \cdot d_{-1} d_{-2} d_{-3} d_{-4} \, 0 \, 0 \, 0 \, 0$$

to

$$0 \cdot d_{-1} d_{-2} d_{-3} d_{-4} \, 1 \, 1 \, 1 \, 1$$

would be truncated to

$$0 \cdot d_{-1} d_{-2} d_{-3} d_{-4}$$

The error in the four-bit result ranges from 0 to 0.0 0 0 0 1 1 1 1. In general, the error in truncating ranges from 0 to approximately 1 in the low-order position of the retained bits—in this case, in the 2^{-4} position.

   Truncation is a fast and simple method for disposing of fraction underflow digits and requires no additional hardware, but it may introduce a significant error. The truncation error is plotted in Fig. 7.2 and indicates that the truncation function lies entirely below the ideal truncation line, touching it only where there is no truncation error.

7.2.2 Adder-based Rounding

The floating-point multiplication of two *n*-bit operands produced a 2*n*-bit product. Recall that the low-order *n* bits were truncated and a 1 was added to the high-order *n* bits if the high-order bit in the lower half was a 1. This is one way of rounding off the low-order bits. The result is rounded to the nearest number that can be contained in *n* bits. When a 1 is added to the remaining bits, the carry, if any, is propagated to the left. If rounding causes a carry-out of the high-order bit position, then the fraction is shifted one bit position to the right and the exponent is incremented by 1.

   The rounding procedure adds a 1 to the low-order bit position of the retained bits if there is a 1 in the high-order bit position of the removed bits. Thus, $0 \cdot d_{-1} d_{-2} d_{-3} d_{-4} \, 1$ rounds to $0 \cdot d_{-1} d_{-2} d_{-3} d_{-4} + 0 . 0 \, 0 \, 0 \, 1$, and $0 \cdot d_{-1} d_{-2} d_{-3} d_{-4} \, 0$ rounds to $0 \cdot d_{-1} d_{-2} d_{-3} d_{-4}$. The former ap-

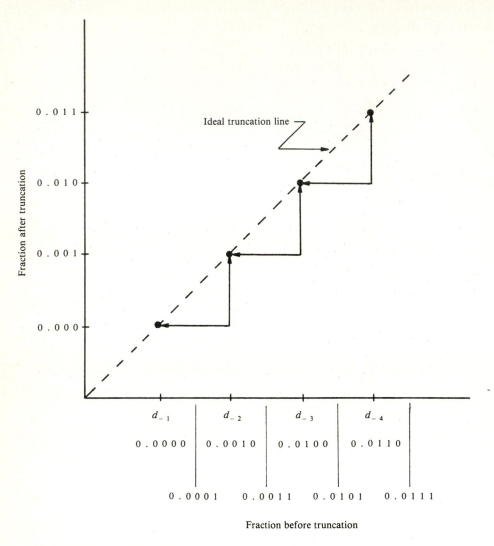

Figure 7.2 Truncation of underflow digits.

proaches the true value from above and the latter approaches the true value from below. This is better illustrated by the examples in Fig. 7.3

Another way to view this is when the low-order portion being rounded off has a value greater than or equal to one-half of its maximum value, then a 1 is added to the high-order portion. This causes the true value to be approached from above; otherwise, it is approached from below. Thus, in Fig. 7.3(*a*), the portion to be rounded off (deleted) has a maximum value of $1\ 1\ 1\ 1_2$, which is 15_{10}, while its actual value is 8_{10}. Since $8 \geqslant 7.5$, a 1 is added to the retained portion. However, in Fig. 7.3(*b*), the actual value of the portion to be deleted is 7_{10}. Since

$$\text{Delete}$$
$$0 . 0 0 1 0 \mid \overbrace{1\ 0\ 0\ 0} \times 2^8 \quad (+40 = \text{true value})$$

Add $\quad 0 . 0 0 0 1$
_____

Rounded $\quad 0 . 0 0 1 1 \mid \qquad \times 2^8 \quad (+48)$
result

$$(a)$$

$$\text{Delete}$$
$$0 . 0 0 1 0 \mid \overbrace{0\ 1\ 1\ 1} \times 2^8 \quad (+39 = \text{true value})$$

Rounded $\quad 0 . 0 0 1 0 \mid \qquad \times 2^8 \quad (+32)$
result

$$(b)$$

Figure 7.3 Rounding procedure: (a) true value approached from above; (b) true value approached from below.

$7 < 7.5$, the low-order portion is simply deleted and no addition takes place on the retained portion.

Figure 7.4 shows a plot of the rounding technique, which is nearly symmetric with respect to the ideal rounding line—a great improvement over truncation. The points halfway between the d_i numbers are always rounded up; that is, they approach the true value from above. Thus, a long sequence of operations involving rounding may create a slight positive bias.

Rounding is clearly a better method than truncation. However, it entails an added cost in both hardware and time, because it requires an extra addition operation. Adder-based rounding is seldom used in floating-point units.

7.2.3 Von Neumann Rounding

The von Neumann rounding technique is also referred to as *jamming*. This technique is similar to truncation, in which the bits to be deleted are truncated and the low-order bit of the retained portion is always set to 1. Thus, when eight-bit fractions are rounded to four-bit fractions using the von Neumann technique, fractions in the range

$$0 \cdot d_{-1} d_{-2} d_{-3}\ 0\ 0\ 0\ 0\ 0 \text{ to } 0 \cdot d_{-1} d_{-2} d_{-3}\ 1\ 1\ 1\ 1\ 1$$

will all be rounded to $0 \cdot d_{-1} d_{-2} d_{-3}\ 1$. Therefore, the error in this method ranges from -1 in the low-order bit of the retained portion for the case in which

$$0 \cdot d_{-1} d_{-2} d_{-3} \, 0 \, 0 \, 0 \, 0 \, 0$$

is rounded to

$$0 \cdot d_{-1} d_{-2} d_{-3} \, 1$$

to almost 1 in the low-order bit of the retained portion for the case in which

$$0 \cdot d_{-1} d_{-2} d_{-3} \, 1 \, 1 \, 1 \, 1 \, 1$$

is rounded to

$$0 \cdot d_{-1} d_{-2} d_{-3} \, 1$$

Although the range of error is larger with this technique than with truncation, the error range is symmetrical about the ideal rounding line, as shown in Fig. 7.5. If it can be assumed that the individual errors are evenly distributed over the error range, then positive errors should tend to offset negative errors for long sequences of computations that involve rounding. The von Neumann method of rounding has the same total bias as the previous rounding method, but it requires no more time than truncation.

7.2.4 Read-Only Memory Rounding

This method can be implemented using a read-only memory (ROM) or combinational logic. The adder-based rounding technique described previously reqires an additional cycle and additional hardware to accommodate the carry propagation resulting from a 1 being added to the low-order bit of the retained portion of the fraction. This additional time required to complete the rounding operation can be eliminated by the ROM rounding technique.

This is an implementation for reducing a floating-point fraction to a smaller fraction with a less precise approximation. The shorter fraction is the correct word size after the appropriate rounding operation has been completed. Consider a floating-point fraction as shown in Fig. 7.6. This fraction is used directly in the ROM rounding method. Assume that ROM requires a k-bit address. This scheme uses the $k - 1$ low-order bits of the portion of the fraction that is to be retained, together with the high-order bit of the portion that is to be rounded off. These bits form the k-bit address to ROM, which has 2^k words and produces a correctly rounded $(k - 1)$-bit result, except when the $k - 1$ low-order bits are all 1s. In this case, truncation is performed instead of rounding. However, this is not critical because the remaining 255 of 256 cases are correctly rounded.

Figure 7.7 shows the logical organization for the ROM rounding method for $k = 8$. The $(k - 1)$-bit output from ROM, which contains the correctly round-

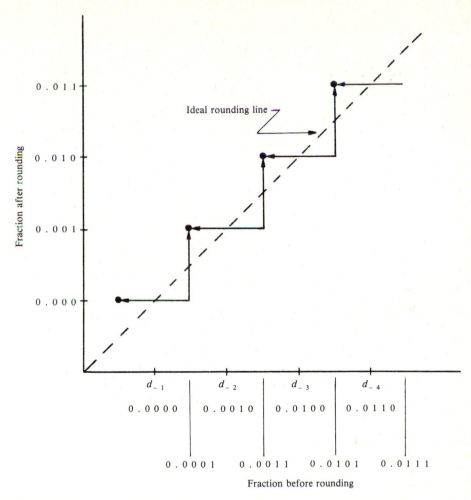

Figure 7.4 Rounding of underflow digits.

ed $k - 1$ bits of the fraction, are loaded back into the same bit positions of the fraction. Since time-consuming addition with full carry lookahead is not required, the ROM table lookup approach can be very fast. The actual rounding is performed with the appropriate addition operation implemented by ROM programming. The technique is inexpensive to implement with present memory technology, and speeds of less than 5 ns can easily be attained.

7.3 GUARD DIGITS

Although the fractions of initial operands and final results contain n bits, it is important to have additional bits, called *guard digits* (or *bits*), during the intermediate steps. This permits maximum accuracy to be retained in the result.

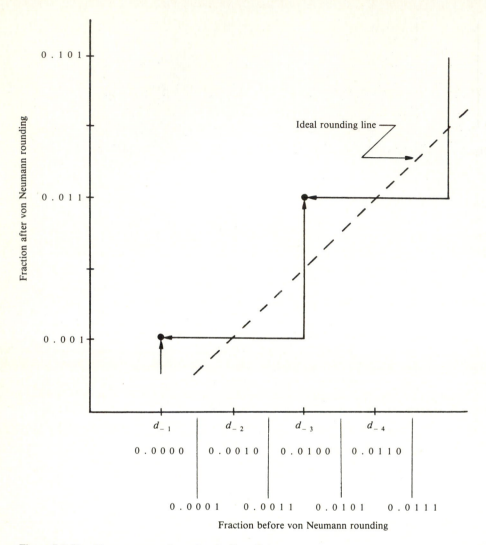

Figure 7.5 Von Neumann rounding of underflow digits.

The guard digits consist of the low-order bits to the right of the n significant bits of the fraction, and may contain one or more bits. The guard digits hold the part of the aligned operand that is shifted right during exponent comparison, and give added precision to the final fraction. These digits may be used with any rounding scheme described previously.

When two n-bit fractions are added and one fraction is shifted right during alignment, the bits that are shifted off the right end can be retained in a guard-digit register and used during the rounding operation. There is no need to save these bits if truncation is to be performed. At minimum, the last bit shifted out must be saved for rounding.

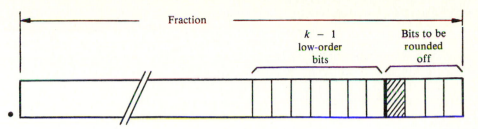

Figure 7.6 Floating-point fraction used in ROM rounding technique.

In normalized floating-point multiplication, two n-bit fractions produce a $2n$-bit result. There may be one leading 0 in the high-order bit position of the result, which requires a left shift of one bit position to postnormalize the result. If truncation is used to obtain an n-bit result, then at least one bit of the lower n-bit portion (the high-order bit) must be retained as a guard bit. This guard bit then becomes the low-order bit of the n-bit result after postnormalization. If rounding is to be performed, then at least two bits of the lower n-bit portion (the two high-order bits) must be retained as guard bits—one for postnormalization and one for rounding.

If no guard bits are retained during a multiplication, then less precise results can be expected. If truncation is performed using one guard bit, then more precise results will be obtained. Even more precise results can be expected using a rounding scheme and two guard bits.

There may also be a third guard bit, which is the low-order bit of the three guard bits. This low-order bit has the property that if a 1 is ever shifted into it during fraction alignment, it is set to 1 and remains in that state; otherwise, it remains a 0. This is useful in some rounding methods in which it is necessary to know if any 1s were shifted right during alignment. This bit will generate any carry sequencs to its left, as would occur if there were additional guard bits.

This discussion on guard bits has been presented for the binary case where the radix is 2. It applies equally well to any radix; for example, radix 16 would refer to guard digits, where each digit is four bits. For a machine with an n-bit fraction, only n bits may be kept in main storage and in the programmable registers of the machine. Therefore, the guard digits are used only within the arithmetic processor. In some operations, it would be advantageous to retain the guard digits throughout the central processing unit and to truncate them when placing the results in storage. This would mean additional hardware in the form of wider registers, but would yield more precise results without having to maintain double precision throughout the machine.

7.4 OVERFLOW AND UNDERFLOW

The fractions in floating-point operands are processed using fixed-point arithmetic. During fixed-point addition or subtraction, an overflow can occur.

The following comments can be made about overflow during an addition operation.

1. When two positive numbers or two negative numbers are added together, an overflow occurs when the carry-in to the high-order bit position is different from the carry-out of the high-order bit position.
2. When a positive number is added to a negative number, an overflow cannot occur.

Although the first rule represents a true overflow in fixed-point arithmetic, it is only a temporary condition in floating-point arithmetic, because the fraction is simply shifted right and the exponent incremented by 1. It is the exponent overflow in floating-point arithmetic that is of primary concern.

When two n-bit numbers are multiplied, the result is a $2n$-bit product. A $2n$-bit accumulator is provided to store the result, and an overflow cannot occur because the product of two numbers can always be correctly represented in a double-length result register. However, in division, it is possible for the quotient to exceed the range of the number representation of the machine.

During floating-point arithmetic, the exponent of the result can exceed its allowable range. Exponent overflow can occur if the exponent exceeds the most positive number or the most negative number of its allowable range. If the exponent exceeds the range in the positive direction, this results in an exponent overflow. If it exceeds the range in the negative direction, this results in an exponent underflow. The overflow bit is set only when the exponent overflows in the positive direction. It is not set when a temporary overflow occurs in the fraction.

During addition or subtraction, normalization of the result fraction may induce an overflow in the result exponent. During multiplication, no temporary fraction overflow can occur; however, the exponent addition caused by the operation can directly cause an exponent overflow. During division, overflow can occur in different ways. If the divisor is 0, the overflow bit can be set as well as the divide-by-0 check bit; the operation is then terminated. Also, exponent overflow can occur in division when exponents of opposite signs are subtracted, for example, $(+e_1) - (-e_2)$. This may result in an exponent integer that is outside the range of the exponent field. Finally, the normalization that takes place to correct a temporary overflow of the quotient fraction can cause an exponent overflow similar to addition.

The conditions that cause an exponent underflow are the same as those that cause an overflow, except that negative numbers are employed. For example, exponent underflow can occur in multiplication when two negative exponents are added, that is, $(-e_1) + (-e_2)$. Exponent underflow can occur in division when two exponents of opposite signs are subtracted, that is, $(-e_1) - (+e_2)$. When an underflow is detected, two actions can take place.

1. An underflow bit is set and corrective action is taken.
2. The fraction and exponent of the result are set to 0.

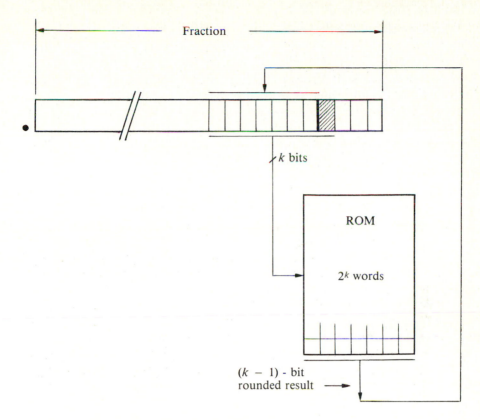

k bits

ROM

2^k words

$(k - 1)$ - bit
rounded result

Figure 7.7 Organization for ROM rounding.

Step 2 may not be sufficiently precise for some programs. Such programs run suc-
cessfully when the underflow is gradual, but fail when the underflow causes the
result to be reset to 0.

An alternative correction of an underflow situation is to dynamically increase
the range of the exponent at the expense of reducing the precision of the fraction.
However, this dynamic expansion of the exponent range may be unacceptable
because of fluctuating precision, increased hardware cost, and more complicated
error analysis.

7.5 MULTIPLE PRECISION

Multiple-precision arithmetic, which is used for high-precision computations, can
be designed into large or small computers when greater precision is needed than
can be obtained from the existing word length of the machine. Double-precision
arithmetic allows a computer to operate with the same precision as a machine
with twice the word length.

Double-precision floating-point numbers are usually stored in two consecutive storage locations. The high-order half is stored in the lower-addressed word of the pair of words, and the low-order half is stored in the higher-addressed word. Consider the floating-point format of Fig. 7.8 for a 32-bit operand. If double-precision operation is specified, then the double-length operand is stored as shown in Fig. 7.9. Bits 24–31 of the low-order half may not be used. This permits use of a 24-bit adder and does not require any special operand alignment. Alternatively, the entire 32 bits of the low-order word could be used, requiring a 32-bit adder with bits 56–63 of the high-order word considered as 0s.

Using the full length of the low-order half of the double-precision operand of Fig. 7.9, and for radix $= 2$, a floating-point operand A can be expressed as

$$A = f \times 2^e$$

where $|f|$ is in the range

$$\frac{1}{2} \leqslant |f| \leqslant 1 - 2^{-56} \tag{7.9}$$

The range of f is equivalent to

$$0 \cdot 1 0 0 \cdots 0 \leqslant |f| \leqslant 0 \cdot 1 1 \cdots 1$$

The right side of Eq. 7.9 is equal to $0 \cdot 1 1 \cdots 1$, because

$$
\begin{array}{r}
1 - 2^{-56} = \quad 1 \cdot 0 0 0 \cdots 0 0 \\
-)\, 0 \cdot 0 0 0 \cdots 0 1 \\
\hline
\end{array}
$$

$$
\begin{array}{r}
1 \cdot 0 0 0 \cdots 0 0 \\
+)\, 1 \cdot 1 1 1 \cdots 1 1 \\
\hline
0 \cdot 1 1 1 \cdots 1 1 \\
\end{array}
$$

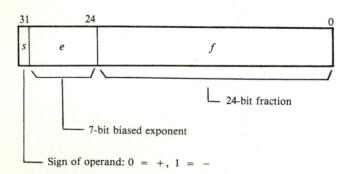

Figure 7.8 Floating-point format for 32-bit operands.

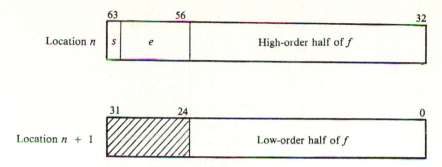

Figure 7.9 Double-precision floating-point operand.

7.5.1 Addition and Subtraction

For the format used in this text, double-precision addition requires a double-length shift register to contain the fraction with the smaller exponent. Consider two double-length floating-point operands A and B, as shown below,

$$A = \boxed{ \quad e_a \quad\quad f_{a_H}} \quad\quad \boxed{\quad\quad\quad f_{a_L} \quad\quad\quad}$$

$$B = \boxed{ \quad e_b \quad\quad f_{b_H}} \quad\quad \boxed{\quad\quad\quad f_{b_L} \quad\quad\quad}$$

and assume that $e_b \geqslant e_a$. Operand A parts (f_{a_H} and f_{a_L}) are loaded into concatenated registers $A_H \cdot A_L$ in Fig. 7.10, where the fraction is shifted right, with corresponding increments to e_a, until $e_a = e_b$. If $\mid e_a - e_b \mid \geqslant 56$, then the operation should be terminated, because all of the significant bits in A will be lost. Operand B part f_{b_L} is loaded into register B, and the sum of $A_L + B$ is formed and stored in register A_L. The carry bit is saved. The following load operation then takes place:

$$B \leftarrow f_{b_H}$$

Then the sum of $A_H + B + C$ is formed and stored in A_H.

The sum in register-pair $A_H \cdot A_L$ is then normalized, if necessary, by shifting left

$$A_H \cdot A_L \leftarrow A_H \cdot A_L \cdot \text{guard bit}$$

Storage bus

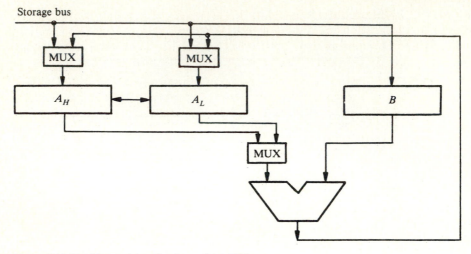

Figure 7.10 Double-precision floating-point addition.

and rounding or truncating as desired. If 56 left shifts are not sufficient for normalization, then the sum should be made 0. The sum is stored as follows:

$$\text{Sum}_n \leftarrow A_{H_S} \cdot e_a \cdot A_H$$
$$\text{Sum}_{n+1} \leftarrow A_L$$

Subtraction is identical to the above description after the B operand has been 2s-complemented.

7.5.2 Multiplication

Given two operands A and B, where

$$\text{Multiplicand} = A = f_a \times 2^{e_a}$$

and

$$\text{Multiplier} = B = f_b \times 2^{e_b}$$

then the computational procedure for $A \times B$ is

$$A \times B = (f_a \times 2^{e_a}) \times (f_b \times 2^{e_b})$$
$$= \text{sign} \cdot (|f_a| \times |f_b|) \times 2^{e_a + e_b} \quad (7.10)$$

Exponent addition is the same as single-precision floating-point multiplication. A problem occurs when attempting to multiply two 56-bit operands (yielding a 112-bit product) using 32-bit hardware in the floating-point unit. The solution is to partition the operation into sequences that produce subproducts and then add the appropriately shifted subproducts to yield the final product. Two double-length operands A and B are formatted below.

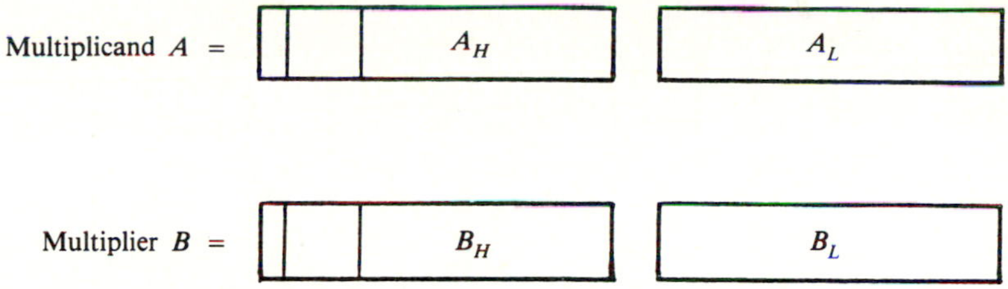

Multiplicand A =

| | A_H | | A_L |

Multiplier B =

| | B_H | | B_L |

The product is defined by

$$
\begin{aligned}
\text{Product} &= A \times B \\
&= (A_H \cdot A_L) \times (B_H \cdot B_L) \\
&= (A_H \times B_H) + (A_H \times B_L) + (A_L \times B_H) + (A_L \times B_L)
\end{aligned}
$$

$$(7.11)$$

Equation 7.11 indicates that four 64-bit subproducts are generated, which, when appropriately aligned and added, produce the desired product.

For simplicity, and without loss of generality, assume that

$$
\begin{aligned}
A &= (A_H = 0\ 1\ 0\ 1) \cdot (A_L = 1\ 1\ 1\ 0) = +94 \\
B &= (B_H = 0\ 0\ 1\ 0) \cdot (B_L = 0\ 0\ 1\ 1) = +35
\end{aligned}
$$

└─ Implied radix point

The operation $A \times B$ is as follows:

$$
\begin{array}{l}
0\ .\ 1\ 0\ 1\ 1\ 1\ 1\ 0\ 0 \times 2^7 \quad (+94) \\
0\ .\ 1\ 0\ 0\ 0\ 1\ 1\ 0\ 0 \times 2^6 \quad (+35)
\end{array}
$$

$$
\begin{array}{rcl}
& 0\ 0\ 0\ 0\ 0\ 0\ 0\ 0 & \\
& 0\ 0\ 0\ 0\ 0\ 0\ 0\ 0 & \\
A_H \times B_L & 1\ 0\ 1\ 1\ 1\ 1\ 0\ 0 & A_L \times B_L \\
& 1\ 0\ 1\ 1\ 1\ 1\ 0\ 0 & \\
& 0\ 0\ 0\ 0\ 0\ 0\ 0\ 0 & \\
& 0\ 0\ 0\ 0\ 0\ 0\ 0\ 0 & \\
A_H \times B_H & 0\ 0\ 0\ 0\ 0\ 0\ 0\ 0 & A_L \times B_H \\
& 1\ 0\ 1\ 1\ 1\ 1\ 0\ 0 &
\end{array}
$$

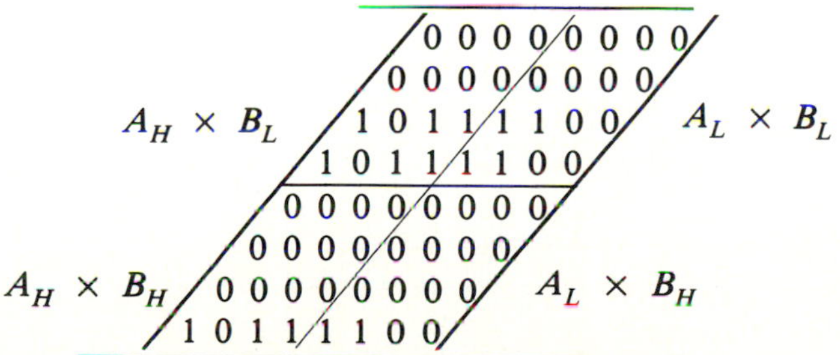

$$
0\ .\ 0\ 1\ 1\ 0\ 0\ 1\ 1\ 0\ 1\ 1\ 0\ 1\ 0\ 0\ 0\ 0 \times 2^{13} \quad (+3290)
$$

The process produces four subproducts: $A_L \times B_L$, $A_H \times B_L$, $A_L \times B_H$, and $A_H \times B_H$. The multiply operation can be subdivided into four distinct multiply partitions, each yielding an eight-bit subproduct. This is shown in Fig. 7.11. The 4 eight-bit subproducts are then aligned and added as shown in Fig. 7.12.

The 32-bit adder is used to add the subproducts, as shown in Fig. 7.12(b). $(A_L \times B_L)_L$ is left unchanged. $(A_L \times B_L)_H$ is added to $(A_H \times B_L)_L$ and the carry C_1 is saved. This sum is added to $(A_L \times B_H)_L$ to produce part of the final product. Carry C_2 is saved. $(A_H \times B_L)_H$ is added to $(A_L \times B_H)_H$ together with C_1. The carry C_3 is saved. The sum thus formed is added to $(A_H \times B_H)_L$ together with C_2, and the carry C_4 is saved. This sum becomes part of the final product. Finally, $(A_H \times B_H)_H$ is added to C_3 and C_4 to yield part of the final product.

The product is normalized and rounded, if necessary, probably by means of firmware, since a pure hardware normalization would necessitate a 112-bit register as well as a guard bit. A small register could also be used if sufficient temporary storage were available and the processor had the capability to merge words. Appropriate adjustment of the exponent $e_a + e_b$ due to normalization must be performed. The final normalized product, together with the final exponent and sign, is stored in four consecutive storage locations.

7.5.3 Division

Given two operands A and B, where

$$\text{Dividend} = A = f_a \times 2^{e_a}$$

and

$$\text{Divisor} = B = f_b \times 2^{e_b}$$

then the computational procedure for A/B is

$$\frac{A}{B} = \frac{f_a \times 2^{e_a}}{f_b \times 2^{e_b}}$$

$$= \text{sign} \cdot \left| \frac{f_a}{f_b} \right| \times 2^{e_a - e_b} \tag{7.12}$$

To prevent overflow, the divisor must be less than the dividend; that is,

$$\left| \frac{f_a}{f_b} \right| < 1 \tag{7.13}$$

$$
\begin{array}{r}
A_L = \quad 1\ 1\ 0\ 0 \\
B_L = \quad \times)\ 1\ 1\ 0\ 0 \\
\hline
0\ 0\ 0\ 0 \\
0\ 0\ 0\ 0 \\
1\ 1\ 0\ 0 \\
1\ 1\ 0\ 0 \\
\hline
\end{array}
$$

$A_L \times B_L = \underbrace{1\ 0\ 0\ 1}\ \underbrace{0\ 0\ 0\ 0}$

$(A_L \times B_L)_H\ (A_L \times B_L)_L$

$$
\begin{array}{r}
A_H = \quad 1\ 0\ 1\ 1 \\
B_L = \quad \times)\ 1\ 1\ 0\ 0 \\
\hline
0\ 0\ 0\ 0 \\
0\ 0\ 0\ 0 \\
1\ 0\ 1\ 1 \\
1\ 0\ 1\ 1 \\
\hline
\end{array}
$$

$A_H \times B_L = \underbrace{1\ 0\ 0\ 0}\ \underbrace{0\ 1\ 0\ 0}$

$(A_H \times B_L)_H\ (A_H \times B_L)_L$

$$
\begin{array}{r}
A_L = \quad 1\ 1\ 0\ 0 \\
B_H = \quad \times)\ 1\ 0\ 0\ 0 \\
\hline
0\ 0\ 0\ 0 \\
0\ 0\ 0\ 0 \\
0\ 0\ 0\ 0 \\
1\ 1\ 0\ 0 \\
\hline
\end{array}
$$

$A_L \times B_H = \underbrace{0\ 1\ 1\ 0}\ \underbrace{0\ 0\ 0\ 0}$

$(A_L \times B_H)_H\ (A_L \times B_H)_L$

$$
\begin{array}{r}
A_H = \quad 1\ 0\ 1\ 1 \\
B_H = \quad \times)\ 1\ 0\ 0\ 0 \\
\hline
0\ 0\ 0\ 0 \\
0\ 0\ 0\ 0 \\
0\ 0\ 0\ 0 \\
1\ 0\ 1\ 1 \\
\hline
\end{array}
$$

$A_H \times B_H = \underbrace{0\ 1\ 0\ 1}\ \underbrace{1\ 0\ 0\ 0}$

$(A_H \times B_H)_H\ (A_H \times B_H)_L$

Figure 7.11 Double-precision multiplication subproducts.

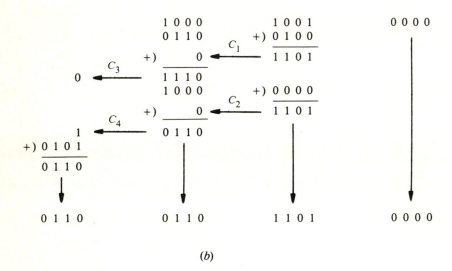

(a)

(b)

Figure 7.12 Double-precision multiplication: (a) subproduct alignment, (b) subproduct addition.

If Eq. 7.13 is not initially true, then the dividend must be shifted one bit position to the right. Equation 7.12 then becomes

$$\frac{A}{B} = \text{sign} \cdot \left| \frac{f_a/2}{f_b} \right| \times 2^{e_a - e_b + 1} \tag{7.14}$$

Double-precision division is frequently executed by firmware. It is a complex routine that is not as readily applicable to hardware implementation as double-precision multiplication. Two double-length operands A and B are formatted as follows:

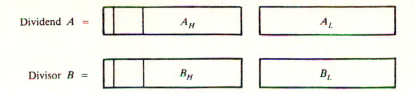

A and B can be written in the form

$$A_H + (A_L \times k)$$

$$B_H + (B_L \times k)$$
(7.15)

where k is the reciprocal of the word size of the processor, typically 2^{-32}. Then the division operation becomes

$$\frac{A_H + (A_L \times k)}{B_H + (B_L \times k)}$$

which can be expanded to

$$\frac{A_H + (A_L \times k)}{B_H + (B_L \times k)} = \frac{A_H + (A_L \times k)}{B_H} \left[\frac{1}{1 + (B_L/B_H)k} \right]$$

and further expanded into an alternating series such that

$$\frac{A_H + (A_L \times k)}{B_H + (B_L \times k)} = \frac{A_H + (A_L \times k)}{B_H} \left[1 - \left(\frac{B_L}{B_H} \right) k + \left(\frac{B_L}{B_H} \right)^2 k^2 - \cdots \right]$$

Since

$$0 \leqslant B_L < 1$$

and

$$\frac{1}{2} \leqslant B_H < 1$$

then the error incurred by deleting the $(B_L / B_H)^2 k^2$ term and all successive terms can be disregarded. Therefore, the division algorithm reduces to

$$\frac{A}{B} = \frac{A_H + (A_L \times k)}{B_H} \left[1 - \left(\frac{B_L}{B_H} \right) k \right]$$
(7.16)

The division of two normalized floating-point operands always results in a normalized quotient if the dividend alignment is performed before the division operation. The exponent is also adjusted at that time. Therefore, no postnormalization is required on the quotient. The final normalized quotient, together with the final exponent and sign, is stored in consecutive storage locations.

7.6   HEXADECIMAL RADIX

A specific format for a floating-point number is shown in Fig. 7.13. The implied base (radix) is 2 and the exponent is a 2s complement integer. The fraction is normalized with the binary point at the left end, as indicated. Thus, the magnitude of the fraction is either 0 or within the range

$$\frac{1}{2} \leqslant |f| < 1$$

The exponent has a range of $1\,0\,0\,0\,0\,0\,0_2$ (-64_{10}) to $0\,1\,1\,1\,1\,1\,1_2$ $(+63_{10})$. Thus, the scale factor with radix 2 has a range of

$$2^{1\,000000} = 2^{-64} \text{ to } 2^{0\,111111} = 2^{63}$$

This range may not be large enough for all applications. The number of bits in the exponent could be increased, but this would mean a reduction in the number of bits in the fraction with a resulting decrease in accuracy, if the 32-bit format is to be maintained. One solution that has been implemented is to increase the value of the implied radix. The radix should be a power of 2 so that shifting the fraction right or left can be accompanied by a corresponding increase or decrease in the exponent, respectively.

An implied radix of 16 is a popular choice. The fraction is considered to be multiplied by a power of 16 and the exponent indicates the power. Thus, the range of the scale factor becomes

$$16^{-64} \leqslant \text{scale factor} \leqslant 16^{63}$$

Since the implied radix is 16, the fraction must be shifted in groups of four bits. Each four-bit shift will increase or decrease the exponent by 1. Hexadecimal normalization is accomplished when any of the four leading bits is a 1. Hexadecimal numbers may have three leading 0s in a digit. This means that less accuracy may be achieved than with a radix of 2 for the same size fraction. However, not as many exponent bits are required with a radix of 16

Table 7.1 compares the number of bits required for a radix 2 exponent versus a radix 16 exponent. For radix 2, three exponent bits are required, whereas for radix 16 only one exponent bit is required. It is easy to see the wider range that is achieved due to the higher radix. The table also indicates that less shifting occurs in radix 16 representation, which may result in a simpler implementation.

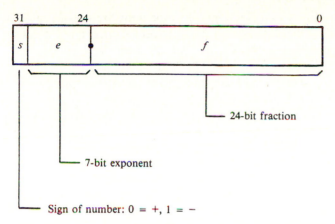

Figure 7.13 A 32-bit floating-point format.

Unbiased exponents are in the range

$$- 64 \leqslant e \leqslant 63$$

An unbiased exponent has a bias of 64 added to it (excess -64 format) for internal machine representation. Thus, a biased exponent is represented as

$$e_{biased} = e_{unbiased} + 64$$

so that the biased exponents have a range

$$0 \leqslant e_{biased} \leqslant 127$$

Table 7.1 Binary versus hexadecimal exponent representation

Number	$r = 2$		$r = 16$	
	f	r^e	f	r^e
0.0001	0.1	r^{-011}	0.0001	r^0
0.0010	0.1	r^{-010}	0.0010	r^0
0.0100	0.1	r^{-001}	0.0100	r^0
0.1000	0.1	r^{000}	0.1000	r^0
1.0000	0.1	r^{001}	0.0001	r^1
10.0000	0.1	r^{010}	0.0010	r^1
100.0000	0.1	r^{011}	0.0100	r^1
1000.0000	0.1	r^{100}	0.1000	r^1
10000.0000	0.1	r^{101}	0.00010000	r^2

The smallest scale factor 16^{-64} is then represented by 0 0 0 0 0 0 0, and the largest scale factor 16^{63} is represented by 1 1 1 1 1 1 1. Biased exponents permit the use of simple magnitude comparators to determine the relative size of two floating-point numbers.

Figure 7.14 shows an unnormalized fraction and the corresponding normalized version for radix 16 representation. The power of 16 shown in the figure is the unbiased exponent value. The value of the exponent within the partitioned floating-point number is the biased value, and thus has 1 0 0 0 0 0 0$_2$ (64_{10}) added to the exponent.

Let us discuss one final point regarding normalization and exponent size for radix 2 representation. After normalization, the leftmost bit is always a 1. This bit could be made implicit, resulting in an increase in the number of bits in the exponent. The one additional bit in the exponent due to the implied leading 1 in the normalized fraction increases the range of the biased exponent.

7.7 IEEE FLOATING-POINT STANDARD

This section summarizes the IEEE proposed standard for floating-point arithmetic. The implementation of a floating-point system based upon this standard can be realized in hardware, software, or a combination of both hardware and software. The standard specifies:

1. The format for floating-point operands
2. The accuracy of arithmetic results for addition, subtraction, multiplication, division, square root generation, obtaining remainders, and comparison operations
3. Conversion between integers and floating-point numbers
4. Conversion between different floating-point formats as specified in the proposal
5. Conversion between binary floating-point numbers and decimal numbers.
6. Floating-point exceptions.

7.7.1 Major Considerations

Three major considerations are contained in the proposal:

1. The format of the floating-point numbers
2. The accuracy of the arithmetic computations
3. The handling of exception conditions

There are two basic formats for floating-point operands: 32 bits and 64 bits. Radix 2 was chosen rather than radix 8 (octal) or radix 16 (hexadecimal) in order to maintain a high degree of precision. The leftmost significant bit of the fraction

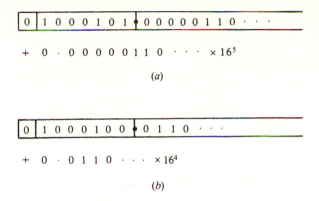

$$+ \quad 0 \cdot 0\ 0\ 0\ 0\ 0\ 1\ 1\ 0 \quad \cdots \quad \times 16^5$$

(a)

$$+ \quad 0 \cdot 0\ 1\ 1\ 0 \quad \cdots \quad \times 16^4$$

(b)

Figure 7.14 Normalization example for radix 16: (a) unnormalized fraction, (b) normalized version.

is not represented for normalized numbers, thus allowing the number of bits in the exponent field to be increased by 1. The exponent bias is chosen such that the reciprocal of all normalized numbers can be represented without causing an exponent overflow. The exponent range for the 64-bit format was chosen so that the product of eight 32-bit numbers would not overflow the 64-bit format.

The proposal also specifies extended-precision operations including intermediate results, which have a range and precision greater than the requirements of a basic format but do not need the number of bits required for double precision. This increases the precision of the final result by reducing rounding errors. Extended precision is supplied in order to obtain higher-precision results without the increased delay normally associated with higher precision. However, the standard requires only single precision to be implemented.

The standard requires accurate arithmetic results and proposes additional bits to achieve this goal. A guard bit, a round bit, and a sticky bit are placed to the immediate right of the low-order fraction bit, as illustrated in Fig. 7.15. Any number of guard digits could be used, but the number can be limited to three by introducing a sticky bit, which is set to 1 and remains set if a 1 is shifted into it during alignment; otherwise, it remains at 0. Recall that if truncation is used to obtain a $2n$-bit product, then a $(2n + 1)$-bit result must be developed to accommodate postnormalization. If rounding is to be used, then $2n + 2$ bits are required—one for postnormalization and one for rounding. During binary subtraction, any sequence of borrows propagates from right to left over a string of 0s in the minuend. The sticky bit will generate any borrow sequences to the left in the same manner as if there were additional guard digits.

Arithmetic operations that produce results beyond the range of normalized floating-point numbers are also handled by the proposal. Operations that have no mathematical interpretation, such as $0 \div 0$, will produce a not-a-number (NaN).

The proposal defines the following additional terms, which have not been previously presented in this text, or which may have expanded meanings.

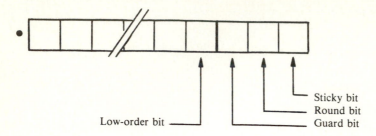

Figure 7.15 Guard digits used in rounding.

Significand. This is the portion of a binary floating-point number that consists of an explicit or implicit leading bit (0 or 1) to the immediate left of the radix point and a fraction to the right of the radix point, as shown below.

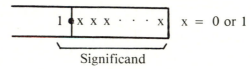

Normal 0. This is defined as a minimum exponent and a 0 significand. The sign of a normal 0 may be positive or negative.

Denormalized. This is defined as a minimum exponent, with the explicit or implicit leading (leftmost) bit of the significand being 0; the number is not a normal 0.

Unnormalized. This occurs only in the extended format, where the value of the exponent is greater than the minimum value of the format being used, and the explicit leftmost bit of the significand is 0. If the significand is 0, then this represents an unnormalized 0.

Normalized. This is defined as a nonzero number in which the leftmost significand bit is a 1. If the significand is 0, then the number becomes a normal 0. Normalization does not change the sign of the number.

7.7.2 Formats

The following four floating-point formats are defined in the standard:

Single format. This is a 32-bit format for binary floating-point numbers, as shown in Fig. 7.16(a). The format consists of a 1-bit sign s, an 8-bit biased exponent e, and a 23-bit fraction f. The value V of the number is as follows:

1. $V = $ NaN, if $e = 255$ and $f \neq 0$.
2. $V = -1^s \times \infty$, if $e = 255$ and $f = 0$; that is, $V = \pm \infty$.
3. $V = -1^s \times 2^{e-127} \times 1.f$, if $0 < e < 255$.
4. $V = -1^s \times 2^{-126} \times 0.f$, if $e = 0$ and $f \neq 0$.
5. $V = -1^s \times 0$, if $e = 0$ and $f = 0$; that is, $V = 0$.

An example is now given that represents case 3 above.

$$+13 = +2^3 \times 1.10100\cdots0 \quad \text{unbiased exponent}$$

After adding the bias of 127 to the unbiased exponent (3), the single-precision format of the number is

$$\boxed{0\;|\;1\;0\;0\;0\;0\;0\;1\;0\;|\;1\;0\;1\;0\;0\;\cdots\;0\;0}$$

$$s \qquad\qquad \text{Biased } e \qquad\qquad f$$

Therefore, using case 3 above,

$$V = -1^0 \times 2^{130-127} \times 1.10100\cdots0$$
$$= 1 \times 2^3 \times 1.10100\cdots0$$
$$= 13$$

A second example using case 3 is

$$-22 = 2^4 \times 1.011000\cdots0$$

After adding the bias, the single-precision format of the number is

$$\boxed{1\;|\;1\;0\;0\;0\;0\;0\;1\;1\;|\;0\;1\;1\;0\;0\;\cdots\;0\;0}$$

$$s \qquad\qquad \text{Biased } e \qquad\qquad f$$

Therefore, using 3 above,

$$V = -1^1 \times 2^{131-127} \times 1.01100\cdots0$$
$$= -1 \times 2^4 \times 1.01100\cdots0$$
$$= -22$$

A third example using the single-precision format is now presented for the operation of addition. The operation is $(+1) + (+1)$.

$$2^0 \times 1.0\,0\cdots0 = \boxed{0\;|\;0\;1\;1\;1\;1\;1\;1\;1\;|\;0\;0\;0\;\cdots\;0\;0}$$

$$2^0 \times 1.0\,0\cdots0 = \boxed{0\;|\;0\;1\;1\;1\;1\;1\;1\;1\;|\;0\;0\;0\;\cdots\;0\;0}$$

After addition, the sum is

$$2^0 \times 10.000\cdots00$$

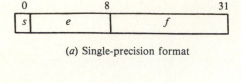

(a) Single-precision format

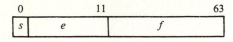

(b) Double-precision format

Figure 7.16 IEEE single- and double-precision formats.

because the leading significant bit is a 1 for each number. Postnormalization is required, which yields

$$2^1 \times 1.000 \cdots 00$$

Double format. This is a 64-bit format for binary floating-point numbers, as shown in Fig. 7.16(*b*). The format consists of a 1-bit sign s, an 11-bit biased exponent e, and a 52-bit fraction f. The value V of the number is as follows:

1. $V = \text{NaN}$, if $e = 2047$ and $f \neq 0$.
2. $V = -1^s \times \infty$, if $e = 2047$ and $f = 0$; that is, $\pm \infty$.
3. $V = -1^s \times 2^{e-1023} \times 1.f$, if $0 < e < 2047$.
4. $V = -1^s \times 2^{-1022} \times 0.f$, if $e = 0$ and $f \neq 0$.
5. $V = -1^s \times 0$, if $e = 0$ and $f = 0$; that is, $V = 0$.

Single-extended format. This format depends on the implementation technique for the floating-point operations. A floating-point number in this format has the following fields: a 1-bit sign s, an exponent e with a range of $-1023 \leqslant e \leqslant +1024$ with a bias that is implementation-dependent, a 1-bit integer j, and a fraction f with at least 31 bits. The value V of the number is as follows:

1. $V = \text{NaN}$, if $e \geqslant +1024$ and $f \neq 0$.
2. $V = -1^s \times \infty$, if $e \geqslant +1024$ and $f = 0$; that is, $V = \pm \infty$.
3. $V = -1^s \times 2^e \times j.f$, if $-1023 < e < +1024$.
4. $V = -1^s \times 0$, if $e \leqslant -1023$ and $j = f = 0$; that is, V is a normal 0.
5. $V = -1^s \times 2^{e'} \times j.f$, if $e \leqslant -1023$ and $j \neq 0$ or $f \neq 0$, where $e' \leqslant -1023$ or $e' \leqslant -1022$. The selection of e' is determined by the implementation scheme.

Double-extended format The double-extended format is the same as the single-extended format except that the exponent range is $-16383 \leqslant e \leqslant +16384$ and the fraction has at least 63 bits.

Rounding deletes one or more of the least-significant digits in a positional number system and adjusts the retained portion in accordance with some rule. The purpose of rounding is to reduce the number of digits in the number so that it can be contained in the size of the destination's format. Rounding usually limits the precision of the number, and this fact should be indicated to the rest of the system.

The implementation scheme for rounding will permit the user to select either positive-directed rounding (round toward $+\infty$), negative-directed rounding (round toward $-\infty$), or truncation (round toward 0) for all operations. A result is usually rounded so that it can be accommodated by the destination.

7.7.3 Operations

All implementations of the standard will facilitate addition, subtraction, multiplication, division, square root generation, remainder generation, conversion between different floating-point formats, conversion between floating-point numbers and integers, conversion between binary and decimal, and comparison operations. When all operands are normalized, the operations will be performed to the precision of the format before rounding is specified.

During arithmetic operations, the destination format will be at least as wide as the format of the operands. All results will be rounded. The square root operation will be provided for all formats and is defined for all normalized numbers that are greater than or equal to 0. The destination format will be at least as wide as the format of the operands, and all results will be rounded. If a floating-point format is converted to a less precise (less wide) format, then the result will be rounded. If the conversion is made to a more precise (wider) format, then the result will be exact.

It is also possible to round a floating-point number to an integer value in the same floating-point format. Any conversions between binary floating-point numbers and decimal numbers will be correctly rounded. It is possible to compare two floating-point numbers that are in the same or in different formats. Four mutually exclusive results are possible:

Less than
Equal to
Greater than
Unordered

The unordered situation arises when at least one operand is NaN, or when ∞ is compared to anything other than ∞. Comparisons do not produce an overflow or underflow.

Unnormalized and denormalized arithmetic. When at least one operand is unnormalized, the operation will conform to the following rules:

1. *Addition or subtraction* ($z = x \pm y$). If at least one of the two operands is normalized and has an exponent m, where m is the maximum of the unbiased exponent of x and the unbiased exponent of y, then z will be normalized before rounding; otherwise, the unbiased exponent of z is set to m.
2. *Multiplication* ($z = x \times y$). The unbiased exponent of z is equal to the sum of the unbiased exponents of x and y.
3. *Division* ($z = x/y$). The unbiased exponent of z is equal to the difference of the unbiased exponents of x and y.
4. *Remainder* ($z = x$ REM y). z is calculated assuming that operand x is normalized.
5. *Square root.* If the operand is unnormalized, then square root is an invalid operation.
6. *Conversion.* The exponent of the result is set equal to the unbiased exponent of the operand to be converted.
7. *Comparison.* Comparison operations will assume that both operands are normalized.

Rounding and overflow/underflow detection are performed after the above operations have been completed and may alter the results.

7.7.4 Exceptions

Five types of exceptions are detected. Each exception has a trap associated with it that can be enabled or disabled by the user. If the trap is disabled, then a status flag is set on the occurrence of any of the exceptions.

1. *Invalid operation.* There are two types of invalid operation exceptions. The first type occurs if an operand is invalid for the operation to be performed. The second occurs if the result is invalid for the destination. An operand is invalid for any of the following reasons:

   (*a*) Detection of NaN
   (*b*) Addition or subtraction of ∞
   (*c*) Multiplication of $0 \times \infty$
   (*d*) Division of 0/0, ∞/∞, or where the divisor is unnormalized and the dividend is not infinite and not a normal 0.
   (*e*) During a remainder operation x REM y, where y is 0 or unnormalized or $x = \infty$
   (*f*) During a square root operation, if the operand is less than zero, is ∞, or is unnormalized

   The result is invalid when the result of any operation is unnormalized, but not denormalized, and has a single- or double-format destination.
2. *Division by 0.* If the dividend is a finite nonzero number and the divisor is a normal 0, then the division by 0 exception will be indicated.

3. *Overflow.* Overflow will be indicated if a rounded result is finite but not invalid, and the exponent is too large to be represented in the applicable floating-point format.

4. *Underflow.* Underflow will be indicated when a result that is not a normal 0 has an exponent that is too small to be represented in the applicable floating-point format. Underflow is also signaled when an extended format product or quotient (with neither operand being a normal 0) is indistinguishable from a normal 0.

5. *Inexact.* If there is no invalid operation exception and the rounded result of an operation is not exact, then the inexact exception will be indicated. This exception will also be signaled when there is no invalid operation exception and the rounded result overflows without the appropriate trap being enabled.

7.7.5 Concluding Remarks

The IEEE Computer Society's Floating-Point Committee, Task 754, considered several proposals for binary floating-point arithmetic. The major proposals considered by the committee are publicly available.

The proposal presented in this section describes binary floating-point operations for single- and double-precision formats. In addition to the normalized numbers of $+0$ and -0, there are representations for denormalized numbers. Denormalized numbers can result from underflow, $+\infty$, $-\infty$, and NaNs, where NaNs represent various types of invalidities. Extended formats are defined for single-extended and double-extended operations.

The proposed standard specifies features that are useful in practical application programs. Studies have indicated that the implementation cost of the proposal is not much greater than the cost of less comprehensive traditional systems for floating-point arithmetic.

PROBLEMS

7.1. What is the purpose of rounding? How is precision affected? What situations can cause rounding to occur?

7.2 Name three methods of rounding and discuss their different attributes regarding:
  (a) How rounding is accomplished
  (b) Error range
  (c) Symmetry in relation to the ideal rounding line for that method
  (d) Relative speeds of the rounding methods
  (e) Additional hardware required to perform rounding

7.3 Explain the following terminologies:
- (*a*) Prenormalization
- (*b*) Postnormalization
- (*c*) Chopping
- (*d*) Jamming
- (e) Double precision
- (*f*) Guard digits
- (*g*) Significand

7.4 A ROM has four address bits. Specify the contents of the ROM when it is used in the ROM rounding method for a 24-bit fraction with three guard bits.

BIBLIOGRAPHY

Allmark, R. H., and Lucking, J. R., "Design of an Arithmetic Unit Incorporating A Nesting Store,"*Proceedings of IFIP Congress,* 1962, pp. 694–698.

Amdahl,G. M., "The Structure of System/360, Part III, Processing Unit Considerations," *IBM System Journal,* vol. 3, no. 1964, pp. 144–164.

———, "Validity of the Single Processor Approach to Achieve Large Scale Computing Capabilities," *AFIPS Conference Proceedings,* vol. 30, 1967, pp. 483–485.

———, Blaauw, G. A., and Brooks, F. P., Jr., "Architecture of The IBM System/360," *IBM Journal of Research and Development,* vol. 8, no. 2, Apr. 1964, pp. 87–101.

Anderson, D. W., Sparacio, F. A., and Tomasulo, R. M., "The IBM System/360 Model 91: Machine Philosophy and Instruction Handling," *IBM Journal of Research and Development,* vol. 11, no. 1, 1967, pp. 8–24.

Anderson, S. F., et al., "The IBM System/360 Model 91: Floating-Point Execution Unit," *IBM Journal of Research and Development,* vol. 11, no. 1, Jan. 1967, pp. 34–53.

Ashenhurst, R. L., and Metropolis, N., "Unnormalized Floating-Point Arithmetic," *Journal of ACM,* vol. 6, Mar. 1959, pp. 415–428.

Atkins, D. E., "Design of the Arithmetic Units of Illiac III: Use of Redundancy and Higher Radix Methods," *IEEE Transactions on Computers,* vol. C-19, no. 8, Aug. 1970, pp. 720–733.

———, "Higher-Radix Division Using Estimates of the Divisor and Partial Remainders," *IEEE Transactions on Computers,* vol. C-17, no. 10, Oct. 1968, pp. 925–934.

Avizienis, A., "Signed-Digit Number Representations for Fast Parallel Arithmetic," *IRE Transactions on Electronic Computers,* vol. EC-10, no. 3, Sept. 1961, pp. 389–400.

Baer, Jean-Loup, *Computer Systems Architecture,* Computer Science Press, 1980.

Baker, P. W., "More Efficient Radix-2 Algorithms for Some Elementary Functions," *IEEE Transactions on Computers,* vol. C-24, Nov. 1975, pp. 1049–1054.

Baugh, C.R., and Wooley, B.A., "A Two's Complement Parallel Array Multiplication Algorithm," *IEEE Transactions on Computers,* vol. C-22, no. 12, Dec. 1973, pp. 1045–1047.

Bedrij, O.J., "Carry-Select Adders," *IRE Transactions,* vol. EC-11, no. 3, June 1962, pp. 340–346.

Bell, C.G., and Newell, A., *Computer Structures: Readings and Examples,* McGraw-Hill, New York, 1971.

Blaauw, G., *Digital System Implementation,* Prentice-Hall, Englewood Cliffs, N.J., 1976.

Booth, A.D., "A Signed Binary Multiplication Technique," *Quarterly Journal of Mechanics and Applied Mathematics*, vol. 4, part 2, 1951, pp. 236–240.

Braun, E.L. *Digital Computer Design*, Academic Press, New York, 1963.

Brent, R., "On the Addition of Binary Numbers," *IEEE Transactions and Computers*, vol. C-19, 1970, pp. 758–759.

———, "On the Precision Attainable With Various Floating-Point Arithmetic," *IEEE Transactions on Computers*, vol. C-22, no. 6, June 1973, pp. 601–607.

———, "The Parallel Evaluation of General Arithmetic Expressions," *Journal of ACM*, vol. 21, 2, Apr. 1974, pp. 201–206.

———, Kuck, D., and Maruyama, K., "The Parallel Evaluation of Arithmetic Expressions without Division," *IEEE Transactions on Computers*, vol. C-22, no. 1, May 1973, pp. 532–534.

Brubaker, T. A., and Becker, J. C., "Multiplication Using Logarithms Implemented with Read-Only Memory," *IEEE Transactions on Computers*, vol. C-24, 1975.

Buchholz, W. (ed.), *Planning a Computer System*, McGraw-Hill, New York, 1962.

Cappa, M., "Cellular Iterative Arrays for Multiplication and Division," Department of Electrical Engineering, University of Toronto, Oct. 1971.

———, and Hamacher, V. C., "An Augmented Iterative Array for High-Speed Binary Division," *IEEE Transactions on Computers*, vol. C-22, Feb. 1973, pp. 172–175.

Chen, S. C., and Kuck, D. J., "Combinational Circuit Synthesis with Time and Component Bounds," *IEEE Transactions on Computers*, vol. C-26, no. 8, Aug. 1977, pp. 712–726.

Chen, T. C., "A Binary Multiplication Scheme Based on Squaring," *IEEE Transactions on Computers*, vol. C-20, no. 6, June 1971, pp. 678-680.

———, "Parallelism, Pipelining and Computer Efficiency," *Computer Design*, vol. 10, Jan. 1971, pp. 69–74.

Chu, Y., *Computer Organization and Microprogramming*, Prentice-Hall, Englewood Cliffs, N.J., 1972.

——— (ed.), *High-Level Language Computer Architecture*, Academic Press, New York, 1975.

Cody, W. J., "Analysis of Proposals for the Floating-Point Standard," *IEEE Transactions on Computers*, vol. 14, no. 3, Mar. 1981, pp. 63–68.

Coonan, J.T., "Underflow and the Denormalized Numbers," *IEEE Transactions on Computers*, vol. 14, no. 3, Mar. 1981, pp. 75–87.

Dadda, L., "On Parallel Digital Multipliers," *Alta Frequency*, no. 45, 1976, pp. 574–580.

Davis, R. L., "Uniform Shift Networks," *IEEE Transactions on Computers*, vol. 7, no. 9, Sept. 1974, pp. 60–71.

Dean, K. J., "Binary Division Using Data Dependent Iterative Arrays," *Electronics Letters*, vol. 4, July 1968, pp. 283–284.

———, "Design of a Full Multiplier," *Proceedings of IEEE*, vol. 115, Nov. 1968, pp. 1592–1594.

———, "Iterative Arrays of Logical Circuits for Performing Arithmetic," *Electronics Engineering*, Dec. 1968, pp. 694–697.

———, "Some Applications of Cellular Logic Arithmetic Arrays," *Radio and Electronic Engineer*, vol. 37, 1969, pp. 225-227.

Deegan, I. D., "Cellular Multiplier for Signed Binary Numbers," *Electronics Letters*, vol. 7, 1971, pp. 436–437.

Deverell, J., "The Design of Cellular Arrays for Arithmetic," *Radio and Electronic Engineer*, vol. 44, no. 1, Jan. 1974, pp. 21–26.

Fenwick, P. M., "Binary Multiplication with Overlapped Addition Cycles," *IEEE Transactions on Computers*, vol. C-18, no. 1, Jan. 1969, pp. 71–74.

Ferrari, D., "A Division Method Using a Parallel Multiplier," *IEEE Transactions on Computers*, vol. EC-16, Apr. 1967, pp. 224–226.

———, "Fast Carry-Propagation Iterative Networks," *IEEE Transactions on Computers*, vol. C-17, no. 2, Feb. 1968, pp.132–145.

Field, J. A., "Optimizing Floating-Point Arithmetic via Post Addition Shift Probabilities," *Proceedings of AFIPS Spring Joint Computer Conference*, AFIPS Press, Montvale, N. J., 1969, pp. 597–603.

Flores, I., *The Logic of Computer Arithmetic*, Prentice-Hall, Englewood Cliffs, N.J., 1963.

———, "Lookahead Control in the IBM System/370 Model 165," *IEEE Transactions on Computers*, vol. 7, no. 11, Nov. 1974, pp. 24–38.

Flynn, M. J. "Very High-Speed Computing Systems," *Proceedings of IEEE*, vol. 54, Dec. 1966, pp. 1901–1909.

———, "On Division by Functional Iteration," *IEEE Transactions on Computers*, vol. C-19, Aug. 1970, pp. 702–706.

———, and Low, P. R., "The IBM System/360 Model 91: Some Remarks on System Development," *IBM Journal*, Jan. 1967, pp. 2–7.

Freedman, M. D., *Principles of Digital Computer Operation*, Wiley, New York, 1972.

Gardiner, A. B., and Hont, J., "Comparison of Restoring and Nonrestoring Cellular Array Dividers," *Electronics Letters*, vol. 7, Apr. 1971, pp. 172–173.

Garner, H. L., "A Survey of Some Recent Contributions to Computer Arithmetic," *IEEE Transactions on Computers*, vol. C-25, no. 12, Dec. 1976, pp.1277–1282.

———, "Number Systems and Arithmetic," *Advances in Computers*, vol. 6, 1965, pp. 168–177.

Gex, A., "Multiplier-Divider Cellular Array," *Electronics Letters*, vol. 7, July 1971, pp. 442–444.

Ghest, C., "Multiplying Made Easy for Digital Assemblies," *Electronics*, Nov. 22, 1971, pp. 56–61.

Gibson, J. A., and Gibbard R. W., "Synthesis and Comparison of Two's Complement Parallel Multipliers," *IEEE Transactions on Computers*, vol. C-24, Oct. 1975, pp. 1020–1027.

Gilchrist, B., et al., "Fast Carry Logic for Digital Computers," *IRE Transactions*, vol. EC-4, Dec. 1955, pp. 133–136.

Gilman, R. E., "A Mathematical Procedure for Machine Division," *Communications of ACM*, vol. 2, no. 4, Apr. 1959, pp 10–12.

Goldstein, M., "Significance Arithmetic on a Digital Computer," *Communications of ACM*, vol. 6, no. 3, Mar. 1963, pp. 111–117.

Gruenberger, F., *Computing: An Introduction*, Harcourt, New York, 1969.

Guild, H. H., "Fully Iterative Fast Array for Binary Multiplication and Fast Addition," *Electronics Letters*, vol. 5, May 1969, pp.263.

———, "Some Cellular Logic Arrays for Nonrestoring Binary Division," *Radio and Electronic Engineer*, vol. 39, June 1970, pp. 345–348.

Habibi, A., and Wintz, P. A., "Fast Multipliers," *IEEE Transactions on Computers*, vol. C-19, no. 2, Feb. 1970, pp. 153–157.

Hallin, T. G., and Flynn, M. J., "Pipelining of Arithmetic Functions," *IEEE Transactions on Computers*, vol. C-21, Aug. 1972, pp. 880–886.

Hamacher, V. C., et al., *Computer Organization*, McGraw-Hill, New York, 1978.

———, and Gavilan, J., "High-Speed Multiplier/Divider Iterative Arrays" *Proceedings of 1973 Sagamore Computer Conference on Parallel Processing*, 1973, pp. 91–100

Hayes, J. P., *Computer Architecture and Organization*, McGraw-Hill, New York, 1978.

Hellerman, H., *Digital Computer System Principles*, 2d ed., McGraw-Hill, New York, 1973.

Hemel, A., "Making Small ROMs Do Math Quickly," *Electronics*, May 11, 1970, pp. 104–110.

———, "Making Small ROMs Do Math Quickly, Cheaply and Easily," In W. B. Riley (ed.), *Electronic Computer Memory Technology*, McGraw-Hill, New York, 1971, pp. 133–140.

Hill, F. J., and Peterson, G. R., *Digital Systems: Hardware Organization and Design*, Wiley, New York, 1973.

Hintze, G., *Digital Machine Computation*, Springer-Verlag, New York, 1967.

Hough, D., "Application of the Proposed IEEE 754 Standard for Floating-Point Arithmetic," *IEEE Computer*, vol. 14, no. 3, Mar. 1981, pp. 70–74.

Hwang, K., *Computer Arithmetic. Principles, Architecture and Design*, Wiley, New York, 1979.

IBM Corporation, "IBM System/370 Principles of Operation," Form GA22-7000-8, Poughkeepsie, N. Y. 1970.

IEEE Computer Society, *IEEE Transactions on Computers*, vol. C-22, no. 6 (special section on computer arithmetic), June 1973.

Kamal, A. A., and Ghanam, M., "High-Speed Multiplication Systems," *IEEE Transactions on Computers*, vol. C-21, no. 9, Sept. 1972, pp. 1017–1021.

Kaneko, T., and Liu, B., "On Local Roundoff Errors in Floating-Point Arithmetic," *Journal of ACM*, vol. 20, no. 3, July 1973, pp. 391–398.

Katzan, H. Jr., *Computer Organization and the System/370*, Van Nostrand-Reinhold, New York, 1971.

Knuth, D. E., *The Art of Computer Programming: Seminumerical Algorithms*, vol. 2, Addison-Wesley, Reading, Mass., 1969.

Kouvaras, N. D., et al., "Digital Systems of Simultaneous Addition of Several Binary Numbers," *IEEE Transactions on Computers*, vol. C-17, no. 10, Oct. 1968, pp. 992–997.

Krishnamurthy, E. V., "On Optimal Iterative Schemes for High-Speed Division," *IEEE Transactions on Computers*, vol. C-19, no. 3, Mar. 1970, pp. 227–231.

Kruy, J. F., "A Fast Conditional Sum Adder Using Carry Bypass Logic," *AFIPS Conference Proceedings*, vol. 27, Fall 1965, pp. 695–703.

Kuck, D., *The Structure of Computers and Computations*, vol. 1, Wiley, New York, 1978.

———, et al., "ROM-Rounding: A New Rounding Scheme," *3rd Symposium on Computer Arithmetic*, IEEE Computer Society catalog no. 75CH1017-3C, 1975, pp. 67–72.

———, Lawrie, D. H., and Sameh, A. H. (eds.), *High Speed Computer and Algorithm Organization*, Academic Press, New York, 1977.

———, and Maruyama, K., "Time Bounds on the Parallel Evaluation of Arithmetic Expressions," *SIAM Journal of Computing*, vol. 4, no. 2, June 1975, pp. 147–162.

———, Parker, D. S., and Sameh, A, H., "Analysis of Rounding Methods in Floating-Point Arithmetic," *IEEE Transactions on Computers*, vol. C-26, no. 7, July 1977, pp. 643–650.

Kuki, H., and Cody, W. J., "A Statistical Study of the Accuracy of Floating-Point Number Systems," *Communications of ACM*, vol. 16, no. 4, Apr. 1973, pp. 223–230.

Kulisch, U., "Mathematical Foundation of Computer Arithmetic," *IEEE Transactions on Computers*, vol. C-26, no. 7, July 1977, pp. 610–620.

Kunz, K. S., *Numerical Analysis*, McGraw-Hill, New York, 1957.

Ling, H., "High-Speed Binary Parallel Adder," *IEEE Transactions on Computers*, vol. EC-15, no. 5, Oct. 1966, pp. 799–802.

———, "High-Speed Computer Multiplication Using a Multiple-Bit Decoding Algorithm," *IEEE Transactions on Computers*, vol. C-19, no. 8, Aug. 1970, pp. 706–709.

MacSorley, O. L., "High-Speed Arithmetic in Binary Computers," *Proceedings of IRE*, vol. 49, no. 1, Jan. 1961, pp. 67–91.

Majithia, J. C., "Nonrestoring Binary Division Using a Cellular Array," *Electronics Letters*, vol. 6, May 1970, pp. 303–304.

———, and Kita, R., "An Interative Array for Muliplication of Signed Binary Number," *IEEE Transactions on Computers*, vol. C-20, Feb. 1971, pp. 214–216.

Mano, M. M., *Computer Logic Design*, Prentice-Hall, Englewood Cliffs, N. J., 1972.

———, *Computer System Architecture*, Prentice-Hall, Englewood Cliffs, N. J., 1976.

Metropolis, N., and Ashenhurst, R. L., "Basic Operations in an Unnormalized Arithmetic System," *IEEE Transactions on Computers*, vol. EC-12, no. 6, Dec. 1963, pp. 896–904.

Mori, R. D., "Suggestion for an IC Fast Parallel Multiplier," *Electronics Letters*, vol. 5, Feb 1969, pp. 50–51.

Mowle, F. J., *A Systematic Approach to Digital Logic Design*, Addison-Wesley, Reading, Mass., 1976.

Pezaris, S. D., "A 40-ns 17-bit Array Multiplier," *IEEE Transactions on Computers*, vol. C-20, Apr. 1971, pp. 442–447.

Ramamoorthy, C. V., and Li, H. F., "Pipeline Architecture," *Computer Survey*, vol. 9, Mar. 1977, pp. 61–102.

Reitwiener, G. W., "Binary Arithmetic," *Advances in Computers*, vol. 1, Academic Press, New York, 1960, pp. 261–265.

———, "The Determination of Carry Propagation Length for Binary Addition," *IRE Transactions on Electronic Computers*, vol. EC-9, Mar. 1960, pp. 35–38.

Richards, R. K., *Arithmetic Operations in Digital Computers*, Van Nostrand, New York, 1955.

———, *Digital Design*, Wiley, New York, 1971.

Robertson, J. E., "A New Class of Digital Division Methods," *IRE Transactions on Electronic Computers*, vol. EC-7, no. 3, Sept. 1958, pp. 218–222.

——— , "Two's Complement Multiplication in Binary Parallel Digital Computers,"*IRE Transactions*, vol. EC-4, no. 3, Sept. 1955, pp. 118–119.

——— , "The Correspondence between Methods of Digital Divison and Multiplier Recording Procedures," *IEEE Transactions on Computers*, vol. C-19, no. 8, Aug. 1970, pp. 692–701.

Schmid, H., *Decimal Computation*, Wiley, New York, 1974.

Singh, S. and Waxman, R., "Multiple Operand Addition and Multiplication," *IEEE Transactions on Computers*, vol. C-22, no. 2, Feb. 1973, pp. 113–119.

Stefanelli, R., "A Suggestion for High-Speed Parallel Binary Divider," *IEEE Transactions on Computers*, vol. C-21, Jan. 1972, pp. 42–55.

Stein, M. L., and Munro, W. D., *Introduction to Machine Arithmetic*, Addison-Wesley, Reading, Mass., 1971.

Sterbenz, P. H., *Floating-Point Computation*, Prentice-Hall, Englewood Cliffs, N.J., 1974.

Stevenson, D., "A Proposed Standard for Binary Floating-Point Arithmetic," *IEEE Computer*, vol. 14, no. 3, Mar. 1981, pp. 51–62.

Stone, H., *Introduction to Computer Architecture*, 2d ed., Science Research Associates, Chicago, 1980.

Swartzlander, E. E. (ed.), *Computer Arithmetic*, Dowden, 1980.

Sweeney, D. W., "An Analysis of Floating-Point Addition," *IBM System Journal*, vol. 4, no. 1, 1965, pp. 31–42.

Szabo, N. S., and Tanaka, R. I., *Residue Arithmetic and Its Applications to Computer Technology*, McGraw-Hill, New York, 1967.

Tocher, T. D., "Techniques of Multiplication and Division for Automatic Binary Computers," *Quarterly Journal of Mechanics and Applied Mathematics*, vol. 2, part 3, 1958, pp. 364–384.

Tomasulo, R. M., An Efficient Algorithm for Exploiting Multiple Arithmetic Units," *IBM Journal of Research and Development*, vol. 11, no. 1, Jan. 1967, pp. 25–33.

Tsao, N. K., "On the Distribution of Significant Digits and Roundoff Errors," *Communications of ACM*, vol. 17, no. 5, May 1974, pp. 269–271.

Wallace, C. S., "A Suggestion for a Fast Multiplier," *IEEE Transactions on Electronic Computers*, vol. EC-13, Feb. 1964, pp. 14–17.

Weinberger, A., Smith, J. L., "A Logic for High-Speed Addition," National Bureau of Standards, Circular 591, 1958, pp. 3–12.

Weller, C.W., "A High-Speed Carry Circuit for Binary Adders," *IEEE Transactions on Computers*, vol. C-18, no. 8, Aug. 1969, pp. 728–732.

Wilkinson, J. H. *Rounding Errors in Algebraic Processes,* Prentice-Hall, Englewood Cliffs, N. J., 1963.

Wilson, J. B. et al., "An Algorithm for Rapid Binary Division," *IRE Transactions*, vol. EC-10, no. 4, Dec. 1961, pp. 662–670.

Winograd, S., "On the Time Required to Perform Addition," *Journal of ACM*, vol. 12, no. 2, Apr. 1965, pp. 277–285.

——— , "On the Time Required to Perform Multiplication," *Journal of ACM*, vol. 14, no. 4, Oct. 1967, pp. 793–802.

——— , "On the Parallel Evaluation of Certain Arithmetic Expressions," *Journal of ACM*, vol. 22, no. 4, Oct. 1975, pp. 477–492.

Yohe, J. M. "Rounding in Floating-Point Arithmetic," *IEEE Transactions on Computers*, vol. C-22, no. 6, June 1973, pp. 577–586.